# Brief Contents

e **LearningCurve** activities and additional multiple-choice grammar exercises are available for the topics in this unit. Visit **macmillanhighered.com/foundationsfirst**.

# Foundations First with Readings

## Sentences and Paragraphs

# Foundations First with Readings

## Sentences and Paragraphs

**Fifth Edition**

**Laurie G. Kirszner**
**University of the Sciences, Emeritus**

**Stephen R. Mandell**
**Drexel University**

**Bedford/St. Martin's**
**Boston ◆ New York**

*For Bedford/St. Martin's*

*Vice President, Editorial, Macmillan Higher Education Humanities:* Edwin Hill
*Editorial Director for English and Music:* Karen S. Henry
*Developmental Editor:* Jill Gallagher
*Senior Production Editor:* Peter Jacoby
*Production Supervisor:* Samuel Jones
*Senior Marketing Manager:* Christina Shea
*Copy Editor:* Alice Vigliani
*Indexer:* Kirsten Kite
*Photo Researcher:* Sheri Blaney
*Director of Rights and Permissions:* Hilary Newman
*Senior Art Director:* Anna Palchik
*Text Design:* Jerilyn Bockorick
*Cover Design:* Donna Lee Dennison
*Cover Art:* © architetta/Getty Images
*Composition:* Graphic World, Inc.
*Printing and Binding:* RR Donnelley and Sons

Manufactured in the United States of America.

9  8  7  6  5  4
f   e   d   c   b   a

*For information, write:* Bedford/St. Martin's, 75 Arlington Street, Boston, MA 02116
(617-399-4000)

ISBN 978-1-4576-3345-4 (Student Edition)
ISBN 978-1-4576-8496-8 (Loose-Leaf Edition)

**Acknowledgments**

*Text acknowledgments and copyrights appear at the back of the book on page 543, which constitutes an extension of the copyright page. Art acknowledgments and copyrights appear on the same page as the art selections they cover. It is a violation of the law to reproduce these selections by any means whatsoever without the written permission of the copyright holder.*

# Preface for Instructors

As experienced teachers, we have learned that in college, writing comes first. For this reason, *Foundations First with Readings: Sentences and Paragraphs* encourages students to begin every chapter with a writing activity. We also know that students learn writing skills most meaningfully in the context of their own writing. Therefore, this text takes a "practice in context" approach, teaching students the skills they need to become better writers by having them practice in the context of their own writing.

In the fifth edition of *Foundations First*, we have introduced TEST, a unique tool to help students assess their writing. The letters T-E-S-T stand for Topic Sentence (or Thesis Statement), Evidence, Summary statement, and Transitions, the key elements found in effective paragraphs and essays. Remembering the four TEST letters helps students to identify these four key elements as they read; more important, it enables them to make sure that all these elements are present in their own paragraphs and essays.

In the classroom and in daily life, writing is an essential skill. For this reason, *Foundations First* begins with thorough coverage of the writing process. Each chapter opens with a Seeing and Writing prompt that asks students to think critically about an image; later in the chapter, they are encouraged to develop their responses into a paragraph.

With comprehensive grammar coverage, online grammar practice, and sixteen professional and student reading selections, *Foundations First* gets students reading, writing, and thinking critically in preparation for academic, career, and life success. Striking images and a brand-new design appeal to today's visual learners, as do the graphic organizers for paragraph organization in Unit Two. And with LaunchPad Solo for *Foundations First with Readings*, we bring the book's instruction into an online, interactive space, where students can continue their practice of key grammar and reading concepts.

We wrote this book for adults—our own interested, concerned, and hardworking students—and we tailored the book's content and approach to them. Instead of offering exercises that reinforce the preconception that writing is a dull, pointless, and artificial activity, we chose fresh, contemporary examples (both student and professional) and developed engaging exercises and writing assignments that are relevant and interesting. Throughout *Foundations First*, we talk *to* students, not *at* or *down to* them. We strive to be concise without being abrupt, thorough without being repetitive, direct without being rigid, specific without being prescriptive, and flexible without being inconsistent. Our most important goal is simple: to create an engaging text that motivates students and gives them the tools and encouragement they need to improve their writing.

# Organization

*Foundations First with Readings* has a flexible organization that permits instructors to teach various topics in the order that works best for them and for their students. The book is divided into seven units. Unit One offers critical reading coverage as well as a brief introduction to the college writing process, while Unit Two explains and illustrates the various kinds of paragraphs and fully explains the process of writing paragraphs. This unit also includes a chapter on writing essays. Units Three through Six focus on sentence skills, grammar, punctuation, and mechanics. Throughout these units, marginal callouts direct students to additional online grammar practice via LaunchPad Solo. In addition, LaunchPad Solo includes LearningCurve: innovative, adaptive online quizzes that let students learn at their own pace, with a game-like interface that keeps them at it. Finally, Unit Seven features sixteen professional and student readings, each preceded by a biographical headnote and followed by critical thinking questions and writing practice prompts.

# Features

When we wrote *Foundations First*, our goal was to create the most useful and student-friendly sentence-to-paragraph text available for developing writers. In preparing the fifth edition, we have retained all the features that instructors told us contributed to the book's accessibility, while also making several important additions.

**A complete resource for improving student writing.**   With one comprehensive unit on paragraphs, two units on sentences, two on grammar, one on reading, and numerous examples of student writing, *Foundations First* provides comprehensive coverage of basic writing in a format that gives instructors maximum flexibility in planning their courses.

**An emphasis on the connection between reading and writing.**   *Foundations First* presents reading as an integral part of the writing process, offering numerous student and professional examples throughout the text. Chapter 1, Reading for Academic Success, introduces the basic techniques of critical reading and shows students how to get the most out of their academic and professional reading. Sixteen reading selections (three of them by students) in Chapter 36, Readings for Writers, provide material for writing assignments and classroom discussion.

**Word Power boxes.**   Throughout the text, marginal Word Power boxes help students build their vocabulary by defining unfamiliar words that appear in the text's explanations and reading selections.

**FYI boxes.**   Throughout the book, these boxes highlight useful information and explain difficult concepts.

> # FYI
>
> ## Stating Your Thesis
>
> At this stage of the writing process, your thesis is **tentative**, not definite. As you write and revise, you are likely to change it—possibly several times.

**Grammar-in-Context boxes.**   These boxes identify grammar problems related to the rhetorical pattern under discussion. Cross-references to *Foundations First*'s grammar chapters direct students to sections where they can get additional help on grammar issues they find challenging.

**Chapter and Unit Reviews.**   Featuring Editing Practices and Review Checklists, these reviews challenge students to think critically about their writing and to practice editing skills in paragraphs and essays.

**Extensive help for ESL students.**   Chapter 29 addresses the concerns of nonnative speakers, and ESL Tips throughout the Instructor's Annotated Edition provide helpful hints for novice and experienced instructors alike.

# New to This Edition

**TEST A unique tool that inspires student confidence and independence.**   This simple yet effective assessment tool helps students to remember the key elements to look for in the paragraphs and essays they read. In addition, it enables them to take inventory of their own paragraphs and essays as they begin the revision process. Using TEST as a guide, they can make sure their paragraphs and essays include all the necessary elements: Topic sentence (or thesis statement), Evidence, Summary statement, and Transitions.

**Seeing and Writing prompts.** These prompts introduce a connected strand of activities, a hallmark of the Kirszner/ Mandell approach: students are prompted to respond to an

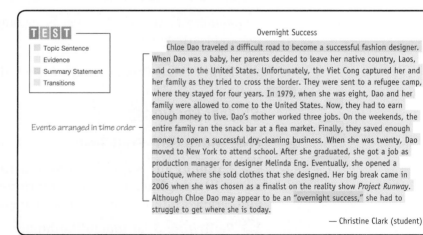

TEST
- Topic Sentence
- Evidence
- Summary Statement
- Transitions

Events arranged in time order

Overnight Success

Chloe Dao traveled a difficult road to become a successful fashion designer. When Dao was a baby, her parents decided to leave her native country, Laos, and come to the United States. Unfortunately, the Viet Cong captured her and her family as they tried to cross the border. They were sent to a refugee camp, where they stayed for four years. In 1979, when she was eight, Dao and her family were allowed to come to the United States. Now, they had to earn enough money to live. Dao's mother worked three jobs. On the weekends, the entire family ran the snack bar at a flea market. Finally, they saved enough money to open a successful dry-cleaning business. When she was twenty, Dao moved to New York to attend school. After she graduated, she got a job as production manager for designer Melinda Eng. Eventually, she opened a boutique, where she sold clothes that she designed. Her big break came in 2006 when she was chosen as a finalist on the reality show *Project Runway*. Although Chloe Dao may appear to be an "overnight success," she had to struggle to get where she is today.

— Christine Clark (student)

image at the beginning of each chapter, to explore their responses in writing, and then to fine-tune their responses by following the instructions in the TEST-Revise-Edit box at the end of the chapter.

**New, streamlined design.** A brand-new design is both visually attractive and functional, helping students to differentiate the various elements of the text, keeping them engaged with the content.

**Online grammar practice with Launch-Pad Solo.** *Foundations First with Readings* now comes with access to LearningCurve: innovative, adaptive online quizzes that let students learn at their own pace, with a game-like interface that keeps them engaged. Quizzes are keyed to grammar instruction in the book, so what is taught in class is reinforced at home. Instructors can also check in on each student's activity in a grade book. Additional multiple-choice grammar exercises offer students even more practice with their most challenging grammar concepts. The exercises are auto-gradable and report directly to the instructor's grade book. Marginal callouts throughout the book direct students to these online exercises, part of the book's LaunchPad Solo. 🄔

## Support for Instructors and Students

*Foundations First with Readings* is accompanied by comprehensive teaching and learning support.

📖 Print     🖥 Online     💿 CD-ROM

### *Student Resources*

**Free with a New Print Text**

🖥 **LaunchPad Solo** for *Foundations First with Readings,* at **macmillanhighered.com/foundationsfirst**, provides students with auto-graded interactive and adaptive grammar exercises.

🖥 *Re:Writing 3*, at **macmillanhighered.com/rewriting**, gives students even more ways to think, watch, practice, and learn about writing concepts. New open online resources with videos and interactive elements engage students in new ways of writing. You'll find tutorials about using common digital writing tools; an interactive peer-review game, Extreme Paragraph Makeover; and more—all for free and for fun.

### Premium

📖 *The Bedford/St. Martin's Textbook Reader,* **Second Edition,** by Ellen Kuhl Repetto, gives students practice in reading college textbooks across the curriculum. This brief collection of chapters from market-leading introductory college textbooks can be packaged inexpensively with *Foundations First.* Beginning with a chapter on college success, *The Bedford/St. Martin's Textbook Reader* also includes chapters from current texts on composition, mass communication, history, psychology, and environmental science. Comprehension questions and tips for reading success guide students in reading college-level materials efficiently and effectively. Package ISBN: 978-1-319-01167-3

## Free Instructor Resources

📖 The *Instructor's Annotated Edition of Foundations First with Readings* contains answers to all grammar practice exercises as well as many of the exercises that appear throughout the reading and writing instructional chapters, in addition to numerous teaching ideas, reminders, and cross-references useful to instructors at all levels of experience. ISBN: 978-1-4576-3361-4

🖥 The *Instructor's Manual for Foundations First with Readings* offers advice for teaching developmental writing as well as general teaching suggestions for important aspects of the course, including structure, diagnostics, conferencing, and syllabi. Additionally, this instructor's manual includes chapter-by-chapter pointers for using *Foundations First with Readings* in the classroom and gives answers to all of the book's practice exercises. To download, go to **macmillanhighered.com/foundationsfirst/catalog.** ISBN: 978-1-4576-8495-1

💿 *Testing Tool Kit: Writing and Grammar Test Bank CD-ROM* enables instructors to create secure, customized tests and quizzes from a pool of nearly 2,000 questions covering 47 topics. It also includes 10 prebuilt diagnostic tests. ISBN: 978-0-3124-3032-0

🖥 *Diagnostic and Mastery Tests for Foundations First with Readings,* Fifth Edition, offer diagnostic and mastery tests that complement the topics covered in *Foundations First.* To download, go to **macmillanhighered .com/foundationsfirst/catalog.** ISBN: 978-1-4576-8979-6

🖥 *Teaching Central* at **macmillanhighered.com/teachingcentral** offers the entire list of Bedford/St. Martin's print and online professional resources in one place. You will find landmark reference works, sourcebooks on pedagogical issues, award-winning collections, and practical advice for the classroom.

## e-Book Options

The e-Book for *Foundations First,* value priced, can be purchased in formats for use with computers, tablets, and e-readers. Visit **macmillanhighered .com/ebooks** for more information.

> ### Ordering Information
>
> To order any of the ancillaries for *Foundations First with Readings*, contact your local Bedford/St. Martin's sales representative, email **sales_support@macmillan.com**, or visit our website at **macmillanhighered.com**.

# Acknowledgments

In our work on *Foundations First*, we have benefited from the help of a great many people.

We are grateful to Randee Falk, who made valuable contributions to the exercises and writing activities in the text, as well as to Mallory Ladd, who helped adapt exercises for online use.

Instructors throughout the country have contributed suggestions and encouragement at various stages of the book's development. For their collegial support, we thank Steven Adkison, Wallace Community College; Matthew Allen, Wright College; Douglas Armendarez, East Los Angeles College; Valerie Bronstein, American River College; Jill Cadwell, Century College; David Cassick, Los Angeles Trade Technical College; Judy Covington, Trident Technical College; Laurel Gardner, Sierra College; Suzanne Hammond, Dodge City Community College; Karen Henderson, University of Montana Helena College of Technology; Mary Anne Keefer, Lord Fairfax Community College; Mary Jae Kleckner, Mid-State Technical College; Steve Lewis, University of Montana Helena College of Technology; Carl Mason, UMass Lowell; Jennifer McCann, Bay College; Kelly Mieszek, Greenville Technical College; Josie Mills, Arapahoe Community College; Christopher Morelock, Walters State Community College; Lori Morrow, Rose State College; Sandra Nichols, Mid-State Technical College; Robin O'Quinn, Connors State College; Brit Osgood-Treston, Riverside City College; Cara Phillips, Greenville Technical College; Cindy Pierce, Northwest Mississippi Community College; Marie Reeves, Cincinnati Christian University; Cathy Rusco, Muskegon Community College; Randall Silvis, Edinboro University of Pennsylvania; Anne Smith, Northwest Mississippi Community College; Roberta Steinberg, Mount Ida College; Jamie Tanzman, Northern Kentucky University; Sharon Tippins, Martin University; Sandra Vandercook, New Orleans Baptist Theological Seminary; Julie Voss, Front Range Community College; Theresa Walther, Rose State College; Julie Warner, Armstrong Atlantic State University; Mary Wilson, Greenville Technical College; and Viktor Zamora, Southwest Los Angeles Community College.

At Bedford/St. Martin's, we thank founder and former president Charles Christensen, former president Joan Feinberg, and former editor in chief Nancy Perry, who believed in this project and gave us support and encouragement from the outset. We thank Denise Wydra, Karen Henry, and Edwin Hill for overseeing this edition. We are also grateful to Val Zaborski,

Samuel Jones, and Peter Jacoby for guiding the book ably through production. Many thanks also go to Christina Shea, senior marketing manager, and Vivian Garcia, market development manager. And finally, we thank our editor, Jill Gallagher, for all her hard work on this project.

It almost goes without saying that *Foundations First with Readings* could not exist without our students, whose work inspired the sample sentences, paragraphs, and essays in this book. We thank all of them, past and present, who have allowed us to use their work.

We are grateful in addition for the continued support of our families. Finally, we are grateful for the survival and growth of the writing partnership we entered into when we were graduate students. We had no idea then of the wonderful places our collaborative efforts would take us. Now, we know.

*Laurie G. Kirszner*
*Stephen R. Mandell*

# A Note to Students

It's no secret that writing will be very important in most of the courses you take in college. Whether you write lab reports or English papers, midterms or final exams, your ability to organize your thoughts and express them in writing will help to determine how well you do. In other words, succeeding at writing is the first step toward succeeding in college. On the job and in everyday life, if you can express yourself clearly and effectively, you will stand a better chance of achieving your goals and making a difference in the world.

Whether you write as a student, as an employee, as a parent, or as a concerned citizen, your writing almost always has a specific purpose. For example, when you write an essay, a memo, a letter, or a research paper, you are writing not just to complete an exercise but also to give other people information or to tell them your ideas or opinions. That is why, in this book, we don't just ask you to do grammar exercises and fill in the blanks; in each chapter, we also ask you to apply the skills you are learning to a writing assignment of your own.

As teachers—and as former students—we know how demanding college can be and how hard it is to juggle assignments with work and family responsibilities. We also know that you don't want to waste your time. That's why in *Foundations First* we make information easy to find and use and include many different features to help you become a better writer.

*Laurie G. Kirszner*
*Stephen R. Mandell*

# Contents

🄴 LearningCurve activities and additional multiple-choice grammar exercises are available for the
topics in this chapter. Visit **macmillanhighered.com/foundationsfirst**.

**XV**

e LearningCurve activities and additional multiple-choice grammar exercises are available for the topics in this chapter. Visit **macmillanhighered.com/foundationsfirst**.

e **LearningCurve** activities and additional multiple-choice grammar exercises are available for the topics in this chapter. Visit **macmillanhighered.com/foundationsfirst**.

:e **LearningCurve** activities and additional multiple-choice grammar exercises are available for the topics in this chapter. Visit **macmillanhighered.com/foundationsfirst**.

e **LearningCurve** activities and additional multiple-choice grammar exercises are available for the topics in this chapter. Visit **macmillanhighered.com/foundationsfirst**.

e **LearningCurve** activities and additional multiple-choice grammar exercises are available for the topics in this chapter. Visit **macmillanhighered.com/foundationsfirst**.

e **LearningCurve** activities and additional multiple-choice grammar exercises are available for the topics in this chapter. Visit **macmillanhighered.com/foundationsfirst**.

---

**e** LearningCurve activities and additional multiple-choice grammar exercises are available for the topics in this chapter. Visit **macmillanhighered.com/foundationsfirst**.

## 29 Grammar and Usage Issues for ESL Writers   403 🄴

## Unit 6 Understanding Punctuation, Mechanics, and Spelling   427

## 30 Using Commas   429 🄴

🄴 **LearningCurve** activities and additional multiple-choice grammar exercises are available for the topics in this chapter. Visit **macmillanhighered.com/foundationsfirst**.

e **LearningCurve** activities and additional multiple-choice grammar exercises are available for the topics in this chapter. Visit **macmillanhighered.com/foundationsfirst**.

# An Introduction to College Writing

Most people would agree that the best way to learn to write is by writing. In a sense, then, you are already something of an expert when it comes to writing; after all, you have been writing for years—not just for your classes but also in your everyday life. For example, on your Facebook page, you update your profile, post and respond to comments, and send messages; you also probably text every day. In these situations, you write confidently and concisely, without self-consciousness, because you know your audience and because you know what you want to say and how you want to say it.

Of course, this kind of writing has its limitations. As you most likely already know, college writing is more structured than personal writing; "textspeak," abbreviations, and shorthand are not acceptable in college writing assignments, and random bursts of words are acceptable only in the very roughest of first drafts or in the writing exercises you do before you start your drafts. The trick is to use the experience you have with informal writing and make it work for you in an academic context.

In college, writing is not just a convenience—a way to make plans, share feelings, or let off steam. College writing tends to be more formal than your personal writing and more focused on a particular assignment; it requires you to pull your thoughts together so you can develop (and support) original ideas and opinions and express them clearly for a variety of audiences. When you write to someone you know well, someone just like you, there is no need to explain, give examples, use precise language, or support your claims; you simply assume your reader will understand what you mean—and will often agree with you. When your audience is a college instructor or your classmates, however, you can't always count on your readers' knowing exactly what you mean or understanding the context for your remarks.

And, of course, academic writing needs to be correct. You can't assume that your readers will be willing to tolerate (or ignore) errors you might make in grammar, sentence structure, word choice, punctuation, or mechanics. Your writing also has to follow certain formal conventions and formats; you can't produce shapeless, slang-filled, punctuation-free documents and expect your readers to figure out what you mean.

Learning some specific strategies you can use in written, electronic, and oral communication will help you to communicate your ideas in various academic situations.

## Learning College Communications Skills

Effective communication is essential in college. Your success depends to a great extent on how effectively you communicate your ideas in speech and in writing—to your instructors and to your fellow students.

## Written Communication

The essays, exams, and research papers that you write for your college courses should use a level of **diction** that is somewhere between formal and informal English. You should sound conversational, but you should not use slang, abbreviations, incorrect grammar, or other nonstandard forms. When the situation calls for it, use the technical vocabulary of the academic field for which you are writing. Choose your words carefully, and make sure you say exactly what you intend to say.

Remember that good writing is not overly complex, pompous, or flowery. Your purpose is not to impress your readers with your vocabulary but to be clear and to use language that is appropriate for the occasion. For this reason, try not to use words like *utilize* when you mean *use* or *terminate* when you mean *end*.

Also, be careful to avoid **offensive language** (language that is sexist or racist or that includes profanity). Sexist language intentionally (or unintentionally) degrades or excludes a group of people. In your writing, always refer to adult females as *women*, not as *girls* or *ladies*. In addition, do not use *he* or *him* when your subject could be either male or female. Instead, use the plural *they* or *them* or the phrase *he or she* (not *he/she*). Whenever possible, use a nonsexist alternative to a sexist usage—for example, *people* instead of *mankind*.

### WORD POWER

**diction** choice of words; style of expression

## Electronic Communication

Many people think of electronic communication as informal, so they use an informal style. In much of the writing you do every day—texts, Facebook updates, blog posts, tweets, and so on—you use first person (*I*), contractions, and slang. For example, if you are planning to make an appointment with your academic adviser, you might send a text like the following to a friend to let him or her know where you'll be.

Even though personal emails and texts may be informal (disregarding the rules of grammar, punctuation, and spelling), the more formal electronic communications you send to your instructors should follow the rules of standard written English. This means that an email to your adviser should not contain abbreviations or shorthand, and it should not omit words or punctuation to save time or space. For example, if you have concerns about a course, you might send the following email to your instructor:

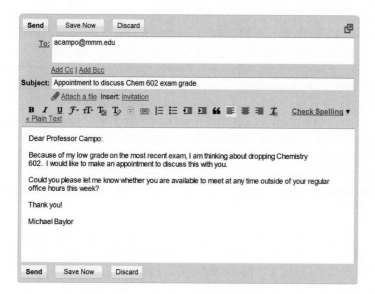

# FYI

## Usages to Avoid

Although the following are acceptable in informal electronic communication, they are *never* acceptable in academic essays or in emails to instructors:

- **Shorthand,** such as *4* for *for*, *r* for *are*, *u* for *you*, and *c* for *see*

- **Abbreviations,** such as *JK* ("just kidding"), *btw* ("by the way"), *GTG* ("got to go"), *BWTM* ("but wait, there's more"), and *TTYL* ("talk to you later")

- **Emoticons,** typed characters such as : - ) or : - ( that indicate a writer's mood or feelings

- **Inappropriate salutations,** such as *Hi Prof* or *Hey*—or the instructor's first name.

## Oral Communication

In general, the same guidelines that apply to written communication also apply to speaking. In one-on-one situations, take cues from your instructor about the level of formality that is required. Remember, it's fine to be friendly, but you need to be respectful and not overly familiar. For example, never call a professor by his or her first name unless you are specifically asked to do so.

When you ask a question in class, let the instructor know that you have read the assignment. For example, introduce your question with a phrase such as "According to the textbook" or "As the article you assigned says." Never begin a question or answer with "I haven't read the assignment, but. . . ."

When you speak in class, be respectful of your fellow students: listen to what they have to say, and don't interrupt. When it's your turn to speak, choose your words carefully, speak slowly, and try to make your points clearly. Use the technical language of a discipline when it is appropriate to do so. For example, use terms like *protagonist* (not *hero*) in literature, *titration* (not *mixture*) in chemistry, and *cohort* (not *group*) in sociology. As you do in written communication, use language that is suitable for the situation. Do not use slang or nonstandard constructions, and never use language that might be seen as offensive.

Remember, to succeed in college, you have to learn to write well—and as you go through this book, you will learn the skills and strategies you need to do so.

# 1 Reading for Academic Success

## 1 Studying Life

### Why are frogs croaking?

Amphibians—frogs, toads, and salamanders—have been around for a long time. They watched the dinosaurs come and go. But today amphibian populations around the world are in dramatic decline, with more than a third of the world's amphibian species threatened with extinction. Why?

Biologists work to answer this question by making observations and doing experiments. A number of factors may be involved, and one possible cause may be the effects of agricultural pesticides and herbicides. Several studies have shown that many of these chemicals tested at realistic concentrations do not kill amphibians. But Tyrone Hayes, a biologist at the University of California at Berkeley, probed deeper.

Hayes focused on atrazine, the most widely used herbicide in the world and a common contaminant in fresh water. More than 70 million pounds of atrazine are applied to farmland in the United States every year, and it is used in at least 20 countries. Atrazine is usually applied in the spring, when many amphibians are breeding and thousands of tadpoles swim in the ditches, ponds, and streams that receive runoff from farms.

In his laboratory, Hayes and his associates raised frog tadpoles in water containing no atrazine and in water with concentrations ranging from 0.01 parts per billion (ppb) up to 25 ppb. The U.S. Environmental Protection Agency considers environmental levels of atrazine of 10 to 20 ppb of no concern; the level it considers safe in drinking water is 3 ppb. Rainwater in Iowa has been measured to contain 40 ppb. In Switzerland, where the use of atrazine is illegal, the chemical has been measured at approximately 1 ppb in rainwater.

In the Hayes laboratory, concentrations as low as 0.1 ppb had a dramatic effect on tadpole development: it feminized the males. In some of the adult males that developed from these larvae, the vocal structures used in mating calls were smaller than normal, female sex organs developed, and eggs were found growing in the testes. In other studies, normal adult male frogs exposed to 25 ppb had a tenfold reduction in testosterone levels and did not produce sperm. You can imagine the disastrous effects these developmental and hormonal changes could have on the capacity of frogs to breed and reproduce.

But Hayes's experiments were performed in the laboratory, with a species of frog bred for laboratory use. Would his results be the same in nature? To find out, he and his students traveled from Utah to Iowa, sampling water and collecting frogs. They analyzed the water

**Frogs Are Having Serious Problems**  An alarming number of species of frogs, such as this tiny leaf frog (*Agalychnis calcarifer*) from Ecuador, are in danger of becoming extinct. The numerous possible reasons for the decline in global amphibian populations have been a subject of widespread scientific investigation.

Page: Courtesy of Sinauer Associates, Inc. | *HMS Beagle* illustration: British Library/Robana/Hulton Fine Art Collection/Getty | Red-eyed tree frog photo: © Aleksey Stemmer/Shutterstock.com

## seeing and writing

The picture above shows a page of a textbook with important information highlighted and notes in the margins. When you read your textbooks, you will understand them better if you write notes directly on the pages. Write a few sentences explaining how you mark your textbooks — or explaining why you don't. Try to use the Word Power words in your response.

### WORD POWER

**annotate** to make explanatory notes on a page

**highlight** to mark a page to emphasize important details

In this chapter, you will learn

- how to become an active reader **(1a)**
- how to preview, highlight, annotate, outline, and summarize a reading assignment **(1b)**
- how to read different kinds of texts **(1c)**

## 1a Becoming an Active Reader

Reading is essential in all your college courses. To get the most out of your college reading, you should be prepared to think critically about what you read—commenting on, questioning, evaluating, and even challenging what the text says. In other words, you should learn to become an active reader.

In practical terms, being an **active reader** means actively participating in the reading process—approaching a reading assignment with a clear understanding of your purpose, and writing in the text to help you understand what you are reading.

You may find it easier to understand the concept of active reading if you see how this strategy applies to "reading" a picture. Like a written text, every **visual text**—a photograph, an advertisement, a chart, or a graph; a work of fine art, such as a painting or a piece of sculpture; and even a web page—has a message to communicate. Visual texts communicate their messages through the specific words and images their creators choose and through the way these words and images are arranged on the page.

When you approach a visual, your first step is to identify the words and images you see. Then, you consider how they are arranged and how they are related to one another.

In the ad for Tropicana orange juice on the next page, the main idea—that the product's juicier pulp gives it a fresh-squeezed taste—is expressed in the heading: "We squeeze the oranges, not the pulp." This message is supported by the large central image, which links the juice carton, the glass of juice, and the orange. The smaller type presents specific information that explains how and why this brand of juice is fresher and tastier than others.

### Questions for Tropicana Ad (p. 9)

☐ Why is the orange labeled "Handle with Care"?

☐ Why is it placed in front of the juice carton?

☐ Do you think this ad would convince consumers to purchase Tropicana rather than another brand of orange juice? If so, why? If not, why not?

*Tropicana Advertisement*

In the visual below, a painting by the American artist Winslow Homer, the images are not supported by written text, but the message is still clear. Here, the central image—the man alone in the middle of the ocean, surrounded by open space—communicates the painting's emotions: fear, desperation, hopelessness. The surrounding images—the choppy waves, the threatening sky, the sharks—support this impression.

*Winslow Homer, The Gulf Stream (1899)*

When you "read" visuals such as these, at first you get just a general sense of what you see. But, as you read more actively, you let your mind take you beyond the page. You ask yourself why certain details were selected, why they are arranged as they are, what comes to mind when you look at the picture, and whether you find the visual effective.

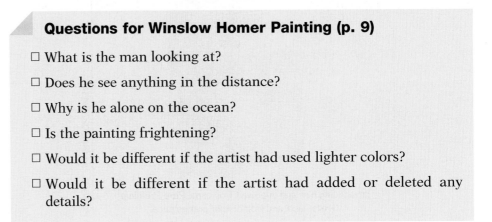

**Questions for Winslow Homer Painting (p. 9)**

☐ What is the man looking at?

☐ Does he see anything in the distance?

☐ Why is he alone on the ocean?

☐ Is the painting frightening?

☐ Would it be different if the artist had used lighter colors?

☐ Would it be different if the artist had added or deleted any details?

Active reading of a written text, like active reading of a visual text, is a writing activity that encourages you to "read between the lines." In this way, it helps you develop a deeper understanding of the material. The process of actively reading written texts is explained and illustrated in the following section.

## 1b  Reading Written Texts

### Determining Your Purpose

Even before you start reading, you should consider some questions about your **purpose**—why you are reading. The answers to these questions will help you understand what kind of information you hope to get out of your reading and how you will use this information.

**Questions about Your Purpose**

☐ Will you be expected to discuss what you are reading? If so, will you discuss it in class? In a conference with your instructor?

☐ Will you have to write about what you are reading? If so, will you be expected to write an informal response (for example, a journal entry) or a more formal one (for example, an essay)?

☐ Will you be tested on the material?

# Previewing

When you **preview** a text, you don't read it word for word; instead, you **skim** the text to get a sense of the writer's main idea, key supporting points, and general emphasis. You should begin by focusing on the title, the first paragraph (which often contains a purpose statement or overview), and the last paragraph (which often contains a summary of the writer's points). You should also look at each paragraph's first sentence. As you skim, you should look for clues to the passage's content and the writer's emphasis in other **visual signals**, such as headings, boxed words, and images.

---

### Using Visual Signals

- Look at the title.
- Look at the opening and closing paragraphs.
- Look at each paragraph's first sentence.
- Look at headings.
- Look at *italicized* and **boldfaced** words.
- Look at numbered lists.
- Look at bulleted lists (like this one).
- Look at visuals (graphs, charts, tables, photographs, and so on).
- Look at any information that is boxed.
- Look at any information that is in color.

---

When you have finished previewing, you should have a general sense of what the writer wants to communicate.

**PRACTICE**

**1-1**   Following is a passage that defines the term *microloans* and explains how they work. Preview the passage in preparation for class discussion and for the other activities that will be assigned throughout section 1b.

As you read, try to identify the writer's main idea and key supporting points, and write that information on the blank lines that follow the passage.

Microloans: Promise and Performance

More than a third of the world's people are "very poor": they survive on less than $2 a day. How can these people raise their standard of living? One answer may be microcredit. *Microcredit* means extending very small loans —

**microloans** — to poor people who are unable to secure loans from traditional banks. Thousands of microcredit institutions operate in countries around the world. In fact, more than 75 million borrowers hold loans totaling more than $40 billion. Supporters and opponents have very different views about the effects of microloans, but the truth probably lies somewhere in between.

To understand the effects that microloans might have, we need to understand the challenges of microcredit for borrowers and lenders. First, microloans are loans, not charity; the loans must be repaid. Second, lenders have to charge high interest rates on these loans to offset the cost of making and keeping track of many small loans.

In order to deal with these challenges, microcredit institutions can use the following techniques to make lending more successful:

1. They can *lend to groups* instead of individuals. With group lending, the group is responsible for repayment. If an individual group member is unable to make a payment, the other members can each pay a little more.

2. They can *lend to women* instead of men. Women are more likely to use the loans to improve a business and to raise their family's standard of living. Women are also more willing to accept very small loans and are more likely to repay.

3. They can use *graduated lending*. With this practice, borrowers begin with very small loans; then, if they repay these first loans, they can get larger loans.

Statistics show that microloans have helped people. Microloans have strengthened businesses, created jobs, and raised incomes. They have also led to better nutrition and better housing. In addition, although interest rates are high, they are much lower than the rates charged by private lenders.

However, statistics also show that microcredit has not been very good at helping the poorest of the poor. Furthermore, microloans can have negative consequences. For example, because of the high interest rates, some borrowers are unable to repay their loans. This means they are always in debt. In addition, some borrowers use the money from their loans to lend to others, thus becoming lenders themselves.

Overall, microcredit has not been nearly as successful as its supporters hope it will be, but the negative consequences have not been as bad as opponents fear.

Microcredit is not a cure-all for poverty, but it certainly can help poor people improve their lives.

**Main idea**

_____

_____

**Key supporting points**

1. _____

_____

2. _____

_____

3. _____

_____

4. _____

_____

# Highlighting

After you have previewed a passage, read it again, this time more carefully. As you read, keep a pen or pencil (or a highlighter pen) handy so you can **highlight**, using underlining and symbols to identify important information. This active reading strategy will reinforce your understanding of the writer's main idea and key supporting points and will help you to see the relationships among them. (If you want to highlight material from a book that you do not own, photocopy the passage first.)

## Highlighting Symbols

- Underline or highlight key ideas.
- Box or circle words or phrases you want to remember.
- Place a check mark (✓) or star (✱) next to an important idea.
- Place a double check mark (✓✓) or double star (✱✱) next to an especially significant idea.
- Draw lines or arrows to connect related ideas.
- Put a question mark beside a word or idea that you do not understand.
- Number the writer's key supporting points or examples.

Highlight freely, but try not to highlight too much. Remember, you will eventually have to read every highlighted word, phrase, and sentence—and your study time is limited. Highlight only the most important, most useful information—for example, definitions, examples, and summaries.

## FYI

### Knowing What to Highlight

You want to highlight what's important—but how do you *know* what's important?

- Look for the same **visual signals** that you looked for when you did your previewing. Many of the ideas you will need to highlight will probably be found in material that is visually set off from the rest of the text—opening and closing paragraphs, lists, and so on.

- Look for **verbal signals**—words and phrases like *however, therefore, another reason,* and *the most important point*—that often introduce key points. (Some of these verbal signals are listed in the box that follows.)

Together, these visual and verbal signals will give you clues to the writer's meaning and emphasis.

### Using Verbal Signals

- Look for phrases that signal emphasis ("The *primary* reason"; "The *most important* idea").

- Look for repeated words and phrases.

- Look for words that signal addition (*also, in addition, furthermore*).

- Look for words that signal time sequence (*first, after, then, next, finally*).

- Look for words that identify causes and effects (*because, as a result, for this reason*).

- Look for words that introduce examples (*for example, for instance*).

- Look for words that signal comparison (*likewise, similarly*).

- Look for words that signal contrast (*unlike, although, in contrast*).

- Look for words that signal contradiction (*however, on the contrary*).

- Look for words that signal a narrowing of the writer's focus (*in fact, specifically, in other words*).

- Look for words that signal summaries or conclusions (*to sum up, in conclusion*).

Here is how a student highlighted a passage from an introductory American history textbook. The passage focuses on the position of African Americans in society in the years immediately following World War II. Because the passage includes no visual signals apart from the title and paragraph divisions, the student looked carefully for verbal signals to guide her highlighting.

"I spent four years in the army to free a bunch of Frenchmen and Dutchmen," an African-American corporal declared, "and I'm hanged if I'm going to let the Alabama version of the Germans kick me around ✓ when I get home." Black veterans as well as civilians resolved that the return to peace would not be a return to the racial injustices of prewar ✓ America. Their political (clout) had grown with the migration of two million African Americans to northern and western cities, where they could vote and participate in ongoing struggles to end discrimination in housing and education. Pursuing civil rights through the courts and Congress, the National Association for the Advancement of Colored People (NAACP) counted half a million members.

In the postwar years, individual African Americans broke through the color barrier, achieving several "firsts." Jackie Robinson integrated major league baseball, playing for the Brooklyn Dodgers and braving abuse from fans and players to win the Rookie of the Year Award in 1947. In 1950, Ralph J. Bunche received the Nobel Peace Prize for his United Nations work, and Gwendolyn Brooks was awarded the Pulitzer Prize for poetry. Charlie "Bird" Parker, Ella Fitzgerald, and a host of other black musicians were hugely popular across racial lines.

✱ ✱ Still, for most African Americans little had changed, especially in the South, where violence greeted their attempts to assert their rights. Armed white men turned back Medgar Evers (who would become a ① key civil rights leader in the 1960s) and four other veterans trying to vote in Mississippi. A mob lynched Isaac Nixon for voting in Georgia, ② and an all-white jury acquitted the men accused of his murder. In the

③ South, <u>political leaders and local vigilantes routinely intimidated potential black voters</u> with threats of violence and warnings that they could lose their livelihoods.

—James L. Roark et al., *The American Promise,* Fifth Edition

The student who highlighted this passage was preparing for a meeting of her study group. Because the class would be taking a midterm the following week, she needed to understand the material.

The student began her highlighting by placing check marks beside two important advances for African Americans cited in paragraph 1 and by drawing arrows to specific examples of blacks' political influence. (Although she thought she knew the meaning of the word *clout,* she circled it anyway and placed a question mark above it to remind herself to check its meaning in a dictionary.)

In paragraph 2, she boxed the names of prominent postwar African Americans and underlined their contributions, circling and starring the key word "firsts." She then underlined and double-starred the entire passage's main idea—the first sentence of paragraph 3—numbering the examples in the paragraph that support this idea.

**PRACTICE**

**1-2**  Review the highlighted passage from the history textbook (pp. 15–16). How would your own highlighting of this passage be similar to or different from the sample student highlighting?

**PRACTICE**

**1-3**  Reread "Microloans: Promise and Performance" (pp. 11–13). As you read, highlight the passage by underlining and starring main ideas, boxing and circling key words, and checkmarking important points. Circle each unfamiliar word, and put a question mark above it.

## Annotating

As you highlight, you should also annotate what you are reading. **Annotating** a passage means reading critically and making notes—of questions, reactions, reminders, and ideas for discussion or writing—in the margins or between the lines. Keeping a record of ideas as they occur to you will help prepare you to discuss the reading with your classmates—and, eventually, to write about it.

Considering the following questions as you read will help you to read critically and to write useful annotations.

## Questions for Critical Reading

☐ What is the writer saying?

☐ What is the writer's purpose—his or her reason for writing?

☐ What kind of audience is the writer addressing?

☐ Is the writer responding to another writer's ideas?

☐ What is the writer's main idea?

☐ How does the writer support his or her points? With facts? Opinions? Both facts and opinions? What supporting details and examples does the writer use?

☐ Does the writer include enough supporting details and examples?

☐ Do you understand the writer's vocabulary?

☐ Do you understand the writer's ideas?

☐ Do you agree with the points the writer is making?

☐ Do you see any connections between this reading assignment and something else you have read?

The following passage reproduces the student's highlighting of the American history textbook from pages 15–16 and also illustrates her annotations.

"I spent four years in the army to free a bunch of Frenchmen and Dutchmen," an African-American corporal declared, "and I'm hanged if I'm going to let the Alabama version of the Germans kick me around when I get home." Black veterans as well as civilians resolved that the return to peace would not be a return to the racial injustices of prewar America. Their political clout had grown with the migration of two million African Americans to northern and western cities, where they could vote and participate in ongoing struggles to end discrimination in housing and education. Pursuing civil rights through the courts and Congress, the National Association for the Advancement of Colored People (NAACP) counted half a million members.

*Achievements of African Americans:*

*Military*

? = power

*Politics*

*Sports*

In the postwar years, individual African Americans broke through the color barrier, achieving several "firsts." Jackie Robinson integrated major league baseball, playing for the Brooklyn Dodgers and braving abuse from fans and players to win the Rookie of the Year Award in 1947. In 1950, Ralph J. Bunche received the Nobel Peace Prize for his United Nations work, and Gwendolyn Brooks was awarded the Pulitzer Prize for poetry. Charlie "Bird" Parker, Ella Fitzgerald, and a host of other black musicians were hugely popular across racial lines.

*World politics*

*Literature*

*Music*

*In South, voters intimidated*

Still, for most African Americans little had changed, especially in the South, where violence greeted their attempts to assert their rights. ① Armed white men turned back Medgar Evers (who would become a key civil rights leader in the 1960s) and four other veterans trying to ② vote in Mississippi. A mob lynched Isaac Nixon for voting in Georgia, and an all-white jury acquitted the men accused of his murder. In the ③ South, political leaders and local vigilantes routinely intimidated potential black voters with threats of violence and warnings that they could lose their livelihoods.

— James L. Roark et al., *The American Promise*, Fifth Edition

In her annotations, this student put some of the writer's key ideas into her own words and recorded ideas she hoped to discuss in her study group.

**PRACTICE**

**1-4**　Reread "Microloans: Promise and Performance" (pp. 11–13). As you reread, refer to the Questions for Critical Reading (p. 17), and use them to guide you as you write your own ideas and questions in the margins. Note where you agree or disagree with the writer, and briefly explain why. Quickly summarize any points you think are particularly important. Take time to look up any unfamiliar words you have circled, and write brief definitions for them.

**PRACTICE**

**1-5**　Trade books with another student, and read over his or her highlighting and annotating of "Microloans: Promise and Performance." How are your written responses similar to the other student's? How are they different? Do your classmate's responses help you to see anything new about the article?

## Outlining

Another technique you can use to understand a reading assignment better is **outlining**. Unlike a **formal outline**, which follows fairly strict conventions—for example, major heads are identified by roman numerals, less important heads by capital letters, and so on—an **informal outline** is easy to construct. An informal outline can also be a valuable reading tool: it shows you which ideas are more important than others, and it shows you how ideas are related.

## FYI

### Constructing an Informal Outline

To construct an informal outline of a reading assignment, follow these guidelines.

1. Write or type the passage's main idea at the top of a sheet of paper.

2. At the left margin, write down the most important idea of the first paragraph or section of the passage.

3. Indent the next line a few spaces, and list the examples or details that support this idea.

4. As ideas become more specific, indent further. (Ideas that have the same degree of importance are indented the same distance from the left margin.)

5. Repeat this process with each paragraph or section of the passage.

*Note:* Your word-processing program's outline function will automatically format the different levels of your outline.

The student who highlighted and annotated the textbook passage on pages 17–18 made the following informal outline to help her understand its content.

Main idea: Although African Americans had achieved a lot by the end of World War II, they still faced prejudice and violence.

    African Americans as a group had made significant advances.
        Many had served in the military.
        Political influence was growing.
           More African Americans could vote.
           NAACP membership increased.

    Individual African Americans had made significant advances.
        Sports: Jackie Robinson
        World politics: Ralph Bunche
        Literature: Gwendolyn Brooks
        Music: Charlie Parker and Ella Fitzgerald

Despite these advances, much remained the same for African Americans, especially in the South.

Blacks faced violence and even lynching if they tried to vote.

Elected officials and vigilantes threatened potential voters.

**PRACTICE**

**1-6**    Working on your own or in a small group, make an informal outline of "Microloans: Promise and Performance" (pp. 11–13). Refer to your highlighting and annotations as you construct the outline. When you have finished, check to make sure your outline shows which ideas the writer is emphasizing and how those ideas are related.

## Summarizing

Once you have highlighted and annotated a passage, you may want to try summarizing it. A **summary** retells, *in your own words,* what a passage is about. A summary condenses a passage, so it leaves out all but the most important ideas. A summary generally omits most details and examples, and it does not include your own ideas or opinions.

# FYI

## Writing a Summary

1. Review your outline.

2. Consulting your outline, restate the passage's main idea *in your own words*.

3. Consulting your outline, restate the passage's supporting points. Add words and phrases between sentences where necessary to connect ideas.

4. Reread the original passage to make sure you haven't left out anything significant.

The student who highlighted, annotated, and outlined the passage from the history textbook wrote the following summary.

Although African Americans had achieved a lot by the end of World War II, they still faced prejudice and even violence. As a group, they had made significant advances, which included military service and increased participation in politics, as indicated by voting and NAACP membership. Individual African Americans had also made significant advances in sports, world politics, literature, and music. Despite these advances, however, much remained the same for African Americans after World War II. Their situation was especially bad in the South. For example, African Americans still faced the threat of violence and even lynching if they tried to vote. Elected officials and vigilantes also discouraged blacks from voting, often threatening them with economic retaliation or even violence.

**PRACTICE**

**1-7** Write a brief summary of "Microloans: Promise and Performance" (pp. 11–13). Use your informal outline as a guide, and remember to keep your summary short and to the point. (Note that your summary will be shorter than the original passage.)

## 1c Reading in College, in the Community, and in the Workplace

In college, in your life as a citizen of a community, and in the workplace, you will read material in a variety of different formats—for example, textbooks, newspapers, websites, and job-related memos, emails, blog posts, and reports.

Although the active reading process you have just reviewed can be applied to all kinds of material, various kinds of reading often require slightly different strategies during the previewing stage. One reason for this is that different kinds of reading may have different purposes—to present information, to persuade, and so on. Another reason is that the various texts you read are aimed at different audiences, and different audiences require different signals about content and emphasis. For these reasons, you need to look for different kinds of verbal and visual signals when you read different kinds of material.

### Reading Textbooks

Much of the reading you do in college is in textbooks (like this one). The purpose of a textbook is to present information, and when you read a textbook, your goal is to understand that information. To do this, you need to figure out which ideas are most important as well as which points support those key ideas and which examples illustrate them.

## checklist

### Reading Textbooks

Look for the following features as you preview.

- [ ] **Boldfaced** and *italicized* words, which can indicate terms to be defined

- [ ] Boxed checklists or summaries, which may appear at the ends of sections or chapters

- [ ] Bulleted or numbered lists, which may list key reasons or examples or summarize important material

*(continued)*

*(continued from previous page)*

- ☐ Diagrams, charts, tables, graphs, photographs, and other visuals that illustrate the writer's points
- ☐ Marginal quotations and definitions
- ☐ Marginal cross-references
- ☐ Web links

## PRACTICE
### 1-8

The following passage from an introductory psychology textbook defines and illustrates the term *attribution*. Preview the passage to identify the main idea and key supporting points. Then, highlight and annotate the passage.

# Attribution
## Explaining Behavior

### Key Theme

- ▪ Attribution refers to the process of explaining your own behavior and the behavior of other people.

### Key Questions

- ▪ What are the fundamental attribution error and the self-serving bias?
- ▪ How do attributional biases affect our judgments about the causes of behavior?
- ▪ How does culture affect attributional processes?

As you're studying in the college library, the activities of two workers catch your attention. The two men are trying to lift and move a large file cabinet. "Okay, let's tip it this way and lift it," the first guy says with considerable authority. The second guy sheepishly nods agreement. In unison, they heave and tip the file cabinet. When they do, the top two file drawers fly out, smashing into the first guy's head. As the file cabinet goes crashing to the floor, you bite your lip to keep from laughing and think to yourself, "What a pair of 40-watt bulbs."

Why did you arrive at that conclusion? After all, it's completely possible that the workers are not dimwits. Maybe the lock on the file drawers slipped or broke when they tipped the cabinet. Or maybe someone failed to empty the drawers.

**Attribution** is the process of inferring the cause of someone's behavior, including your own. Psychologists also use the word *attribution* to refer to the explanation you make for a particular behavior. The attributions you make strongly influence your thoughts and feelings about other people.

If your explanation for the file cabinet incident was that the workers were a couple of clumsy doofuses, you demonstrated a common cognitive bias. The **fundamental attribution error** is the tendency to spontaneously attribute the behavior of others to internal, personal characteristics, while ignoring or underestimating the role of external, situational factors (Ross, 1977). Even though it's entirely possible that situational forces were behind another person's behavior, we tend to automatically assume that the cause is an internal, personal characteristic (Bauman & Skitka, 2010; Zimbardo, 2007).

Notice, however, that when it comes to explaining our *own* behavior, we tend to be biased in the opposite direction. Rather than internal, personal attributions, we're more likely to explain our own behavior using *external, situational* attributions. He dropped the file cabinet because he's a dimwit; you dropped the file cabinet because there wasn't a good way to get a solid grip on it. Some jerk pulled out in front of your car because she's a reckless, inconsiderate moron; you pulled out in front of her car because an overgrown hedge blocked your view (Hennessy & others, 2005). And so on.

Why the discrepancy in accounting for the behavior of others as compared to our own behavior? Part of the explanation is that we simply have more information about the potential causes of our own behavior than we do about the causes of other people's behavior. When you observe another driver turn directly into the path of your car, that's typically the only information you have on which to judge his or her behavior. But when *you* inadvertently pull in front of another car, you perceive your own behavior in the context of the various situational factors that influenced your action. You're aware of such factors as visual obstacles, road conditions, driving distractions, and so forth. You also know what motivated your behavior and how differently you have behaved in similar situations in the past. Thus, you're much more aware of the extent to which your behavior has been influenced by situational factors (Jones, 1990).

The fundamental attribution error plays a role in a common explanatory pattern called **blaming the victim**. The innocent victim of a crime, disaster, or serious illness is blamed for having somehow caused the misfortune or for not having taken steps to prevent it. For example, many people blame the poor for their dire straits, the sick for bringing on their illnesses, and battered women and rape survivors for somehow "provoking" their attackers.

The blaming the victim explanatory pattern is reinforced by another common cognitive bias.

*AP Photo/Tom Gannam*

**Blaming the Victim** *Fifteen-year-old Shawn Hornbeck is shown at a press conference shortly after being reunited with his family. Four years earlier, Shawn had been kidnapped and held captive. When the FBI suspected Shawn's kidnapper in the abduction of another boy, both boys were rescued. As details of Shawn's captivity became public, many people asked why Shawn hadn't tried to escape or call the police while his kidnapper was at work. As it turned out, the kidnapper had abused and terrorized Shawn for months. At one point, he tried to strangle Shawn. When Shawn pleaded for his life, the kidnapper made the boy promise that he would never try to escape. "There wasn't a day when I didn't think that he'd just kill me," Shawn later recalled. Why do people often "blame the victim" after crimes, accidents, or other tragedies?*

**Hindsight bias** is the tendency, after an event has occurred, to overestimate one's ability to have foreseen or predicted the outcome. In everyday conversations, this is the person who confidently proclaims *after* the event, "I could have told you that would happen" or "I can't believe they couldn't see that coming." In the case of blaming the victim, hindsight bias makes it seem as if the victim should have been able to predict—and prevent—what happened (Goldinger & others, 2003).

Why do people often resort to blaming the victim? People have a strong need to believe that the world is fair—that "we get what we deserve and deserve what we get." Social psychologist Melvin Lerner (1980) calls this the **just-world hypothesis**. Blaming the victim reflects the belief that, because the world is just, the victim must have done something to deserve his or her fate. Collectively, these cognitive biases and explanatory patterns help psychologically insulate us from the uncomfortable thought "It could have just as easily been me" (Alves & Correia, 2008, Ijzerman & Van Prooijen, 2008).

> — Don H. Hockenbury and Sandra K. Hockenbury,
> *Psychology*, Sixth Edition

## Reading News Articles

As a student, as an employee, and as a citizen, you read school, community, local, and national newspapers in print and online. Like textbooks, newspapers communicate information. In addition to containing relatively straightforward news articles, newspapers also contain editorials (which aim to persuade) as well as feature articles (which may be designed to entertain as well as to inform).

## checklist

### Reading News Articles

Look for the following features as you preview.

- [ ] Headlines
- [ ] Boldfaced headings within articles
- [ ] Labels like *editorial*, *commentary*, or *opinion*, which indicate that an article is the writer's opinion
- [ ] Brief biographical information at the end of an opinion piece
- [ ] Phrases or sentences set in **boldface** (to emphasize key points)
- [ ] The article's first sentence, which often answers the questions *who*, *what*, *why*, *where*, *when*, and *how*
- [ ] The **dateline**, which tells you the city the writer is reporting from
- [ ] Photographs, charts, graphs, and other visuals

In *print news articles*, related articles that appear on the same page—for example, boxed information or **sidebars**, which are short articles that provide additional background on people and places mentioned in the article

In *online news articles*, links to related articles, reader comments, or other useful material

**PRACTICE**

**1-9**   Using the checklist above as a guide, preview the following newspaper article. When you have finished, highlight and annotate the article.

# Are Smartphones Turning Us into Bad Samaritans?
## Busy with our tablets and smartphones in public places, we may be losing our sense of duty to others

Christine Rosen

*We can't afford to be so preoccupied with our gadgets when we're in public spaces, says writer Christine Rosen in a conversation with WSJ's Gary Rosen.*

In late September, on a crowded commuter train in San Francisco, a man shot and killed 20-year-old student Justin Valdez. As security footage shows, before the gunman fired, he waved around his .45 caliber pistol and at one point even pointed it across the aisle. Yet no one on the crowded train noticed because they were so focused on their smartphones and tablets. "These weren't concealed movements—the gun is very clear,"

District Attorney George Gascon later told the Associated Press. "These people are in very close proximity with him, and nobody sees this. They're just so engrossed, texting and reading and whatnot. They're completely oblivious of their surroundings."

Another recent attack, on a blind man walking down the street in broad daylight in Philadelphia, garnered attention because security footage later revealed that many passersby ignored the assault and never called 911. Commenting to a local radio station, Philadelphia's chief of police Charles Ramsay said that this lack of response was becoming "more and more common" and noted that people are more likely to use their cellphones to record assaults than to call the police.

Indeed, YouTube features hundreds of such videos—outbreaks of violence on sidewalks, in shopping malls and at restaurants. Many of these brawls, such as the one that broke out between two women during a victory parade for the New York Giants in 2012, feature crowds of people gathered around, cameras aloft and filming the spectacle.

Our use of technology has fundamentally changed not just our awareness in public spaces but our sense of duty to others. Engaged with the glowing screens in front of us rather than with the people around us, we often honestly don't notice what is going on. Adding to the problem is the ease with which we can record and send images, which encourages those of us who are paying attention to document emergencies rather than deal with them. The fascination with capturing images of violence is nothing new, as anyone who has perused Weegee's photographs of bloody crime scenes from the early 20th century can attest. But the ubiquity of camera-enabled cellphones has shifted the boundaries of acceptable behavior in these situations. We are all Weegee now.

© Frances Roberts/Getty Images

*Our screens often keep us from noticing what's going on around us.*

But if everyone is filming an emergency, who is responsible for intervening in it? Consider an event from December 2012, when a man was pushed onto the subway tracks in New York City. Struggling unsuccessfully to heave himself onto the platform, he turned, in his final seconds, to see the train barreling down on him. We know this because a freelance photographer who happened to be on the platform took a picture of the awful episode and sold it to the *New York Post*, which ran it on the front page the next day, prompting public outrage about profiting from a man's death. The photographer noted that others on the platform closer to the man made no effort to rescue him and quickly pulled out their phones to capture images of his dead body.

The brutal nighttime stabbing of Kitty Genovese on a New York City sidewalk in 1964 became a symbol of the uninvolved bystander: Many people heard her screams, but no one went outside to assist her or to intervene in the attack. The incident spawned much hand-wringing and some intriguing social-science research about why we don't always come to each other's aid.

In a 1968 study, the sociologists John Darley and Bibb Latané tested the willingness of individuals to intervene in various emergency situations (a "lady in distress," a smoke-filled room). They found that the larger the number of people present, the more the sense of responsibility was diffused for any given individual. When alone, people were far more likely to help.

In subsequent experiments, carried out by Irving Piliavin, bystanders were much more likely to help an actor on a subway car who pretended to be ill and asked for help. Why? As psychologist Elliot Aronson wrote in his classic textbook *The Social Animal*, "People riding on the same subway car do have the feeling of sharing a common fate, and they were in a face-to-face situation with the victim, from which there was no immediate escape."

The problem with many of our new gadgets, as the San Francisco shooting suggests, is that they often keep us from experiencing these face-to-face situations and the unspoken obligations that go with them. Most of these duties—to be aware of others, to practice basic civility—are not onerous. But on rare occasions, we are called upon to help others who are threatened or whose lives are in danger. At those moments, we should not be anticipating how many views we will get on YouTube if we film their distress; we should act. To do otherwise is to risk becoming a society not just of apathetic bystanders but of cruel voyeurs.

## Reading Web Pages

In schools, businesses, and community settings, people turn to the web for information. However, because many websites are busy and crowded, reading them can require you to work hard to distinguish important information from not-so-important material.

## checklist

### Reading Web Pages

Look for the following features as you preview.

☐ The site's URL designation (.com, .org, .gov, and so on)

☐ Links to other sites (often underlined in blue)

☐ Graphics

☐ Color

☐ Headings

☐ Boxed material

☐ Placement of images and text on the page

☐ Type size

☐ Photographs

**PRACTICE**

**1-10**  The following is the home page of the U.S. Environmental Protection Agency. Preview this page, looking closely at the features listed in the checklist above. What information attracts your attention? Why? Do you think this page communicates its information effectively? Why or why not? How could its presentation be improved?

*Environmental Protection Agency (EPA) home page*

## Reading on the Job

In your workplace, you may be called on to read memos, letters, emails, and reports. These documents are often addressed to a group rather than to a single person. (Note that the most important information is often presented *first*—in a subject line or in the first paragraph.)

## checklist

### Reading on the Job

Look for the following features as you preview.

- [ ] Numbered or bulleted lists of tasks or problems (numbers indicate the order of the items' importance)

- [ ] The first and last paragraphs and the first sentence of each body paragraph, which often contain key information

- [ ] **Boldfaced**, underlined, or *italicized* words

- [ ] In a report, visuals that illustrate key concepts

- [ ] In electronic communications, the person(s) addressed, the subject line, and links to the web

- [ ] In a memo or a report, headings that highlight key topics or points

**PRACTICE**

**1-11** Preview the following two examples of on-the-job writing, and answer the following two questions.

- What is each writer's purpose (that is, what does the writer want to accomplish)?
- What is the most important piece of information each writer wants to communicate?

Then, highlight and annotate each of the two examples, and write a brief summary of each in your own words.

1. A memo

September 8, 2013
To: Hector Garzon, Executive Director
From: Marco Morales, Director, Drug and Alcohol Unit
Subject: Marta Diaz-Gold

Marta Diaz-Gold has returned to work from her maternity leave. I have assigned her a caseload that consists of our clients who have been referred from the Road to Recovery program. This means that the funds for substance abuse counseling that go to Road to Recovery can now be used to pay

Marta's salary and that the Road to Recovery case managers can provide support for our counseling services.

Marta and I have agreed on the following:

- Regular monthly meetings with Road to Recovery case managers
- Weekly reports to me from Marta regarding progress on the Road to Recovery caseload
- Joint review of Marta's work by Miriam Cabrera and myself after six months

Marta will be meeting with the current counselor and each individual client this week so she can make a smooth transition into her new position. As of next week, she will have full responsibility for all these clients. Because the Road to Recovery clients will not constitute a full caseload, it is understood that Marta will also be getting clients on a regular rotation from our other drug and alcohol programs.

Cc: Miriam Cabrera, Human Resources Director
Marta Diaz-Gold

2. An email
To: University Faculty, Staff, and Students
Re: Network Maintenance

The college network and all systems, including email, online registration, and BlackBoard, will be undergoing routine maintenance from 11 p.m. on Friday, December 20, until 7 a.m. on Sunday, December 22. During this time, all access to the network and its systems will be unavailable. When leaving campus for the holiday break, be sure to properly and completely shut down all computers and devices. Network access will be restored at 7 a.m. on Sunday, December 22. For more information, visit www.bbcc.edu/ithelpdesk, or email us at ithelpdesk@bbcc.edu.

# Skills Check

Look back at your response to the Seeing and Writing prompt on page 7. Now that you have read this chapter, you should be able to answer the following questions.

- How do you think highlighting can help you to understand your reading assignments?
- How do you think annotating can help you to understand your reading assignments?

Expand your Seeing and Writing response so it answers these two questions.

# review checklist

## Reading for Academic Success

☐ Become an active reader. (See 1a.)

☐ Preview your reading assignment. (See 1b.)

☐ Highlight your reading assignment. (See 1b.)

☐ Annotate your reading assignment. (See 1b.)

☐ Outline your reading assignment. (See 1b.)

☐ Summarize your reading assignment. (See 1b.)

☐ Learn how to read different kinds of texts. (See 1c.)

# unit
# 2 Writing Effective Paragraphs

# 2 Writing a Paragraph

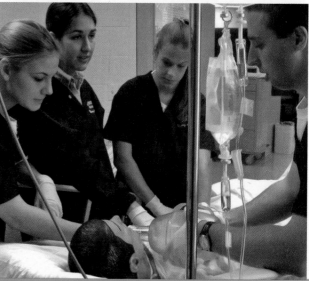

## seeing and writing

The pictures above show college students in different settings, both traditional and nontraditional. Look at the pictures, and then consider all the reasons you decided to go to college. Think about this question carefully before you read the pages that follow. As you move through this chapter, you will be developing a paragraph in response to the question, "Why did you decide to go to college?" Think about how you could use the Word Power words in your paragraph.

### WORD POWER

**self-esteem** pride in oneself; self-respect
**curriculum** courses offered in a school or in a field of study

It's no secret that writing is essential in most of the courses you will take in college. Whether you write a lab report or a psychology essay, a midterm or a final exam, your ability to organize your ideas and express them in writing will help to determine how well you do. In other words, succeeding at writing is the first step toward succeeding in college. Writing is also a key to success outside the classroom. On the job and in everyday life, if you can express yourself clearly and effectively, you will stand a better chance of achieving your goals and influencing the world around you.

This chapter will guide you through the process of writing a paragraph. Because paragraphs play an important part in almost all the writing you do, learning to write a paragraph is central to becoming an effective writer.

## 2a  Understanding Paragraph Structure

Before you can begin the process of writing a paragraph, you need to have a basic understanding of paragraph structure.

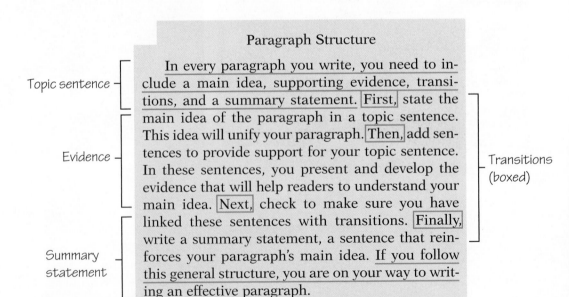

**Paragraph Structure**

Topic sentence — Evidence — Summary statement — Transitions (boxed)

In every paragraph you write, you need to include a main idea, supporting evidence, transitions, and a summary statement. First, state the main idea of the paragraph in a topic sentence. This idea will unify your paragraph. Then, add sentences to provide support for your topic sentence. In these sentences, you present and develop the evidence that will help readers to understand your main idea. Next, check to make sure you have linked these sentences with transitions. Finally, write a summary statement, a sentence that reinforces your paragraph's main idea. If you follow this general structure, you are on your way to writing an effective paragraph.

A **paragraph** is a group of sentences that is unified by a single main idea. The **topic sentence** states the main idea, and the rest of the sentences in the paragraph provide **evidence** (examples and details) to support the main idea. The sentences in a paragraph are linked by **transitions**, words and phrases (such as *also* and *for example*) that show how ideas are related. At the end of the paragraph, a **summary statement** reinforces the main idea.

The first letters of these four elements—Topic sentence, Evidence, Summary statement, and Transitions—spell TEST. Whenever you write a paragraph, you should TEST it to make sure it is complete.

## FYI

### Paragraph Structure

Note that the first sentence of a paragraph is **indented**, starting about half an inch from the left-hand margin. Every sentence begins with a capital letter, and most end with a period. (Sometimes, a sentence ends with a question mark or an exclamation point.)

## 2b Focusing on Your Assignment, Purpose, and Audience

In college, a writing task almost always begins with an assignment. Before you begin to write, stop to consider some questions about this **assignment** (*what* you are expected to write) as well as about your **purpose** (*why* you are writing) and your **audience** (*for whom* you are writing). If you answer these questions now, you will save yourself a lot of time later.

### Questions about Assignment, Purpose, and Audience

**Assignment**

☐ What is your assignment? Is it a written assignment? Is it on your class syllabus or posted on the class website?

☐ Do you have a word or page limit?

☐ When is your assignment due?

☐ Will you be expected to do your writing at home or in class?

*(continued)*

*(continued from previous page)*

☐ Will you be expected to work on your own or with other students?

☐ Will you be allowed to revise before (or after) you hand in your work?

**Purpose**

☐ Are you expected to express your personal reactions—for example, to tell how you feel about the ideas expressed in an essay?

☐ Are you expected to present information—for example, to describe a scientific process or answer an exam question?

☐ Are you expected to take a position on a controversial issue—for example, to respond to an editorial?

**Audience**

☐ Who will read your essay—just your instructor or your classmates as well?

☐ Do you have an audience beyond the classroom—for example, your supervisor at work or the readers of your school newspaper?

☐ How much are your readers likely to know about your topic?

☐ Will your readers expect you to use a formal or an informal style? (For example, are you writing a research paper or a personal essay?)

**PRACTICE**

**2-1**    Each of the following writing assignments has a different audience and purpose. On the lines following each item, write a few notes about how you would approach the task. (The Questions about Assignment, Purpose, and Audience above can help you decide on the best approach.) Be prepared to discuss your responses with the class or in a group of three or four students.

1. For the other students in your writing class, describe the best or worst class you have ever had.

   _____

   _____

2. Write an email to your school newspaper in which you try to convince readers that a certain course should no longer be required at your school.

   _____

   _____

3. Write a letter applying for a job. Explain how the courses you have taken qualify you for that job.

_____

_____

_____

_____

## 2c   Finding Ideas to Write About

Once you know what, why, and for whom you are writing, you can begin to look for ideas to write about. This process can be challenging, and it is different for every writer. You may be the kind of person who likes a structured way to find ideas, or you may prefer a looser, more relaxed way to find things to write about. As you gain more experience as a writer, you will learn which of the strategies discussed in the pages that follow work best for you.

Julia Reyes, a student in an introductory writing course, was given the following assignment.

> **ASSIGNMENT**   Is it better to go to college right after high school or to wait? Write a paragraph in which you answer this question.

Before she could begin to draft her paragraph, Julia needed to think of ideas to write about. To help students in the class practice using different ways to find ideas, Julia's instructor required them to try four different strategies—_freewriting, brainstorming, clustering,_ and _journal writing_. The pages that follow explain each of these strategies and show how Julia used them.

## Freewriting

When you **freewrite**, you write down whatever comes into your mind, and you write for a set period of time without stopping. Grammar and spelling are not important at this point; what is important is to get your ideas down on paper. Even if your words don't seem to be going anywhere, keep on writing. Sometimes you freewrite to find a topic. Most often, however, you freewrite in response to a specific assignment that your instructor gives you. In these cases, you are doing **focused freewriting**.

When you finish freewriting, read what you have written, and try to find at least one idea you think you might be able to write more about. Underline this idea, and then freewrite again, using the underlined idea as a starting point.

Here is Julia's focused freewriting on the topic "Is it better to go to college right after high school or to wait?"

> *Which is better? To start college right away? To wait? I waited, but last year was such a waste of time. Such a waste. Every job I had was stupid. Telemarketing — the worst worst job. Why didn't I just quit the first day? (Money.) Waitressing was a hard job. Everybody had an attitude. The customer was always right, blah blah. Another waste of time. Why didn't I just go right to college? I needed money. And I was sick of school. School was hard. I wasn't good at it. But work was boring. But now I hate how all my friends are a year ahead of me. So I guess it's better not to wait.*

*Freewriting*

### PRACTICE
### 2-2

Read Julia's freewriting. Which ideas do you think she should write more about? Write your suggestions on the following lines.

_____

_____

_____

_____

_____

# Freewrite

Now, it is time for you to begin working on your own paragraph. You already have your assignment from the Seeing and Writing box on page 33:

> Why did you decide to go to college?

Your first step is to freewrite about this assignment. On a blank sheet of lined paper (or on your computer), write for at least five minutes without stopping. If you can't think of anything to write, just write the last word over and over again until something else comes to mind.

### PRACTICE
### 2-3

Reread your freewriting. Underline the sentence that you think expresses the most interesting idea. Use this sentence as a starting point for another five-minute focused freewriting exercise.

## Brainstorming

When you **brainstorm**, you write down all the ideas you can think of about your topic. Brainstorming is different from freewriting, and it looks different on the page. Instead of writing lines of text, you write all over the page. You can star, check, box, or underline words, and you can ask questions, make lists, and draw arrows to connect ideas.

Here are Julia's brainstorming notes on the topic "Is it better to go to college right after high school or to wait?"

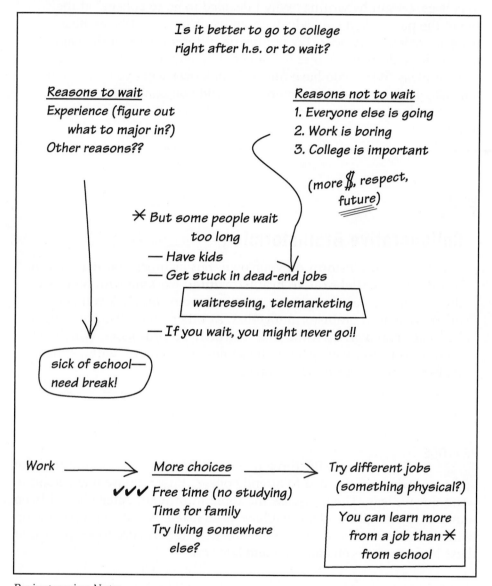

*Brainstorming Notes*

## PRACTICE

**2-4** Read Julia's brainstorming notes. How is her brainstorming similar to her freewriting (p. 40)? How is it different? Which ideas do you think she should write more about? Which ones should she cross out? Write your suggestions on the lines that follow.

_____

_____

_____

_____

# Brainstorm

On a sheet of *unlined* paper, brainstorm about why you decided to go to college. (Begin by writing "Why I decided to go to college" at the top of the page.) Write quickly, without worrying about being neat or using complete sentences. Try writing on different parts of the page, making lists, drawing arrows to connect related ideas, and starring important ideas. When you have finished, look over what you have written. Which ideas seem most interesting? Did you come up with any new ideas in your brainstorming that you did not think of in your freewriting?

# FYI

## Collaborative Brainstorming

Usually, you brainstorm on your own, but at times you may find it helpful to do **collaborative brainstorming**, working with other students to find ideas. Sometimes, your instructor may ask you and another student to brainstorm together. At other times, the class might brainstorm as a group while your instructor records ideas. Whichever method you use, your goal is the same—to come up with as much material about your topic as you can.

**PRACTICE**

**2-5**   Brainstorm with three or four other students on the topic of why you decided to attend college. First, choose one person to write down ideas. Then, discuss the topic informally. After about fifteen minutes, review all the ideas that have been listed. Has the group come up with any ideas that you can use in your writing? Be sure to keep a list of these ideas so that you can use them later on.

## Clustering

**Clustering**, which is sometimes called *mapping*, is another strategy you can use to find ideas. To create a cluster diagram, you begin by writing your topic in the center of a sheet of paper. Then, you draw lines from the general topic to related ideas, moving out from the center to the corners of the page. (These lines may look like spokes of a wheel or branches of a tree.) Your ideas will get more and more specific as you move from the center to the edges of the page.

When your diagram is complete, you can create a new one on a new sheet of paper, this time beginning with a specific idea that you thought of the first time.

Here is Julia's cluster diagram on the topic "Is it better to go to college right after high school or to wait?"

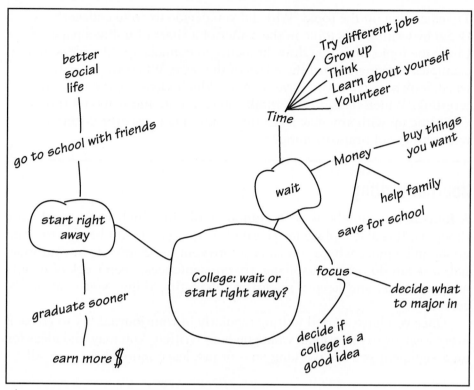

*Cluster Diagram*

## PRACTICE

**2-6**   How is Julia's cluster diagram similar to her brainstorming notes on the same subject (p. 41)? How is it different? Which branch of her cluster diagram do you think Julia should focus on when she writes her paragraph? Why? Should she add any other branches? Write your responses on the following lines. Be prepared to discuss your ideas with your class or in a small group of students.

# Make a Cluster Diagram

Try clustering on the topic "Why did you decide to go to college?" Begin by writing this topic in the center of a sheet of unlined paper. Circle the topic, and then draw branches to connect specific ideas and examples, moving toward the edges of the page. When you have finished, look over what you have written. Which ideas are the most interesting? Which ones do you think you can write more about? Have you come up with any new ideas that you did not discover during your freewriting and brainstorming?

## Journal Writing

A **journal** is a notebook or a computer file in which you record your thoughts. It is also a place to record ideas that you might be able to write about and a place where you can explore your assignments. In your journal, you can do problem solving, try out sentences, keep track of details and examples, and keep a record of interesting things you read or observe.

Once you have started writing regularly in your journal, try to go back every week or so and reread what you have written. You may find ideas for an assignment you are working on—or just learn more about yourself.

# FYI

## Journals

Here are some subjects you can write about in a journal.

- *Your school work*  Writing regularly about the topics you are studying in school is one way to become a better student. For example, you can react to what you are learning, write down questions about topics you are having trouble understanding, and examine new ideas.

- *Your job*  You can write about the day-to-day triumphs and frustrations of your job. For example, you can record conversations with coworkers, or you can list problems and remind yourself how you solved them. Rereading your journal may help you understand your strengths and weaknesses as an employee.

- *Your ideas about your community and your world*  As you learn more about the social and political world around you, you can explore your reactions to new ideas. For example, you may read an interesting story in the newspaper or see something on television or on the Internet that challenges your beliefs. Even if you are not ready to talk to others about what you are thinking, you can still "talk" to your journal.

- *Your impressions of what you see around you*  Many writers carry their journals with them and record interesting, unusual, or funny things they notice as they go about their daily business. If you get into the habit of writing down your observations and reactions, you may be able to use them later in your writing.

- *Personal thoughts*  Although you may not feel comfortable writing about your personal thoughts and experiences — especially if your instructor will read your journal — you should try to be as honest as you can. Writing about relationships with family and friends, personal problems, and hopes and dreams can help you get to know (and understand) yourself better.

Here is Julia's journal entry on the topic "Is it better to go to college right after high school or to wait?"

---

*This is a hard topic for me to write about. When I finished high school, I never wanted to go to school again. High school was hard. I worked hard, but teachers always said I could do better. Studying was boring. I couldn't concentrate. I never seemed to get things right on homework or on tests. Things seemed easier for everyone else. Sometimes I hated school. So I decided I'd work and not go to college right away, or maybe ever. But after a year, here I am. I'm still not sure why. School always felt hard. Work was boring, but it was easy. For the first time, I could do everything right. I got raises and promotions and better hours because I was a good worker. I wasn't judged by how I did on some dumb test. For once, I had some self-esteem. So why am I here? Good question.*

---

*Journal Entry*

# Write a Journal Entry

Set aside a time to write in your journal for fifteen minutes or so — during lunch, for example, or right before you go to bed — every day. Then, write your first journal entry. Being as honest with yourself as possible, try to explain why you really decided to go to college.

# 2d Identifying Your Main Idea and Writing a Topic Sentence

**ⓔ macmillanhighered.com /foundationsfirst**
LearningCurve > Topics and Main Ideas

When you think you have enough material to write about, it is time for you to identify your **main idea**—the central idea you will develop in your paragraph.

Begin by looking over what you have already written. As you read through your freewriting, brainstorming, clustering, and journal entries, look for a key idea that your material seems to support. The sentence that states this main idea and gives your writing its focus will be your paragraph's **topic sentence**.

The topic sentence of your paragraph is important because it tells both you and your readers what the focus of your paragraph will be. An effective topic sentence has three characteristics.

1. **A topic sentence is a complete sentence.** There is a difference between a *topic* and a *topic sentence*. The **topic** is what the paragraph is about.

   TOPIC    Whether to start college right after high school

   A **topic sentence**, however, is a complete sentence that includes a subject and a verb and expresses a complete thought.

   TOPIC SENTENCE    Students should not start college right after they finish high school.

2. **A topic sentence is more than just an announcement of what you plan to write about.** A topic sentence makes a point about the topic the paragraph discusses.

   ANNOUNCEMENT    In this paragraph, I will explain my ideas about whether students should go to college right after high school.

   TOPIC SENTENCE    My ideas about the best time to start college changed when I became a college student.

3. **A topic sentence presents an idea that can be discussed in a single paragraph.** If your topic sentence is too broad, you will not be able to discuss it in just one paragraph. If your topic sentence is too narrow, you will not be able to say much about it.

   TOPIC SENTENCE TOO BROAD    Students have many different reasons for deciding whether to go to college right after high school.

   TOPIC SENTENCE TOO NARROW    Most students begin college right after high school.

   EFFECTIVE TOPIC SENTENCE    Students who begin college right after high school may be too immature to do well in school.

When Julia Reyes reviewed her notes, she saw that most of her material supported the idea that it was better to wait instead of starting college right after high school. She stated this idea in a topic sentence.

> I think it's better to wait a few years instead of beginning college right after high school.

When Julia thought about how to express her topic sentence, she knew it had to be a complete sentence, not just a topic, and that it would have to make a point, not just announce what she planned to write about. When she reread the topic sentence she had written, she decided that it did these things and that it was neither too broad nor too narrow for her to support in a paragraph.

### PRACTICE
### 2-7

Read the following items. Put a check mark next to each one that you think would make an effective topic sentence for a paragraph.

**Examples**

Raccoons in the suburbs. _____

Raccoons often find food and shelter in suburban communities. ____✔____

1. The country's most exciting roller coasters. _____

2. Some of the country's most exciting roller coasters are made of wood.

_____

3. It is dangerous to text while driving. ___✓____

4. In this paragraph, I am going to write about texting while driving.

_____

5. Reality shows can be addictive. ____✓____

6. Some facts about reality shows. _____

### PRACTICE
### 2-8

The following topic sentences are either too broad or too narrow. On the line after each sentence, write *Too broad* if the sentence is too broad and *Too narrow* if the sentence is too narrow. Then, rewrite each sentence—making it more specific or more general—so that it could be an effective topic sentence for a paragraph.

**Examples**

Eating in a restaurant is interesting.

*Too broad. Possible rewrite: Eating in an ethnic restaurant is interesting*

*because the food choices are different from those I have at home.*

I text my friends every day.

*Too narrow. Possible rewrite: Texting is a good way to keep in touch with friends.*

1. Textbooks can be expensive.

_____

_____

2. At the supermarket, I can never find healthy snacks.

_____

_____

3. The United States is a beautiful country.

_____

_____

4. Everyone should be computer literate.

_____

_____

5. In some offices, workers can wear jeans and sneakers on casual Fridays.

_____

_____

# Identify Your Main Idea, and Write a Topic Sentence

Now that you have practiced freewriting, brainstorming, and clustering, and have written a journal entry, you are ready to write a paragraph in response to the Seeing and Writing prompt on page 35.

Why did you decide to go to college?

Your first step is to decide on a main idea for your paragraph. Look over the work you have done so far, and identify the idea your material can best support. On the lines below, write a topic sentence that expresses this idea.

Topic sentence: _____

_____

_____

# 2e  Choosing Supporting Points

After you identify your paragraph's main idea and state it in a topic sentence, it is time to review your notes again. Now, you are looking for specific evidence (examples and details) to support your topic sentence. Copy your topic sentence at the top of a sheet of paper. As you review your notes and continue to think about your topic, list all the supporting points you think you might be able to use in your paragraph.

After you list your supporting points, review them to make sure each point is *relevant*, *distinct*, and *specific*.

- **Relevant** points are directly related to your paragraph's main idea.

- **Distinct** points do not overlap with other supporting points.

- **Specific** points are not general or vague; they communicate just what you meant to say.

Julia listed the following points she thought she could use to support her paragraph's topic sentence. When she reviewed her points, she crossed out three of them.

**TOPIC SENTENCE (MAIN IDEA)**   I think it's better to wait a few years instead of beginning college right after high school.

- Work experience
- Chance to earn money
- ~~Avoid friends from high school~~
- Chance to develop self-esteem
- ~~Look for a job~~
- Time to grow up
- Chance to decide if college is right for you
- ~~Some things can be difficult~~

When she looked over her list, Julia crossed out three points.

- She crossed out "Avoid friends from high school" because it was not *relevant*; it was not related to her paragraph's main idea.

- She crossed out "Look for a job" because it was not *distinct*; it overlapped with "Work experience."

- She crossed out "Some things can be difficult" because it was not *specific*; it did not explain what "things" could be hard, and it did not specify whether she was referring to high school or to college.

**macmillanhighered.com /foundationsfirst**
LearningCurve > Topic Sentences and Supporting Details

# Choose Supporting Points

Now, continue to work on your paragraph about why you decided to go to college. Reread your freewriting, brainstorming, and clustering exercises as well as your journal entry, and list below all the points you can use to support your topic sentence. Then, cross out any points that are not relevant, distinct, and specific. (You can also list any new points you think of.)

Topic sentence: _____

_____

Supporting points:

■ _____

■ _____

■ _____

■ _____

## 2f   Arranging Your Supporting Points

Once you have decided which supporting points you want to write about, arrange them in the order in which you plan to discuss them. Julia arranged her supporting points in the following informal outline.

**TOPIC SENTENCE**  I think it's better to wait a few years instead of beginning college right after high school.
1. Waiting gives people time to work and earn money.
2. Waiting gives people time to think about life and grow up.
3. Waiting helps people decide if college is right for them.
4. Waiting gives people a chance to develop self-esteem.

# Arrange Your Supporting Points

Reread your list of supporting points. On the following lines, create an informal outline by arranging your points in the order in which you plan to write about them.

1. _____

2. _____

3. _____

4. _____

# 2g   Drafting Your Paragraph

So far, you have found a main idea for your paragraph, written a topic sentence, listed supporting points, and arranged these points in the order in which you will write about them. Now, you are ready to write a first draft.

Begin drafting your paragraph by stating your topic sentence. Then, referring to your list of supporting points, write down your ideas without worrying about correct sentence structure, word choice, spelling, or punctuation. If you think of a good idea that is not on your list, include it in your draft. (Don't worry at this point about where it fits or whether you will keep it.)

Remember, your first draft is a rough draft that you will revise. If you type your draft, leave extra space between lines. If you plan to revise on your handwritten draft, make things easy for yourself by leaving wide margins and skipping lines so you have room to write in new ideas.

When you have finished your rough draft, don't start revising it right away. Take a break, and then return to your draft and read it over very carefully.

Here is the first draft of Julia's paragraph on the topic "Is it better to go to college right after high school or to wait?"

---

Waiting

I think it's better to wait a few years instead of beginning college right after high

school. Many people start college right after high school just because that's what

everybody else is doing. But that's not always the right way to go. Different things

are right for different people. There are other possible choices. Taking a few years

off can be a better choice. During this time, people can work and earn money. They

also have time to think and grow up. Waiting can even help people decide if college is

right for them. Finally, waiting gives them a chance to develop self-esteem. For all

these reasons, waiting a year or two between high school and college is a good idea.

---

*First Draft*

**PRACTICE**

**2-9**    Read Julia's first draft. What do you think she should change? What should she add? What should she take out? Write your suggestions on the following lines. Be prepared to discuss your suggestions with the class or in a small group.

_____

_____

_____

# Draft Your Paragraph

Now, write a draft of your paragraph about why you decided to go to college, using the material you have come up with so far. Be sure that your paragraph states your main idea in the topic sentence and that you support the topic sentence with specific evidence. When you have finished, give your paragraph a title that accurately reflects what you are writing about.

## 2h  TESTing Your Paragraph

When you have finished your draft, you are ready to start revising. The first thing you should do is "test" what you have written to make sure it includes all the elements of an effective paragraph. You do this by asking the following four **TEST** questions.

**T** ▪ **Topic sentence**—Does your paragraph have a topic sentence that states its main idea?

**E** ▪ **Evidence**—Does your paragraph include specific evidence (examples and details) that supports your topic sentence?

**S** ▪ **Summary statement**—Does your paragraph end with a statement that reinforces its main idea?

**T** ▪ **Transitions**—Does your paragraph include transitional words and phrases that show readers how your ideas are related?

If your paragraph includes these four **TEST** elements, you are off to a very good start. If it does not, you will need to add whatever is missing.

When Julia reread her draft, she **TEST**ed it to take a quick inventory of her paragraph.

▪ She thought her **topic sentence** clearly expressed her main idea, but she decided it could be more specific.

- She thought she needed to add more **evidence** to support her topic sentence.

- She thought her paragraph's **summary statement** could be expanded so it applied to other students as well as to her.

- She thought she had enough **transitions** to connect her ideas, but she decided to revise some of them to make her emphasis clearer.

## TEST Your Paragraph

TEST the first draft of your paragraph to make sure it includes all four elements of an effective paragraph: Topic sentence, Evidence, Summary statement, and Transitions. If any elements are missing, plan to add them as you continue revising.

## 2i    Revising Your Paragraph

Keep in mind that **revision** means much more than correcting a few commas or crossing out one word and putting another one in its place. Often, it means moving sentences around, adding words and phrases, and even changing the topic sentence. To get the most out of revision, begin by slowly rereading your draft—first aloud, then to yourself. Then, carefully consider each of the questions on the checklist that follows.

## self-assessment checklist

### Revising Your Paragraph

- ☐ Does your topic sentence clearly state your main idea?

- ☐ Have you included enough examples and details?

- ☐ Should you cross out any examples or details?

- ☐ Does every sentence say what you mean?

- ☐ Does the order of your sentences make sense?

- ☐ Is every word necessary?

- ☐ Have you used the right words?

- ☐ Does your paragraph include a concluding statement that sums up your main idea?

WORD POWER

**peer** someone with equal standing; an equal

Sometimes your instructor may suggest that you get feedback from your classmates. The process of giving and receiving constructive feedback is called **peer review**. Peer review is most productive if you know how to make helpful comments and how to use the comments you get from others.

**Giving feedback** on a classmate's draft means making specific comments and pointing to particular sections of the draft. A general comment like "This is a good draft" or "Your ideas need more support" is not as helpful as more specific comments like "Your draft is convincing because you give lots of detail about your community service experience, especially in your fourth and fifth sentences" and "You need support for the point you make in sentence 6."

**Using feedback** means carefully evaluating the suggestions you get and deciding whether or not taking a classmate's advice will strengthen your draft. Remember, not every suggestion is worth adopting, but every one is worth considering.

After Julia drafted the paragraph on page 51, she used her **TEST** responses and the Self-Assessment Checklist on page 53 (as well as comments from her peer-review group) to help her revise her paragraph.

Waiting

~For students who are not getting much out of school, it is often~ I think it's better to wait a few years instead of beginning college right after high school. Many people start college right ~after high school~ *away* just because ~that's~ *that is* what everybody else is doing. ~But that's~ *However, that is* not always the right ~way to go. Different things are right for different people.~ *thing to do.* ~There are other possible choices.~ Taking a few years off can *often* be a better choice. During this time, people can work and earn money. ~They also have~ *for college. Working at different jobs can help them decide on a career.* *Taking a year or two off also gives people* time to think and grow up. Waiting can even help people decide if college *really* is right for them. ~Finally,~ *Most important of all,* waiting gives them a chance to develop self-esteem. For ~all these reasons,~ waiting a year ~or two~ between high school and (college ~is~ *was* a good idea, *and I think it can be a good idea for other students, too.*

*I was a poor student in high school. School always felt hard. When I took a year off, everything changed. In high school, I always saw all the things I couldn't do. At work, I learned what I could do. Now, I think I can succeed.*

*Revised Draft*

When she revised her paragraph, Julia crossed out sentences, added sentences, and changed the way she worded her ideas. Her biggest change was adding an explanation of how taking a year off had helped her. She also revised her topic sentence so that it suggested *why* she thought wait-ing was a better choice. Here is the final version of her revised paragraph.

TEST
☐ Topic Sentence
☐ Evidence
☐ Summary Statement
☐ Transitions

### Waiting

For students who are not getting much out of school, it is often better to wait a few years instead of beginning college right after high school. Many people start college right away just because that is what everybody else is doing. However, that is not always the right thing to do. Taking a few years off can often be a better choice. During this time, people can work and earn money for college. Working at different jobs can help them decide on a career. Taking a year or two off also gives people time to think and grow up. Waiting can even help people decide if college is really right for them. Most important of all, waiting gives them a chance to develop self-esteem. I was a poor student in high school. School always felt hard. When I took a year off, everything changed. In high school, I always saw all the things I couldn't do. At work, I learned what I could do. Now, I think I can succeed. For me, waiting a year between high school and college was a good idea, and I think it can be a good idea for other students, too.

## FYI

### Editing

Don't confuse revision with editing, which comes *after* revision. When you **edit**, you check for correct grammar, punctuation, mechanics, and spelling. Then, you **proofread** carefully for typing errors that a spell checker may not identify. You also make sure that you have indented the first sentence of your paragraph and that every sentence begins with a capital letter and ends with a period.

Remember, editing is a vital last step in the writing process. Read-ers may not take your ideas seriously if your writing includes errors in grammar or spelling.

### PRACTICE

**2-10** Read the final version of Julia's revised paragraph (above), and compare it with her first draft (p. 51). What specific changes did she make? Which do you think are her best changes? Why? Answer these questions on the following lines. Then, with the class or in a small group, discuss your reaction to the revised paragraph.

_____

_____

_____

_____

_____

# Revise and Edit Your Paragraph

Consulting the Self-Assessment Checklist on page 53, continue revising your paragraph, adding, crossing out, and rewording material as needed. Then, **edit** your paragraph, checking grammar, punctuation, mechanics, and spelling—and **proofread** carefully for typing errors.

## review checklist

### Writing a Paragraph

- [ ] Be sure you understand paragraph structure. (See 2a.)
- [ ] Consider your assignment, purpose, and audience. (See 2b.)
- [ ] Use different strategies—freewriting, brainstorming, clustering, and journal writing—to help find ideas to write about. (See 2c.)
- [ ] Identify your main idea, and write a topic sentence. (See 2d.)
- [ ] Choose supporting points from your notes. (See 2e.)
- [ ] Arrange your supporting points in a logical order. (See 2f.)
- [ ] Write a draft of your paragraph. (See 2g.)
- [ ] TEST your paragraph. (See 2h.)
- [ ] Revise and edit your draft. (See 2i.)

# 3 TESTing Your Paragraphs

© D Dipasupil/Getty

## seeing and writing

The picture above shows the annual Mermaid Parade in Coney Island. Look at the picture, and then write a paragraph about a memorable event or celebration — for example, a baseball game or a birthday party — as if it were unfamiliar to the person reading about it. How would you describe the event? What is so special about it? Try to use the Word Power words in your paragraph.

**In this chapter, you will learn**
- to write unified paragraphs (3a)
- to write well-developed paragraphs (3b)
- to write coherent paragraphs (3c)

As you learned in Chapter 2, TEST is the first step in the revision process. TESTing your paragraph will tell you whether it includes all the elements of an effective paragraph.

The following paragraph includes all the elements of an effective paragraph.

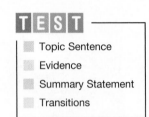

Topic Sentence
Evidence
Summary Statement
Transitions

> My high school has three silly rules. The first silly rule is that only seniors can go outside the school building for lunch. In spite of this rule, all students go outside to eat because the cafeteria is too small to hold everyone. Understanding the problem, the teachers just look the other way. The second silly rule is that students have to attend 95 percent of all the classes for each course, If they do not, they are supposed to fail. Of course, this rule is never enforced, because if it were, most of the students in the school would fail everything. The third silly rule is that students are not allowed to throw their hats into the air at graduation. The explanation is that a parent—no one can remember who—complained that a falling hat could poke someone in the eye. As a result, all graduating classes are told that under no circumstances should they throw their hats. Of course, on graduation day every class does the same thing—ignores the rule and tosses its hats. Although these silly rules still remain on the books, no administrator seems to have the time—or the courage—to change them.

The rest of this chapter explains and illustrates the process of TESTing a paragraph.

## 3a TESTing for a Topic Sentence

The first thing you do when you TEST a paragraph is to look for a **topic sentence (T)**. An effective paragraph focuses on a single main idea, and it includes a topic sentence that states this main idea.

A paragraph is **unified** when all its sentences support the main idea stated in the topic sentence. A paragraph is **not unified** when its sentences do not support the main idea stated in the topic sentence. When you revise, you can make your paragraphs unified by crossing out any sentences that do not support your main idea and, if necessary, adding sentences that do.

The following paragraph is not unified because it includes information that does not support the topic sentence.

**Paragraph Not Unified**

Applying for a Bank Loan

<u>Although applying for a bank loan can be confusing, the process is not all that difficult.</u> The first step is to determine which bank has the lowest interest rate. There are a lot of banks in my neighborhood, but they aren't very friendly. The last time I went into one, I waited for twenty minutes before anyone bothered to talk to me. Once you have chosen a bank, you have to go to the bank in person and apply, and if the bank isn't friendly, you don't want to go there. This is a real problem when you apply for a loan. If you have any questions about the application, you won't be able to get anyone to answer them. After you have submitted the application comes the hard part—waiting for approval.

The revised paragraph below is unified. When the writer reread his paragraph, he deleted the sentences that did not support his topic sentence. Then, he added some sentences that did.

**Unified Paragraph**

Applying for a Bank Loan

<u>Although applying for a bank loan can be confusing, the process is not all that difficult.</u> The first step is to determine which bank has the lowest interest rate. ~~There are a lot of banks in my neighborhood, but they aren't very friendly. The last time I went into one, I waited for twenty minutes before anyone bothered to talk to me.~~ *Irrelevant information deleted* Although a half-percent difference in rates may not seem like much, over the course of a four-year loan, the savings can really add up. *Support added* Once you have chosen a bank, you have to go to the bank in person and apply.~~, and if the bank isn't friendly, you don't want to go there. This is a real problem when you apply for a loan. If you have any questions about the application, you won't be able to get anyone to answer them.~~ *Irrelevant information deleted* Make sure you tell the loan officer exactly what rate you are applying for. Then, take the application home and fill it out, being careful not to omit any important information. If you have any problems with your credit, explain them on the application or in a separate letter. When the application is complete, take it back to the bank, and ask any questions you might have. (Do not sign the application until all your questions have been answered.) After you have submitted the application comes the hard part—waiting for approval. *Support added*

— Hector de la Paz (student)

**PRACTICE**

**3-1**    Underline the topic sentence in each of the following para-graphs. Keep in mind that the topic sentence may not always be the first sentence of the paragraph.

1. The Innocence Project arranges for lawyers and law students to help free innocent people who have been wrongly convicted. Some-times, a DNA test can prove that these people are innocent, but this testing is often not done. The test is expensive, and prisoners can-not afford it. Unfortunately, they have no other way to prove their innocence, except to hope that the Innocence Project will choose their cases. The lawyers and law students in the Innocence Project study the cases and take those they think they can win. As a result of the Innocence Project, more than 170 people in the United States have been released from jail. Fourteen of these people had been sentenced to death. Thousands of other prisoners are waiting and hoping that they will be released from jail as a result of the work of the Innocence Project.

2. What were your parents thinking when they gave you your name? Did they give you a popular name? If so, other children in your class probably had the same name. Some popular names change over time. Biblical names have been popular for boys for many years. In recent years, for example, the top boys' names have come from the Bible—Jacob, Michael, and Joshua. Girls' names are dif-ferent. In the past, many girls were named Mary, but recently some of the most popular girls' names have been Emily, Emma, and Madison. Today, girls are often named after characters from books, movies, or television shows. Most likely, your name is a name that was popular when you were born.

**PRACTICE**

**3-2**    The following paragraph has no topic sentence. Read the para-graph, and then choose the best topic sentence from the list below.

People cheat on taxes, people cheat on their spouses, and people cheat on their insurance claims. People cheat on this, and they cheat on that. Politicians skim a little off the top here and add a little over there. No one seems to be playing by the rules anymore. It's time we started challenging people for their dishonesty. What does all this cheating say about our society? Maybe it says that we're incapable of succeeding honorably. Maybe it suggests that honesty is just for people who don't understand how the world works. When we cheat or accept the fact that someone else cheats, we are really only cheating ourselves. In the long run, we have to live with the problems that cheating creates and pay the price for our dishonesty.

Put a check mark next to the topic sentence that best expresses the main idea in the paragraph above.

1. Everyone, regardless of age or gender, seems to be cheating. _____

2. Cheating is bad for society. _____

3. The widespread cheating in our society has to stop. _____

4. Lots of people cheat. _____

5. There is nothing we can do to stop the cheating that we see around us.

_____

**PRACTICE
3-3**
The following paragraphs do not have topic sentences. Think of a topic sentence that sums up each paragraph's main idea, and write it on the line above the paragraph.

**Example**

*Books can be banned from schools and libraries for various reasons.*

_____

Each year, the American Library Association puts out a list of the books that people want removed from libraries and classrooms. Books like *The Catcher in the Rye* by J. D. Salinger and *Forever* by Judy Blume have been challenged for sexual content and offensive language. The Harry Potter series by J. K. Rowling is often criticized for supposedly encouraging witchcraft. Books like *Daddy's Roommate* have been challenged for promoting homosexuality. Finally, *The Adventures of Huckleberry Finn* by Mark Twain has been challenged for being racist.

1. _____

_____

Until the 1960s, wearing a hat was a mark of adulthood. It was a more formal time when many men wore suits and hats even at sports events. For women, dresses, white gloves, and hats were essential for many occasions. By 1960, though, going hatless was more common. Many people resisted the formal look of the past and began to dress much more casually. They abandoned their suits, dresses, white gloves, and hats. Going bareheaded became the rule except on very special occasions. Even though designers have often predicted that hats are coming back in style, this hasn't happened yet.

2. _____

_____

Tupperware, a type of plastic food storage container, was first sold in 1951 at home parties. In a friend's living room, housewives would be invited to check out the various sizes and shapes of the plastic storage containers with the famous "burping" seal. They would pick the ones they wanted and order them from the Tupperware consultant—a housewife like them. Today, you can still find Tupperware parties in some places, but so many women work outside the home that they need other ways to buy Tupperware. Shopping malls may have Tupperware showcases—booths where shoppers can purchase Tupperware. Shoppers can also buy Tupperware online, directly from the company. They may even get an email invitation to an online party, where they can buy Tupperware.

3. _____

_____

_____

A mystery shopper goes to a store, checks it out, and completes a questionnaire about its prices, customer service, cleanliness, and other things that affect a customer's experience. Typical locations for mystery shopping are department stores, supermarkets, restaurants, and bars. As a result of the shopper's report, the store might improve its staff training or lower its prices to be more competitive. Most mystery shoppers earn between $12 and $20 for a shopping trip of less than an hour. They usually work part-time. It is not a very highly paid job, but for someone who likes to shop, it might be perfect.

**PRACTICE**
**3-4**    Read the following paragraphs. Underline the topic sentence of each paragraph. Then, check to see if every sentence in the paragraph supports that topic sentence. Write *unified* after the paragraphs that are unified and *not unified* after the ones that are not unified. Be prepared to explain why a paragraph is (or is not) unified.

**Example:**    Many species of animals are becoming extinct. Children love to see all different kinds of animals in zoos. Parents and children watch nature programs on TV for fun and education. For example, the Siberian tiger is an endangered species, with fewer than 400 individual tigers still existing. Some species of birds are endangered too, such as a type of parrot called the Puerto Rican Amazon, with fewer than 100 remaining. Soon, many different species of animals will probably disappear, or else they will just exist in zoos and laboratories. It is interesting to explore the website of the U.S. Fish and Wildlife Service. ___*not unified*___

1. Drivers must be careful to avoid road rage incidents. Road rage occurs when a driver loses control over his or her emotions in a stressful situation. Driving in bad weather can be very stressful. A car does not handle as easily on snowy or icy roads as it does on dry ones. Snow tires can make winter driving safer. Even with snow

tires, though, driving on slippery roads requires concentration. Road rage can lead to property damage and even injury. Therefore, drivers should always keep their emotions under control. _____

2. Carbon paper—thin paper with a waxy ink coating—has an interesting history. It was invented around 1800 by Ralph Wedgwood, an Englishman, and Pellegrino Turri, an Italian. The men invented it separately, in both cases as part of a system enabling blind people to write. Wedgwood then saw a more general use, which he tried to promote. When people wrote an important letter or other document, they often also wrote a copy. By putting carbon paper between two sheets of paper, they could simultaneously write the original and a copy. However, Wedgwood's idea did not catch on until the development of commercial typewriters, beginning in the 1870s. With improvements in typewriters and in carbon paper, in the mid-twentieth century carbon paper was essential to businesses. Technological change continued, however, soon making carbon paper obsolete. First, in the 1960s, came the photocopier, which could produce any number of copies of any document. Then, by the 1980s, computers were taking the place of typewriters. Today, carbon paper has just a few special uses—for example, to transfer patterns onto clay pottery. A final tribute to carbon paper can be found at the top of emails, where "cc" stands for "carbon copy." _____

3. Georgia O'Keeffe was a bold and influential painter. Her most famous paintings are of flowers and of scenes from the Southwest. Many tourists visit the Southwest to enjoy its beautiful deserts. Taos, New Mexico, is an especially busy tourist spot. O'Keeffe developed a unique painting style. She created dramatic images that went against the artistic fashion of her times. In fact, her rich use of color has inspired many artists. Quite a few artists today work in video and collage as well as in paint. O'Keeffe's work is on display in many of the world's leading museums. _____

### PRACTICE

**3-5**   Review the paragraphs in Practice 3-4 that you decided were not unified. Reread the topic sentences you underlined in each of these paragraphs. Then, cross out the sentences in each paragraph that do not support the topic sentence.

**Example**

Many species of animals are becoming extinct. ~~Children love to see all different kinds of animals in zoos. Parents and children watch nature programs on TV for fun and education.~~ For example, the Siberian tiger is an endangered species, with fewer than 400 individual tigers still existing. Some species of birds are endangered too, such as a type of parrot called the Puerto Rican Amazon, with fewer than 100 birds remaining. Soon, many different species of animals will prob-ably disappear, or else they will just exist in zoos and laboratories. ~~It is interesting to explore the website of the U.S. Fish and Wildlife Service.~~

1. Drivers must be careful to avoid road rage incidents. Road rage occurs when a driver loses control over his or her emotions in a stressful situation. Driving in bad weather can be very stressful. A car does not handle as easily on snowy or icy roads as it does on dry ones. Snow tires can make winter driving safer. Even with snow tires, though, driving on slippery roads requires con centration. Road rage can lead to property damage and even injury. Therefore, drivers should always keep their emotions under control.

2. Georgia O'Keeffe was a bold and influential painter. Her most fa-mous paintings are of flowers and of scenes from the Southwest. Many tourists visit the Southwest to enjoy its beautiful deserts. Taos, New Mexico, is an especially busy tourist spot. O'Keeffe de-veloped a unique painting style. She created dramatic images that went against the artistic fashion of her times. In fact, her rich use of color has inspired many artists. Quite a few artists today work in video and collage as well as in paint. O'Keeffe's work is on dis-play in many of the world's leading museums.

**PRACTICE**
**3-6**  On the lines below, write a paragraph that develops the main idea stated in each topic sentence. After you finish, check to make sure that each paragraph is unified.

1. Many people simply cannot afford to pay their bills on time.

_____

_____

_____

_____

_____

2. A neighborhood is more than just houses and stores.

_____

_____

_____

_____

_____

3. If I were president of this college, I would make a few changes.

_____

_____

_____

_____

_____

## 3b   TESTing for Evidence

The next thing you do when you TEST a paragraph is to make sure that you have enough **evidence** (E)—examples and details—to support the main idea stated in the topic sentence.

A paragraph is **well developed** when it includes enough evidence to explain and support its main idea. The amount of evidence you need depends on the idea you state in your topic sentence. If your topic sentence is relatively limited, two or three well-chosen examples may be enough to support it: *My school's registration process has three problems.* If your topic sentence is broader, however, then you will have to include more support: *The plans for the new sports stadium are seriously flawed.*

## FYI

### Developing Paragraphs with Examples and Details

Specific evidence (examples and details) can make a paragraph convincing. For example, in a paragraph on a history test, you could say that many soldiers were killed during the American Civil War. Your paragraph would be far more effective, however, if you said that over 500,000 soldiers were killed during the Civil War—more than in all the other wars in U.S. history combined.

The following paragraph is not well developed because it does not supply enough evidence to support the claim that bottled water is bad for the environment (which is what the topic sentence promises).

**Paragraph Not Well Developed**

Why We Need to Stop Buying Bottled Water

America's love affair with bottled water is harming our environment. Americans have become major consumers of bottled water. Drinking bottled water rather than tap water has a significant environmental cost. Fortunately,

Americans are becoming more aware of the issue, as shown by the dozens of college campuses that have banned sales of bottled water.

In the following revised paragraph, the writer added evidence—examples and details—that helps support the point made in the topic sentence.

**Well-Developed Paragraph**

Why We Need to Stop Buying Bottled Water

America's love affair with bottled water is harming our environment. Americans have become major consumers of bottled water. We drink about 30 gallons of bottled water per person in a year, twice as much as we did 15 years ago. In fact, Americans drink about 60 percent of all the bottled water drunk in the world. Drinking bottled water rather than tap water has a significant environmental cost. For example, 17 million barrels of oil a year are used to make the plastic bottles for water. Many more millions of barrels are used to transport and refrigerate the bottles. Moreover, only about 25 percent of the bottles are recycled. The rest clog our landfills or pollute our oceans. We buy this bottled water even though most of us can get healthy, clean, good-tasting water free from our taps. Fortunately, Americans are becoming more aware of the issue, as shown by the dozens of college campuses that have banned sales of bottled water.

Examples and details support topic sentence

*Note:* Length is no guarantee that a paragraph is well developed. A paragraph composed of one generalization after another can be quite long and still not provide enough support.

**PRACTICE**

**3-7**  Some of the following paragraphs are well developed; others are not. On the line after each paragraph, write *well developed* if the paragraph is well developed and *not well developed* if it is not.

**Example**

The National Spelling Bee has many purposes. It encourages children to improve their spelling, vocabulary, and English usage. As a result, children can read and write better and get higher scores on standardized tests. Spelling bees also encourage friendly competition among children and their schools. *not well developed*

1. PlumpyNut can help starving people survive. PlumpyNut is a peanut-based paste that was invented by a French scientist in 1999. It comes in a foil wrapper and does not need to be refrigerated. PlumpyNut is a high-energy, high-protein food that can save people's lives. Before PlumpyNut came into use, the most common nutritious food given to starving people was based on powdered milk. However, this milk-based food needed clean water and careful preparation by medical staff. PlumpyNut is much simpler to use. It can be fed to a child by a parent. The contents of the foil

packet can be used after it has been opened. PlumpyNut is truly a life-saver. _____

2. Jeans have a long history. They were invented by Levi Strauss in 1873. Strauss had a dry goods store in San Francisco. One of his customers kept ripping his pants, so Strauss made pants that would be stronger. He got a patent on his invention, and blue jeans were born. At first, they were called "waist overalls." In the 1960s, the term "jeans" became popular. Today, there are many kinds of jeans sold by many different companies. _____

3. Tattoos have become widely accepted in the American workplace. In the past, employers, like most other people, tended to view tattoos as a sign that a potential employee was a biker, sailor, or gang member. Today, many Americans, especially younger Americans, have tattoos; according to one study, 40 percent of people in their twenties have at least one tattoo. As a result, attitudes toward tattoos have changed significantly. This change in attitude means that employers are now less likely to turn someone down for a job because he or she has tattoos. In fact, employers in the arts and other creative fields, such as fashion or music, may have positive views of tattoos. Although not every employer accepts tattoos, times and employer dress codes have certainly changed. _____

**PRACTICE**

**3-8**   The following paragraphs are not well developed. On the lines below each paragraph, write three questions or suggestions that might help the writer develop his or her ideas more fully.

### Example

Justin Timberlake is a great musician. He was in a band called 'NSync but now has his own solo career. He sings several of my favorite songs. He is also a talented performer. He often appears on television. He is truly a great performer.

- *Identify some of your favorite songs that Justin Timberlake sings.*

- *Describe some of Timberlake's talents.*

- *What television shows has Timberlake appeared in?*

1. For me, having a regular study routine is important. I need to do the same things at the same times. If I have important school work to do, I stick to my routine. As long as I follow my schedule, everything works out all right.

- _____

- _____

- _____

2. Religion is a deeply personal issue. Attitudes toward religion vary from person to person. One person I know considers religion an essential part of life. Another feels just the opposite. Because of such differences, it is impossible to generalize about religious attitudes.

- _____
- _____
- _____

**PRACTICE**

**3-9**    Choose one of the paragraphs from Practice 3-8. Reread it, and review your suggestions for improving it. Then, rewrite the paragraph, adding specific details and examples to make it well developed.

_____

_____

_____

_____

_____

_____

_____

_____

# 3c TESTing for a Summary Statement

The third thing you do when you TEST a paragraph is to make sure that it ends with a **summary statement** (S)—a sentence that reinforces your paragraph's main idea. By reminding readers what your paragraph is about, a summary statement helps to further **unify** your paragraph.

The following paragraph has no summary statement.

### Colorful Rooms

Visitors to the White House in Washington, D.C., are surprised to see how varied and colorful some of the rooms are. For example, in front of the Visitor's Entrance is the Library, furnished in the style of the Federal period and used for teas and meetings. To the left of the Library is the Vermeil Room, decorated in gold and silver and used occasionally as a women's lounge. To the right and front of the Library is the East Room, an expansive oblong space where formal receptions take place. Next to the East Room is the Green Room, a square drawing room decorated in shades of green that is used for small receptions and teas. Beside the Green Room is the Blue Room, an oval-shaped room used as a reception area. From the Blue Room, visitors enter the Red Room, which is actually a parlor that is used to entertain small groups.

The summary statement in the following revised paragraph reinforces the paragraph's main idea and brings the paragraph to a close.

### Colorful Rooms

Visitors to the White House in Washington, D.C., are surprised to see how varied and colorful the rooms are. For example, in front of the Visitor's Entrance is the Library, furnished in the style of the Federal period and used for teas and meetings. To the left of the Library is the Vermeil Room, decorated in gold and silver and used occasionally as a women's lounge. To the right and front of the Library is the East Room, an expansive oblong space where formal receptions take place. Next to the East Room is the Green Room, a square drawing room decorated in shades of green that is used for small receptions and teas. Beside the Green Room is the Blue Room, an oval-shaped room used as a reception area. From the Blue Room, visitors enter the Red Room, which is actually a parlor that is used to entertain small groups. Because these rooms have such distinctive styles and colors, they are especially interesting to visitors.

### PRACTICE
**3-10**  Read the following two paragraphs, which do not include summary statements. Then, on the lines below each paragraph, write a summary statement that reinforces the paragraph's main idea and brings it to a close. Be careful not to use the same wording as the topic sentence.

1. Although the character Hello Kitty was developed for young children, it has found great success with adult consumers. Created in Japan by Sanrio, Hello Kitty made her first appearance in 1974, on a coin purse. Hello Kitty was marketed to teenagers and adults starting in the 1990s, with products such as purses, laptops, and televisions. As the character's audience grew, so did the range of products. Today, products include high-end collectibles such as Hello Kitty electric guitars, fine jewelry, and even a collection of wines. The Hello Kitty character can be found on 50,000 products in 60 countries, earning Sanrio $5 billion a year.

**Summary Statement**

_____

_____

2. Google Glass may appear to be just a pair of glasses, but in reality, it is an innovation that will revolutionize the way we live. When the first pair of Google Glass was developed in 2011, it weighed eight pounds. Now, each pair weighs less than a typical pair of sunglasses. A group of test users, called Explorers, were able to begin using the device in 2013. It cost $1,500 to buy a pair. Google Glass is outfitted with a tiny camera in the upper corner of the right lens, which allows users to take pictures, record video, and see information such as maps, weather forecasts, and video clips. The screen is voice-activated, but there is also a touch-pad on the arm of the glasses. Users can make phone calls and send messages with the device as well.

**Summary Statement**

_____

_____

# 3d  TESTing for Transitions

The final thing you do when you TEST a paragraph is to make sure the paragraph includes **transitions** (T) that connect ideas clearly and logically.

**Transitional words** and **phrases** create **coherence** by indicating how ideas are connected in a paragraph. In general, you can arrange the ideas in a paragraph in three ways—in *time order*, in *spatial order*, or in *logical order*. By signaling the order of ideas in a paragraph, transitional words and phrases make it easier for readers to follow your discussion.

## Time Order

You use **time signals** to show readers the order in which events occurred. News reports, historical accounts, and process explanations are usually arranged like this.

The following paragraph presents events in time order. (Transitional words and phrases are highlighted.)

### Ralph Ellison

No other American writer achieved as great a reputation on the basis of a single book as Ralph Ellison did. Ellison was born in 1914 in Oklahoma City, Oklahoma, and grew up in the segregated South. In 1936, he came to New York City to earn money to pay his tuition at Tuskegee Institute, where he was a senior majoring in music. After becoming friends with many writers who were part of the Harlem Renaissance—a flowering of art, music, and literature among African Americans—he decided to remain in New York. During this period, Richard Wright, author of *Native Son* and *Black Boy*, encouraged Ellison to write his first short story. Later, Ellison published two collections of essays and some

**WORD POWER**

**renaissance** a rebirth or revival

short fiction. Eventually, in 1952, he wrote *Invisible Man*, the novel that established him as a major twentieth-century writer.

— Mike Burdin (student)

Notice that throughout the paragraph, the writer uses transitional words and phrases that signal time order—*in 1914, in 1936, after, during this period, in the years that followed,* and *eventually.* These words and phrases help to make the paragraph coherent.

## Some Transitional Words and Phrases That Signal Time Order

| | | | |
|---|---|---|---|
| after | finally | soon | dates (for example, |
| afterward | first . . . next | still | "in 1920") |
| at first | later | then | times (for example, |
| before | meanwhile | today | "at 8 o'clock," |
| during | now | until | "that night") |
| earlier | recently | when | |
| eventually | since | while | |

## PRACTICE

**3-11**   Read the following paragraphs, whose sentences are organized in time order. Underline the transitional words and phrases that make each paragraph coherent.

1. A job interview is most likely to go well when you are prepared for it. The first step is to determine your strengths. Do you have the right level of education for the job? Are you experienced in the field? What special skills do you have? The next step is to research the company and the kind of business it does. If you have a thorough knowledge of the company, you will make a good impression and be able to answer many questions. Finally, decide what points you want to emphasize in the interview. Although the interviewer will guide the conversation, you should be ready to offer your own thoughts as well.

2. Director Wes Anderson has had a successful career making unusual movies. Before he started making movies professionally, he went to school at the University of Texas at Austin, where he met actor Owen Wilson, who now co-writes many of Anderson's films. In 1996, he released his first feature film, *Bottle Rocket*. Although it was critically praised, it did not do well at the box office. Following *Bottle Rocket*, Anderson made such acclaimed movies as *The Royal Tenenbaums*, *The Life Aquatic*, and *Moonrise Kingdom*. Anderson's films are distinctive for their visual style and unusual characters. In 2009, he released *The Fantastic Mr. Fox*, an animated film that was nominated for an Academy Award for Best

Animated Feature. Recently, he released *The Grand Budapest Hotel*, a quirky film that takes place in Europe.

**PRACTICE
3-12** The following paragraph includes no transitional words and phrases to connect its ideas. Read the paragraph carefully. Then, after consulting the list of transitional words and phrases on page 71, add appropriate transitions to connect the paragraph's ideas in time order.

### A Killer Disease

The worst pandemic in the history of the world occurred in 1918, when the flu killed between 20 and 40 million people. _____, soldiers in American military camps began to get sick during their training for combat in World War I. _____, as military units moved from one battlefield to another in Europe, the disease spread from soldier to soldier. _____, it started to spread to civilians. _____, the war ended, and as people came together to celebrate, they continued to spread the flu. _____, the flu attacked people all over the world, especially young people who had previously been healthy. _____, doctors were trying desperately to find ways to treat their flu patients, but nothing worked. To stop the spread of the disease, gauze masks and quarantines were tried, but these efforts had little effect. _____, millions of people all over the world were dying. _____, we are still learning more about the 1918 flu.

## Spatial Order

You use **spatial order** to show readers how people, places, and things stand in relation to one another. For example, you can move from top to bottom, from right to left, from far to near, and so on. Spatial order is used most often in paragraphs that describe something—for example, in a lab report describing a piece of equipment.

The following paragraph uses spatial order. (Transitional words and phrases are highlighted.)

### My Great-Grandmother's House

When I was fourteen, my family and I traveled to Michigan to visit the town where my great-grandmother had lived. Somerset was hardly a town; in fact, it was just a collection of farms and cow pastures. Scattered through the fields were about twenty buildings. One of them was my great-grandmother's old brick farmhouse, which was sold after she died. Next to the house were a rusting silo and a faded barn. In front of the house was a long wooden porch that needed painting. On the porch were a potted plant, two white wooden rocking chairs, and a swing. The house was locked, so all we could do was walk around it and look. The lace curtains that my great-grandmother had made before she died still hung in each window. In back of the house was a small cemetery that contained eight graves. There, off in the corner, on the oldest-looking stone, was the name "Azariel Smith"—the name of my great-grandmother's father.

— Molly Ward (student)

Notice how transitional words and phrases that signal spatial order—*next to, in front, on the porch, in back of, there,* and *in the corner*—help make the paragraph coherent.

## Some Transitional Words and Phrases That Signal Spatial Order

| | | | |
|---|---|---|---|
| above | below | inside | on/to the right |
| along | beneath | near | outside |
| around | beside | next to | over |
| at/on the top | in | on the bottom | there |
| at/on the bottom | in back (of) | on the top | under |
| behind | in front (of) | on/to the left | within |

**PRACTICE**

**3-13** Read the following paragraph, whose details are arranged in spatial order. Underline the transitional words and phrases that make the paragraph coherent.

The most spectacular sight I have ever seen is Machu Picchu, an ancient Incan city in Peru. Machu Picchu is built high on a ridge in the Andes Mountains. Below it is the Urabamba River, which runs swiftly north and raises a white mist. Behind Machu Picchu, the mountain Huayna Picchu stands like an enormous dark guard. Its triangular faces look like arrowheads pointing to the sky. All around Machu Picchu, thick brush covers the land, including the steps cut into the mountain. These steps were used for growing crops. To me, however, they seem to have been carved for giants to walk on. Within the city of Machu Picchu, houses and temples are made of carved stones. In the center of the city is the main plaza, where one of my favorite sites, the Temple of the Three Windows, is located. Inside this temple, tourists can look out of three large stone windows and see the mountains beyond. I do not need photographs to remember the view from this temple. It will always be with me.

**PRACTICE**

**3-14**  The following paragraph includes no transitional words and phrases to connect ideas. Read the paragraph carefully. Then, after consulting the list of transitional words and phrases on page 73, add appropriate transitions to connect the paragraph's ideas in spatial order.

*Nighthawks:* A Painting by Edward Hopper

One of the most familiar images in American art is a painting of three customers and a counterman in a diner on a city street corner at night: Edward Hopper's *Nighthawks*, painted in 1942. The scene is viewed from the perspective of someone standing _____ the diner and looking in. _____ the diner, a man and woman are sitting _____ each other but not speaking. _____, another man is sitting with his back to the viewer. _____, on the countertop, are two large coffeemakers. _____ the counter, the counterman is bending down to reach for something, maybe saying something to one of the men. _____ the diner, the street is deserted, and the store and apartment windows are dark. Many people get an intense feeling of loneliness from this painting, but Hopper said that the painting is actually about the possibility of danger in the night.

## Logical Order

You use **logical order** to show readers how one idea logically follows another. For example, you can move from the least important idea to the most important one. Logical order is often used in paragraphs that provide information or in paragraphs with a persuasive purpose—for example, in a paragraph trying to convince readers to get an annual flu shot.

The following paragraph presents ideas in logical order. (Transitional words and phrases are highlighted.)

Priorities

As someone who is both a parent and a student, I have had to develop strategies for coping. For example, I try to do my studying at night after I have put my son to bed. I want to give my son all the attention that he deserves, so after I pick him up from day care, I play with him, read to him, and watch a half hour of TV with him. When I am sure he is asleep, I begin doing my schoolwork. I also try to use every spare moment that I have during the day. For instance, if I have an hour between classes, I go to the computer lab and do some work. While I eat lunch, I get some of my reading out of the way. When I ride home from work on the bus, I review my class notes. Most important, I always keep my priorities in mind. My first priority is my son, my second priority is my schoolwork, and my last priority is keeping my apartment clean.

— Vanessa Scully (student)

The writer of this paragraph moves from her least important to her most important point. Notice how transitional words and phrases that signal logical order—*for example, also, for instance,* and *most important*—help make the paragraph coherent.

---

### Some Transitional Words and Phrases That Signal Logical Order

| | | |
|---|---|---|
| all in all | for this reason | not only . . . but also |
| also | furthermore | one . . . another |
| finally | in addition | similarly |
| first . . . second . . . third | in conclusion | the least important |
| for example | in fact | the most important |
| for instance | last | therefore |
| for one thing | moreover | |

---

**PRACTICE**

**3-15** Read the following paragraphs, whose sentences are organized in logical order. Underline the transitional words and phrases that make the paragraphs coherent.

1. Even though only one out of every ten people is left-handed, "left-ies" have a surprising amount of influence on our society. For one thing, five of the last seven presidents were left-handed. In addi-tion, one in four of the *Apollo* astronauts was left-handed. Also, the late computer whiz Steve Jobs was left-handed; so is Bill Gates, along with many of the employees at Apple and Microsoft. More-over, left-handed people are disproportionately represented among Nobel Prize winners. Researchers who have tried to explain this phenomenon have discovered some interesting facts. For example, left-handed people seem to have high IQs. Moreover, many left-handers are good at big-picture and visual thinking. For this rea-son, they may be able to see things in ways that right-handers cannot. In conclusion, it appears that many left-handed people excel both because they are smart and because—in the words of the Apple slogan—they "think different."

2. Hybrid foods are very popular these days. One of the most popular hybrid foods is the cronut, a combination croissant and donut. At first, they were sold only at one bakery in New York City, but their popularity has gone global, with imitations being sold everywhere from South Korea to Australia. In fact, they are so popular that people will wait in line for hours just to taste them. Many other hybrid desserts have gained popularity; for example, the townie, a tartlet-brownie confection, is in demand in the United Kingdom. In addition to the sweet foods, savory hybrids are also on the rise. The most famous of these is the turducken, which consists of a chicken inside a duck inside a turkey.

**PRACTICE**

**3-16**   The following paragraph lacks the transitional words and phrases needed to connect its ideas. Read the paragraph carefully. Then, after consulting the list of transitional words and phrases on page 75, add appropriate transitions to connect the paragraph's ideas in logical order.

### More Than Just a Fad

_____ awareness bracelets became popular in 2004, they seemed likely to

be a brief fad, _____, more and more people are wearing them. _____,

Livestrong, an organization that helps people who are fighting cancer, introduced

its yellow cancer awareness bracelet. _____, awareness bracelets come in almost

every color, and each color can symbolize many different causes. Several reasons

explain their continuing popularity. _____, awareness bracelets give charities

an inexpensive way to raise money. They are often made from silicone, an

inexpensive material. _____, colorful silicone bracelets are appropriate for

everyone. _____, students like them, and older people do, too. _____,

the bracelets give people an easy way to show support for the causes that are

most important to them. _____, awareness bracelets really do raise awareness.

_____, if a person wears a bracelet related to an illness, other people ask

about the bracelet and about the illness. Often, the person has a story to share,

and such stories make the illness more meaningful to other people. _____,

awareness bracelets remain popular because they appeal both to people's sense of

style and to their ideals.

# TEST · Revise · Edit

Review the paragraph you drafted in response to the Seeing and Writing prompt on page 57. Then, TEST your paragraph by asking the following questions:

- Does your paragraph include a topic sentence?
- Does your paragraph include enough evidence?
- Does your paragraph include a summary statement?
- Does your paragraph include enough transitions?

Now, continue revising your draft. When you have finished, prepare a final edited draft of your paragraph.

## EDITING PRACTICE

TEST each of the following student paragraphs to make sure that it is *unified*, *well developed*, and *coherent*. Begin by underlining the **topic sentence**. Then, cross out any sentences that do not support the topic sentence. If necessary, add **evidence** (examples and details) to support the topic sentence. Then, decide if you need to make any changes to the paragraph's **summary statement**. (If the paragraph does not include a summary statement, write one now.) Finally, add **transitional words** and **phrases** where needed.

1. At a young age, pirate Anne Bonny traded a life of wealth and privilege for one of adventure and crime. In 1716, she ran away from home to marry a sailor. Sailors passed through the place where she lived, on the East Coast of the United States, on a regular basis. Later, she met a pirate named Calico Jack Rackham. Bonny soon left her husband to join Rackham's crew. She developed a reputation as a fierce fighter. In 1720, Bonny met another female pirate named Mary Read. They were captured by authorities. Bonny, who was pregnant, was not sentenced to death because executing a pregnant woman was against the law. Read received a death sentence. Before it could be carried out, she died of a fever in prison. No one knows what finally became of Bonny.

2. Just like Jell-O itself, the history of Jell-O is full of shakes and bounces. Easy-to-use powdered gelatin was patented in 1845. The formula was sold to a cough syrup manufacturer who added fruit flavorings and gave the product the name Jell-O. The dessert still didn't catch on. The Genesee Pure Food Company bought the Jell-O brand. Sales turned around after Jell-O advertisements appeared in the *Ladies' Home Journal* and door-to-door salesmen began distributing free Jell-O cookbooks. Jell-O can be used to make aspics and congealed salads. Jell-O sales jumped as a result of the baby boom but began falling steadily until Bill Cosby became the brand's spokesperson in the mid-1970s. Since that time, despite some ups and downs, Jell-O has retained its place as one of America's favorite family desserts.

3.  NASCAR, which stands for the National Association for Stock Car Auto Racing, sponsors one of the most popular sporting events in the United States. In the past, NASCAR events used to be held mainly in the South, where most of the fans lived. To lower the risks of terrible accidents, NASCAR drivers have to wear special seat belts and restraints for the head and neck. There are offices of the organization all over the country, including Los Angeles and New York City, and races are held worldwide. The biggest race of the season is the Daytona 500, which is 200 laps long and has more television viewers than the Indianapolis 500. NASCAR drivers are like rock stars for fans. Danica Patrick attracted many fans when she became the first woman to take the lead in the Daytona 500. Fans follow the careers of their favorite drivers and sometimes spend an entire week at the racetrack, cheering on their favorites as they prepare for a big race.

# review checklist

## TESTing Your Paragraph

☐ Your topic sentence should state the paragraph's main idea. (See 3a.)

☐ Your paragraph should include enough evidence—examples and details—to support its main idea. (See 3b.)

☐ Your paragraph should end with a summary statement that reinforces its main idea and helps to unify the paragraph. (See 3c.)

☐ Your paragraph should include transitional words and phrases that indicate how ideas are connected. (See 3d.)

# 4 Exemplification

© WENN photos/Newscom

## seeing and writing

The picture above shows the cast members from the television show *Lost*, a series that followed the lives of survivors of a plane crash on a mysterious tropical island. Look at the picture, and then brainstorm about the skills you would need to survive on a deserted island. Try to use the Word Power words in your brainstorming.

*Note:* If you like, you may choose instead to brainstorm on one of the additional topics listed on the following page.

In this chapter, you will learn to write an exemplification paragraph.

**PREVIEW**

## additional topics

| TOPIC | WORD POWER WORDS | DEFINITIONS |
|---|---|---|
| the dangers of social networking | restrict | ▪ to limit in number or scope |
| | divulge | ▪ to disclose or reveal |
| the demands of being a parent | nurture | ▪ to encourage the development of |
| | fatigue | ▪ extreme tiredness |
| problems you face | obstacle | ▪ something that stands in the way |
| | overwhelm | ▪ to overpower |
| peer pressure | conform | ▪ to behave as others do |
| | self-esteem | ▪ pride in oneself; self-respect |

**macmillanhighered.com /foundationsfirst**
LearningCurve > Patterns of Organization

## 4a What Is Exemplification?

What do we mean when we say that an instructor is *good* or that a football team is *bad*? What do we mean when we say that a particular government policy is *misguided* or that a particular war was *wrong*? To clarify general statements like these, we use **exemplification**—that is, we give **examples**, specific instances that illustrate a general idea.

| GENERAL STATEMENT | SPECIFIC EXAMPLES |
|---|---|
| Today is going to be a hard day. | Today is going to be a hard day because I have a history test in the morning and a lab quiz in the afternoon. I also have to go to work an hour earlier than usual. |
| My car is giving me problems. | My car is burning oil and won't start on cold mornings. In addition, I need a new set of tires. |

An **exemplification paragraph** explains or clarifies a general idea—stated in the topic sentence—by providing specific examples. Personal experiences, class discussions, observations, conversations, and reading can all be good sources of examples.

When you TEST an exemplification paragraph, make sure it includes these four elements.

T ■ An exemplification paragraph begins with a **topic sentence** that clearly states the main idea of the paragraph.

E ■ An exemplification paragraph presents **evidence**—in the form of examples—that supports and clarifies the general statement made in the topic sentence. Examples are arranged in **logical order**—for example, from least to most important or from general to specific.

S ■ An exemplification paragraph closes with a **summary statement** that reinforces the main idea stated in the topic sentence.

T ■ An exemplification paragraph includes **transitions** that introduce the examples and connect them to one another and to the topic sentence.

**Paragraph Map: Writing an Exemplification Paragraph**

**Topic sentence** _____

_____

*Example #1* _____

_____

*Example #2* _____

_____

*Example #3* _____

_____

*Summary statement* _____

_____

The following paragraph uses several examples to support the idea that state lotteries are a bad way to raise money.

## The Trouble with Lotteries

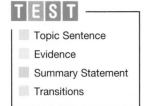

TEST
- Topic Sentence
- Evidence
- Summary Statement
- Transitions

Examples presented in logical order

Even for states that are financially troubled, lotteries are a bad way to raise money. First, lotteries can create financial problems for all but the few people who win. For example, in states that have lotteries, the average player spends nearly $150 each year on tickets. Some even spend $500 or more. Because the odds of winning are low, much of this money is wasted. Second, state lotteries send the message that gambling is risk-free and acceptable. Specifically, ticket buyers may ask themselves, "If the government sponsors gambling, how bad can it be?" They may therefore be less likely to see the possible dangers. Finally, lotteries are not necessarily a good or consistent revenue source. For instance, states spend millions of dollars on prizes and advertising for lotteries. These costs eat into the money that is made. Furthermore, lotteries are not immune to economic downturns. For example, some states saw double-digit drops in ticket sales during the recent recession. For these reasons, lotteries are a big gamble for states and their citizens.

*Examples presented in logical order*

— Jeffrey Smith (student)

## Some Transitional Words and Phrases for Exemplification

| | | |
|---|---|---|
| also | furthermore | the most important |
| finally | in addition | example |
| first . . . second . . . | moreover | the next example |
| (and so on) | one example . . . | |
| for example | another example | |
| for instance | specifically | |

## grammar in context

### Exemplification

When you write an exemplification paragraph, always use a comma after the introductory transitional word or phrase that introduces your examples.

First, lotteries can create financial problems for all but the few people who win.

Second, state lotteries send the message that gambling is risk-free and acceptable.

Finally, lotteries are not necessarily a good or consistent revenue source.

*For information on using commas with introductory and transitional words and phrases, see 30b.*

## 4b  Reading an Exemplification Paragraph

When you read an **exemplification paragraph**, TEST it to make sure that it contains all the elements of an effective paragraph.

**PRACTICE**

**4-1**   Read this exemplification paragraph, and follow the instructions that come after it.

### The Little World of Matchbox Cars

Matchbox cars are tiny die-cast models that come in a wide variety of styles. The most common Matchbox models, the ones most often seen in toy stores, are about 2.5 inches long. There are also larger cars, called "Major" or "Super Kings." Because Majors are unusual and fairly expensive, they are usually bought by collectors. Matchbox does not restrict itself to making model cars. For instance, the company has made airplanes called "Sky Busters" that it sold in stores and supplied to the major airlines. Matchbox has also made a series of fantasy vehicles called "Ultra Heroes." In addition to these items, Matchbox makes double-decker buses, helicopters, and trucks as well as play sets that include fire stations and car washes. Because of this wide variety of models, people who like Matchbox cars have no trouble finding new and unusual items to buy.

— Michael Graham (student)

> **WORD POWER**
>
> **die-casting** a process of forcing very hot metal into a mold

1. Underline the topic sentence of the paragraph.

2. Consider the paragraph's evidence. List the specific examples the writer uses to support the topic sentence. The first example has been listed for you.

   *Small cars that are found in toy stores.* _____

   _____

   _____

   _____

   _____

3. Circle the transitional words and phrases that the writer uses to connect examples in the paragraph.

4. Underline the paragraph's summary statement.

**PRACTICE**

**4-2**   Following are four topic sentences for exemplification paragraphs. After each sentence, list three examples that could support the main idea. For example, if you were writing about the poor quality of food in your school cafeteria, you could list mystery meat, weak coffee, and stale bread.

1. Many of the skills learned by our grandparents are not needed in today's high-tech world.

_____

_____

_____

_____

2. People who want to get their news from the Internet have many options.

_____

_____

_____

_____

3. I have always been very unlucky (or lucky) in love.

_____

_____

_____

_____

4. Although many people criticize television shows as mindless, there are a few exceptions.

_____

_____

_____

_____

## 4c  Writing an Exemplification Paragraph

Now, it is time to write an exemplification paragraph. Review the brainstorming you did in response to the Seeing and Writing prompt on page 80, and then complete the Practice activities that follow.

**PRACTICE**

**4-3**　Do some further brainstorming, or use one of the other strategies discussed in 2c, to help you come up with more examples for an exemplification paragraph on the topic that you have chosen.

_____

_____

_____

_____

_____

**PRACTICE**

**4-4**　Review all of your examples, and list below the four or five that can best help you develop a paragraph on the topic you have chosen.

_____

_____

_____

_____

_____

**PRACTICE**

**4-5**　Reread your list of examples. Then, draft a topic sentence that states your paragraph's main idea.

Topic sentence: _____

_____

**PRACTICE**

**4-6**　On the lines below, create an informal outline for your paragraph by arranging the examples you listed in Practice 4-4 in a logical order—for example, from least important to most important.

1. _____

2. _____

3. _____

4. _____

5. _____

**PRACTICE**

**4-7**  Draft your exemplification paragraph. Begin with the topic sentence you developed in Practice 4-5, and follow the informal outline you created in Practice 4-6. Try to use the Word Power words on pages 80 or 81 in your paragraph.

---

# TEST · **Revise · Edit**

Look back at the draft of your exemplification paragraph. Using the **TEST** checklist below, evaluate your paragraph to make sure it includes a topic sentence, evidence, a summary statement, and transitions. Then, prepare a revised and edited draft of your paragraph.

---

# TESTing an exemplification paragraph

## **T** opic Sentence Unifies Your Paragraph

☐ Do you have a clearly worded **topic sentence** that states your paragraph's main idea?

☐ Does each topic sentence state an idea that can be supported by examples?

## **E** vidence Supports Your Paragraph's Topic Sentence

☐ Does all your **evidence**—the examples you present—support your paragraph's main idea?

☐ Do you need to add more examples?

## **S** ummary Statement Reinforces Your Paragraph's Unity

☐ Does your paragraph end with a **summary statement** that reinforces your main idea?

## **T** ransitions Add Coherence to Your Paragraph

☐ Do you use **transitions** to introduce each example your paragraph discusses?

☐ Do you need to add transitions to make your paragraph clearer and to help readers follow your ideas?

1. The following student exemplification paragraph is missing a topic sentence, transitional words and phrases, and a concluding statement. After reading the paragraph, fill in the missing elements on the appropriate lines below. (Look on p. 83 for a list of transitions.)

Preparing a Résumé: What Not to Do

_____

_____. _____, people should never exaggerate

on a résumé. Employers can usually spot exaggerations. They know that "food

professional" at a fast-food restaurant means that a person was flipping hamburgers

or working at the counter. _____, people should not be vague about

their accomplishments. For instance, they shouldn't just say that they saved the

company money or that they have management experience. Instead, they should

include the exact amount of money they saved or the specific management

duties they performed. _____, people should never try to cover up gaps in

their employment history. They should not invent jobs or lie about the amount

of time they worked. Instead, they should explain any gaps in a cover letter.

_____

_____

2. Create an exemplification paragraph by adding examples that support the topic sentence below. Connect the examples with appropriate transitions, and end the paragraph with a clear summary statement. Finally, add an appropriate title on the line provided.

_____

Eating fast food on a regular basis can have a number of drawbacks.

_____

_____

_____

_____

_____

1. The following student narration paragraph is missing a topic sentence, transitional words and phrases, and a concluding statement. After reading the paragraph, fill in the missing elements on the appropriate lines below. (See p. 92 for a list of transitions.)

The Date from Hell

_____

_____

The date started when I picked Tracy up at her apartment. _____

we left, I had to get the approval of her roommates. Apparently, I passed

the test. _____, we drove to a small Italian restaurant that I like.

_____ the owner tried to seat us, Tracy said that she didn't like the

table. _____, she found a table she liked. _____, we sat down

and ordered. When the food came, Tracy sent it back because she said it wasn't

what she had expected. When the waiter brought her another platter, she sent

it back because she said it was too cold. _____, dinner was over, and

we went back to her apartment to talk. We didn't agree about anything. I told

her I liked a certain movie, and she said she didn't. I told her who I voted for

in the last election, but she voted for another person. If I had an opinion about

anything, she had the opposite opinion. _____, I had had enough.

I told Tracy that I had to get up early the next morning, and I went home.

_____

_____

2. Create a narrative paragraph by adding events to support the topic sentence below. Connect the events with appropriate transitions, and end the paragraph with a clear summary statement that sums up the main idea. Finally, add an appropriate title on the line provided.

_____

When I was young, I had an experience that caused me to grow up

suddenly. _____

_____

# 6 Description

© Peter Bowster/Photo Researchers, Inc.

## seeing and writing

The picture above shows a building in Barcelona, Spain, designed by the famous architect Antoní Gaudi. Look at the picture, and then brainstorm about what you see. Include enough specific details so that readers will be able to "see" what you are describing without looking at the picture. Try to use the Word Power words in your brainstorming.

*Note:* If you like, you may choose instead to brainstorm on one of the additional topics listed on the following page.

In this chapter, you will learn to write a descriptive paragraph.

**PREVIEW**

## additional topics

| TOPIC | WORD POWER WORDS | DEFINITIONS |
|---|---|---|
| a person you admire | esteem<br><br>commend | ▪ to have great regard for<br><br>▪ to express approval of |
| your workplace | environment<br><br>culture | ▪ surroundings<br><br>▪ ideas, customs of a group |
| your car, truck, or bike | efficient<br><br>transportation | ▪ operating with little waste<br><br>▪ a means of conveyance |
| someone (or something) you see every day | remarkable<br><br>recurring | ▪ worthy of notice<br><br>▪ occurring again and again |

macmillanhighered.com
/foundationsfirst
LearningCurve > Patterns of Organization

## 6a  What Is Description?

When you write a **description**, you use language that creates a vivid impression of what you have seen, heard, smelled, tasted, or touched. The more specific details you include, the better your description will be.

The following description is flat because it includes no specific details.

**FLAT DESCRIPTION**

I saw a beautiful sunrise.

In contrast, the description below is full of details that convey the writer's experience to readers.

**RICH DESCRIPTION**

Early this morning, as I walked along the sandy beach, I saw the sun rise slowly out of the ocean. At first, the ocean looked red. Then, it turned slowly to pink, to green, and finally to blue. As I stood watching the sun, I heard the waves hit the shore, and I felt the cold water swirl around my toes. For a moment, even the small grey and white birds that hurried along the shore seemed to stop and watch the dazzling sight.

The revised description relies on sight (*saw the sun rise slowly out of the ocean; looked red; turned slowly to pink, to green, and finally to blue*), touch (*the sandy beach; felt the cold water*), and sound (*heard the waves hit the shore*).

## FYI

### Description

Vague, overused words—such as *good, nice, bad,* and *beautiful*—do not help readers see what you are describing. When you write a descriptive paragraph, try to use specific words and phrases that make your writing come alive.

A **descriptive paragraph** paints a picture of a person, place, or object. When you TEST a descriptive paragraph, make sure it includes these four elements.

**T** ■ A descriptive paragraph includes a **topic sentence** that states the main idea or general impression that you want to convey with your paragraph.

**E** ■ A descriptive paragraph presents **evidence** in the form of descriptive details that support the topic sentence. Details are arranged in definite **spatial order**, the order in which you observed the scene you are describing—for example, from near to far.

**S** ■ A descriptive paragraph ends with a **summary statement** that reinforces the main idea stated in the topic sentence.

**T** ■ A descriptive paragraph includes **transitions** that connect details to one another and to the topic sentence.

**Paragraph Map: Writing a Descriptive Paragraph**

> **Topic sentence** _____
> _____
>
> *Detail #1* _____
> _____
>
> *Detail #2* _____
> _____
>
> *Detail #3* _____
> _____
>
> **Summary statement** _____
> _____

The following paragraph uses descriptive details to support the idea that the Lincoln Memorial is a monument to American democracy.

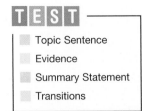

TEST

■ Topic Sentence
■ Evidence
■ Summary Statement
■ Transitions

### The Lincoln Memorial

The Lincoln Memorial was built to celebrate American democracy. In front of the monument is a long marble staircase that leads from a reflecting pool to the Memorial's entrance. Thirty-six columns surround the building.

Inside the building are three rooms. The first room contains the nineteen-Ofoot-tall statue of Lincoln. Seated in a chair, Lincoln looks exhausted after the long Civil War. One of Lincoln's hands is a fist, suggesting his strength, and the other is open, suggesting his kindness. On either side of the first room are two other rooms. On the wall of one room are the words of the Gettysburg Address. On the wall of the other room, Lincoln's Second Inaugural Address is displayed. Above the Gettysburg Address is a mural that shows an angel freeing the slaves. Above the Second Inaugural Address is another mural, which shows the people of the North and the South coming back together. As its design shows, the Lincoln Memorial was built to celebrate both the sixteenth president and the nation's struggle for equality.

*Descriptive details arranged in spatial order*

— Nicole Lentz (student)

## Some Transitional Words and Phrases for Description

| | | |
|---|---|---|
| above | in front of | on top of |
| behind | inside | outside |
| below | nearby | the first . . . the second |
| between | next to | the next |
| beyond | on | under |
| in | on one side . . . | |
| in back of | on the other side . . . | |

# grammar in context

## Description

When you write a descriptive paragraph, you sometimes use **modifiers**—words and phrases that describe another word or group of words.

A modifier should be placed as close as possible to the word it is supposed to modify. If you place modifying words or phrases too far from the words they modify, you create a **misplaced modifier** that will confuse readers.

CONFUSING    Seated in a chair, the long Civil War has clearly exhausted Lincoln. (*Was the Civil War seated in a chair?*)

CLEAR    Seated in a chair, Lincoln is clearly exhausted by the long Civil War.

*For information on how to identify and correct misplaced modifiers, see Chapter 23.*

# 6b   Reading a Descriptive Paragraph

When you read a **descriptive paragraph**, TEST it to make sure that it contains all the elements of an effective paragraph.

**PRACTICE 6-1**   Read this descriptive paragraph, and follow the instructions that come after it.

### Morning on the Bus

Early this morning, the people on the bus were strangely quiet. When the doors to the bus opened, I saw that it was almost empty. Inside the bus, way in the back, two people who were coming home from a night of clubbing were sleeping. Nearby, I saw a small woman dressed in a black and white waitress uniform. She held a paper container of coffee in both hands and looked out the window into the soft morning light. At the next stop, several people boarded the bus. They slumped down in their seats, closed their eyes, and tried to catch a few more minutes of sleep. At the front of the bus, a short, unshaven man took out a newspaper, folded it so that only a small bit was showing, and tried to read. As I watched him, I realized that he was reading the same page again and again. The only sounds were the engine and the screeching of the brakes as the bus came to a stop. No one was really awake yet. It was as if everyone was quietly waiting for the day to start.

— Caitlin McNally (student)

1. Underline the topic sentence of the paragraph.

2. Consider the paragraph's evidence. List some of the details the writer uses to describe the people on the bus. The first detail has been listed for you.

   *Two people coming home were sleeping*

   _____

   _____

   _____

3. Circle some of the transitions the writer uses to lead readers from one detail to another.

4. Underline the paragraph's summary statement.

**PRACTICE**

**6-2**  Following are four topic sentences for descriptive paragraphs. After each topic sentence, list three details that could help convey why you are writing the description. For example, to describe an interesting person, you could tell what the person looked like, how he or she behaved, and what he or she said.

1. It was a long hike, but when we finally got to the top of the mountain, the view was incredible.

   _____

   _____

   _____

2. Every community has a house that all the kids think is haunted.

   _____

   _____

   _____

3. In every living situation, there is one person who is a slob.

   _____

   _____

   _____

4. I'll never forget the first time I did something really risky.

   _____

   _____

   _____

## 6c  Writing a Descriptive Paragraph

Now, it is time to write a descriptive paragraph. Review the brainstorming you did in response to the Seeing and Writing prompt on page 100, and then complete the Practice activities that follow.

**PRACTICE**

**6-3** Do some further brainstorming, or use one of the other strategies discussed in 2c to help you come up with more details for a descriptive paragraph on the topic that you have chosen.

_____

_____

_____

_____

**PRACTICE**

**6-4** Review all of your examples, and list below the four or five details that can best help you develop a paragraph on the topic you have chosen.

_____

_____

_____

_____

**PRACTICE**

**6-5** Reread your list of details. Then, draft a topic sentence that summarizes your paragraph's main idea.

Topic sentence: _____

_____

**PRACTICE**

**6-6** On the lines below, create an informal outline for your paragraph by arranging the details you listed in Practice 6-4 in spatial order—for example, from left to right, near to far, or top to bottom.

1. _____

2. _____

3. _____

4. _____

5. _____

**PRACTICE**

**6-7** Draft your descriptive paragraph. Begin with the topic sentence you developed in Practice 6-5, and follow the informal outline you created in Practice 6-6. Try to use the Word Power words on pages 100 or 101 in your paragraph.

# TEST · Revise · Edit

Look back at the draft of your descriptive paragraph. Using the **TEST** checklist below, evaluate your paragraph to make sure it includes a topic sentence, evidence, a summary statement, and transitions. Then, prepare a revised and edited draft of your paragraph.

# TESTing a descriptive paragraph

## **T** opic Sentence Unifies Your Paragraph

☐ Do you have a clearly worded **topic sentence** that states your paragraph's main idea—the general impression you want to convey?

☐ Does your topic sentence identify the person, place, or thing you will describe in your paragraph?

## **E** vidence Supports Your Paragraph's Topic Sentence

☐ Does all your **evidence**—descriptive details—support your paragraph's main idea?

☐ Do you have enough descriptive details, or do you need to include more?

## **S** ummary Statement Reinforces Your Paragraph's Unity

☐ Does your paragraph end with a **summary statement** that reinforces your main idea?

## **T** ransitions Add Coherence to Your Paragraph

☐ Do your **transitions** lead readers from one detail to the next?

☐ Do you need to add transitions to make your paragraph clearer and to help readers follow your ideas?

1. The following student descriptive paragraph is missing a topic sentence, transitional words and phrases, and a concluding statement. After reading the paragraph, fill in the missing elements on the appropriate lines below. (See p. 103 for a list of transitions.)

Disaster Area

_____

_____

When I open the door to her room, the clutter is overwhelming. Directly

_____ the room, under the windows, is my sister's desk. Surprisingly,

this is the neatest, most organized part of her room. _____ side of

her desk is a large blue dictionary. Next to that are two large white loose-leaf

binders. _____ side of the desk is her iPod dock and a small televi-

sion set. On another wall is my sister's bed. It is almost always unmade and

covered with clothes, books, magazines, an empty bag of potato chips, a half-

eaten sandwich, and three or four stuffed animals. _____ the bed

is her dresser. Usually, the drawers are open, and their contents are draped

over the front of the drawers. If she has had a particularly bad time decid-

ing what to wear, the floor will be covered with clothes. _____ of

the dresser is a jumbled collection of make-up, perfume bottles, hair spray,

brushes, cotton balls, at least one hairdryer, and several empty soda cans.

_____

_____

2. Create a descriptive paragraph by adding details to support the topic sentence below. Connect details with appropriate transitions, and end the paragraph with a clear concluding summary that reinforces the main idea. Finally, add an appropriate title on the line provided.

_____

My picture in my high school yearbook reveals a lot about me. _____

_____

_____

# 7 Process

## WORD POWER

**challenge** something that requires special effort

**replacement** something that takes the place of another thing

**unanticipated** not expected

## seeing and writing

The picture above shows someone trying to fix a burst water pipe. Look at the picture, and then brainstorm about how you would attempt to fix a mechanical problem of some sort. Try to use the Word Power words in your brainstorming.

*Note:* If you like, you may choose instead to brainstorm on one of the additional topics listed on the following page.

# additional topics

| TOPIC | WORD POWER WORDS | DEFINITIONS |
|---|---|---|
| how to succeed in college | discipline | ▪ to train oneself to do something |
| | gratification | ▪ a source of pleasure |
| getting out of debt | strategy | ▪ a plan to achieve a specific goal |
| | consolidate | ▪ to combine into one thing |
| planning a road trip | destination | ▪ the place to which someone is going |
| | attractions | ▪ things that evoke interest |
| cooking your favorite food | prepare | ▪ to put together |
| | ingredients | ▪ foods combined to make a particular dish |

e macmillanhighered.com
/foundationsfirst
LearningCurve > Patterns of Organization

# 7a  What Is Process?

When you describe a **process**, you tell readers how something works or how to do something. For example, you could explain how the optical scanner at the checkout counter of a food store works or how to shorten a pair of jeans.

A **process paragraph** presents a series of steps to explain how something works (or happens) or how to perform an action. When you TEST a process paragraph, make sure it includes these four elements.

- **T** ▪ A process paragraph begins with a **topic sentence** that identifies the process. It should also state the point you want to make about it.

- **E** ▪ A process paragraph presents **evidence** in the form of the steps in the process. These steps are presented one at a time, in strict **time order**—the order in which they occur or are to be performed.

- **S** ▪ A process paragraph ends with a **summary statement** that brings the process to a close and reinforces the main idea stated in the topic sentence.

- **T** ▪ A process paragraph includes **transitions** that connect steps in the process to one another and to the topic sentence.

**Paragraph Map: Writing a Process Paragraph**

**Topic sentence** _____

_____

*Step #1* _____

_____

*Step #2* _____

_____

*Step #3* _____

_____

**Summary statement** _____

_____

There are two types of process paragraphs: **process explanations** and **instructions**.

## Process Explanations

In a **process explanation**, your purpose is to tell how something works or how something happens—for example, how a cell phone operates or how the body digests food. In this case, you do not expect readers to perform the process.

The following paragraph explains how a fire extinguisher works.

TEST
- Topic Sentence
- Evidence
- Summary Statement
- Transitions

Steps presented in time order

How a Fire Extinguisher Works

Even though many people have fire extinguishers in their homes, most people do not know how they work. A fire extinguisher is a metal cylinder filled with a substance that will put out a fire. All extinguishers operate the same way. First, the material inside the cylinder is put under pressure. Next, when a lever on top of the metal cylinder is squeezed, a valve is opened, and the pressure inside the fire extinguisher is released. As the compressed gas in the cylinder rushes out, it carries the material in the fire extinguisher along with it. Then, a nozzle at the top of the cylinder concentrates the stream of liquid, gas, or powder coming from the fire extinguisher so it can be aimed at a fire. Finally, the material comes in contact with the fire and puts it out. Every home should have at least one fire extinguisher located where it can be easily reached when it is needed. Most important, everyone should know how to use a fire extinguisher.

— David Turner (student)

## Instructions

When you write **instructions**, your purpose is to give readers the information they need to perform a task or activity—for example, to fill out an application or to operate a piece of machinery. Because you expect readers to follow your instructions, you address them directly, using **commands** (*check the gauge . . . pull the valve*).

The following paragraph gives humorous instructions on how to get food out of a vending machine.

Man vs. Machine

Long ago, the first food machines were the servants of people, but now, these machines have turned against their creators. The result is a generation of machines that will take a little girl's allowance and keep her Cheetos, too. Luckily, there is a foolproof method for getting a vending machine to give up its food. First, approach the vending machine coolly. Make sure that you don't seem frightened or angry. The machine will sense these emotions and steal your money. Second, be polite. Say hello, compliment the machine on its selection of goodies, and smile. Be careful. If the machine thinks you are trying to take advantage of it, it will keep your money. Third, if the machine steals your money, remain calm. Ask it nicely to give you the food you paid for. Finally, it is time to get serious. Hit the side of the vending machine with your fist. If this doesn't work, lower your shoulder, and throw yourself at the machine. (A good kick or two might also help.) When the machine has had enough, it will drop your snack, and you can grab it. If you follow these few simple steps, you should have no trouble walking away from vending machines with the food you paid for.

— Adam Cooper (student)

<table>
<tr><td>T E S T</td></tr>
<tr><td>☐ Topic Sentence</td></tr>
<tr><td>☐ Evidence</td></tr>
<tr><td>☐ Summary Statement</td></tr>
<tr><td>☐ Transitions</td></tr>
</table>

## Some Transitional Words and Phrases for Process

| | | |
|---|---|---|
| after that | first | soon |
| as | immediately | the first (second, third) step |
| as soon as | later | the last step |
| at the same time | meanwhile | then |
| at this point | next | the next step |
| before | now | when |
| finally | once | while |

# grammar in context

## Process

When you write a process paragraph, you may find yourself making **illogical shifts** in tense, person, number, and voice. If you shift from one tense, person, or voice to another without good reason, you may confuse readers.

**CONFUSING**   First, the vending machine should be approached coolly. Make sure that you don't seem frightened or angry. (illogical shift from passive to active voice)

**CLEAR**   First, approach the vending machine coolly. Make sure that you don't seem frightened or angry. (consistent use of active voice)

*For information on how to avoid illogical shifts in tense, person, and voice, see Chapter 22.*

## 7b   **Reading a Process Paragraph**

When you read a **process paragraph**, TEST it to make sure that it contains all the elements of an effective paragraph.

**PRACTICE**

**7-1**   Read this process paragraph, and follow the instructions that come after it.

Getting a Tattoo

Before getting a tattoo, a customer should understand the process. First, the customer should find an experienced and responsible tattoo artist, one who has state certification. Also, the shop should be clean, and all equipment that is not disposable should be carefully sterilized. Next, the customer should work with the tattoo artist to select a design from the artist's portfolio. Later, while the customer sits in a chair, the artist will transfer a stencil of the design onto the skin. After this step, the artist will use an inked needle to create the tattoo. Once the tattoo is completed, the artist should apply ointment and a bandage to the affected area. Eventually, the tattoo will scab over and heal. Most customers find the process less painful than they had expected, and they are usually pleased with the results.

—Ryan Felder (student)

1. Underline the topic sentence of the paragraph.

2. Consider the paragraph's evidence. List the steps in the process on the lines below.

_____

_____

_____

_____

_____

_____

_____

3. Circle the transitions that tell you that the writer is moving on to the next step in the process.

4. Underline the paragraph's summary statement.

**PRACTICE**

**7-2** Following are four topic sentences for process paragraphs. List three steps that might occur in each process.

1. Registering for college courses can be a frustrating process.

_____

_____

_____

2. Balancing a checkbook is not as complicated as it may seem.

_____

_____

_____

3. Driving on a snowy road is not difficult if you follow a few simple steps.

_____

_____

_____

4. Buying products online can save you time and money.

_____

_____

_____

# 7c Writing a Process Paragraph

Now, it is time to write a process paragraph. Review the brainstorming you did in response to the Seeing and Writing prompt on page 110, and then complete the Practice activities that follow.

**PRACTICE 7-3**

Do some further brainstorming, or use one of the other strategies discussed in 2c to help you come up with two or three more steps for a process paragraph on the topic that you have chosen.

_____

_____

_____

_____

**PRACTICE 7-4**

Review your notes, and decide whether to write a process explanation or a set of instructions. Then, choose the steps you want to include from the list you made in Practice 7-3, and list them below.

_____

_____

_____

_____

**PRACTICE 7-5**

Reread your list of steps. Then, draft a topic sentence that identifies the process you will discuss and states your paragraph's main idea.

Topic sentence: _____

_____

**PRACTICE 7-6**

On the lines below, create an informal outline for your paragraph by arranging your steps in time order, moving from the first step to the last.

1. _____

2. _____

3. _____

4. _____

5. _____

**PRACTICE 7-7**

Draft your process paragraph. Begin with the topic sentence you developed in Practice 7-5, and follow the informal outline you created in Practice 7-6. Try to use the Word Power words on pages 110 or 111 in your paragraph.

# TEST · Revise · Edit

Look back at the draft of your process paragraph. Using the TEST checklist below, evaluate your paragraph to make sure it includes a topic sentence, evidence, a summary statement, and transitions. Then, prepare a revised and edited draft of your paragraph.

# TESTing a process paragraph

### **T** opic Sentence Unifies Your Paragraph

☐ Do you have a clearly worded **topic sentence** that states your paragraph's main idea?

☐ Does your topic sentence identify the process you will discuss?

☐ Does your topic sentence indicate whether you will be explaining a process or giving instructions?

### **E** vidence Supports Your Paragraph's Topic Sentence

☐ Have you included all the steps in the process?

☐ Have you included enough **evidence**—examples and details—to explain the steps and make the process clear to readers?

☐ If your paragraph is a set of instructions, have you included all the information readers need to perform the process?

### **S** ummary Statement Reinforces Your Paragraph's Unity

☐ Does your paragraph end with a **summary statement** that reinforces your main idea?

### **T** ransitions Add Coherence to Your Paragraph

☐ Do your **transitions** move readers from one step in the process to the next?

☐ Do you need to add transitions to make your paragraph clearer and to help readers follow your ideas?

1. The following student process paragraph is missing a topic sentence, transitional words and phrases, and a summary statement. After reading the paragraph, fill in the missing elements on the appropriate lines below. (See p. 113 for a list of transitions.)

Starting Over

_____

_____

Before you begin dating, keep in mind that you should date only when you are ready. _____, once you decide to go out on a date, is to take things slowly. Both you and your children need to get used to the fact that you are dating. _____, make sure that your children are well cared for when you are on a date. Parents or close friends are best because your children will feel safe with them. _____, talk to your children. Explain that you would like to spend time with someone you like. Do not talk about marriage or getting them a "new parent." _____, if you decide you would like to introduce the person you are dating to your children, keep the first visit short, and schedule additional visits far apart. Also, do not show your date too much affection in front of your children. _____, be patient. It may take a long time for both you and your children to become comfortable with your new life. _____

_____

2. Create a process paragraph by adding details to support the topic sentence below. Connect the steps in the process with appropriate transitions, and end the paragraph with a clear summary statement that sums up the main idea. Finally, add an appropriate title on the line provided.

_____

Facebook and other social networking sites can be good places to meet new friends, provided you follow a few simple steps to protect your privacy.

_____

_____

# 8 Cause and Effect

© Tyler Golden/NBCU via Getty Images

WORD POWER

**conceited** self-important
**empower** to give power
or confidence
**humble** modest
**self-esteem** pride in
oneself; self-respect

## seeing and writing

The picture above shows finalists from a recent season of *The Voice*. Look at the picture, and then brainstorm about how your life would be different if you won this competition. How would winning affect you and the people you know? Try to use the Word Power words in your brainstorming.

*Note:* If you like, you may choose instead to brainstorm on one of the additional topics listed on the following page.

In this chapter, you will learn to write a cause-and-effect paragraph.

**PREVIEW**

# additional topics

| TOPIC | WORD POWER WORDS | DEFINITIONS |
|---|---|---|
| why people shop online | convenient | ▪ easy, accessible |
| | discount | ▪ to sell below the usual price |
| the effects of social networking sites | network | ▪ to cultivate people who can be helpful |
| | socialize | ▪ to mix with others |
| why you chose the college you did | assistance | ▪ money or resources that help someone |
| | reputation | ▪ the opinion that people have about someone or something |
| the effects of divorce on children | cope | ▪ to deal with something difficult |
| | conflict | ▪ a serious disagreement |

ⓔ **macmillanhighered.com /foundationsfirst**
LearningCurve > Patterns of Organization

# 8a What Is Cause and Effect?

Why is the cost of college so high? How does smoking affect a person's health? How dangerous is swine flu? All these familiar questions have one thing in common: they try to determine the causes or effects of an action, event, or situation.

A **cause** is something or someone that makes something happen. An **effect** is something brought about by a particular cause.

| CAUSE | EFFECT |
|---|---|
| Increased airport security ⟶ | Long lines at airports |
| Weight gain ⟶ | Decision to exercise |
| Seat belt laws passed ⟶ | Increased use of seat belts |

A **cause-and-effect paragraph** helps readers understand why something happened or is happening or shows readers how one event or situation affects something else. When you TEST a cause-and-effect paragraph, make sure it includes the following four elements.

T ■ A cause-and-effect paragraph begins with a **topic sentence** that states the paragraph's main idea; it tells readers whether the paragraph is focusing on causes or on effects.

E ■ A cause-and-effect paragraph presents **evidence**—examples and details—to support the topic sentence and explain each cause and effect. Points are arranged in **logical order**—for example, from the least to most important cause or effect.

S ■ A cause-and-effect paragraph ends with a **summary statement** that reinforces the main idea stated in the topic sentence.

T ■ A cause-and-effect paragraph includes **transitions** that connect causes or effects to one another and to the topic sentence.

### Paragraph Map: Writing a Cause-and-Effect Paragraph

**Topic sentence** _____

*Cause (or effect) #1* _____

*Cause (or effect) #2* _____

*Cause (or effect) #3* _____

**Summary statement** _____

**TEST**

    Topic Sentence
    Evidence
    Summary Statement
    Transitions

The following paragraph focuses on *causes*.

### Health Alert

For a number of reasons, Americans are gaining weight at an alarming rate. The first reason is that many Americans do not eat healthy foods. Instead, they eat a lot of food that is high in salt and contains a lot of saturated fat. Also, many Americans eat on the run, grabbing a doughnut or muffin on the way to work and eating fast food for lunch or dinner. Another reason Americans are gaining weight is that they eat too much. They take too much food and think they must eat everything on their plates. They do not stop eating when they are full, and they often have second helpings and dessert. The most important reason for this alarming weight gain is that Americans do not exercise. They sit on the couch and watch hours of television and get up only to have a snack or a soda. The effect of this unhealthy lifestyle is easy to predict. Unless Americans begin eating better, many will develop severe health problems in the future.

— Jen Toll (student)

The paragraph below focuses on *effects*.

### Second Thoughts

When I dropped out of high school before my senior year, I had no idea how this action would affect my life. The first effect was that I became a social outcast. At the beginning, my friends called and asked me to go out with them. Gradually, however, school activities took up more and more of their time. Eventually, they had no time for me. Another effect was that I became stuck in a dead-end job. When I was in school, working part-time at a bookstore didn't seem bad. Once it became my full-time job, however, I saw that I was going nowhere, but without a diploma or some college education, I couldn't get a better job. The most important effect was that my girlfriend broke up with me. One day, she told me that she didn't like dating a dropout. She said I had no goals and no future. I had to agree with her. When I heard that she had started dating a sophomore in college, something clicked. I enrolled in night school and got my GED, and then I applied to community college. Now that I am taking college classes, I realize how wrong I was to drop out of high school and how lucky I am to have a second chance.

— Dan Tarr (student)

## Some Transitional Words and Phrases for Cause and Effect

| | | |
|---|---|---|
| another cause | moreover | the first (second, third, |
| another effect | one cause | final) reason |
| another reason | (effect, reason) | the most important cause |
| as a result | since | the most important |
| because | so | effect |
| besides | the first (second, | the most important |
| consequently | third, final) cause | reason |
| finally | the first (second, | therefore |
| for | third, final) effect | |
| for this reason | | |

## grammar in context

### Cause and Effect

When you write a cause-and-effect paragraph, be careful not to confuse the words *affect* and *effect*. *Affect* is a verb meaning "to influence." *Effect* is a noun meaning "result."

      *effect*
The first ~~affect~~ is that I became a social outcast. (*effect* is a noun)

When I dropped out of high school before my senior year, I
                  *affect*
had no idea how this action would ~~effect~~ my life. (*affect* is a verb)

*For more information on* effect *and* affect, *see Chapter 35.*

## 8b Reading a Cause-and-Effect Paragraph

When you read a **cause-and-effect paragraph**, TEST it to make sure that it contains all the elements of an effective paragraph.

**PRACTICE**

**8-1** Read this cause-and-effect paragraph, and follow the instructions that come after it.

Why I Had to Move

It's hard to imagine why someone would go to all the trouble and expense of moving, but I had some very good reasons for moving to a new apartment. My first reason for moving was that I had noisy neighbors. When I looked at the apartment, the rental agent promised me that it would be quiet. He didn't bother to tell me that the apartment across the hall was rented by two guys who came and went at all hours of the day and night. Every weekend, and most nights, they had friends over, and this made it impossible for me to sleep or to study. Another reason that I moved was that the landlord never fixed things. The stove never worked right, and I could never be sure if I would have heat or hot water. My most disturbing reason for moving was that the landlord made a habit of coming into my apartment without telling me. As soon as I moved in, I began to notice that something wasn't right. I would come home from classes and notice that the door wasn't locked — even though I remembered locking it. Once I noticed that my DVD player had been disconnected and that a drawer that I had closed was open. Later, a neighbor told me that the landlord came around and inspected all the apartments once a month. When I told the rental agent that the landlord shouldn't come into my apartment anytime he felt like it, he told me to read my lease. By the end of the year, I decided that I had had enough, and I moved.

— Jenny Wong (student)

1. Underline the topic sentence of the paragraph.

2. Consider the paragraph's evidence. Does the paragraph focus on causes or effects? How do you know?

_____

_____

_____

3. List the causes on the lines below.

_____

_____

_____

4. Circle the transitions that tell you the writer is moving from one cause to another.

5. Underline the paragraph's summary statement.

**PRACTICE**

**8-2**  Following are four topic sentences for cause-and-effect paragraphs. List three causes or effects for each sentence.

1. Indoor air pollution is caused by products we use every day.

_____

_____

2. Secondhand smoke can have harmful effects on everyone's health.

_____

_____

3. Twitter is popular for many reasons.

_____

_____

4. Smartphones have changed our society.

_____

_____

## 8c  Writing a Cause-and-Effect Paragraph

Now, it is time to write a cause-and-effect paragraph. Review the brainstorming you did in response to the Seeing and Writing prompt on page 120, and then complete the Practice activities that follow.

**PRACTICE**

**8-3** Do some further brainstorming, or use one of the other strategies discussed in 2c, to help you come up with several additional causes or effects for a cause-and-effect paragraph on the topic that you have chosen.

_____

_____

_____

_____

_____

**PRACTICE**

**8-4** Review your notes, and create a cluster diagram. Write your topic in the center of the page, and draw arrows branching out to specific causes or effects.

**PRACTICE**

**8-5** Choose the most important causes or effects from your cluster diagram, and list them on the lines that follow.

_____

_____

_____

**PRACTICE**

**8-6** Reread your list of causes or effects from Practice 8-5. Then, draft a topic sentence that states the main idea your paragraph will develop.

Topic sentence: _____

_____

**PRACTICE**

**8-7** On the lines below, create an informal outline for your paragraph by arranging the causes or effects you have decided to discuss in your paragraph in an effective order—for example, from least important to most important.

1. _____

2. _____

3. _____

4. _____

5. _____

Draft your cause-and-effect paragraph. Begin with the topic sentence you developed in Practice 8-6, and follow the informal outline you created in Practice 8-7. Try to use the Word Power words on pages 120 or 121 in your paragraph.

## TEST · Revise · Edit

Look back at the draft of your cause-and-effect paragraph. Using the **TEST** checklist below, evaluate your paragraph to make sure it includes a topic sentence, evidence, a summary statement, and transitions. Then, prepare a revised and edited draft of your paragraph.

## TESTing a cause-and-effect paragraph

### **T**opic Sentence Unifies Your Paragraph

☐ Do you have a clearly worded **topic sentence** that states your paragraph's main idea?

☐ Does your topic sentence identify the cause or effect on which your paragraph will focus?

### **E**vidence Supports Your Paragraph's Topic Sentence

☐ Do you need to add any important causes or effects?

☐ Do you need to explain your causes or effects more fully?

☐ Does all your **evidence**—examples and details—support your paragraph's main idea?

### **S**ummary Statement Reinforces Your Paragraph's Unity

☐ Does your paragraph end with a **summary statement** that reinforces your main idea?

### **T**ransitions Add Coherence to Your Paragraph

☐ Do your **transitions** clearly introduce each cause or effect?

☐ Do you need to add transitions to make your paragraph clearer and to help readers follow your ideas?

1. The following student cause-and-effect paragraph is missing a topic sentence, transitional words and phrases, and a summary statement. After reading the paragraph, fill in the missing elements on the appropriate lines below. (See p. 123 for a list of transitions.)

Doing My Part

_____

_____

_____ is that I recycle. I try to separate bottles, cans, and paper. I even recycle used cooking oil and old batteries that I replaced. Our township requires us to separate trash, but many people just put everything into a big plastic bag and throw it away. I choose to recycle. _____ is that I take public transportation when I commute to school. That way, I use less gas and oil. If more people took the train, we would all help to cut down on the pollution in the world. Besides, when I leave my car at home, I save money. I don't have to pay for gas, parking, or bridge tolls. _____ is that I buy items that can be reused before they are thrown away. For example, instead of using paper towels, I use cloth hand towels that I wash. I even refill the empty ink cartridges from my printer so that I can use them again.

_____

_____

2. Create a cause-and-effect paragraph by adding causes to support the topic sentence below. Connect the effects with appropriate transitions, and end the paragraph with a clear summary statement that sums up the main idea. Finally, add an appropriate title on the line provided.

_____

A number of factors can cause students to do poorly on exams. _____

_____

_____

_____

# 9 Comparison and Contrast

© Danielle Donders — Mothership Photography/Getty

## seeing and writing

The picture above shows a dog and a cat. Look at the picture, and brainstorm about how dogs and cats are alike and how they are different. Try to use the Word Power words in your brainstorming.

*Note:* If you like, you may choose instead to brainstorm on one of the additional topics listed on the following page.

## additional topics

| TOPIC | WORD POWER WORDS | DEFINITIONS |
|---|---|---|
| online classes versus traditional classes | flexible | ■ easy to modify or adapt |
| | interact | ■ to act together |
| two different teachers | inspire | ■ to make someone want to do something |
| | encouraging | ■ giving support |
| two different websites | cluttered | ■ crowded, disordered |
| | navigate | ■ to get around a website |
| men's and women's shopping habits | economical | ■ giving good value |
| | satisfaction | ■ gratification, fulfillment |

ⓔ **macmillanhighered.com /foundationsfirst**
LearningCurve > Patterns for Organization

## 9a  What Is Comparison and Contrast?

When you **compare**, you consider how two things are similar. When you **contrast**, you consider how they are different.

**Comparison-and-contrast paragraphs** can examine just similarities or just differences, or they can examine both. When you TEST a comparison-and-contrast paragraph, make sure it includes these four elements.

**T** ■ A comparison-and-contrast paragraph begins with a **topic sentence** that states its main idea and tells readers whether the paragraph is going to discuss similarities or differences.

**E** ■ A comparison-and-contrast paragraph includes **evidence**—examples and details—to make the similarities and differences clear to readers. A comparison-and-contrast paragraph discusses the same or similar points for both subjects. Points are arranged in **logical order**—for example, from least to most important.

**S** ■ A comparison-and-contrast paragraph ends with a **summary statement** that reinforces the main idea stated in the topic sentence.

**T** ■ A comparison-and-contrast paragraph includes **transitions** that connect the two subjects being compared and that link the points about each subject.

There are two kinds of comparison-and-contrast paragraphs: *subject-by-subject comparisons* and *point-by-point comparisons*.

## Subject-by-Subject Comparisons

In a **subject-by-subject comparison**, you divide your comparison into two parts and discuss one subject at a time. In the first part of the paragraph, you discuss all your points about one subject. Then, in the second part, you discuss all your points about the other subject.

A subject-by-subject comparison is best for short paragraphs in which you do not discuss too many points. Readers will have little difficulty remembering the points you discuss for your first subject as you move on to discuss the second subject.

**Paragraph Map: Writing a Subject-by-Subject Comparison Paragraph**

> **Topic sentence** _____
> _____
>
> **Subject A** _____
>   Point 1 _____
>   _____
>   Point 2 _____
>   _____
>   Point 3 _____
>   _____
>
> **Subject B** _____
>   Point 1 _____
>   _____
>   Point 2 _____
>   _____
>   Point 3 _____
>   _____
>
> **Summary Statement** _____
> _____

**T·E·S·T**
- Topic Sentence
- Evidence
- Summary Statement
- Transitions

The following paragraph develops a subject-by-subject comparison to compare two ways of telling time.

### Why I Wear a Watch

Subject A: My watches ⎡ Cell phones may be the modern way to check the time, but I prefer a good, old-fashioned watch. A watch is always right there when I need it, allowing me to do a quick time check. Also, watches let me show my style. My sleek chrome watch helps me look professional when I am at work, and my retro-style digital watch lets me show a funkier side at school or on the weekends. In addition, watches can have sentimental value. My chrome watch was a high-school graduation gift from my grandmother, and I bought the digital watch while on a road trip with my best friend. Cell phones also tell time, but they are not as practical or as much fun as watches. Compared to my watches, my cell phone is often hard to find when I'm out. Sometimes, I have to stop on the street or in a busy train station and dig around in my backpack for it. Also, unlike watches, cell phones do not let me show my style. Of course, I can get different covers for my phone, but I cannot change its shape. Finally, I cannot imagine forming a sentimental attachment to a phone. My watches remind me of people and important occasions, but my cell phone has no special memories associated with it. As long as my watches keep ticking, I will save my cell phone for talking and texting.

*Subject A: My watches*

*Subject B: My cell phone*

— Tonya Jones (student)

## Point-by-Point Comparisons

In a **point-by-point comparison**, you discuss a point about one subject and then discuss the same point about the second subject. You use this alternating pattern throughout the paragraph.

A point-by-point comparison is a good strategy for paragraphs in which you discuss many points. It is also a good choice if the points you are discussing are technical or complicated.

### Paragraph Map: Writing a Point-by-Point Comparison Paragraph

**Topic sentence** _____

_____

***Point 1*** _____

    Subject A _____

_____

    Subject B _____

_____

***Point 2*** _____

    Subject A _____

_____

    Subject B _____

_____

***Point 3*** _____

    Subject A _____

_____

    Subject B _____

_____

**Summary Statement** _____

_____

The following paragraph develops a point-by-point comparison to compare two characters in a short story.

```
T E S T
  Topic Sentence
  Evidence
  Summary Statement
  Transitions
```

### Two Sisters

Point 1: Different personalities

Point 2: Different attitudes toward life

Point 3: Different attitudes toward tradition

Although they grew up together, Maggie and Dee, the two sisters in Alice Walker's short story "Everyday Use," are very different. Maggie, who was burned in a fire, is shy and has low self-esteem. When she walks, she shuffles her feet and looks down at the ground. Dee, however, is confident and outgoing. She looks people in the eye when she talks to them and is very opinionated. Maggie seems satisfied with her life. She never complains or asks for anything more than she has, and she has remained at home with her mother in rural Georgia. In contrast, Dee has always wanted nicer things. She has gone away to school and hardly ever visits her mother and Maggie. The biggest difference between Maggie and Dee is their attitude toward tradition. Although Maggie values her family's traditions, Dee values her African roots. Maggie cherishes her family's handmade quilts and furniture, hoping to use them with her own family. Unlike Maggie, Dee sees the handmade objects as things to be displayed, not used. The many differences between Maggie and Dee add conflict and tension to the story.

— Margaret Caracappa (student)

### Some Transitional Words and Phrases for Comparison and Contrast

| | |
|---|---|
| although | nevertheless |
| but | one difference . . . another difference |
| compared to | one similarity . . . another similarity |
| even though | on the contrary |
| however | on the one hand . . . on the other hand |
| in comparison | similarly |
| in contrast | though |
| like | unlike |
| likewise | whereas |

## grammar in context

## Comparison and Contrast

When you write a comparison-and-contrast paragraph, you should state the points you are comparing in **parallel** terms—using the same patterns of words to expresss similarities or differences.

**NOT PARALLEL** Although Maggie values her family's traditions, the African heritage of their family is the thing that Dee values.

**PARALLEL**   Although Maggie values her family's traditions, Dee values their African roots.

*For more information on revising to make ideas parallel, see Chapter 18.*

# 9b  Reading a Comparison-and-Contrast Paragraph

When you read a **comparison-and-contrast paragraph**, TEST it to make sure that it contains all the elements of an effective paragraph.

**PRACTICE**

**9-1**   Read this comparison-and-contrast paragraph, and follow the instructions that come after it.

### Life after Smoking

Having been both a smoker and a nonsmoker, I believe I am qualified to compare the two ways of life. When I smoked, I often found myself banished from public places such as offices, restaurants, and stores when I felt the urge to smoke. I would huddle with my fellow smokers outside, in all kinds of weather, just for a cigarette. As more and more people stopped smoking, I found myself banished from private homes, too. I spent a lot of money on cigarettes, and the prices seemed to rise faster and faster. I worried about lung cancer and heart disease. My colds wouldn't go away, and they often turned into bronchitis. Climbing stairs and running left me breathless. Now that I have stopped smoking, my life is different. I can go anywhere and socialize with anyone. The money I have saved in the last year on cigarettes is going to pay for a winter vacation in Florida. After not smoking for only a few weeks, I could breathe more easily, and I had more energy for running and climbing stairs. I have also avoided colds so far, and I'm not as worried about lung and heart disease. In fact, I've been told that my lungs should be as healthy as those of a nonsmoker within another year or so. All in all, quitting smoking was one of the smartest moves I ever made.

— Margaret Gonzales (student)

**WORD POWER**

**banished** sent away from a place as punishment

1. Underline the topic sentence of the paragraph.

2. Does this paragraph deal mainly with similarities or differences?

   _____

   How do you know?

   _____

   _____

3. Is this paragraph a subject-by-subject or a point-by-point comparison? How do you know?

   _____

   _____

   _____

   _____

4. Consider the paragraph's evidence. List some of the contrasts the writer describes. The first contrast has been listed for you.

   _When she was a smoker, she often had to smoke outside of public and private_

   _places. As a nonsmoker, she can go anywhere._

   _____

   _____

   _____

   _____

   _____

5. Underline the paragraph's summary statement.

**PRACTICE**
**9-2**   Following are four topic sentences for comparison-and-contrast paragraphs. First, identify the two things being compared. Then, list three similarities or differences between the two subjects. For example, if you were comparing two authors, you could show the similarities and/or differences in the subjects they write about, in their styles of writing, and in the kinds of readers they attract.

1. All things considered, I would rather be happy than rich.

   _____

   _____

   _____

2. The media's portrayal of young people is often very negative, but the true picture is more positive.

_____

_____

_____

3. Two styles of music that I like are very similar.

_____

_____

_____

4. As soon as I arrive at work, I become a different person.

_____

_____

_____

# 9c   Writing a Comparison-and-Contrast Paragraph

Now, it is time to write a comparison-and-contrast paragraph. Review the brainstorming you did in response to the Seeing and Writing prompt on page 130, and then complete the Practice activities that follow.

**PRACTICE**
**9-3**   Do some further brainstorming, or use one of the other strategies discussed in 2c, to help you identify two or three additional similarities or differences that could help you develop a comparison-and-contrast paragraph on the topic you have chosen. (If you decide to use clustering, create a separate cluster diagram for each of the two subjects you are comparing).

_____

_____

_____

_____

_____

_____

**PRACTICE**

**9-4**   Review your notes, and decide whether to focus on similarities or differences. On the following lines, list the similarities or differences that can best help you develop a comparison-and-contrast paragraph on the topic you have chosen.

_____

_____

_____

_____

_____

**PRACTICE**

**9-5**   Reread your list of similarities or differences. Then, draft a topic sentence that introduces your two subjects, indicates whether your paragraph will focus on similarities or differences, and states the main idea your paragraph will develop.

Topic sentence: _____

_____

**PRACTICE**

**9-6**   Decide whether you will write a subject-by-subject or a point-by-point comparison. Then, use the appropriate outline below to help you create an informal outline for your paragraph. Before you begin, decide on the order in which you will present your points—for example, from least important to most important. (For a subject-by-subject paragraph, begin by deciding which subject you will discuss first.)

**Subject-by-Subject Comparison**

Subject A _____

   Point 1 _____

   Point 2 _____

   Point 3 _____

Subject B _____

   Point 1 _____

   Point 2 _____

   Point 3 _____

**Point-by-Point Comparison**

Point 1 _____

   Subject A _____

   Subject B _____

Point 2 _____

   Subject A _____

   Subject B _____

Point 3 _____

   Subject A _____

   Subject B _____

**PRACTICE**

**9-7**   Draft your comparison-and-contrast paragraph. Begin with the topic sentence you developed in Practice 9-5, and follow the outline you created in Practice 9-6. Try to use the Word Power words on pages 130 or 131 in your paragraph.

# TEST · Revise · Edit

Look back at the draft of your comparison-and-contrast paragraph. Using the TEST checklist below, evaluate your paragraph to make sure it includes a topic sentence, evidence, a summary statement, and transitions. Then, prepare a revised and edited draft of your paragraph.

# TESTing a comparison-and-contrast paragraph

## T opic Sentence Unifies Your Paragraph

☐ Do you have a clearly worded **topic sentence** that states your paragraph's main idea?

☐ Does your topic sentence indicate whether you are focusing on similarities or on differences?

## E vidence Supports Your Paragraph's Topic Sentence

☐ Does all your **evidence**—examples and details—support your paragraph's main idea?

☐ Do your examples and details show how your two subjects are alike or different?

☐ Do you need to discuss additional similarities or differences?

## S ummary Statement Reinforces Your Paragraph's Unity

☐ Does your paragraph end with a **summary statement** that reinforces your main idea?

## T ransitions Add Coherence to Your Paragraph

☐ Do your **transitions** indicate whether you are focusing on similarities or on differences?

☐ Do transitional words and phrases lead readers from one subject or point to the next?

☐ Do you need to add transitions to make your paragraph clearer and to help readers follow your ideas?

1. The following student comparison-and-contrast paragraph is missing a topic sentence, transitional words and phrases, and a summary statement. After reading the paragraph, fill in the missing elements on the appropriate lines below. (See p. 134 for a list of transitions.)

Farmers' Markets and Supermarkets

_____

_____

_____ to supermarket produce, locally grown food comes in many unusual varieties. In the fall, for instance, many farmers' markets are loaded with different varieties of apples, such as Autumn Gold, Cherry Pippin, and Eddie April.

_____the owners of large factory farms that supply supermarket chains, local farmers are willing to invest the time and energy in growing unusual varieties of fruits and vegetables. Also, _____ the produce at supermarkets, the local food at farmers' markets is always fresh because it has been transported only a few miles. The produce in the supermarket, _____, may have been transported across the country or around the world. The biggest advantage of buying locally grown food is the social atmosphere at farmers' markets. _____ most people want to get in and out of the supermarket as fast as possible, they seem to like spending time at the farmers' market. They enjoy talking to the farmers and meeting other people who are interested in locally grown food. Also, the farmers' market often features bands, cooking demonstrations, and other entertainment, so it's often hard to leave.

_____

2. Create a comparison-and-contrast paragraph by adding points that support the topic sentence below, contrasting your goals in high school and your goals today. Connect the points with appropriate transitions, and end the paragraph with a clear summary statement that sums up the main idea. Finally, add an appropriate title on the line provided.

When I was in high school, my goals were different from those I have today. _____

_____

_____

_____

_____

_____

_____

_____

_____

_____

_____

_____

_____

_____

_____

_____

# 10 Classification

© Ambient Images Inc./Alamy

## seeing and writing

The picture above shows a small neighborhood store. Look at the picture, and then brainstorm about several kinds of stores in your neighborhood — for example, mom-and-pop stores (such as bodegas), convenience stores (such as 7-11s), and superstores (such as Walmart). Try to use the Word Power words in your brainstorming.

*Note:* If you like, you may choose instead to brainstorm on one of the additional topics listed on the following page.

In this chapter, you will learn to write a classification paragraph.

**PREVIEW**

# additional topics

| TOPIC | WORD POWER WORDS | DEFINITIONS |
|-------|------------------|-------------|
| kinds of fitness routines | aerobic | ▪ involving exercise that strengthens the heart and lungs |
| | strenuous | ▪ requiring great effort or strength |
| types of sports fans | diehard | ▪ determined, loyal |
| | passive | ▪ not actively participating |
| parenting styles | permissive | ▪ allowing great freedom |
| | authoritarian | ▪ enforcing strict obedience |
| kinds of success | material | ▪ having to do with physical objects or money |
| | fulfillment | ▪ satisfaction, happiness |

**macmillanhighered.com /foundationsfirst**
LearningCurve > Patterns of Organization

# 10a What Is Classification?

**Classification** is the act of sorting items (people, things, or ideas) into categories. You classify when you organize your bills into those you have to pay now and those you can pay later. You also classify when you sort the clothes in a dresser drawer into piles of socks, T-shirts, and underwear.

In a **classification paragraph**, you tell readers how items can be sorted into categories or groups. When you TEST a classification paragraph, make sure it includes these four elements.

T ▪ The **topic sentence** states the main idea of the paragraph (and often identifies the categories you will discuss).

E ▪ A classification paragraph includes **evidence**—examples and details—to explain each category and to show how it is distinct from the other categories. The categories are arranged in **logical order**—for example, from least important to most important.

S ▪ A classification paragraph ends with a **summary** statement that reinforces its main idea stated in the topic sentence.

T ▪ A classification paragraph includes **transitions** to introduce the categories and to connect them to one another and to the topic sentence.

**Paragraph Map: Writing a Classification Paragraph**

Topic sentence _____

_____

*Category #1* _____

_____

*Category #2* _____

_____

*Category #3* _____

_____

**Summary Statement** _____

_____

The writer of the following paragraph classifies items into three distinct groups.

### Types of Bosses

- Topic Sentence
- Evidence
- Summary Statement
- Transitions

I have had three kinds of bosses in my life — the uninterested boss, the interested supervisor, and the over-interested micromanager. The first type is the uninterested boss. This boss doesn't care what workers do as long as they leave him alone. When I was a counselor at summer camp, my boss fell into this category. As long as no campers (or, worse yet, parents) complained, he left you alone. He never cared if you followed the activity plan for the day or gave the kids an extra snack to keep them quiet. The second type of boss is the helpful supervisor. This kind of boss will check you periodically and give you advice. You'll have a certain amount of freedom but not too much. When I was a salesperson at the Gap, my boss fell into this category. She helped me through the first few weeks of the job and encouraged me to do my best. By the end of the summer, I had learned a lot about the retail business and had good feelings about the job. The last, and worst, type of boss is the micromanager. This kind of boss gets involved in everything. My boss at Taco Bell was this kind of person. No one could do anything right. There was always a better way. If you rolled a burrito one way, he would tell you to do it another way. If you did it the other way, he would tell you to do it the first way. Because of the constant criticism, people quit all the time. This boss never seemed to understand that people need praise every once in a while. Even though the second type of boss — the supervisor — expects a lot and makes you work, it is clear to me that this boss is better than the other types.

— Melissa Burrell (student)

### Some Transitional Phrases for Classification

one kind . . . another kind

the first (second, third) category

the first group . . . the next group . . . the final group

the first type . . . the second type

the most (or least) important group

## grammar in context

### Classification

When you write a classification paragraph, you often list the categories you are going to discuss. If you use a colon to introduce your list, make sure that a complete sentence comes before the colon.

INCORRECT   Basically, bosses can be divided into: the uninterested boss, the supervisor, and the micromanager.

CORRECT   Basically, I've had three kinds of bosses in my life: the uninterested boss, the supervisor, and the micromanager.

*For more information on how to use a colon to introduce a list, see 32b.*

## 10b   Reading a Classification Paragraph

When you read a **classification paragraph**, TEST it to make sure that it contains all the elements of an effective paragraph.

**PRACTICE**

**10-1**   Read the classification paragraph below, and follow the instructions that come after it.

International Symbols

Because many people travel to different countries, international symbols have been created to help them find what they need when they don't know the language. These symbols substitute for words. One group of symbols is for transportation. For example, airports post easy-to-understand pictures of planes, taxis, buses, and trains to help people get where they need to go. Another group of symbols is for travelers' personal needs. For example, men's and women's toilets have different symbols. There are signs for drinking fountains and baby-changing tables. A final group of symbols helps travelers when they get to their destinations. For example, international travelers often have to change their money in a new country. They can find a currency exchange at a sign that shows an American dollar, a British pound, and a Japanese yen. If they need to find a hotel or a restaurant, they can look for the sign with a bed or a knife and fork. Clearly, these symbols make it easier for people to travel in countries where they do not speak the language.

— Laurent Fischer (student)

1. Underline the paragraph's topic sentence.

2. Consider the paragraph's evidence. List the categories that the writer uses to classify the types of international symbols discussed.

_____

_____

_____

3. Underline the paragraph's summary statement.

4. Circle the transitional words and phrases that let the reader know that a new category is being introduced.

**PRACTICE**

**10-2**  Following are four topic sentences for classification paragraphs. For each sentence, list three or four categories under which information could be discussed.

1. On every road in the United States, motorists encounter three types of drivers.

_____

_____

_____

_____

2. Students can be sorted into a number of distinct categories.

_____

_____

_____

_____

3. Part-time jobs can range from tolerable to terrible.

_____

_____

_____

4. Reality shows fall into several categories.

_____

_____

_____

## 10c   Writing a Classification Paragraph

Now, it is time to write a classification paragraph. Review the brainstorming you did in response to the Seeing and Writing prompt on page 142, and then complete the Practice activities that follow.

**PRACTICE**

**10-3**   Do some further brainstorming, or use one of the other strategies discussed in 2c, to help you think of one or two additional categories for a classification paragraph on your topic.

_____

_____

_____

_____

_____

**PRACTICE**

**10-4**   Review your list of categories. On the following lines, list the three or four categories you can best develop in your paragraph.

_____

_____

_____

_____

**PRACTICE**

**10-5**   On the lines below, create an informal outline for your paragraph by listing the categories in the order in which you will discuss them.

1. _____

2. _____

3. _____

4. _____

**PRACTICE**

**10-6**   Reread your list of categories. Then, draft a topic sentence that states your main idea (and perhaps introduces the categories you will discuss).

Topic sentence: _____

_____

**PRACTICE**

**10-7**   Draft your classification paragraph. Begin with the topic sentence you developed in Practice 10-7, and follow the informal outline you created in Practice 10-6. Try to use the Word Power words on pages 142 or 143 in your paragraph.

---

# TEST · Revise · Edit

Look back at the draft of your classification paragraph. Using the TEST checklist below, evaluate your paragraph to make sure that it includes a topic sentence, evidence, a summary statement, and transitions. Then, prepare a revised and edited draft of your paragraph.

---

# TESTing a classification paragraph

## T opic Sentence Unifies Your Paragraph

☐ Do you have a clearly worded **topic sentence** that states your paragraph's main idea?

☐ Does your topic sentence identify the categories you will discuss?

## E vidence Supports Your Paragraph's Topic Sentence

☐ Does all your **evidence**—examples and details—support your paragraph's main idea?

☐ Do your examples and details explain each category and indicate how each is distinct from the others?

☐ Do you need to include more examples or details?

## S ummary Statement Reinforces Your Paragraph's Unity

☐ Does your paragraph end with a **summary statement** that reinforces your main idea?

## T ransitions Add Coherence to Your Paragraph

☐ Do your **transitions** clearly indicate which categories are more important than others?

☐ Do you need to add transitions to make your paragraph clearer and to help readers follow your ideas?

1. The following student classification paragraph is missing a topic sentence, transitional words and phrases, and a summary statement. After reading the paragraph, fill in the missing elements on the appropriate lines below. (See p. 144 for a list of transitions.)

Types of Rocks

_____

_____

_____, igneous rock, is molten rock that has cooled and solidified. Igneous rocks, such as pumice and granite, are formed when volcanic eruptions bring molten rock to the earth's surface. Other types of igneous rocks are formed when molten rock solidifies slowly underground. _____, sedimentary rock, is formed from the sediment that is deposited at the bottom of the ocean. Sedimentary rocks, such as sandstone and shale, are deposited in layers, with the oldest sediments on the bottom and the newest on top. _____, metamorphic rock, is created by heat and pressure. These rocks are buried deep below the earth's surface for millions of years. The weight and high temperatures that they are exposed to change their structure and mineral composition. The most common metamorphic rocks are marble, slate, gneiss, and quartzite. _____

_____

_____

2. Create a classification paragraph by adding information about the three categories to support the topic sentence below. Make sure you connect the categories with appropriate transitions, and end the paragraph with a clear summary statement that sums up the main idea. Finally, add an appropriate title on the line provided.

_____

There are three kinds of friends—those who are useful, those who are fun to be with, and those who make us better people. _____

_____

_____

# 11 Definition

© Roberto Schmidt/AFP/Getty Images

## seeing and writing

The picture above shows firefighters leaving the rescue area near the World Trade Center after their shift on September 13, 2001. Look at the picture, and then brainstorm about how you would define the word *hero*. What qualities do you think heroes should possess? Who are your heroes? Try to use the Word Power words in your brainstorming.

*Note:* If you like, you may choose instead to brainstorm on one of the additional topics listed on the following page.

> **WORD POWER**
>
> **courageous** brave
> **daring** bold
> **determined** firm, strong-minded
> **invincible** unbeatable

3. What patterns of development does the writer use in this definition?

_____

_____

_____

4. Circle some of the transitional words and phrases used in this paragraph.

5. Underline the paragraph's summary statement.

**PRACTICE**

**11-2** Following are four topic sentences for definition paragraphs. Each sentence contains an underlined word or phrase. List two patterns of development you could use in an extended definition of the underlined word or phrase.

1. Surveillance cameras help communities to fight crime.

_____

_____

2. Terrorism is a world-wide problem.

_____

_____

3. Alternate energy sources can help the United States become energy independent.

_____

_____

4. A sense of humor is an important quality for a person to have.

_____

_____

## 11c Writing a Definition Paragraph

Now, it is time to write a definition paragraph. Review the brainstorming you did in response to the Seeing and Writing prompt on page 151, and then complete the Practice activities that follow.

**PRACTICE**

**11-3**   Do some further brainstorming, or use one of the other strategies discussed in 2c, to help you find more information about the term you have chosen for your definition paragraph. (Remember, your goal is to identify the term's distinctive features or characteristics.)

_____

_____

_____

_____

_____

**PRACTICE**

**11-4**   Review your notes. On the following lines, list the ideas that can best help you develop your definition paragraph.

_____

_____

_____

_____

_____

**PRACTICE**

**11-5**   On the lines below, create an outline for your paragraph by listing the ideas you will discuss in an effective order.

1. _____

2. _____

3. _____

4. _____

**PRACTICE**

**11-6**   Reread your list of ideas. Then, draft a topic sentence that states your paragraph's main idea.

Topic sentence: _____

_____

_____

**PRACTICE**

**11-7**  Draft your definition paragraph. Begin with the topic sentence you developed in Practice 11-6, and follow the informal outline you created in Practice 11-5. Try to use the Word Power words on pages 151 or 152 in your paragraph.

# TEST · Revise · Edit

Look back at the draft of your definition paragraph. Using the **TEST** checklist below, evaluate your paragraph to make sure that it includes a topic sentence, evidence, a summary statement, and transitions. Then, prepare a revised and edited draft of your paragraph.

## TESTing a definition paragraph

### **T** opic Sentence Unifies Your Paragraph

☐ Do you have a clearly worded **topic sentence** that states your paragraph's main idea?

☐ Does your topic sentence identify the term you are defining?

### **E** vidence Supports Your Paragraph's Topic Sentence

☐ Does all your **evidence**—examples and details—support your paragraph's main idea?

☐ Do you need to add more examples or details to help you define your term?

### **S** ummary Statement Reinforces Your Paragraph's Unity

☐ Does your paragraph end with a **summary statement** that reinforces your main idea?

### **T** ransitions Add Coherence to Your Paragraph

☐ Are your **transitions** appropriate for the pattern (or patterns) of development you use?

☐ Do you need to add transitions to make your paragraph clearer and to help readers follow your ideas?

1. The following student definition paragraph is missing a topic sentence, transitional words and phrases, and a summary statement. After reading the paragraph (and possibly consulting a dictionary), fill in the missing elements on the appropriate lines below. (See p. 154 for a list of transitions.)

Internet Fraud

_____

_____.

Internet fraud takes many forms. _____ , in *purchase fraud*, the fraudsters use stolen credit cards or counterfeit money orders to pay for a purchase or may accept payment for an item and not send it. In *charity fraud*, people are tricked into thinking they are donating money to a legitimate charity when they are actually not. In *dating fraud*, someone on an online dating site asks for money. _____ other kinds of fraud, Internet fraud involves causing harm to people through lies and misrepresentation. _____ other kinds of fraud, however, Internet fraud makes use of the Internet. This difference has some important consequences. _____ , Internet fraud can easily affect large numbers of people and can have serious repercussions, especially if identity theft is involved. _____ , on the Internet people can easily create false identities, which makes Internet fraud more difficult to detect and combat. As the Internet changes, Internet fraud also changes to take advantage of the new technology.

_____

_____

2. Create a definition paragraph by adding sentences to support the topic sentence below. Use several different patterns of development, and be sure to include transitional words and phrases to lead readers through your discussion and end the paragraph with a clear summary statement. Finally, add an appropriate title on the line provided.

Success is a concept that is difficult to define. _____

_____

_____

_____

_____

_____

_____

_____

_____

_____

_____

_____

_____

_____

_____

_____

_____

# 12 Argument

AP Photo/FX, Prashant Gupta

## seeing and writing

The picture above shows actors from the television show *Sons of Anarchy* on their motorcycles. Almost all U.S. states once had laws requiring motorcycle riders and passengers to wear helmets. Today, largely because of motorcyclists' objections, fewer than half of the states have a helmet requirement. Look at the picture, and then brainstorm about a law that you think should be changed, identifying the specific reasons for your objections. Try to use the Word Power words in your brainstorming.

*Note:* If you like, you may choose instead to brainstorm on one of the additional topics listed on the following page.

## additional topics

| TOPIC | WORD POWER WORDS | DEFINITIONS |
|---|---|---|
| Should undocumented immigrants be given amnesty? | plight<br><br>amnesty | ▪ a difficult situation<br><br>▪ a pardon |
| Is a college education worth the money? | outlay<br><br>opportunity | ▪ an expense<br><br>▪ an occasion that makes it possible to do something |
| Should plastic grocery bags be banned? | disposable<br><br>reusable | ▪ designed to be thrown away<br><br>▪ capable of being used again |
| Should assisted suicide be legalized in all states? | option<br><br>euthanasia | ▪ the opportunity to choose something<br><br>▪ mercy killing |

ⓔ macmillanhighered.com
/foundationsfirst
LearningCurve > Patterns of
Organization

# 12a  What Is Argument?

When most people hear the word *argument*, they think of the heated exchanges they hear on television interview programs or on radio talk shows. These discussions, however, are more like shouting matches than arguments.

A true **argument**—the kind you are expected to make in college—involves taking a well-thought-out position on a *debatable issue*—an issue on which reasonable people may disagree.

- Should intelligent design be taught in high school classrooms?
- Should teenagers who commit felonies be tried as adults?

In an argument, you attempt to convince people of the strength of your ideas not by shouting but by presenting **evidence**—facts and examples. In the process, you also consider opposing ideas, and if they are strong, you acknowledge their strengths. If your evidence is solid and your logic is sound, you will present a convincing argument.

The purpose of an **argument paragraph** is to persuade readers that a particular position has merit. When you TEST an argument paragraph, make sure it includes these four elements.

**T** ■ An argument paragraph begins with a **topic sentence** that clearly states the paragraph's position. Words like *should, should not,* or *ought to* in the topic sentence make that position clear to readers.

> The federal government should lower the tax on gasoline.

> The city should not build a new sports stadium.

**E** ■ In an argument paragraph, each point is supported with **evidence**—facts or examples that illustrate or explain the point. (A fact is a piece of information that can be verified; an example is a specific illustration of a general statement.) An argument paragraph presents points in **logical order**—for example, from least to most important. An argument paragraph also identifies and **refutes** opposing arguments by showing how they are inaccurate, weak, or misguided.

**S** ■ An argument paragraph ends with a strong **summary statement** that reinforces the main idea stated in the topic sentence.

**T** ■ An argument paragraph includes **transitions** to connect the supporting points to one another and to the topic sentence.

**Paragraph Map: Writing an Argument Paragraph**

Topic sentence _____

_____

*Point #1* _____

_____

*Point #2* _____

_____

*Point #3* _____

_____

*Opposing argument #1* _____

_____

*Opposing argument #2* _____

_____

Summary statement _____

_____

The following argument paragraph presents three reasons to support the writer's position.

Taxing Soda

Point 1 and support —

Recently, some people have suggested taxing soda because they think it is not healthy for young people. I am against this tax because it is unfair, it is unnecessary, and it will not work. The first reason this kind of tax is bad is that it is not fair. The American Medical Association (AMA) thinks the tax will fight obesity in the United States. However, people should be allowed to decide for themselves whether they should drink soda. It is not right for a group of doctors to decide what is best for everybody.

Point 2 and support —

Another reason this kind of tax is bad is that it is unnecessary. It would be better to set up educational programs to help children make decisions about what they eat. In addition, the AMA could educate parents so they will stop buying soda for their children. Education will do more to help children than a tax will.

Point 3 and support —

Finally, this kind of tax is bad because it will not work. As long as soda is for sale, children will drink it. The only thing that will work is outlawing soda completely, and no one is suggesting this.

Opposing arguments and refutation —

Of course, some people say that soda should be taxed because it has no nutritional value. This is true, but many snack foods have little nutritional value, and no one is proposing a tax on snack food. In addition, not everyone who drinks soda is overweight, let alone obese. A tax on soda would hurt everyone, including people who are healthy and don't drink it very often. The key to helping young people is not to tax them but to teach them what a healthy diet is.

— Ashley Hale (student)

**T E S T**

- [ ] Topic Sentence
- [ ] Evidence
- [ ] Summary Statement
- [ ] Transitions

## Some Transitional Words and Phrases for Argument

| | | |
|---|---|---|
| accordingly | finally | on the one hand . . . |
| admittedly | however |    on the other hand |
| although | in addition | since |
| because | in conclusion | the first reason . . . |
| but | in fact |    another reason |
| certainly | in summary | therefore |
| consequently | meanwhile | thus |
| despite | moreover | to be sure |
| even so | nevertheless | truly |
| even though | nonetheless | |
| first . . . second . . . | of course | |

# grammar in context

## Argument

When you write an argument paragraph, you need to show the relationships among your ideas. You do this by combining simple sentences to create compound and complex sentences.

**COMPOUND SENTENCE**  The only thing that will work is outlawing soda completely. *, and no* ~~No~~ one is suggesting this.

|  |  |
|---|---|
| COMPLEX SENTENCE | Recently, some people have suggested taxing |

soda. ~~They~~ *because they* think it is not healthy for young

people.

*For more information on how to create compound sentences, see Chapter 15. For more information on how to create complex sentences, see Chapter 16.*

# 12b   Reading an Argument Paragraph

When you read an **argument paragraph,** TEST it to make sure that it contains all the elements of an effective paragraph.

**PRACTICE**

**12-1**   Read this argument paragraph, and follow the instructions that come after it.

### The Importance of Voting

Americans should vote in every election. Unfortunately, many American citizens never cast a ballot, and voter turnout is often below 50 percent even in presidential elections. It is sad that people give up this hard-won right. It is in every citizen's best interest to vote. One reason to vote is that government affects every part of our lives. It is foolish not to have a say about who makes the laws and regulations people have to live with. If a citizen does not vote, he or she has no voice on issues such as taxes, schools, health care, the environment, and even the building and repairing of roads and bridges. Another reason to vote is to support a particular political party. If a person believes in a party's policies, it is important to vote to elect that party's candidates and keep them in power. A third reason to vote is that voting enables people to influence public policy. Many people seem to think a single vote doesn't matter. However, even if a voter's candidate does not win, his or her vote isn't wasted. The voter has expressed an opinion by voting, and the government in power is affected by public opinion. Therefore,

to keep our democracy working, all citizens should exercise their right
to vote.

— Lori Wessier (student)

1. Underline the paragraph's topic sentence.

2. What issue is the writer addressing?

_____

_____

_____

_____

   What is the writer's position on the issue?

_____

_____

3. List some of the reasons the writer uses to support her position. The
   first reason has been listed for you.

   *The most important reason to vote is that government affects every part of our lives.*

_____

_____

_____

4. What opposing argument does the writer address?

_____

_____

_____

5. Circle some of the transitional words and phrases used in this
   paragraph.

6. Underline the paragraph's summary statement.

**PRACTICE**

**12-2** Following are four topic sentences for argument paragraphs.
For each statement, list three points that could support the
statement. For example, if you were arguing in favor of banning smoking

in all public places, you could say that smoking is a nuisance, a health risk, and a fire hazard.

1. The dangers of climate change have (or have not) been overstated.

_____

_____

_____

2. Becoming a volunteer in your community can be personally and professionally rewarding.

_____

_____

_____

3. High school students should (or should not) be required to take four years of a foreign language.

_____

_____

_____

4. Congress should (or should not) act to forgive federal student loans.

_____

_____

_____

# 12c Writing an Argument Paragraph

Now, it is time to write an argument paragraph. Review the brainstorming you did in response to the Seeing and Writing prompt on page 161, and then complete the Practice activities that follow.

**PRACTICE**

**12-3** Write a journal entry exploring the issue you have chosen to write about. As you write, consider the following questions.

- What is your position?
- Why are you taking this position?

- What specific actions do you think should be taken?
- What objections might be raised against your position?
- How might you respond to these objections?

### PRACTICE
**12-4** Review your journal entry, and make some additional notes about the issue you have chosen. Next, select the points that best support your position, and list those points below. Then, list the strongest objections to your position.

Supporting Points

_____

_____

_____

_____

Objections

_____

_____

### PRACTICE
**12-5** Review the supporting points you listed in Practice 12-4. Then, draft a topic sentence that clearly expresses the position you will take in your paragraph.

Topic sentence: _____

_____

### PRACTICE
**12-6** On the lines below, create an informal outline by arranging the points that best support your position in an effective order (for example, from least to most important).

1. _____

2. _____

3. _____

4. _____

### PRACTICE
**12-7** Draft your argument paragraph. Begin with the topic sentence you developed in Practice 12-5, and follow the informal outline you created in Practice 12-6. Try to use the Word Power words on pages 161 or 162 in your paragraph.

## TEST · Revise · Edit

Look back at the draft of your argument paragraph. Using the **TEST** checklist below, evaluate your paragraph to make sure that it includes a topic sentence, evidence, a summary statement, and transitions. Then, prepare a revised and edited draft of your paragraph.

## TESTing an argument paragraph

### T opic Sentence Unifies Your Paragraph

☐ Do you have a clearly worded **topic sentence** that states your paragraph's main idea?

☐ Does your topic sentence state your position on a debatable issue?

### E vidence Supports Your Paragraph's Topic Sentence

☐ Does all your **evidence** support your paragraph's main idea?

☐ Have you included enough facts and examples to support your points, or do you need to add more?

☐ Do you summarize and refuse opposing arguments?

### S ummary Statement Reinforces Your Paragraph's Unity

☐ Does your paragraph end with a strong **summary statement** that reinforces your main idea?

### T ransitions Add Coherence to Your Paragraph

☐ Do you use **transitions** to let readers know when you are moving from one point to another?

☐ Do you use transitional words and phrases to indicate when you are addressing opposing arguments?

☐ Do you need to add transitions to make your paragraph clearer and to help readers follow your ideas?

1. The following student argument paragraph is missing a topic sentence, transitional words and phrases, and a summary statement. After reading the paragraph, fill in the missing elements on the appropriate lines below. (See p. 164 for a list of transitions.)

Stop Animal Experimentation

_____. The work done by scientists on animal behavior suggests that animals feel, think, and even communicate with each other. _____, work with whales and dolphins shows that these animals can be trained and can also think. For instance, researchers have found that dolphins identify themselves with unique whistles. These whistles allow each dolphin to be distinguished from others over great distances. _____, it seems that the gap between human beings and the rest of the animal kingdom is getting smaller. _____, wild chimpanzees have been seen using tools to pry termites out of termite mounds. _____, some chimps have been taught to use sign language. _____ many people assume that animals cannot grieve, some animals have been observed mourning their dead. _____, elephants may stand for hours around a dead member of their clan, touching the body with their trunks and feet.

_____, some animals, such as mice, are not as intelligent as dolphins or elephants. _____, research has shown that they can react to positive and negative emotions in other mice. These developments are making it increasingly difficult to justify animal experiments. _____, some people will say that animal experimentation is necessary to save human lives. _____, experts point out that many, if not most, experiments currently done with animals can be duplicated with computer models. _____

_____.

2. Create an argument paragraph by adding several points to support the topic sentence below. Be sure to include transitional words and phrases to introduce your points. If possible, try to address at least one argument against your position, and end the paragraph with a clear summary statement. Finally, add an appropriate title.

_____

Spanking children is never a good way to discipline them. _____

_____

_____

_____

_____

_____

_____

_____

_____

_____

_____

_____

_____

_____

_____

_____

_____

# 13 Writing an Essay

© Jon Kopaloff/Getty

WORD POWER

**competition** a contest
**conflict** a serious disagreement
**regulate** to control

## seeing and writing

The picture above shows two mixed martial arts fighters. Look at the picture, and then think about whether there is too much violence in some sports. As you read the pages that follow, think carefully about this question. You will be writing an essay about the topic of violence in sports as you move through this chapter. As you develop ideas, think about how you could use the Word Power words in your essay.

In this chapter, you will learn

PREVIEW

- to understand essay structure (13a)
- to focus on your assignment, purpose, and audience (13b)
- to find ideas to write about (13c)
- to identify your main idea and state your thesis (13d)
- to choose and arrange your supporting points (13e)
- to draft your essay (13f)
- to TEST your essay (13g)
- to revise and edit your essay (13h)

## 13a Understanding Essay Structure

Understanding the structure of a paragraph can help you understand the structure of an essay. In a paragraph, the main idea is stated in a **topic sentence**, and the rest of the paragraph supports this main idea with **evidence** (details and examples). **Transitional words and phrases** help readers follow the discussion. The paragraph ends with a **summary statement** that reinforces the main idea.

**Paragraph**

> The **topic sentence** states the main idea of the paragraph.
> **Evidence** supports the main idea.
> **Transitional words and phrases** show the connections between ideas.
> A **summary statement** reinforces the main idea of **the paragraph**.

The structure of an essay is similar to the structure of a paragraph:

- The essay's first paragraph—the **introduction**—begins with opening remarks that create interest, and it closes with a **thesis statement**. This thesis statement, like a paragraph's topic sentence, states the main idea.

- The **body** of the essay includes several paragraphs that support the thesis statement. Each body paragraph begins with a **topic sentence** that states the main idea of the paragraph. The other sentences in the paragraph support the topic sentence with **evidence** (examples and details).

- **Transitional words and phrases** lead readers from sentence to sentence and from paragraph to paragraph.

- The last paragraph—the **conclusion**—ends the essay. The conclusion includes a **summary statement** that reinforces the thesis. It ends with concluding remarks.

## FYI

### Testing Your Essays

The first letters of these four key elements—thesis statement, **e**vidence, **s**ummary statement, and **t**ransitions—spell TEST. Just as you did with paragraphs, you can TEST your essays to see whether they include all four elements of an effective essay.

Many of the essays you will write in college will have a **thesis-and-support** structure.

### Essays

**Opening remarks** introduce the subject being discussed in the essay.

The **thesis statement** presents the essay's main idea.

— Introduction

The **topic sentence** states the essay's first point.

**Evidence** supports the topic sentence.

**Transitional words and phrases** connect the examples and details and show how they are related.

— First body paragraph

The **topic sentence** states the essay's second point.

**Evidence** supports the topic sentence.

**Transitional words and phrases** connect the examples and details and show how they are related.

— Second body paragraph

The **topic sentence** states the essay's third point.

**Evidence** supports the topic sentence.

**Transitional words and phrases** connect the examples and details and show how they are related.

— Third body paragraph

The **summary statement** reinforces the thesis.

**Concluding remarks** present the writer's final thoughts on the subject.

— Conclusion

Here is an essay that follows this thesis-and-support structure.

### My Grandfather's Lessons

My grandfather, Richard Weaver, is seventy years old and lives in Leola, a small town outside of Lancaster, Pennsylvania. He has lived there his entire life. As a young man, he apprenticed as a stone mason and eventually started his own business. He worked as a stone mason until he got silicosis and had to retire. He now works part time for the local water department. When I was eight, my mother was very sick, and I lived with my grandparents for almost a year. During that time, my grandfather taught me some important lessons about life.

One thing my grandfather taught me was that I did not have to spend money or go places to have a good time. An afternoon in his workshop was more than enough to keep me entertained. We spent many hours together working on small projects, such as building a wagon, and large projects, such as building a tree house. My grandfather even designed a pulley system that carried me from the roof of his house to the tree house. Working next to my grandfather, I also learned the value of patience and hard work. He never cut corners or compromised. He taught me that it was easier to do the job right the first time than to do it twice.

Another thing my grandfather taught me was the importance of helping others. Whenever anyone needs help, my grandfather is always there — whatever the cost or personal inconvenience. One afternoon a year ago, a friend called him from work and asked him to help fix a broken water pipe. My grandfather immediately canceled his plans and went to help. When he was a member of the volunteer fire department, my grandfather refused to quit even though my grandmother thought the job was too dangerous. His answer was typical of him: he said that people depended on him, and he could not let them down.

The most important thing my grandfather taught me was that honesty is its own reward. One day, when my grandfather and I were in a mall, I found a wallet. I held it up and proudly showed it to my grandfather. When I opened it up and saw the money inside, I couldn't believe it. I had wanted a mountain bike for the longest time, but every time I had asked my grandfather for one, he had told me to be thankful for what I already had. So when I saw the money, I thought that my prayers had been answered. My grandfather, however, had other ideas. He told me that we would have to call the owner of the wallet and tell him that we had found it. Later that night, we called the owner (his name was on his driver's license inside the wallet), and he came over to pick up his money. As soon as I saw him, I knew that my grandfather was right. The man looked as if he really needed the money. When he offered me a reward, I told him no. After he left, my grandfather told me how proud of me he was.

---

Introduction

Thesis statement

Topic sentence (states essay's first point)

**First body paragraph**

Evidence (supports topic sentence)

Topic sentence (states essay's second point)

**Second body paragraph**

Evidence (supports topic sentence)

Topic sentence (states essay's third point)

**Third body paragraph**

Evidence (supports topic sentence)

Summary statement (reinforces essay's thesis)
Conclusion

> The lessons I learned from my grandfather—doing a job right, helping others, and being honest—were important. Now that I have grown up, I have adopted these special qualities of his. I hope that someday I can pass them on to my own children and grandchildren the way my grandfather passed them on to me.

The rest of this chapter explains the process of writing a thesis-and-support essay. Keep in mind that although the steps in the process are discussed one at a time, they often overlap. For example, while you are writing your first draft, you may also be trying to find more ideas to write about.

## 13b Focusing on Your Assignment, Purpose, and Audience

Most of the essays you write in college will be in response to **assignments** that your instructors give you. Before you can begin to write about these assignments, however, you need to determine why you are expected to write (your **purpose**) and for whom you will be writing (your **audience**). Once you understand your purpose and audience, you are ready to focus on your assignment.

In your writing class, you may be given general assignments such as the following ones.

- Discuss something your school could do to improve the lives of returning older students.
- Examine a decision you made that changed your life.
- Write about the advantages or disadvantages of social networking.

Before you can respond to these general assignments, you will need to ask yourself some questions. Exactly what could your school do to improve the lives of older students? What decision did you make that changed your life? Exactly what dangers or benefits of social networking do you want to discuss? By asking yourself questions like these, you can narrow these general assignments to specific **topics** that you can write about:

| ASSIGNMENT | TOPIC |
|---|---|
| Discuss something your school could do to improve the lives of nontraditional students. | Free day care on campus |
| Examine a decision you made that changed your life. | My struggle to give up smoking |
| Write about the advantages or disadvantages of social networking. | The dangers of Facebook |

**PRACTICE**

**13-1**   The following topics are too general for a short essay. On the line that follows each assignment topic, narrow the topic down so it is suitable for a brief essay.

**Example:**   A personal problem

*How I learned to deal with stress* _____

1. A problem at your school

   _____

2. Blended families

   _____

3. Unwanted presents

   _____

4. Current styles of body art

   _____

5. Censorship

   _____

# Decide on a Topic

Look back at the Seeing and Writing Prompt on page 172. To move from this assignment to a topic you can write about, you need to first identify some sports that you think may be too violent. Begin by listing several sports you could discuss.

## 13c   Finding Ideas to Write About

Once you have a topic, you need to find ideas to write about. You do this by using *freewriting*, *brainstorming*, *clustering*, or *journal writing*—just as you do when you write a paragraph.

# Find Ideas

Choose two or three of the sports you listed. After reviewing section 2c, use whatever strategies you like—for example, freewriting or brainstorming—to help you think of ideas to develop in your essay. Then, decide which of these ideas to write about.

## 13d Identifying Your Main Idea and Stating Your Thesis

After you have decided on a topic and identified some ideas to write about, you are then ready to draft a **thesis statement**—a single sentence that clearly states the main idea that you will discuss in the rest of your essay.

| TOPIC | THESIS STATEMENT |
|---|---|
| Free day care on campus | Free day care on campus would improve the lives of the many students who are also parents. |
| My struggle to give up smoking | Giving up smoking was hard, but it saved me money and gave me self-respect. |
| The dangers of Facebook | Despite its popularity, Facebook has created some serious problems. |

Like a topic sentence, a thesis statement tells readers what to expect. An effective thesis statement does two things.

■ *An effective thesis statement makes a point about your topic.* For this reason, it must do more than simply state a fact or announce what you plan to write about.

| STATEMENT OF FACT | Free day care is not available on our campus. |
|---|---|
| ANNOUNCEMENT | In this essay, I will discuss free day care on campus. |
| EFFECTIVE THESIS STATEMENT | Free day care on campus would improve the lives of the many students who are also parents. |

■ *An effective thesis statement is specific and clearly worded.*

| VAGUE THESIS STATEMENT | Giving up smoking helped me a lot. |
|---|---|
| EFFECTIVE THESIS STATEMENT | Giving up smoking was hard, but it saved me money and gave me self-respect. |

## FYI

### Stating Your Thesis

At this stage of the writing process, your thesis is **tentative**, not definite. As you write and revise, you are likely to change it—possibly several times.

**PRACTICE**

**13-2** In the space provided, indicate whether each of the following items is a fact (*F*), an announcement (*A*), a vague statement (*VS*), or an effective thesis (*ET*). If your instructor gives you permission, you can break into groups and do this exercise collaboratively.

**Examples**

Domestic violence is a problem. ___VS___

The federal government should provide more funding for programs that help victims of domestic violence. ___ET___

1. Americans have a life expectancy of more than seventy-seven years.

   _____

2. There are several reasons why life expectancy has risen in the past century. _____

3. Slavery was a bad practice. _____

4. In 2009, the federal minimum wage was raised to $7.25 an hour.

   _____

5. An increase in the federal minimum wage is necessary. _____

6. In this essay, I will describe some funny incidents that occurred when my father went camping. _____

7. Most Americans say they believe in God. _____

8. Religious institutions can help drug addicts in three ways. _____

9. The post office is really slow. _____

10. Email has some clear advantages over regular mail. _____

# State Your Thesis

Carefully review the material you have gathered for your essay about violence in sports. Then, write a tentative thesis statement for your essay on the lines below.

Tentative thesis statetment: _____

_____

## 13e  Choosing and Arranging Your Supporting Points

Once you have decided on a tentative thesis statement, your next step is to look over your freewriting and brainstorming again and identify the specific **evidence**—details and examples—that best supports your thesis. Once you have selected these supporting points, arrange them in the order in which you plan to discuss them. For example, you might arrange the points from most general to most specific or from least important to most important. You can use this list of points as a rough outline for your essay.

# Choose and Arrange Your Supporting Points

Review your tentative thesis statement. Then, look again at the supporting material you have gathered, and decide which points you will use to support your thesis statement. List those points on the lines below.

_____

_____

_____

_____

Now, arrange these points in the order in which you plan to write about them. (Cross out any points that do not support your thesis statement.)

1. _____

2. _____

3. _____

4. _____

5. _____

## 13f  Drafting Your Essay

After you have decided on a thesis and have arranged your points in the order in which you will present them, you are ready to draft your essay.

Keep in mind that you are writing a rough draft, one that you will revise and edit later. Your goal at this point is simply to get your ideas down so that you can react to them. Even so, your draft should have a thesis-and-support structure.

Here is the first draft of an essay by Anna Habos, a student in an introductory writing class. As she developed her essay, Anna followed the process discussed in this chapter.

Facebook: Pros and Cons

Using Facebook is a good way to keep up with friends. Facebook makes it easy to invite people to parties, share photographs, connect with others, and announce big news. However, despite its popularity, Facebook creates some serious problems.

Facebook can interrupt school or work. Email alerts from Facebook can become a major distraction. Once on the site, a person can get sucked into all the activities that are available. It is easy to waste time on Facebook.

Posting inappropriate comments or pictures can have serious consequences. For example, it can lead to being fired, denied admission to a school, or not offered a job. In addition, friends may embarrass each other on Facebook. In most cases, they do not mean to, but they accidentally say something wrong.

One major mistake people make on Facebook is revealing too much information. Listing addresses, phone numbers, hobbies, or a current work address can lead to problems. A stranger with bad intentions can use this information to track down someone to stalk or rob.

Despite these drawbacks, it is possible to use Facebook responsibly and safely. Because I understand the trouble with Facebook, I feel confident using the site.

**PRACTICE**

**13-3**  Reread Anna's first draft. What changes would you suggest she make? What might she add? What might she delete? Write your suggestions on the following lines. (If your instructor gives you permission, you can form groups and do this exercise collaboratively.)

_____

_____

_____

# Draft Your Essay

Write a draft of your essay about violence in sports. Be sure to include the thesis statement you drafted as well as the supporting points you listed. When you are finished, you can give your essay a working title.

# 13g  TESTing Your Essay

When you have finished drafting your essay, you are ready to start revising. The first thing you do when you revise is to **TEST** your essay to make sure that it contains the four elements that make it clear and effective.

T ▪ **Thesis statement**—Does your essay include a thesis statement that states your main idea?

E ▪ **Evidence**—Does your essay include evidence—examples and details—that supports your thesis statement?

S ▪ **Summary statement**—Does your essay's conclusion include a summary statement that reinforces your thesis?

T ▪ **Transitions**—Does your essay include transitional words and phrases that show readers how your ideas are related?

If your essay is missing any of these elements, add them as you continue revising.

When Anna Habos **TEST**ed the draft of her essay about Facebook, she made the following decisions.

▪ She decided to change her **thesis statement** so that it was more specific and better reflected what she wanted to say.

▪ She decided to add **evidence**—examples and details—to make her discussion more specific and more convincing.

▪ She thought that her **summary statement** adequately summed up the idea expressed in her thesis statement.

▪ She decided to add **transitional words and phrases** to make the relationship between her ideas clear.

# TEST Your Essay

**TEST** your draft to make sure that it includes all the elements of an effective essay. Note any elements that are missing, and be prepared to add them as you continue to revise.

## 13h Revising and Editing Your Essay

When you **revise** your essay, you reconsider the choices you made when you wrote your first draft. As a result, you rethink (and frequently rewrite) parts of your essay. Some of your changes will be major—for example, deleting several sentences or even crossing out or adding whole paragraphs. Other changes will be minor—for example, adding or deleting a word or phrase.

Before you begin to revise, try to put your essay aside for at least an hour or two. Time away from your essay will help you distance yourself from your writing so you can see it critically. When you start to revise, don't be afraid to mark up your first draft with lines, arrows, and cross-outs or to write between the lines and in the margins.

When you are finished revising, **edit** and **proofread** your essay.

# self-assessment checklist

## Revising Your Essay

- [ ] Does your essay have an introduction, a body, and a conclusion?
- [ ] Does your thesis statement clearly state your essay's main idea?
- [ ] Does each body paragraph have a topic sentence?
- [ ] Does each body paragraph focus on one point that supports the thesis statement?
- [ ] Does your conclusion include a statement that reinforces your thesis?

# self-assessment checklist

## Editing Your Essay

**EDITING FOR COMMON SENTENCE PROBLEMS**

- [ ] Have you avoided run-ons? (See Chapter 19.)
- [ ] Have you avoided fragments? (See Chapter 20.)
- [ ] Do your subjects and verbs agree? (See Chapter 21.)
- [ ] Have you avoided illogical shifts? (See Chapter 22.)
- [ ] Have you avoided dangling and misplaced modifiers? (See Chapter 23.)

**EDITING FOR GRAMMAR**

- [ ] Are your verb forms and verb tenses correct? (See Chapters 24 and 25.)
- [ ] Have you used nouns and pronouns correctly? (See Chapters 26 and 27.)
- [ ] Have you used adjectives and adverbs correctly? (See Chapter 28.)

**EDITING FOR PUNCTUATION, MECHANICS, AND SPELLING**

- [ ] Have you used commas correctly? (See Chapter 30.)
- [ ] Have you used apostrophes correctly? (See Chapter 31.)
- [ ] Have you used other punctuation marks correctly? (See Chapter 32.)
- [ ] Have you used capital letters where they are required? (See Chapter 33.)
- [ ] Have you used quotation marks correctly where they are needed? (See Chapter 33.)
- [ ] Have you spelled every word correctly? (See Chapter 34.)

## FYI

### Choosing a Title

Every essay should have a **title** that suggests the subject of the essay and makes people want to read it.

As you choose a title for your paper, think about the following options.

- *A title can highlight a key word or term.*

  > Tortillas

  > Learning Tagalog

- *A title can be a straightforward announcement.*

  > It's Possible to Graduate Debt Free. Here's How.

  > Getting a Tattoo

- *A title can establish a personal connection with readers.*

  > Do What You Love

  > Don't Hang Up, That's My Mom Calling

- *A title can be a familiar saying or a quotation from your essay itself.*

  > What Are Friends For?

  When you write your title, keep the following guidelines in mind.

- Capitalize all words except for articles (*a, an, the*), prepositions (*at, to, of, around,* and so on), and coordinating conjunctions (*and, but,* and so on), unless they are the first or last word of the title.

- Do not underline or italicize your title or enclose it in quotation marks.

- Center the title at the top of the first page. Double-space between the title and the first line of your essay.

When Anna Habos revised her essay about Facebook, she changed her tentative thesis statement so that it was more specific and better reflected what she wanted to say. In addition, she added topic sentences to focus her paragraphs and to help readers see how her body paragraphs related to her thesis statement. To make these relationships clearer, she added transitional words and phrases (*one way; another way; the most important way*). She also added examples to make her discussion more interesting and more convincing. (She took some examples from her journal and some from her personal knowledge of Facebook.) Finally, she expanded her introduction and conclusion, which she thought were too short to be effective.

After she finished revising and editing her essay, Anna proofread it to correct any errors in spelling, grammar, and punctuation that she might have missed. Finally, she checked to make sure that her essay followed her instructor's guidelines.

## FYI

### Guidelines for Submitting Your Papers

Always follow your instructor's guidelines for submitting papers.

- Unless your instructor tells you otherwise, type your name, your instructor's name, the course name and number, and the date (day, month, year) in the upper left-hand corner of your paper's first page, one-half inch from the top.

- Print on one side of each sheet of paper.

- Double-space your work.

- Leave one-inch margins on all sides of the page.

- Type your last name and the page number in the upper right-hand corner of each page (including the first page).

Here is the final draft of Anna's essay. Note that the final draft includes all the elements Anna looked for when she TESTed her essay.

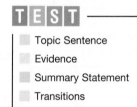

T E S T
- Topic Sentence
- Evidence
- Summary Statement
- Transitions

---

Habos 1

Anna Habos
Professor Smith
Composition 101
18 November 2014

The Trouble with Facebook

Facebook is a popular way for busy people — particularly students — to keep up with friends. This social-networking site makes it easy for them to invite people to parties, share photographs, connect with others, and announce big news. However, because communicating on the site is so easy, some students get themselves into difficulty. To avoid problems, students should be aware of the dangers they can face when they use Facebook.

One way students can get into trouble is by letting Facebook distract them from school or work. If they are not careful, they can let email alerts draw them into Facebook over and over again throughout the day. For example, alerts may tell users whenever a new comment is posted on one of their conversations. If users respond to all these

*Introduction*

*Topic sentence (First point)*

**Evidence (examples and details)**

alerts, they will find themselves spending an excessive amount of time online socializing with their "friends" instead of studying or working. Even Facebook users who do not use email alerts still log in frequently just to stay up-to-date. Once on the site, students can waste a lot of valuable time. For example, during a recent visit to Facebook, I spent forty minutes reviewing new posts, updating my status, and responding to a friend's message.

**Topic sentence (second point)**

Another way students can get into trouble on Facebook is by sharing personal thoughts and photographs too freely. An off-color comment or a revealing photograph posted on the site may seem harmless. However, a boss, a human resources employee, or a college admissions officer may not see these posts as meaningless fun. To them, they may indicate that a person is immature, unreliable, or unmotivated — in short, someone who cannot be trusted to act responsibly. Thus, inappropriate posts can damage a student professionally as well as personally. Of course, it is fine to reveal a personal secret on the phone to a friend. However, posting the same secret on a Facebook page that can be accessed by hundreds of friends, acquaintances, coworkers, and potential employers might be both hurtful and embarrassing.

**Evidence (examples and details)**

**Body Paragraphs**

**Topic sentence (third point)**

The most serious way students can get into trouble on Facebook is by revealing too much about themselves — for example, by posting addresses, phone numbers, employment information, and interests and hobbies. Posting this kind of information is particularly dangerous for women. For example, if a woman indicates that she lives in a particular small town and likes bowling, a stalker might go to the local bowling alley to look for her. Even worse, if a woman accepts a Facebook invitation to a party, a stranger will know exactly where and when to find her. Finally, sexual predators frequently search Facebook pages. As a result, many young adults — and even children — have been tricked into starting online relationships with adults who pose as teenagers. In some cases, these adults were sex offenders who used Facebook to locate victims. By revealing personal information, young Facebook users made it possible for these predators to find and harm them.

**Evidence (examples and details)**

**Conclusion**

Despite these drawbacks, it is possible to use Facebook both responsibly and safely. Students should not allow Facebook activities to intrude excessively into their school day or workplace. They should think twice before posting comments that could hurt themselves or others. Finally, they should be careful about revealing personal information. By taking a few simple precautions, students who use Facebook can enjoy social networking and still be reasonably certain that people who access their pages will not be able to harm them personally or professionally.

**PRACTICE**

**13-4** What specific ideas did Anna add to her draft? What did she delete? What other changes could she have made? Write your suggestions on the following lines.

_____

_____

_____

_____

_____

_____

_____

# Revise and Edit Your Essay

Reread the draft of your essay, and complete the following tasks.

- Using the Self-Assessment Checklist for revising your essay on page 183 as your guide, evaluate your essay on violence in sports.

- Edit your revised draft, using the Self-Assessment Checklist for editing your essay on page 183.

- Proofread for typos and errors in punctuation, mechanics, spelling, and essay format.

## EDITING PRACTICE

After reading the following incomplete student essay, write a thesis statement on the lines provided. (Make sure the thesis statement clearly communicates the essay's main idea.) Next, fill in the topic sentences for the second, third, and fourth paragraphs. Finally, restate the thesis (in different words) in the conclusion.

### Make the DREAM a Reality

Carlos, who is now 18, has lived in Arizona ever since his parents moved there from Mexico when he was a baby. In high school, Carlos got straight As, was on the basketball and baseball teams, played several instruments, and performed community service. He was also class valedictorian. Still, Carlos was not able to apply to college because his family was in the United States illegally. Carlos's story illustrates the need for a federal DREAM Act, a law that would give legal status to undocumented immigrants who were brought to the United States as children.

[Thesis statement] _____

_____

    [Topic sentence] _____

_____

_____

The Development, Relief and Education for Alien Minors Act, or DREAM Act, was first introduced in Congress in 2001. It has been reintroduced at various times, including in 2007, 2009, and 2010, but it has failed each time. The details have varied, but its basic outline has remained the same. The DREAM Act would apply only to young people who came to the United States illegally when they were under sixteen and have lived in the United States continuously for at least five years. If they have a high school diploma or GED and are of good moral character, applicants could obtain conditional residency status that would allow them to stay in the United States for a six-year-period. At the end of this period, if they have been in the military or in college for at least two years, they could apply for permanent resident status and ultimately for citizenship.

[Topic sentence] _____

_____

Opponents say the act would reward illegal behavior. They say that by granting amnesty, the act would actually encourage future illegal immigration. In addition, opponents say that the act would be unfair to legal immigrants. For example, if these young people were given legal residency by the Dream Act, many more would apply to college. Because colleges have only a limited number of slots available, Dream Act children would take places away from legal immigrants (as well as from citizens). In addition, opponents of the act are concerned that Dream Act children would compete for the limited amount of financial aid available.

[Topic sentence] _____

_____

They point out that Dream Act children have done nothing that is illegal. They argue that the act would not encourage others to immigrate illegally because it would apply only to people already in the United States. Because the Dream Act children have grown up in the United States, they are, for all intents and purposes, American. They speak English and often know little or nothing about their parents' country of origin. In short, their home is the United States. Supporters say the act would acknowledge this fact and would encourage Dream Act children to go to college and to contribute to the United States. As a result, the Dream Act children would benefit, and so would the country, which needs well-educated workers.

[Restatement of thesis] _____

_____

By passing the DREAM act, Congress can help individuals like Carlos and, at the same time, help the United States.

# review checklist

## Writing an Essay

- [ ] Many essays have a thesis-and-support structure: the thesis statement presents the main idea, and the body paragraphs support the thesis. (See 13a.)

- [ ] Begin by focusing on your assignment, purpose, and audience. (See 13b.)

- [ ] Narrow your general assignment to a topic you can write about. (See 13b.)

- [ ] Use one or more strategies to find ideas to write about. (See 13c.)

- [ ] State your main idea in a thesis statement. (See 13d.)

- [ ] List the points that best support your thesis, and arrange them in the order in which you plan to discuss them. (See 13e.)

- [ ] As you write your first draft, make sure your essay has a thesis-and-support structure. (See 13f.)

- [ ] Begin revising by TESTing your essay to make sure that it contains the four elements that will make it clear and effective. (See 13g.)

- [ ] Continue revising, and then edit and proofread your essay. (See 13h.)

# 14 Writing Simple Sentences

© Pat Canova/Alamy

## seeing and writing

If you met a person who had never been to McDonald's, what would you tell him or her about this fast-food restaurant? The picture above shows a typical McDonald's restaurant. Look at the picture, and then write a paragraph that answers this question. Try to use the Word Power words in your paragraph.

**In this chapter, you will learn**

- to identify a sentence's subject (14a)
- to recognize singular and plural subjects (14b)
- to identify prepositions and prepositional phrases (14c)
- to distinguish a prepositional phrase from a subject (14c)
- to identify action verbs (14d)
- to identify linking verbs (14e)
- to identify helping verbs (14f)

A **sentence** is a group of words that expresses a complete thought. Every sentence includes both a <u>subject</u> and a <u>verb</u>. A **simple sentence** consists of a single **independent clause**—one <u>subject</u> and one <u>verb</u>.

SUBJECT    VERB
McDonald's <u>is</u> an American institution.

## 14a Identifying Subjects

e macmillanhighered.com /foundationsfirst
Additional Grammar Exercises > Identifying Subjects

The **subject** of a sentence tells who or what is being talked about in the sentence.

Marissa did research on the Internet.

A reference librarian helped her find a topic for her paper.

It was due in March.

The subject of a sentence can be a noun or a pronoun. A **noun** names a person, place, or thing—*Marissa, librarian*. A **pronoun** takes the place of a noun—*I, you, he, she, it, we, they*.

### PRACTICE
### 14-1

On the lines below, write in a subject (a noun or pronoun) that tells who or what is being talked about in the sentence.

**Example:** The _____*wind*_____ howled.

1. _____ was terrified.

2. The fierce _____ was very loud.

3. _____ banged on the roof.

4. A wild _____ barked in the distance.

5. Suddenly, a _____ rapped on the window.

6. _____ screamed and ran to the door.

7. Opening the door, _____ saw a frightening sight.

8. _____ closed the door immediately.

9. Outside, the howling _____ grew stronger.

10. Finally, _____ and _____ arrived.

# FYI

## Simple and Complete Subjects

A sentence's **simple subject** is just a noun or a pronoun.

    Marissa     librarian     it

A sentence's **complete subject** is the simple subject along with all the words that describe it.

    a reference librarian

*Note:* A two-word name, such as *Marissa Johnson*, is a simple subject.

**PRACTICE**

**14-2**   Underline each sentence's simple subject—the noun or pronoun that tells who or what the sentence is about. Then, put brackets around the complete subject.

> **WORD POWER**
> **obsolete** no longer in use

**Example:**   [Older <u>Americans</u>] may remember icemen delivering big blocks of ice to people's homes.

(1) Many occupations have become obsolete. (2) For example, the neighborhood iceman no longer visits homes. (3) Before the 1940s, most people kept food cold in iceboxes. (4) These chests were usually made of wood and had insulated walls and doors. (5) A large compartment held a block of ice for keeping the whole inside cold. (6) Back then, neighborhood icemen were a common sight. (7) Wearing leather vests, they drove wagons loaded with blocks of ice. (8) In the summer, playful children would climb on the wagons, grabbing fallen chips of ice and eating them as treats. (9) Today, this nearly obsolete occupation exists mainly among people without electric refrigerators, such as the Amish.

**PRACTICE**

**14-3** The following sentences have no subjects. Fill in each line below with a complete subject—a simple subject along with all the words that describe it. Remember to begin each sentence with a capital letter.

**Example:** ___My energetic sister___ runs a small business.

1. _____ crashed through the picture window.

2. _____ is my least favorite food.

3. _____ fell from the sky.

4. _____ disappeared into a black hole.

5. _____ ate five pounds of cherries.

---

# 14b Recognizing Singular and Plural Subjects

The subject of a sentence can be *singular* or *plural*. A **singular subject** is one person, place, or thing.

Marissa did research on the Internet.

A **plural subject** is more than one person, place, or thing.

Students often do research on the Internet.

A plural subject that joins two or more subjects with *and* is called a **compound subject**.

Marissa and Jason did research on the Internet.

**PRACTICE**

**14-4** Each item listed here could be the subject of a sentence. Write *S* after each item that could be a singular subject, and write *P* after each item that could be a plural subject.

**Examples**

Joey Ramone ___S___

The Ramones ___P___

Joey and Johnny Ramone ___P___

1. hot-fudge sundaes _____

2. the USS *Enterprise* _____

3. life and death _____

4. the McCaughey septuplets _____

5. our class blog _____

6. three blind mice _____

7. Betty and Barney Rubble _____

8. her two children _____

9. Texas _____

10. Ruben Blades _____

**PRACTICE**

**14-5**   First, underline the simple subject in each sentence. Then, label each singular subject *S*, and label each plural subject *P*. (Remember that a compound subject is plural.)

> **Example:**   The Vietnam Veterans <u>Memorial</u> opened to the public on
>
> November 11, 1982.

1. The memorial honors men and women killed or missing in the Vietnam War.

2. More than 58,000 names appear on the black granite wall.

3. More than two and a half million people visit the memorial each year.

4. Visitors leave mementoes at the site.

5. Some men and women, for example, leave letters and photographs.

6. Other people leave combat boots, stuffed animals, rosaries, or dog tags.

7. One man leaves a six-pack of beer each year.

8. Visitors also leave cigarettes, flowers, canned food, and clothing.

9. Spouses, children, and friends leave gifts for men and women lost in the war.

10. A Persian Gulf War veteran left his medal for his father.

# 14c   Identifying Prepositional Phrases

As you try to identify the subject of a sentence (a noun or pronoun), you may be confused by prepositional phrases, which include nouns or pronouns.

A **prepositional phrase** is made up of a **preposition** (a word like *on, to, in,* or *with*) and its **object** (the noun or pronoun it introduces).

| PREPOSITION | + | OBJECT | = | PREPOSITIONAL PHRASE |
|---|---|---|---|---|
| on | | the roof | | on the roof |
| to | | Leah's apartment | | to Leah's apartment |
| in | | my Spanish class | | in my Spanish class |
| with | | her | | with her |

macmillanhighered.com
/foundationsfirst
LearningCurve > Parts of
Speech: Prepositions and
Conjunctions; Additional
Grammar Exercises >
Identifying Prepositional
Phrases

Because the object of a preposition is a noun or a pronoun, it may look like the subject of a sentence. However, the object of a preposition can never be a subject. To identify a sentence's subject, cross out all the prepositional phrases. (Remember, every prepositional phrase is introduced by a preposition.)

SUBJECT ┌──────────── PREPOSITIONAL PHRASES ────────────┐

The price ~~of a new home in the San Francisco Bay area~~ is very high.

### Frequently Used Prepositions

| | | | | |
|---|---|---|---|---|
| about | behind | for | off | toward |
| above | below | from | on | under |
| across | beneath | in | onto | underneath |
| after | beside | including | out | until |
| against | between | inside | outside | up |
| along | beyond | into | over | upon |
| among | by | like | through | with |
| around | despite | near | throughout | within |
| at | during | of | to | without |
| before | except | | | |

### PRACTICE

**14-6**  Each of the sentences in the following paragraph includes at least one prepositional phrase. To identify each sentence's subject—the noun or pronoun that the sentence is about—first cross out every prepositional phrase. Then, underline the simple subject.

**Example:**   Sudoku <u>puzzles</u> are popular ~~around the world~~.

(1) People are wild about sudoku puzzles. (2) They can be full of challenges. (3) Each puzzle consists of nine 3x3 squares. (4) A player must write numbers in the squares. (5) However, each number may appear only once in each column, each row, and each 3x3 square. (6) The level of difficulty of each puzzle is determined by the "giv-

ens." (7) The "givens" of an individual puzzle make that puzzle unique. (8) Mathematicians with an interest in sudoku have discovered billions of unique grids. (9) However, solvers of these puzzles are not usually mathematicians. (10) In fact, sudoku players do not need an expert knowledge of math.

# 14d  Identifying Action Verbs

An **action verb** tells what the subject does, did, or will do.

Carmelo Anthony <u>plays</u> basketball.

Columbus <u>sailed</u> across the ocean.

Andrea <u>will go</u> to Houston next month.

Action verbs can also show mental or emotional action.

Nirav often <u>thinks</u> about his future.

Wendy <u>loves</u> backpacking.

When the subject of a sentence performs more than one action, the sentence includes two or more action verbs.

Lois <u>left</u> work, <u>drove</u> to Somerville, and <u>met</u> Carmen for dinner.

macmillanhighered.com
/foundationsfirst
LearningCurve > Parts of
Speech: Verbs, Adjectives,
and Adverbs; Additional
Grammar Exercises >
Identifying Action Verbs

**PRACTICE**

**14-7**  In each of the following sentences, underline each action verb twice. (Some sentences include more than one action verb.)

**Example:**  Many nineteenth-century Americans <u>left</u> their homes and

<u>journeyed</u> to unfamiliar places.

(1) During the 1840s, thousands of Americans traveled west to places like Oregon, Nevada, and California. (2) Many travelers began their journey in Independence, Missouri. (3) In towns all around Missouri, travelers advertised in newspapers for strong young companions for the journey west. (4) Thousands of wagons eventually departed from Independence

on the dangerous four-month trip to California. (5) Whole families packed their bags and joined wagon trains. (6) The wagons carried food, supplies, and weapons. (7) Some travelers wrote letters to friends and relatives back east. (8) Others wrote in journals. (9) In these letters and journals, we see the travelers' fear and misery. (10) Traveling 2,500 miles west across plains, deserts, and mountains, many people suffered and died.

**PRACTICE**

**14-8**    Write an action verb in each space to show what action the subject is, was, or will be performing.

**Example:**    I ___*drove*___ my car to the grocery store.

1. Good athletes sometimes _____ but often _____.

2. After opening the letter, Michele _____.

3. The dolphin _____ and _____ on top of the waves.

4. The hurricane _____ the residents and _____ the town.

5. Smoke _____ out of the windows.

## 14e  Identifying Linking Verbs

A **linking verb** does not show action. Instead, it connects the subject to a word or words that describe or rename it. The linking verb tells what the subject is (or what it was, seems to be, or will be).

macmillanhighered.com
/foundationsfirst
LearningCurve > Parts of
Speech: Verbs, Adjectives,
and Adverbs; Additional
Grammar Exercises >
Identifying Linking Verbs

SUBJECT    LINKING VERB    WORDS THAT DESCRIBE SUBJECT

Calculus is a difficult course.

Many linking verbs, such as *is*, are forms of the verb *be*. Other linking verbs refer to the senses (*look, feel, seem,* and so on).

Tremaine looks very handsome today.

Time seemed to pass quickly.

### Frequently Used Linking Verbs

| | | | |
|---|---|---|---|
| act | become | look | sound |
| appear | feel | remain | taste |
| be (am, is, are, | get | seem | turn |
| was, were) | grow | smell | |

**PRACTICE**

**14-9**   Underline the verb in each of the following sentences twice. Then, in the blank, indicate whether the verb is an action verb (*AV*) or a linking verb (*LV*).

**Example:**   U.S. labor officials <u>predict</u> growth in service jobs through at least 2016. ___*AV*___

1. An aging population is one trend that is creating more service jobs. _____

2. For example, older citizens need nursing care and other health services. _____

3. With a home health aide, many elderly people feel confident about staying in their homes instead of moving to assisted living or a nursing home. _____

4. For this reason, home health workers are in demand. _____

5. Related service fields, such as home maintenance, look strong, too. _____

6. Also, officials see rapid growth in education services, including teaching. _____

7. More and more students today realize the benefits of a college degree. _____

8. Other rapidly growing service fields include retail sales and management. _____

9. Consumers seem ready to shop even in tough economic times. _____

10. Customer-service jobs, in fields like information technology and finance, are also likely to experience growth. _____

**PRACTICE**

**14-10**   In the following sentences, underline each linking verb twice. Then, circle the complete subject and the word or words that describe or rename it.

**Example:**   (The juice) <u>tasted</u> (sour).

1. The night grew cold.

2. The song seems very familiar.

3. In January 2008, Barack H. Obama became the forty-fourth president of the United States.

4. College students feel pressured by their families, their instructors, and their peers.

5. Many people were outraged at the mayor's announcement.

6. The cheese smelled terrible.

7. The fans appeared upset by their team's defeat.

8. After the game, the crowd turned ugly.

9. Charlie got sick after eating six corn dogs.

10. My love for my cat remains strong and true.

## 14f Identifying Helping Verbs

Many verbs are made up of more than one word. For example, the verb in the following sentence is made up of two words.

> Andrew <u>must make</u> a choice.

In this sentence, *make* is the **main verb**, and *must* is a **helping verb**. A sentence's complete verb is made up of the main verb plus all the helping verbs that accompany it.

In each of the following sentences, the complete verb is underlined twice, and the helping verbs are checkmarked.

> Ana h√as worked at the diner for two years.

> D√oes Ana still work at the diner?

> Ana d√oes not work on Saturdays.

> Ana c√an choose her own hours.

> Ana m√ay work this Saturday.

> Ana sh√ould take a vacation this summer.

> Ana m√ust work hard to earn money for college.

**e** macmillanhighered.com
/foundationsfirst
LearningCurve > Parts of
Speech: Verbs, Adjectives,
and Adverbs; Additional
Grammar Exercises >
Identifying Helping Verbs

### Frequently Used Helping Verbs

| | | | | |
|------|-------|------|--------|-------|
| am | did | has | might | were |
| are | do | have | must | will |
| can | does | is | should | would |
| could | had | may | was | |

**PRACTICE**

**14-11**  Each of these sentences includes one or more helping verbs as well as a main verb. Underline the complete verb (the main verb and all the helping verbs) in each sentence twice. Then, put a check mark above each helping verb.

**Example:**    Elizabeth II <u>has been</u> queen of England since 1952.

1. Obese adolescents may risk serious health problems as adults.

2. The candidates will name their running mates within two weeks.

3. Henry has been thinking about changing careers for a long time.

4. Do you want breakfast now?

5. I could have been a French major.

6. This must be the place.

7. I have often wondered about my family's history.

8. You should have remembered the mustard.

9. Jenelle has always loved animals.

10. Research really does take a long time.

# Skills Check

Look back at your response to the Seeing and Writing prompt on page 193. Reread it carefully, and then complete the following tasks.

■ Underline the simple subject of every sentence once.

■ Underline the complete verb (the main verb plus all the helping verbs) of every sentence twice.

■ Circle the main verb in each sentence, and put a check mark above each helping verb.

# TEST · Revise · Edit

Starting with **TEST**, revise your paragraph. Then, edit and proofread your work.

## EDITING PRACTICE

Read the following student paragraph. Underline the simple subject of each sentence once, and underline the complete verb twice. To help you locate the subject, cross out the prepositional phrases. The first sentence has been done for you.

The Triangle Shirtwaist Company Fire

~~On March 25, 1911,~~ a terrible <u>event</u> <u>revealed</u> the unsafe conditions ~~in factories across the United States.~~ On that day, a fire at the Triangle Shirtwaist Company killed 146 workers, mainly young immigrant women. These women could not leave the building during working hours. In fact, the factory owners locked most of the exit doors during the day. On the day of the fire, flames spread quickly through the ten-story building. Workers were trapped behind locked doors. Fire engine ladders could not reach the upper floors. In their terror, some people leaped to their deaths from the burning building. After this tragedy, American labor unions grew stronger. Workers eventually gained the right to a shorter workweek and better working conditions. Today, fire safety is very important at most workplaces. A tragedy like the one at the Triangle Shirtwaist Company should never happen again.

## review checklist

### Writing Simple Sentences

☐ The subject tells who or what is being talked about in the sentence. (See 14a.)

☐ A subject can be singular or plural. (See 14b.)

☐ The object of a preposition cannot be the subject of a sentence. (See 14c.)

☐ An action verb tells what the subject does, did, or will do. (See 14d.)

☐ A linking verb connects the subject to a word or words that describe or rename the subject. (See 14e.)

☐ Many verbs are made up of more than one word—a main verb and one or more helping verbs. (See 14f.)

# 15 Writing Compound Sentences

© USA @ Photo Company/Corbis

## seeing and writing

The picture above shows a car that is truly one of a kind. Suppose you wanted to sell this car. Study the picture carefully, and then write a paragraph in which you describe the car in a way that would make someone want to buy it. Try to use the Word Power words in your paragraph.

**In this chapter, you will learn**

- to form compound sentences with coordinating conjunctions (15a)
- to form compound sentences with semicolons (15b)
- to form compound sentences with transitional words and phrases (15c)

As you have seen, the most basic kind of sentence, a **simple sentence**, consists of a single **independent clause**—one <u>subject</u> and one <u>verb</u>.

Many college <u>students</u> <u>major</u> in psychology.

Many other <u>students</u> <u>major</u> in business.

A **compound sentence** is made up of two or more simple sentences (independent clauses).

macmillanhighered.com /foundationsfirst

LearningCurve > Coordination and Subordination; Additional Grammar Exercises > Using Coordinating Conjunctions

## 15a Forming Compound Sentences with Coordinating Conjunctions

One way to create a compound sentence is by joining two simple sentences with a **coordinating conjunction**.

Many college students major in psychology, but many other students major in business.

### WORD POWER

**coordinating** equal in importance, rank, or degree

### Coordinating Conjunctions

| and | nor | so |
| but | or | yet |
| for | | |

## FYI

### Using Commas with Coordinating Conjunctions

When you use a coordinating conjunction to join two simple sentences into a compound sentence, always place a comma before the coordinating conjunction.

We can see a movie, <u>or</u> we can go to a club.

**PRACTICE**

**15-1**   Each of the following compound sentences is made up of two simple sentences joined by a coordinating conjunction. Underline the coordinating conjunction in each compound sentence. Then, bracket the two simple sentences. Remember that each simple sentence includes a subject and a verb.

**Example:**   [I do not like unnecessary delays], <u>nor</u> [do I like lame

excuses].

1. Speech is silver, but silence is golden.

2. I fought the law, and the law won.

3. The house was dark, so she decided not to ring the doorbell.

4. He agreed to sign the contract, for he did not want to lose the job.

5. They will not surrender, and they will not agree to a cease-fire.

6. I could order the chicken fajitas, or I could have chili.

7. She has lived in California for years, yet she remembers her childhood in Kansas very clearly.

8. Professor Blakemore was interesting, but Professor Salazar was inspiring.

9. Melody dropped French, and she signed up for Italian.

10. Give me liberty, or give me death.

Coordinating conjunctions join two ideas of equal importance. Coordinating conjunctions describe the relationship between the two ideas, showing how and why the ideas are connected. Different coordinating conjunctions have different meanings.

■ To indicate addition, use *and*.

> Edgar Allan Poe wrote horror fiction in the nineteenth century, and Stephen King writes horror fiction today.

■ To indicate contrast or contradiction, use *but* or *yet*.

> Poe wrote short stories, but King writes both stories and novels.
>
> Poe died young, yet his stories live on.

■ To indicate a cause-and-effect connection, use *so* or *for*.

> I liked *Carrie*, so I decided to read King's other novels.
>
> Poe's "The Tell-Tale Heart" is a chilling tale, for it is about a horrible murder.

■ To present alternatives, use *or*.

> I have to finish reading *Under the Dome*, or I won't be able to sleep.

■ To eliminate alternatives, use *nor*.

> I have not read *The Green Mile*, nor have I seen the movie.

**PRACTICE**

**15-2** Fill in the coordinating conjunction—*and, but, for, nor, or, so,* or *yet*—that most logically links the two parts of each of the following compound sentences.

> **Example:** The meteorologist predicted sun, ___*so*___ we planned a
>
> trip to the beach.

1. Katya does not eat meat, _____ does she eat dairy products.

2. Malik planned to stay single, _____ then he met Alyssa.

3. The Russells wanted to save money on their heating bill, _____ they sealed cracks around their windows.

4. Some students buy textbooks online, _____ prices may be lower there than in the campus bookstore.

5. Campers can stay in wooden cabins, _____ they can sleep in their own tents.

6. Tony hates the sight of blood, _____ his favorite shows are crime dramas.

7. Good used cars can be inexpensive, _____ they often cost less to insure than new cars.

**PRACTICE**

**15-3** In the following paragraph, fill in the coordinating conjunction—*and, but, for, nor, or, so,* or *yet*—that most logically links the two ideas in each compound sentence.

> **Example:** Three teenagers met in Newark, New Jersey, ___*and*___ they
>
> decided to try to beat the odds.

(1) George Jenkins, Sampson Davis, and Rameck Hunt decided to go to college to become doctors, _____ they made a pact to help each other

succeed. (2) The odds were against them, _____ they lived in inner-city neighborhoods devastated by drugs and violence. (3) They did not have many opportunities, _____ did they have many positive role models. (4) Two of them were involved in crime, _____ one had spent time in jail. (5) Things did not look good for them, _____ then all three were accepted at University High, a school for gifted students. (6) At this point, they made their pact, _____ they vowed to help one another work toward their goal. (7) None of them wanted to disappoint the others, _____ they all worked hard to make their dream of becoming doctors a reality. (8) The young men's success was a result of their intelligence and determination, _____ it was also a result of their loyal friendship. (9) Jenkins, Davis, and Hunt hoped that their story would inspire others, _____ they wrote a book called *The Pact* about their promise. (10) They also started The Three Doctors Foundation, _____ they wanted to create opportunities for inner-city youths.

## PRACTICE
### 15-4
Using the coordinating conjunctions provided, add a complete independent clause to each sentence in the following pairs to create two different compound sentences. Remember that each coordinating conjunction indicates a different relationship between ideas.

**Example**

They married at age eighteen, and *they had four children*_____.

They married at age eighteen, so *they had to grow up together*_____.

1. Adoption is a complex and emotional process, so _____

   _____.

   Adoption is a complex and emotional process, but _____

   _____.

2. Drunk drivers should lose their licenses, for _____

   _____.

   Drunk drivers should lose their licenses, or _____

   _____.

3. A smoke-free environment has many advantages, and _____

_____ .

A smoke-free environment has many advantages, but _____

_____ .

4. Female pilots have successfully flown combat missions, yet _____

_____ .

Female pilots have successfully flown combat missions, so _____

_____ .

5. The death penalty can be abolished, or _____

_____ .

The death penalty should not be abolished, nor _____

_____ .

**PRACTICE**

**15-5** Add coordinating conjunctions to combine sentences where necessary to relate one idea to another. Remember to put a comma before each coordinating conjunction that you add.

*, but dating*

**Example:** In India, some people look for their own mates. ~~Dating~~ is not widespread there.

(1) Arranged marriages may seem old-fashioned to some. (2) They are very important in India. (3) In fact, "love matches" are often seen as unlucky. (4) Many Indians prefer arranged marriages. (5) The matchmaking process can vary. (6) The following steps are typical. (7) First, the parents of a single man or woman put out the word that their child is available. (8) Then, the parents gather information about potential mates. (9) They evaluate this information carefully. (10) For example, they consider the potential mate's profession, educational background, and horoscope. (11) At this point, either set of parents may find a potential spouse unacceptable. (12) The process may stop. (13) Otherwise, the parents will meet to learn more about one another and their potential son-in-law or daughter-in-law. (14) In Japan, arranged marriage—known as *omiai*—is less common than it is in India. (15) It still occurs. (16) A go-between, or *nakodo*, helps to make the match. (17) The man and woman matched by a

*nakodo* meet. (18) They may decide to pursue a relationship. (19) They do not have to follow the *nakodo*'s advice. (20) They do not feel pressured to dismiss it. (21) People who are busy or shy especially appreciate a *nakodo*. (22) He can help them avoid the time-consuming and awkward process of finding a mate on their own.

**PRACTICE**

**15-6**  Write an original compound sentence on each of the following topics. Use the coordinating conjunction provided, and remember to put a comma before the coordinating conjunction in each compound sentence.

**Example:**  *Topic:* course requirements
*Coordinating conjunction:* but

*Composition is a required course for all first-year students, but biology is not*

*required.*

1. *Topic:* rising college tuition
   *Coordinating conjunction:* so

   _____

   _____

2. *Topic:* interracial families
   *Coordinating conjunction:* but

   _____

   _____

3. *Topic:* two things you hate to do
   *Coordinating conjunction:* and

   _____

   _____

4. *Topic:* why you made a certain decision
   *Coordinating conjunction:* for

   _____

   _____

5. *Topic:* something you regret
   *Coordinating conjunction:* yet

   _____

   _____

6. *Topic:* two possible career choices
   *Coordinating conjunction:* or

   _____

   _____

   _____

7. *Topic:* two household chores you would rather not do
   *Coordinating conjunction:* nor

   _____

   _____

---

## 15b  Forming Compound Sentences with Semicolons

Another way to create a compound sentence is by joining two simple sentences (independent clauses) with a **semicolon**.

> The Democrats held their convention in Charlotte; the Republicans held their convention in Tampa.

ⓔ **macmillanhighered.com**
/foundationsfirst
Additional Grammar
Exercises > Using Semicolons

## FYI

### Avoiding Fragments

A semicolon can join two complete sentences. It cannot join a sentence and a fragment.

FRAGMENT

INCORRECT  Because New York City has excellent public transportation; it was a good choice for the convention.

CORRECT  New York City has excellent public transportation; it was a good choice for the convention.

*For more on identifying and correcting fragments, see Chapter 20.*

**PRACTICE**

**15-7**  Each of the following items consists of a simple sentence followed by a semicolon. For each item, add another simple sentence to create a compound sentence.

**Example:**  Some people love to watch sports on television; *others* _____

*would rather play a game than watch one.* _____ .

1. Baseball is known as "America's pastime"; _____

_____.

2. The most-played sport in the United States is probably basketball; ___

_____.

3. Soccer has gained popularity in recent years; _____

_____.

4. American football requires size and strength; _____

_____.

5. Professional sports teams usually give their fans something to cheer

about; _____

_____.

## 15c Forming Compound Sentences with Transitional Words and Phrases

e macmillanhighered.com
/foundationsfirst
Additional Grammar
Exercises > Using Transitional
Words and Phrases

Another way to create a compound sentence is by joining two simple sentences with a **transitional word or phrase**. When a transitional word or phrase joins two sentences, a semicolon always comes *before* the transitional word or phrase, and a comma always comes *after* it.

Women's pro basketball games are often sold out; <u>however</u>, not many people watch the games on television.

Soccer has become very popular in the United States; <u>in fact</u>, more American children play soccer than any other sport.

| **Frequently Used Transitional Words** | | |
| --- | --- | --- |
| also | however | otherwise |
| besides | instead | still |
| consequently | later | subsequently |
| eventually | meanwhile | then |
| finally | moreover | therefore |
| furthermore | nevertheless | thus |

## Frequently Used Transitional Phrases

| | | |
|---|---|---|
| after all | in addition | of course |
| as a result | in comparison | on the contrary |
| at the same time | in contrast | that is |
| for example | in fact | |
| for instance | in other words | |

Different transitional words and phrases convey different meanings.

- Some transitional words and phrases signal addition: *also, besides, furthermore, in addition, moreover,* and so on.

  Golf can be an expensive sport; in addition, public golf courses are not always available.

- Some transitional words and phrases show a cause-and-effect connection: *as a result, therefore, consequently, thus,* and so on.

  Professional baseball players are bigger and stronger than ever before; therefore, home runs have become more common.

- Some transitional words and phrases indicate contradiction or contrast: *nevertheless, however, in contrast, still,* and so on.

  Some of the world's best athletes are track stars; nevertheless, few of their names are widely known.

- Some transitional words and phrases present alternatives: *instead, on the contrary, otherwise,* and so on.

  Shawn got a football scholarship; otherwise, he could not have gone to college.

  He didn't make the first team; instead, he backed up other players.

- Some transitional words and phrases indicate time sequence: *at the same time, eventually, finally, later, meanwhile, subsequently, then,* and so on.

  The popularity of women's tennis has been growing; meanwhile, the popularity of men's tennis has been declining.

### PRACTICE

**15-8**  Each item below consists of a simple sentence followed by a semicolon and a transitional word or phrase. For each item, add an independent clause to create a complete compound sentence.

**Example:** Shopping malls appear throughout the country; in fact, *they have replaced many main streets.*

1. Nearly every community is near one or more shopping malls; as a

   result, _____

   _____.

2. Some malls include hundreds of stores; moreover, _____

   _____

   _____.

3. Malls offer many employment opportunities; for example, _____

   _____

   _____.

4. Malls provide a safe, climate-controlled atmosphere; nevertheless, ___

   _____

   _____.

5. Some people think malls are wonderful; still, _____

   _____

   _____.


**PRACTICE**

**15-9**    In each of the following sentences, underline the transitional word or phrase that joins the two independent clauses. Then, add a semicolon and a comma to set off each transitional word or phrase.

**Example:**   Most Americans see the one-room schoolhouse as a thing

of the past; <u>however</u>, about 400 one-room schools still operate in the

United States.

1. Most one-room schools are in isolated rural areas that is they exist in

   places far from towns with large school systems.

2. Montana and Nebraska still have some one-room schools in contrast

   more densely populated states do not have any.

3. Most one-room schools have only one teacher and a few students

   therefore one room is all they need.

4. A growing community can easily outgrow its one-room school as a

   result the town may have to build a larger school.

5. More often, declining population causes one-room schools to close in other words the town does not have enough students to make operating the school worthwhile.

6. Running a one-room school can be expensive consequently many rural communities share a larger school with nearby towns.

7. Supporters of one-room schools see many benefits for example students in these schools get a lot of individual attention from their teachers.

8. One-room schools tend to produce confident, thoughtful students moreover these students tend to do well on state-wide tests.

9. One-room schools also give a town's residents a sense of community and tradition therefore many towns fight hard to keep their schools.

10. So far, the one-room Croydon Village School in New Hampshire remains open still residents do not take their school for granted.

**PRACTICE**

**15-10**   Consulting the lists of transitional words and phrases on pages 213 and 214, choose a word or expression that logically connects each pair of sentences below into one compound sentence. Be sure to punctuate appropriately.

**Example:**   Temporary memorials along roadways are a familiar sight
these days/ ~~Some~~ people find them distracting and even dangerous.
*; however, some*

1. Many memorials honor the victims of car accidents. Locating them along the roadways makes sense.

2. Some memorials are nearly invisible. Some are almost impossible to miss.

3. A memorial is sometimes just a simple white cross. People often add flowers, photos, toys, or teddy bears.

4. No one wants victims to be forgotten. These memorials can cause problems.

5. The memorials can create obstacles for snowplows and lawnmowers. They can distract drivers.

6. Delaware has taken steps to limit the number of memorials on its roads. Officials want mourners to use an established memorial park.

7. This seems to be a sensible compromise. It does not address one essential issue.

8. The exact location of the victim's death is important to mourners. Mourners sometimes put themselves in danger to reach the right spot.

9. Most states do not enforce their regulations about temporary memorials. some memorials remain beside roads for many months.

10. A public outlet for people's grief is clearly needed. The debate about roadside memorials is likely to continue.

**PRACTICE**

**15-11** Using the specified topics and transitional words or phrases, create five compound sentences. Be sure to punctuate correctly.

**Example:** *Topic:* popular music
*Transitional word:* nevertheless

*Many popular groups today seem to have been put together by a committee;*

*nevertheless, some of these groups sell millions of records.*

1. *Topic:* finding a job
*Transitional phrase:* for example

_____

_____

2. *Topic:* gun safety
*Transitional word:* otherwise

_____

_____

3. *Topic:* Instagram
*Transitional phrase:* as a result

_____

_____

4. *Topic:* credit-card debt
*Transitional word:* still

_____

_____

5. *Topic:* watching television
*Transitional word:* however

_____

_____

# Skills Check

Look back at your response to the Seeing and Writing prompt on page 205. Reread it, underlining every compound sentence. Then, answer the following questions, and make any necessary corrections.

- Have you used the coordinating conjunction or transitional word or phrase that best communicates your meaning?
- Have you punctuated these sentences correctly?

Now, look for a pair of short simple sentences in your writing that you could combine, and use one of the three methods discussed in this chapter to join them into one compound sentence.

# TEST · Revise · Edit

Starting with TEST, revise your paragraph. Then, edit and proofread your work.

## EDITING PRACTICE

Read the following student paragraph. Then, create compound sentences by linking pairs of simple sentences where appropriate. You can join sentences with a coordinating conjunction, a semicolon, or a transitional word or phrase. Remember to put commas before coordinating conjunctions that join two simple sentences and to use semicolons and commas correctly with transitional words and phrases. The first two sentences have been combined for you.

*Murderball* Slays Stereotypes

The 2005 documentary *Murderball* introduced many people to an unfamiliar sport. *; at the same time, it* ~~It~~ helped change people's views of disabled athletes. Most audiences had never heard of quadriplegic rugby. They were not prepared for the full-contact nature of the sport. In quad rugby, players in wheelchairs smash into one another. They often fall out of their chairs. For many spectators, this is difficult to watch. Physically disabled people are usually seen as fragile. *Murderball* tells a different story. The players clearly love the roughness of the game. They refuse to wear pads, helmets, or other protective gear. The audience is not allowed to pity these players. The audience is encouraged to admire them and their fast-paced, demanding sport. Quad rugby is exciting to watch. Spectators are easily caught up in the game. The players are also highly competitive, strong, and even arrogant. They resemble many able-bodied professional athletes. For many players, this resemblance is key. They do not want the emphasis to be on their disabilities. They want people to recognize their abilities. The movie *Murderball* makes people do just that.

## Writing Compound Sentences

☐ A compound sentence is made up of two simple sentences (independent clauses).

☐ A coordinating conjunction—*and, but, for, nor, or, so,* or *yet*—can join two simple sentences into one compound sentence. A comma always comes before the coordinating conjunction. (See 15a.)

☐ A semicolon can join two simple sentences into one compound sentence. (See 15b.)

☐ A transitional word or phrase can join two simple sentences into one compound sentence. When it joins two sentences, a transitional word or phrase is always preceded by a semicolon and followed by a comma. (See 15c.)

# 16 Writing Complex Sentences

© Bill Aron/PhotoEdit, Inc.

## seeing and writing

Look at the picture above, which shows an elementary school class picture. Then, write a paragraph about the childhood friends you've lost touch with. Why do you think you don't see these friends anymore? Which, if any, would you like to see again? Try to use the Word Power words in your paragraph.

WORD POWER

**diverge** to separate and go in different directions
**estranged** separated from someone else by feelings of hostility or indifference

**In this chapter, you will learn**

- to form complex sentences with subordinating conjunctions (16a)
- to punctuate with subordinating conjunctions (16b)
- to form complex sentences with relative pronouns (16c)

A **complex sentence** is made up of one independent clause and one or more dependent clauses.

COMPLEX SENTENCE    Because Tanya was sick yesterday,
┌─── INDEPENDENT CLAUSE ───┐
I had to work a double shift.

Note that sometimes the independent clause comes first in a complex sentence.

I had to work a double shift because Tanya was sick yesterday.

## 16a Forming Complex Sentences with Subordinating Conjunctions

WORD POWER

**subordinate** lower in rank or position; secondary in importance

You can create a complex sentence by joining two simple sentences (independent clauses). Add a **subordinating conjunction**—a word like *although* or *because*—to one of the sentences, turning it into a dependent clause.

TWO SENTENCES    The election was close. The state supreme court did not order a recount.

┌─────── DEPENDENT CLAUSE ───────┐ ┌─── INDEPENDENT ───
COMPLEX SENTENCE    Although the election was close, the state supreme
CLAUSE ───────────────────────────┐
court did not order a recount.

Keep in mind that once you add a subordinating conjunction to a simple sentence, it can no longer stand alone. It needs an independent clause to complete its meaning.

ⓔ macmillanhighered.com /foundationsfirst
LearningCurve > Coordination and Subordination; Additional Grammar Exercises > Using Subordinating Conjunctions

### Frequently Used Subordinating Conjunctions

| | | | |
|---|---|---|---|
| after | even though | since | whenever |
| although | if | so that | where |
| as | if only | than | whereas |
| as if | in order that | though | wherever |
| as though | now that | till | whether |
| because | once | unless | while |
| before | provided | until | |
| even if | rather than | when | |

**PRACTICE**

**16-1**   Write an appropriate subordinating conjunction on each blank line below. Consult the list of subordinating conjunctions on page 222 to make sure you choose one that establishes a logical relationship between ideas. (The required punctuation has been provided.)

**Example:**   _Before_ there were refrigerators in homes and refrigerated trucks, everyone ate locally grown food.

(1) _____ the term *locavore* was only coined in 2005, the locavore movement is changing the way many Americans eat. (2) The term, invented by four women in California, means "someone who eats locally." (3) _____ the locavore movement started, most Americans bought produce grown far from their homes. (4) _____ it is possible to get summer fruit in winter, this fruit is grown hundreds or even thousands of miles away. (5) According to locavores, _____ we buy produce locally, we benefit small farmers as well as the environment. (6) For example, _____ long-distance trucking is eliminated, less carbon dioxide is released into the air. (7) _____ definitions of *local* vary, the word is commonly defined as "within a 100-mile radius." (8) In addition, _____ strict locavores eat only foods grown locally, others will buy foods that cannot be grown in their local area, such as coffee, chocolate, sugar, and bananas. (9) _____ most of us are not locavores, the locavore movement is giving us more options. (10) _____ the movement began, large stores like Wal-Mart and Whole Foods have been offering more locally grown produce.

**PRACTICE**

**16-2**   Complete each of the following complex sentences by finishing the dependent clause on the line provided.

**Example:**   Some students succeed in school because _they have good study habits._

1. After _____, these students review their lecture notes and reread the assignment.

2. They memorize facts from their notes even though _____
_____.

3. Sometimes these students copy key facts from lectures onto note cards so that _____.

4. Teachers sometimes give surprise quizzes because _____ _____.

5. Students might do poorly on these quizzes unless _____ _____.

6. Even if _____, they are prepared for the unexpected.

7. Whenever _____, good students ask questions to be sure they understand the assignment.

8. When _____, good students begin their research early.

9. They narrow the topic and develop a tentative thesis before _____ _____.

10. Because _____, good students are always prepared.

macmillanhighered.com
/foundationsfirst
Additional Grammar
Exercises > Punctuating with
Subordinating Conjunctions

# 16b Punctuating with Subordinating Conjunctions

To punctuate a complex sentence that contains a subordinating conjunction, follow these rules.

■ Use a comma after the dependent clause.

DEPENDENT CLAUSE
Although they had no formal training as engineers, Orville and
INDEPENDENT CLAUSE
Wilbur Wright built the first airplane.

■ Do not use a comma after the independent clause.

INDEPENDENT CLAUSE
Orville and Wilbur Wright built the first airplane although they had
DEPENDENT CLAUSE
no formal training as engineers.

**PRACTICE**

**16-3**   Some of the following complex sentences are punctuated correctly, and some are not. Put a *C* next to every sentence that is punctuated correctly. If the punctuation is not correct, edit the sentence to correct it.

**Example:**   Skateboarding has come a long way since the first commercial boards became available in the 1950s. __*C*__

1. Teenagers used to skate wherever they could find a tempting stretch of concrete. _____

2. When a drought hit southern California in the 1970s homeowners had to leave their pools empty. _____

3. While they were away, daring groups of teenagers trespassed into their backyards. _____

4. The teens skateboarded along the sides of the pools, as if the walls were concrete waves. _____

5. As skateparks became more common, the sport lost some of its bad-boy character. _____

6. Now that skateboarding is more popular skating gear has become fashionable. _____

7. While skaters used to wear slip-on Van shoes, they now wear sneakers. _____

8. Old-time skaters liked loose pants, because the relaxed fit offered freedom of movement. _____

9. Whether they know it or not teens wearing baggy pants today are following a skater trend. _____

10. Although some old-time skaters are disappointed by the mainstream appeal of skateboarding, others are excited about their sport's influence on our culture. _____

**PRACTICE**

**16-4** Combine each of the following pairs of sentences to form one complex sentence, using the subordinating conjunction that follows each pair. Make sure you include a comma where one is required.

**Example:** *Even though people* ~~People~~ fear deadly viruses such as Ebola*, not* ~~Not~~ enough has been done to provide medical supplies to health-care workers in Africa. (even though)

1. Many Westerners hardly ever think about problems in Africa. The lack of medical supplies should concern everyone. (although)

2. Diseases in African countries often spread. Hospitals and medical personnel there do not have enough equipment. (because)

3. An outbreak of Ebola virus occurred in the Democratic Republic of Congo in 2009. Angola closed part of its border with this country to prevent the spread of the disease. (when)

4. Aid organizations arrived with disinfectant, gloves, and surgical masks. Local medical workers worried about their ability to control the disease. (until)

5. Ebola spreads. Bodily fluids from an infected person come into contact with the skin of a healthy person. (whenever)

6. The Ebola virus makes a patient bleed heavily. Medical workers are in danger. (because)

7. Health-care workers must wear gloves. Their skin never touches the skin of their patients. (so that)

8. At first doctors and nurses in the Democratic Republic of Congo did not have the right equipment to handle the outbreak. They did their best to control it. (even though)

9. International organizations arrived with "Ebola kits" containing protective clothing. Health-care workers were able to aid the sick without fear of infection. (when)

10. Wealthier nations should help poorer countries stockpile supplies. Local medical workers can respond effectively as soon as an outbreak occurs. (so that)

**PRACTICE**

**16-5**    Use each of the subordinating conjunctions below in an original complex sentence. Make sure you punctuate your sentences correctly.

**Example**

*subordinating conjunction:* even though

*My little sister finally agreed to go to kindergarten even though she was afraid.*

1. *subordinating conjunction:* because

_____

_____

_____

2. *subordinating conjunction:* after

_____

_____

_____

3. *subordinating conjunction:* even if

_____

_____

_____

4. *subordinating conjunction:* until

_____

_____

_____

5. *subordinating conjunction:* whenever

_____

_____

_____

# 16c Forming Complex Sentences with Relative Pronouns

You can also create a complex sentence by joining two simple sentences (independent clauses) with a **relative pronoun** (*who, which, that,* and so on).

TWO SENTENCES    The Miami Heat's LeBron James was the Cleveland Cavaliers' first pick in the 2003 NBA draft. He was only eighteen years old at the time.

COMPLEX SENTENCE    The Miami Heat's LeBron James, who was only eighteen years old at the time, was the Cleveland Cavaliers' first pick in the 2003 NBA draft. (The relative pronoun *who* creates a dependent clause that describes LeBron James.)

macmillanhighered.com
/foundationsfirst
Additional Grammar
Exercises > Using Relative
Pronouns

## Relative Pronouns

| that | which | whoever | whomever |
|------|-------|---------|----------|
| what | who | whom | whose |

*Note:* *Who* and *whom* always refer to people. *Which* and *that* refer to things.

**PRACTICE 16-6**    In each of the following complex sentences, underline the dependent clause, and circle the relative pronoun. Then, draw an arrow from the relative pronoun to the noun or pronoun it describes.

**Example:**    Indians who wish to maintain their heritage celebrate Diwali, the Festival of Lights.

1. This holiday, which lasts five days, involves special foods, candles, prayers, and presents.

2. The roots of this celebration are in Hinduism, which is one of the oldest religions in the world.

3. Among the special sweets baked for this holiday are cakes that contain saffron, almonds, butter, and milk.

4. Offerings are made to Krishna, who is one of the three main gods of Hinduism.

5. In the evenings, families light candles that stand for the banishing of ignorance and darkness.

6. On the first day of the celebration, people who want good fortune during the coming year decorate their houses with rice flour and red footprints.

7. The second day celebrates a legend about Krishna, who is said to have rescued sixteen thousand daughters of gods and saints from a demon king.

8. The third and most important day consists of feasts, gifts, pilgrimages to temples, and visits to friends whom the family wishes to see.

9. The fourth day, which is associated with legends about mountains, is considered a good day to start a new project.

10. On the last day, families, who meet to exchange gifts, express their love for one another.

**PRACTICE**

**16-7**   Combine each of the following pairs of sentences into one complex sentence, using the relative pronoun that follows each pair.

**Example:**   Whaling was once an important part of American culture. , *which inspired the great American novel* Moby-Dick,
~~Whaling inspired the great American novel *Moby-Dick.*~~ (which)

1. In the nineteenth century, American whalers sailed around the world to hunt whales. Their jobs were very dangerous. (whose)

2. Whale oil provided light in many American homes. It burns very brightly. (which)

3. Today, U.S. laws protect several whale species. They are considered to be in danger of extinction. (that)

4. Most Americans approve of the U.S. ban on whaling. They no longer need whale oil for lighting. (who)

5. Whale hunting is the source of a disagreement between the United States and Japan. The two countries have different ideas about whaling. (which)

6. Japanese fleets operate with permission from the International Whaling Commission. The commission allows whales to be killed for scientific research. (which)

7. Japanese merchants are allowed to sell whale meat. This meat is left over after the research. (that)

8. In recent years, the U.S.-based conservation group Sea Shepherd has claimed victories against Japan's whaling industry. The group attempts to disable Japanese whaling ships. (which)

9. The organization has saved hundreds of whales from Japanese harpoons. The organization's activities have been publicized widely. (whose)

10. Sea Shepherd and other groups see the Japanese whale hunt as benefiting not research but businesses. The businesses sell whale meat to restaurants. (that)

**PRACTICE**

**16-8** Complete each of the following items to create a complex sentence. Make sure that each clause of the complex sentence contains a subject and a verb.

**Example:** A hamburger that *has been barbecued on a grill is one of my favorite things.*

1. When my mother _____

_____.

2. My best friend, who _____

_____.

3. If you ever _____

_____.

4. Although most people _____

_____.

5. My dream job, which _____

_____.

# Skills Check

Look back at your response to the Seeing and Writing prompt on page 221. Reread it, and complete the following tasks.

- Underline every complex sentence.
- Circle the subordinating conjunction or relative pronoun that joins the clauses in each complex sentence.

Now, find a pair of simple sentences that could be combined with a subordinating conjunction or a relative pronoun, and revise the two sentences to create a complex sentence.

# TEST · Revise · Edit

Starting with TEST, revise your paragraph. Then, edit and proofread your work.

## EDITING PRACTICE

Read the following student paragraph, and then revise it by using subordinating conjunctions or relative pronouns to combine some simple sentences. Be sure to punctuate correctly. The first revision has been done for you.

### The Importance of Birth Order

Apparently, birth order can affect a child's personality. Oldest children are achievers, *while youngest* ~~Youngest~~ children are free spirits. Oldest children are serious. Youngest children like to make people laugh. Families have noticed such differences for years. There was no evidence to back up their observations until recently. Several researchers studied children of different birth orders. They made some startling discoveries. For instance, oldest children have a slightly higher IQ score than children following them. Oldest children usually get the most attention from their parents. Some of this advantage might result from helping younger brothers and sisters. Younger brothers and sisters may come to rely on the oldest child. The IQ difference may seem small. It can have major consequences in life. Oldest children are more likely than younger children to go into certain professions. These professions have high pay and high status. In one study, researchers found that 43 percent of CEOs were oldest children, 33 percent were middle children, and 23 percent were youngest children. The study observed a range of businesses. Youngest children may become the family comedian or take risks. They stand out from their brothers and sisters. Famous funny people include Mark Twain and Stephen Colbert. These famous funny people were youngest children. Oldest and youngest children demand (and usually get) a lot of attention. Middle children may feel ignored and lost. However, most eventually find their own identities. These identities may be as a helper or a peacemaker. Such roles are common among middle children. Middle children may feel caught between the strong personalities of the oldest and youngest child. Research backs up old ideas about birth order. Some family members may say, "I told you so."

## Writing Complex Sentences

☐ A complex sentence consists of one independent clause and one or more dependent clauses.

☐ Subordinating conjunctions—such as *after, although, because, when,* and *while*—can join two simple sentences into one complex sentence. (See 16a.)

☐ Always use a comma after a dependent clause that is introduced by a subordinating conjunction. Do not use a comma after an independent clause. (See 16b.)

☐ Relative pronouns—such as *which* or *that*—can join two simple sentences into one complex sentence. (See 16c.)

# 17 Fine-Tuning Your Sentences

© Getty Images Perspectives/Getty

## WORD POWER

**commission** to place an order for something
**priority** an important or urgent goal
**subsidize** to give financial support to a project

## seeing and writing

The picture above shows *Cloud Gate*, also known as "The Bean," a reflective sculpture in Chicago's Millennium Park. Do you think publicly funded artworks like this one enrich our cities, or do you think the money they cost could be put to better use elsewhere? Look at the picture, and then write a paragraph in which you explain your position. Try to use the Word Power words in your paragraph.

**In this chapter, you will learn**
- to vary sentence openings (17a)
- to combine sentences (17b)
- to choose exact words (17c)
- to use concise language (17d)
- to avoid clichés (17e)

## 17a Varying Sentence Openings

When all the sentences in a paragraph begin in the same way, the paragraph is likely to seem dull and repetitive. In the following paragraph, for example, every sentence begins with the subject.

> The AIDS Memorial quilt contains thousands of panels. Each panel commemorates a death from AIDS. One panel is for a young college student. Another panel is for an eight-year-old boy. This panel displays his baseball cap. A third panel displays a large picture of a young man. This panel includes a quotation: "Blood saved his life, and it took it away."

**WORD POWER**

**commemorate** to serve as a memorial to something or someone

### Beginning with Adverbs

Instead of beginning every sentence with the subject, try begining some sentences with **adverbs**, as the following paragraph illustrates.

> The AIDS Memorial quilt contains thousands of panels. Sadly, each panel commemorates a death from AIDS. One panel is for a young college student. Another panel is for an eight-year-old boy. This panel displays his baseball cap. Finally, a third panel displays a large picture of a young man. This panel includes a quotation: "Blood saved his life, and it took it away."

Adding the adverbs *sadly* and *finally* makes the paragraph's sentences flow more smoothly.

### Beginning with Prepositional Phrases

As the following paragraph shows, you can also begin some sentences with **prepositional phrases**. A prepositional phrase is made up of a preposition (*of, by, along,* and so on) and all the words that go along with it (*of the people, by the curb, along the road*).

> The AIDS Memorial quilt contains thousands of panels. Sadly, each panel commemorates a death from AIDS. One panel is for a young college student. Another panel is for an eight-year-old boy. In the center, this panel displays his baseball cap. Finally, a third panel displays a large picture of a young man. Under the picture, this panel includes a quotation: "Blood saved his life, and it took it away."

macmillanhighered.com /foundationsfirst
LearningCurve > Parts of Speech: Verbs, Adjectives, and Adverbs

## PRACTICE

**17-1**　Every sentence in the following paragraph begins with the subject, but several sentences contain adverbs and prepositional phrases that could be moved to the beginning. To vary the sentence openings, move adverbs to the beginnings of three sentences, and move prepositional phrases to the beginnings of two other sentences. Be sure to place a comma after these adverbs and prepositional phrases.

　　　　　　　　　　　　　*In 1940, the*
**Example:**　~~The~~ U.S. government issued the first "green cards" ~~in 1940.~~
　　　　　　　　　　^　　　　　　　　　　　　　　　　　　　　　　　^

(1) Green cards allow citizens of other countries to work in the United States. (2) The cards were white originally. (3) They were one of many different kinds of permits issued to non-U.S. citizens. (4) Green was eventually used for permits allowing permanent residence. (5) Permanent residence status has long been in high demand. (6) Therefore, the government has had to limit the number of green cards offered each year. (7) Green cards were issued by the U.S. Immigration and Naturalization Service until 2003. (8) They are currently issued by a division of the U.S. Department of Homeland Security. (9) Green card applications were examined more closely after the 9/11 terrorist attacks. (10) This trend has continued, creating long waits for green cards.

## PRACTICE

**17-2**　Listed below are three adverbs and three prepositional phrases. To vary sentence openings in the paragraph that follows, add one of these words or phrases to the beginning of a sentence. Be sure your additions connect the passage's ideas clearly and logically. Remember to add commas where they are needed.

| ADVERBS | PREPOSITIONAL PHRASES |
|---|---|
| Eventually | Until then |
| Ideally | At a minimum |
| Surprisingly | For security reasons |

　　　　　　　　　　　　　　*Eventually, someone*
**Example:**　~~Someone~~ may design a safe and convenient way for people
　　　　　　　　^
to access their online accounts without passwords.

(1) The most popular computer passwords are the names of family members, sports teams, and pets. (2) One of the most common passwords is "password." (3) Such words may be easy for users to remember, but they

are also easy for others to guess. (4) Experts recommend using combinations of letters, numbers, and punctuation marks totaling eight or more characters. (5) The characters should not form words or other familiar patterns. (6) For example, "abc12345" would be a bad choice. (7) Passwords should be changed six times a year. (8) However, experts acknowledge the difficulty of keeping track of multiple passwords. (9) Fingerprints or eye scans might replace passwords. (10) We will have to be careful as well as creative when choosing passwords.

## 17b   Combining Sentences

You can also create sentence variety by experimenting with different ways of combining short simple sentences.

### Creating Compound and Complex Sentences

Two simple sentences can be combined into one **compound sentence**.

| TWO SIMPLE SENTENCES | Many young adults do not vote. They have no right to complain about politicians. |
|---|---|
| COMBINED (COMPOUND SENTENCE) | Many young adults do not vote, so they have no right to complain about politicians. |

Two simple sentences can also be combined into one **complex sentence**.

| TWO SIMPLE SENTENCES | Many young adults do not vote. They do not trust politicians. |
|---|---|
| COMBINED (COMPLEX SENTENCE) | Many young adults do not vote because they do not trust politicians. |

Paragraphs like the following one, which consists entirely of short simple sentences, can be boring.

Many young adults do not vote. They do not trust politicians. Maybe they are too lazy to vote. Maybe they don't think their votes will do any good. Some vote in national elections. They don't bother to vote in local elections. Others don't vote at all. They have no right to complain about politicians. Voter turnout in the United States is low. It is much higher in many other countries. Citizens of other countries vote in high numbers. They know how important their votes are. Americans should follow their example.

2. The house needs major repairs. It has been neglected for years.

_____

3. The fans were shouting and stamping their feet. They showed their impatience.

_____

4. The survivors were stranded on a desert island. They considered their options.

_____

5. The ten coworkers won the lottery. They were holding the winning ticket.

_____

## Creating a Series

Another way to vary your sentences is to combine a group of simple sentences into one sentence that includes a **series** of words.

| | |
|---|---|
| **GROUP OF SENTENCES** | Consumers are buying more tablets. They are also buying more smartphones. They are buying more bottled water, too. |
| **COMBINED (SERIES OF NOUNS)** | Consumers are buying more tablets, smartphones, and bottled water. |
| **GROUP OF SENTENCES** | Samantha registered for fall classes. She bought her books. She went back to work. |
| **COMBINED (SERIES OF VERBS)** | Samantha registered for fall classes, bought her books, and went back to work. |
| **GROUP OF SENTENCES** | On his graduation day, Alex was excited. He was also proud. He was a little nervous as well. |
| **COMBINED (SERIES OF ADJECTIVES)** | On his graduation day, Alex was excited, proud, and a little nervous. |

**PRACTICE**

**17-5**   Combine each group of simple sentences to create one simple sentence that uses a series of words.

**Example:**   Labrador retrievers are popular dogs for families. Golden retrievers are also popular dogs for families. In addition, Yorkshire terriers are popular dogs for families.

*Labrador retrievers, golden retrievers, and Yorkshire terriers are popular* _____

*dogs for families.* _____

1. The police officer pulled over the sports car. She asked the driver for his license. Then, she gave the driver a speeding ticket.

   _____

   _____

2. Snowshoeing is fun. It is also invigorating. It is easy to learn, too.

   _____

   _____

3. Camping is an inexpensive way to spend vacation time. Visiting a local pool or lake is another inexpensive way to spend vacation time. Relaxing at home is a third inexpensive way to spend vacation time.

   _____

   _____

4. After getting a raise, Donna called her mother with the news. She celebrated with friends. She also opened a savings account.

   _____

   _____

5. A ripe cantaloupe sounds hollow. It smells sweet. It looks orange.

   _____

   _____

# 17c   Choosing Exact Words

When you revise your writing, check to make sure you have used words that clearly express your ideas. Try to avoid vague, overused words like *good, nice, great, terrific, bad,* and *interesting.*

   **Specific** words refer to particular people, places, and things. **General** words refer to entire classes of things. Sentences that contain specific words create a clearer picture for readers than sentences containing only general ones.

| | |
|---|---|
| GENERAL | The old car went down the street. |
| SPECIFIC | The pink 1959 Cadillac convertible glided smoothly down Main Street. |
| GENERAL | I would like to apply for the job you advertised. |
| SPECIFIC | I would like to apply for the assistant manager's job you posted on Monster.com. |

**PRACTICE**

**17-6**    In the following paragraph, underline the specific words that help you picture the scene the writer describes. The first sentence has been done for you.

(1) *Anna in the Tropics,* a Pulitzer Prize–winning play by Nilo Cruz, brings audiences into the <u>simmering heat of a Cuban cigar factory</u>. (2) The story is set in 1929 in Ybor City, a lively immigrant community in Tampa, Florida. (3) This was a time before the rumbling and buzzing of machinery filled most factories. (4) In this hot, humid world, a whirring ceiling fan was sometimes the only sound workers heard as they hunched over their sticky, repetitive work. (5) The play's action begins when Juan Julian, an elegant man in a sharply pressed white linen suit, arrives to fill the silence. (6) The calm and romantic Julian sits on a wooden platform in the center of the hollow room and reads aloud as the workers roll the moist, brown tobacco leaves between their stained fingers. (7) However, Julian does not read a local newspaper or an instructive textbook; instead, he reads *Anna Karenina,* Leo Tolstoy's novel about doomed Russian lovers. (8) Thus, he brings Anna to the steamy, tropical coast of Florida. (9) At the same time, he also brings his eager listeners to the harsh, frozen landscape of nineteenth-century Russia. (10) *Anna in the Tropics* connects these two very different worlds.

**PRACTICE**

**17-7**  Below are five general words. In the blank beside each, write a more specific word related to the general word. Then, use the more specific word in a sentence.

**Example**

tool _____ *claw hammer* _____

*Melanie pried the rusty nails out of each weather-beaten board with a*

*claw hammer.*

1. game _____

_____

_____

2. magazine _____

_____

_____

3. job _____

_____

_____

4. exercise _____

_____

_____

5. animal _____

_____

_____

**PRACTICE**

**17-8**  The following paragraph is a vaguely worded job-application letter. Rewrite the paragraph, substituting specific words for the general words of the original and adding details where necessary. Start by making the first sentence, which identifies the applicant and the job, more specific. Then, add details about the applicant's background and qualifications, expanding the original paragraph into a three-paragraph letter.

I am currently attending college and would like to apply for the position advertised. I have a strong interest in the field. My background includes high school and college coursework that relates to this position. I also have personal experience that would make me a good choice. I am qualified for this job, and I would appreciate the opportunity to be considered. Thank you for your consideration.

## 17d Using Concise Language

**Concise language** says what it has to say in as few words as possible. When you revise, cross out words that do not add anything to your meaning, and substitute more concise language where necessary.

**macmillanhighered.com
/foundationsfirst**
LearningCurve > Word Choice
and Appropriate Language;
Additional Grammar
Exercises > Using Concise
Language

**WORDY**  In spite of the fact that the British troops outnumbered them, the colonists fought on.

**CONCISE**  Although the British troops outnumbered them, the colonists fought on.

**WORDY**  There are many people who have serious allergies.

**CONCISE**  Many people have serious allergies.

**WORDY**  It is my opinion that everyone should have good health care.

**CONCISE**  Everyone should have good health care.

**WORDY**  During the period of the Great Depression, many people were out of work.

**CONCISE**  During the Great Depression, many people were out of work.

**WORDY**  In the editorial, it warned that the situation was serious.

**CONCISE**  The editorial warned that the situation was serious.

# FYI

## Using Concise Language

The wordy phrases listed below add nothing to a sentence. If you spot them in your writing, see if you can delete them or substitute a more concise phrase.

| WORDY | CONCISE |
|---|---|
| It is clear that | (delete) |
| It is a fact that | (delete) |
| The reason is that | Because |
| It is my opinion that | (delete) |
| Due to the fact that | Because |
| Despite the fact that | Although |
| At the present time | Today/Now |
| At that time | Then |
| In most cases | Usually |
| In order to | To |

**Unnecessary repetition**—saying the same thing twice for no reason—can also make your writing wordy. When you revise, delete repeated words and phrases that add nothing to your sentences.

| | |
|---|---|
| WORDY | Seeing the ocean for the first time was the most exciting and thrilling experience of my life. |
| CONCISE | Seeing the ocean for the first time was the most exciting experience of my life. |
| WORDY | Some people can't make their own decisions by themselves. |
| CONCISE | Some people can't make their own decisions. |
| WORDY | They were repeatedly told time and time again to follow safety procedures. |
| CONCISE | They were repeatedly told to follow safety procedures. |

**PRACTICE**

**17-9**  In the following sentences, cross out wordy expressions and unnecessary repetition, substituting more concise expressions where necessary.

**Example:**  *Tiny*
It is a fact that tiny feet were once a symbol of status and
^
beauty for Chinese women.

1. Foot binding gave women three-inch "lotus feet," which helped them attract rich and prosperous mates.

2. The practice began during the time of the tenth century, when a Chinese ruler fell in love with a dancer who had tiny, bound feet.

3. Due to the fact that a child's bones are easy to bend, foot binding was started at a young age.

4. In order to create a tiny foot, a girl's toes were broken and bound to the sole of her foot with bandages.

5. From then on, it was difficult for her to walk, and she sometimes suffered severe and serious pain.

6. Foot binding was outlawed in 1912, but it continued for several years afterward, despite being illegal.

7. There were some families who were fined for binding their daughters' feet.

8. The government expected citizens to do farm work, which was impossible and out of the question for women with bound feet.

9. Some of these women are alive at the present time despite the fact that they are old and frail.

10. While some of them are proud of their tiny little feet, many wish that their feet had been left alone.

### PRACTICE

### 17-10

The following paragraph is wordy. Cross out unnecessary words, and make any revisions that may be needed.

**Example:**   Germs may be found in the most ~~surprising and~~ unexpected places.

(1) Soap and water are now favored over antibacterial germ-fighting products. (2) Several years ago, antibacterial cleaning products were introduced throughout the American market all across the country. (3) In commercial advertisements, these products were promoted as being better than soap at killing germs. (4) Researchers pointed out that while the new products might kill more germs than soap does, some of these germs are beneficial to humans and have positive effects. (5) These products may also strengthen dangerous bacteria due to the fact that resistant germs will survive. (6) Consequently, scientists recommend and strongly advise that antibacterial products not be used. (7) Recently, however, the public has become concerned about outbreaks of certain germ-based diseases caused by bacteria and viruses. (8) One illness that caused concern and distress was the H1N1 (swine flu) virus. (9) In order to control the spread of this virus, public-health officials urged people to wash their hands frequently. (10) Because not everyone has access to soap and water at all times, officials recommended that people carry antibacterial hand gels that fight germs. (11) In the final analysis, the bottom line is that soap and water are the best way to keep hands clean. (12) However, if soap and water are not available, sanitizing gels are useful and helpful substitutes.

macmillanhighered.com
/foundationsfirst
LearningCurve > Word Choice
and Appropriate Language
Additional Grammar
Exercises > Avoiding Cliches

## 17e  Avoiding Clichés

**Clichés** are phrases—such as *threw him under the bus* and *it is what it is*—that have been used so often that they have lost their impact and, in many cases, their meaning. Clichés do nothing to improve writing; in fact, they may even get in the way of clear communication.

To make your point effectively, try to replace a cliché with a direct statement—or, if posssible, with a fresher expression.

CLICHÉ   After a year of college, I learned that what goes around comes around.

REVISED   After a year of college, I learned that if I don't study, I won't do well.

CLICHÉ   With the pressures of working and going to school, I feel like a rat in a maze.

REVISED   With the pressures of working and going to school, I feel as if I never know where to turn next.

### PRACTICE
### 17-11

Cross out any clichés in the following paragraph. Then, either substitute a fresher expression or restate the idea in more direct language.

**Example:**   A cup of coffee is a needed ~~shot in the arm~~ for many hard-

working Americans.
                                  *boost*

(1) Many Americans get their get up and go from a morning cup of coffee. (2) Many of them find that designer coffees go down smooth as silk. (3) In fact, there are more designer coffees than you can shake a stick at. (4) Some coffees are made from beans imported from the four corners of the globe, from such places as Hawaii, Sumatra, and Kenya. (5) Others have flavors that melt in your mouth, such as hazelnut, vanilla, and raspberry. (6) Still other coffee drinks, such as cappuccino and lattes, include lots of milk straight from the cow. (7) Some designer coffees skillfully combine all three elements—exotic beans, strong flavors, and milk—to create a taste that is out of this world. (8) Consumers pay an arm and a leg for these designer coffees. (9) In fact, Seattle, the home of the Starbucks chain, even went out on a limb and tried to tax designer coffees.

(10) Although the Starbucks chain is top dog in the designer coffee business today, other chains and individual coffee shops offer just as much bang for the buck.

## Skills Check

Look back at your response to the Seeing and Writing prompt on page 234. Reread it, and then answer the following questions.

- Are your sentence openings varied?
- Can you combine any sentences?
- Is your language as exact and concise as possible?
- Have you avoided clichés in your writing?

Check to make sure your sentences are as varied and interesting as possible.

## TEST · Revise · Edit

Starting with TEST, revise your paragraph. Then, edit and proofread your work.

## EDITING PRACTICE

Read the following student paragraph, and then revise it by moving at least two adverbs and at least two prepositional phrases to the beginnings of sentences. Combine sentences wherever possible. Then, revise the paragraph's sentences so that they use exact words and concise language and do not include clichés. The first sentence has been revised for you.

### Changing Views of Vampires

Vampires, "undead" creatures who drink the blood of living and breathing people, have long fascinated humans. Eastern Europe is the source and origin of much vampire superstition. Vampire tales from that region did not include blood drinking originally. Instead, vampires were said to do annoying stuff, such as stealing livestock or firewood. Suspecting the recently dead, townspeople would dig up their graves. They would drive stakes through the bodies. Today's media, television shows, and movies often portray vampires as sexy. Vampires used to be thought of in negative ways. They were described as smelly creatures with rotting skin and bloated faces. Scholars are now of the opinion that these traits were the result of decomposition of dug-up corpses. The idea of a vampire as a mysterious caped man first gained wide appeal among many people with the 1897 publication of Bram Stoker's novel *Dracula*. The novel was made into a play. Later, the play was turned into a highly successful movie. The Count Dracula tells his guests, "I never drink . . . wine" in a famous and well-known line in the movie. Like many movie vampires, he meets his maker eventually. Vampires have been transformed from scary monsters into hot dates over the years. A small-town waitress, Sookie Stackhouse, falls head over heels in love with a handsome vampire, Bill Compton, in the Southern Vampire Mysteries series. The *Twilight* series of books features a love story between a young teenage girl and a vampire. A few hundred years ago in eastern Europe, such relationships would have been unthinkable and beyond belief. In today's world, however, these stories are wildly popular.

# review checklist

## Fine-Tuning Your Sentences

☐ You can make your sentences more interesting by varying your sentence openings. (See 17a.)

☐ Try combining sentences to add variety to your writing. (See 17b.)

☐ Try to replace general words with specific ones. (See 17c.)

☐ Delete wordy expressions, substituting concise language where necessary. (See 17d.)

☐ Avoid clichés (overused expressions). (See 17e.)

# 18 Using Parallelism

NC1 WENN Photos/Newsroom

## seeing and writing

The picture above shows pop star Madonna's high school yearbook photo. Look at the picture, and then write a paragraph in which you discuss how you have changed since you graduated from high school. Try to use the Word Power words in your paragraph.

**In this chapter, you will learn**
- to recognize parallel structure (18a)
- to use parallel structure (18b)

## 18a Recognizing Parallel Structure

**Parallelism** means using the same pattern of words to express similar ideas.

> Paul Robeson was an actor and a singer.
>
> When my brother comes home from college, he eats, sleeps, and watches television.
>
> Elephants are big, strong, and intelligent.
>
> Jan likes to run, to do spinning, and to lift weights.

**Faulty parallelism** occurs when different patterns of words are used to express similar ideas.

> **NOT PARALLEL**  I like composition, history, and doing math.
>
> **PARALLEL**  I like composition, history, and math. (All three items are nouns.)
>
> **NOT PARALLEL**  The wedding guests danced, ate, and were drinking.
>
> **PARALLEL**  The wedding guests danced, ate, and drank. (All three verbs are in the past tense.)
>
> **NOT PARALLEL**  The Manayunk bike race is long and climbs steeply and is difficult.
>
> **PARALLEL**  The Manayunk bike race is long, steep, and difficult.
>
> **NOT PARALLEL**  We can go to the movies, or playing miniature golf is an option.
>
> **PARALLEL**  We can go to the movies, or we can play miniature golf.

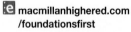 macmillanhighered.com
/foundationsfirst
LearningCurve > Parallelism
Additional Grammar
Exercises > Recognizing
Parallel Structure

**PRACTICE**

**18-1** In each of the following sentences, underline the words that are parallel.

**Example:**  The pitcher <u>threw a tantrum in the dugout</u>, <u>threatened his teammates in the locker room</u>, and <u>called a press conference to criticize the coaches</u>.

1. The tornado was sudden, unexpected, and destructive.

2. Petra ordered an egg-white omelet, a green salad with no dressing, and two slices of cheesecake.

3. After the test, I wanted to lie down and take a nap.

4. The intruders broke the windows, painted graffiti on the walls, and threw garbage on the floor.

5. Maria bought a bicycle, Terence bought a bus pass, and Sheila bought a pair of hiking boots.

**PRACTICE**

**18-2**   In each of the following sentences, decide whether the underlined words are parallel. If so, write *P* in the blank. If not, edit the sentence to make the words parallel.

**Examples**

The contestants argued, sunbathed, and ~~they~~ watched each other suspiciously. _____

A retired Navy SEAL, a river guide, and a corporate trainer were the last contestants left on the island. ___*P*___

1. Hundreds of people wanted to be on a game show that required them to live on an island, catch their own food, and they could not have contact with the outside world. _____

2. The contestants had to be resourceful and healthy. _____

3. The last person on the island would win a car and a million dollars.

   _____

4. *Survivor* was modeled on a Swedish game show that had forty-eight contestants and a thirty-thousand-dollar prize. _____

5. The contestants held their breath underwater, rowed a canoe, and rats and caterpillars were eaten by them. _____

6. Many viewers decided that it was much more fun to watch *Survivor* than watching summer reruns. _____

7. Each week, the television audience saw <u>one person win a contest</u> and <u>another person would get voted off the island</u>. _____

8. The corporate trainer was <u>manipulative</u>, <u>argumentative</u>, and <u>he often schemed</u>. _____

9. <u>Some viewers loved him</u>, <u>some viewers hated him</u>, but <u>all of them talked about his victory</u>. _____

10. The show became so popular that the contestants came home to <u>endorsements</u>, <u>acting roles</u>, and <u>becoming famous</u>. _____

**macmillanhighered.com
/foundationsfirst**
Additional Grammar
Exercises > Using Parallel
Structure

## 18b Using Parallel Structure

Parallel structure is especially important in *paired items, comparisons, items in a series,* and *items in a list.*

### Paired Items

Use parallel structure for paired items connected by a **coordinating conjunction**—*and, but, for, nor, or, so,* or *yet.*

> Jemera <u>takes Alex to day care</u> and then <u>goes to work</u>.
> You can <u>register to vote now</u>, or <u>you can register next week</u>.

Also, use parallel structure for paired items joined by **correlative conjunctions**.

| Correlative Conjunctions | | |
|---|---|---|
| both . . . and | neither . . . nor | rather . . . than |
| either . . . or | not only . . . but also | |

> Darryl is good both <u>in English</u> and <u>in math</u>.
> The movie was not only <u>long</u> but also <u>boring</u>.
> I would rather <u>take classes in the morning</u> than <u>take them in the afternoon</u>.

### Comparisons

Use parallel structure for comparisons formed with *than* or *as.*

> It often costs less <u>to rent a house</u> than <u>to buy one</u>.
> In basketball, <u>natural talent</u> is as important as <u>hard work</u>.

## Items in a Series

Use parallel structure for a series of three or more items.

> At the zoo, we saw the penguins <u>walk</u>, <u>swim</u>, and <u>fish</u>.

> To do well in school, you should <u>attend class regularly</u>, <u>take careful notes</u>, and <u>set aside time to study</u>.

## Items in a List

Use parallel structure for items in a numbered or bulleted list.

> Students go to college for the following reasons:
> 1. To learn
> 2. To increase self-esteem
> 3. To get a better job

**PRACTICE**

**18-3**   In each of the following sentences, underline the parts of the sentence that should be parallel. Then, edit each sentence to make it parallel.

> **Example:**   In Spain, people <u>greet each other with two kisses</u> and al-
> <sub> </sub>*start*
> ways <u>~~starting~~ with the right cheek</u>.
> ^

1. Most countries have a standard greeting—a handshake, a series of kisses, a hug, a bow, or they nod their heads.

2. In the United States, there is no accepted custom, so often it can get confusing.

3. Most Americans greet each other with a handshake, a cheek kiss, by waving, or a hug.

4. However, greetings vary widely, and predicting them can be difficult.

5. A greeting often depends on people's ages, what their genders are, and the situation.

6. For instance, a man might greet a woman with a kiss but a slap on the back might be his choice for a man.

7. Businesspeople are often more comfortable shaking hands with each other than to kiss each other.

8. In general, most people would rather stick out a hand than they would risk a kiss.

9. An unexpected kiss can result not only in bumped noses but also it can be embarrassing.

10. For the time being, how to greet others will continue to puzzle people both in their jobs and when they socialize.

**PRACTICE**

**18-4**    In each of the following sentences, fill in the blanks with parallel words of your own that make sense in context.

**Example:**    When I am at school, my favorite things to do are *hang out* *with friends*, *go to the cafeteria*, and *play Frisbee*.

1. My favorite classes are ————————— and —————————.

2. If I could take any class at school, it would be ————————— or —————————.

3. The subjects I am most interested in are —————————, —————————, and —————————.

4. When I'm not at school, I like to —————————, —————————, and —————————.

5. After I graduate, I hope to ————————— or —————————.

# Skills Check

Look back at your response to the Seeing and Writing prompt on page 251. Reread it, and then complete the following tasks.

- Underline any paired items in your paragraph.
- Underline any series of words in your paragraph.
- Check to be sure that you use the same pattern of words to express similar ideas in each pair or series you have underlined.
- Cross out any words that are not parallel, and substitute parallel words where necessary.

# TEST · Revise · Edit

Starting with TEST, revise your paragraph. Then, edit and proofread your work.

## EDITING PRACTICE

Read the following student paragraph, which contains examples of faulty parallelism. Then, identify the sentences you think need to be corrected, and make the changes necessary to create parallelism. The first error has been corrected for you.

The Need for Organ Donors

Currently, the shortage of transplant organs is widespread, demands serious

attention, and is growing. More than 100,000 people are waiting for a kidney ~~and~~ *or a heart.*

~~the same number need a heart.~~ Each month, the waiting list grows by more than

three hundred people. The shortage is worsening because the conditions that may

lead to organ failure are increasing. These conditions include kidney disease, heart

trouble, and getting diabetes. For patients, the wait for donated organs is not

only long but uncertainty is also a factor. In fact, sixteen people die each day

because they have not gotten an organ transplant. Health officials are trying to

increase the number of organs by educating the public, and they are disproving

myths about organ donation. For example, it is untrue that organ donors are

refused life support or doctors pronounce them dead while they are still alive.

Becoming an organ donor is neither time-consuming nor is difficulty an issue.

People can sign and carry a donor card, join their state's organ registry, or another

option is to indicate a willingness to be a donor on their driver's license application.

These simple steps might save another person's life. Unfortunately, however, the

waiting list for organs is growing three times faster than the rate of organ donation.

## review checklist

### Using Parallelism

- ☐ Use the same pattern of words to express similar ideas. (See 18a.)
- ☐ Use parallel structure with paired items. (See 18b.)
- ☐ Use parallel structure in comparisons formed with *than* or *as.* (See 18b.)
- ☐ Use parallel structure for items in a series or in a numbered or bulleted list. (See 18b.)

Read the following student essay, which contains some sentences that could be clearer or more forceful. Revise the sentences whenever possible by moving prepositional phrases or adverbs to the beginnings of sentences; combining short, choppy sentences; using more exact words; editing out wordy expressions and clichés; and correcting faulty parallelism. The first editing change has been made for you.

## A College Bargain

Community colleges have changed since they started at the beginning of the twentieth century. These public colleges began when ~~people involved in education~~ *educators* decided that some students would benefit from two years of schooling after high school. Veterans began attending community colleges after World War II. There are many students since then who have gone to community colleges to save money. Community colleges today are a big part of the higher education system in the United States.

The first community colleges were often called "junior colleges." They started when some students needed more than a high school education. Still, some students were not right for four-year colleges. Some students, for example, were preparing for technical jobs. These students needed practical training. They did not need a four-year diploma. They went to community college for one or two years. Then, jobs were found by them. For example, they might repair radios, or they could become cooks. Many community colleges were "normal schools." Normal schools trained new teachers. There were many people who were out of a job during the Great Depression of the 1930s. Community colleges at that time stressed job preparation.

The next period of community college development began after World War II ended in 1945. Many veterans went to college on the GI Bill. The U.S. government paid $500 for college tuition and fees. This money also covered the cost of books. Veterans often used their GI Bill benefits to go to community colleges. They lived at home while they went to school. Adult education was growing rapidly at this time. Community colleges were good places for adults to continue their education. Most adults wanted to live at home and commute to school. The cost

**259**

was low for students. The cost was also low for the taxpayers who paid for community colleges.

Community colleges eventually became a way for college students to get a good education, and saving money could be done at the same time. Low cost has always been an important factor for community college students. They can save money by living at home for two years. Tuition is lower there than at four-year colleges. Students who attend community college spend much less on their education than students who choose to attend four-year colleges. Students can transfer to four-year colleges after two years. Community colleges work with four-year colleges to make sure that their students' college credits can be transferred.

At this point in time, more than half of all U.S. college students attend community colleges. These colleges attract students who want to get a big bang for their education buck. Many students get associate's degrees with two years of community college education. There are others who transfer to four-year colleges after their two years at a community college. They can earn more money than students with only a high school diploma in either case. All in all, these colleges provide a wonderful thing for students and their communities.

# 19 Run-Ons

© Scott Houston / Sygma / Corbis

## seeing and writing

The picture above shows Barbie dolls dressed for playing basketball. Do you think Barbie is a positive role model for young girls? Why or why not? Look at the picture, and then write a paragraph in which you answer these questions. Try to use the Word Power words in your paragraph.

WORD POWER

**peer pressure** pressure from friends to behave in a way they see as acceptable

**role model** a person who serves as a model of behavior

In this chapter, you will learn

- to recognize two kinds of run-ons—fused sentences and comma splices (19a)
- to correct run-ons in five different ways (19b)

## 19a Recognizing Run-Ons

A **sentence** consists of at least one independent clause—one subject and one verb.

<u>SUBJECT</u>        <u>VERB</u>
The <u>economy</u> <u>has improved</u>.

A **run-on** is an error that occurs when two sentences are joined incorrectly. There are two kinds of run-ons—*fused sentences* and *comma splices*.

A **fused sentence** occurs when two sentences are incorrectly joined without any punctuation.

FUSED SENTENCE    [The economy has improved] [many people still do not have jobs.]

A **comma splice** occurs when two sentences are incorrectly joined with just a comma.

COMMA SPLICE    [The economy has improved], [many people still do not have jobs.]

> **WORD POWER**
>
> **fused** melded together
> **splice** a connection made by joining two ends

> e macmillanhighered.com
> /foundationsfirst
> LearningCurve > Run-On
> Sentences; Additional
> Grammar Exercises >
> Recognizing Run-Ons

### PRACTICE 19-1

Some of the sentences below are correct, but others are run-ons (fused sentences or comma splices). In the blank after each sentence, write *C* if the sentence is correct and *RO* if it is a run-on.

**Example:** *Once upon a Mattress* is playing at the community theater tonight, it is a musical version of the fairy tale "The Princess and the Pea." _____RO_____

1. Miami was founded by a citrus farmer named Julia Tuttle, it is the only major U.S. city founded by a woman. _____

2. Millions of Internet users visit Google each day. _____

3. Halloween is based on an Irish harvest festival, it was introduced in North America by Irish immigrants. _____

4. Eighty million people attended Major League Baseball games last year, many others watched at home. _____

5. Because people always need clean water for drinking, jobs in water treatment plants are quite secure. ———

6. I took just a carry-on bag, I wanted to avoid paying a fee for checked baggage. ———

7. The advice columnists Dear Abby and Ann Landers were identical twins they did not always get along. ———

8. Ice cream is a common dessert in Japan, green tea and red bean are two popular flavors. ———

9. My sister writes science fiction, her stories focus on dystopian societies. ———

10. Howell Peacock was a college basketball coach he was a medical student at the same time. ———

**PRACTICE**

**19-2**   Some of the sentences in the following passage are correct, but others are run-ons (fused sentences or comma splices). In the blank after each sentence, write *C* if the sentence is correct, *FS* if it is a fused sentence, and *CS* if it is a comma splice.

> **Example:**   Imaginary creatures really are imaginary, Bigfoot is not
>
> real. _CS_

(1) The idea of a strange humanlike creature roaming the American Northwest is fascinating, maybe Bigfoot really exists. ——— (2) However, that is very unlikely, it is mainly based on questionable eyewitness reports. ——— (3) Many people have claimed to see this creature it looked like a giant hairy ape walking upright. ——— (4) Of course, some of these claims have gone viral on the Internet, in addition many so-called Bigfoot footprints have been found. ——— (5) The most convincing evidence was a 1967 film it showed a large creature walking upright across a hillside. ——— (6) Not surprisingly, this film was a hoax. ——— (7) An acquaintance of the filmmakers was actually the creature in the film, he was wearing an ape costume. ——— (8) No living Bigfoot has ever been captured, no bones or other remains have ever been uncovered. ——— (9) When evaluating unusual and surprising claims,

it is important to examine hard scientific evidence. _____ (10) In this case, that evidence doesn't exist neither does Bigfoot. _____

**:e** macmillanhighered.com
**/foundationsfirst**
Additional Grammar
Exercises > Correcting
Run-Ons

# 19b Correcting Run-Ons

## FYI

### Correcting Run-Ons

You can correct run-ons in five ways.

1. **Use a period to create two separate sentences.**

   The economy has improved. Many people still do not have jobs.

2. **Use a coordinating conjunction** *(and, but, or, nor, for, so, yet)* **to connect ideas.**

   The economy has improved, but many people still do not have jobs.

3. **Use a semicolon to connect ideas.**

   The economy has improved; still, many people do not have jobs.

4. **Use a semicolon followed by a transitional word or phrase to connect ideas.**

   The economy has improved; however, many people still do not have jobs.

5. **Use a dependent word** *(although, because, when,* and so on) **to connect ideas.**

   Although the economy has improved, many people still do not have jobs.

**1. Use a period to create two separate sentences.** Be sure each sentence begins with a capital letter and ends with a period.

| | |
|---|---|
| **INCORRECT (FUSED SENTENCE)** | Frances Perkins was the first female cabinet member she was President Franklin D. Roosevelt's secretary of labor. |
| **INCORRECT (COMMA SPLICE)** | Frances Perkins was the first female cabinet member, she was President Franklin D. Roosevelt's secretary of labor. |
| **CORRECT (TWO SEPARATE SENTENCES)** | Frances Perkins was the first female cabinet member. She was President Franklin D. Roosevelt's secretary of labor. |

## PRACTICE
**19-3**    Correct each of the following run-ons by using a period to create two separate sentences. Be sure both sentences begin with a capital letter and end with a period.

> **Example:** In 1933, Charles Darrow began selling the board game
> Monopoly/ ~~he~~ adapted this game from several others on the market.
> <small>. He</small>

1. Parker Brothers turned down Darrow's first offer to sell Monopoly, the company has now sold over 250 million games.

2. The race car was voted America's favorite token, other Monopoly tokens include the dog, the hat, and the thimble.

3. Monopoly was recently updated the company asked the public to vote on possible new settings for the game.

4. The original game used locations in Atlantic City the updated version uses landmarks from cities across the country.

5. The old version of Monopoly had railroads on the board, the new version has airports instead.

**2. Use a coordinating conjunction to connect ideas.** If you want to indicate a particular relationship between ideas—for example, a cause-and-effect link or a contrast—use a coordinating conjunction (*and, but, or, nor, for, so,* or *yet*) to connect the ideas. Always place a comma before the coordinating conjunction.

> **INCORRECT**
> **(FUSED SENTENCE)**    "Strange Fruit" is best known as a song performed by Billie Holiday it was originally a poem.
>
> **INCORRECT**
> **(COMMA SPLICE)**    "Strange Fruit" is best known as a song performed by Billie Holiday, it was originally a poem.
>
> **CORRECT**
> **(IDEAS CONNECTED WITH *BUT*)**    "Strange Fruit" is best known as a song performed by Billie Holiday, but it was originally a poem.

## PRACTICE
**19-4**    Correct each of the following run-ons by using a coordinating conjunction (*and, but, or, nor, for, so,* or *yet*) to connect ideas. Be sure to put a comma before each coordinating conjunction.

> **Example:** Most advertisements are found in commercials/ some advertisers use product placement in TV shows and movies.
> <small>, but</small>

1. A company pays a fee, a TV or movie character uses its product onscreen.

2. For example, E.T. ate Reese's Pieces the candy company paid the movie's producers.

3. Car companies want to show off a new model, how do they reach their audience?

4. The automaker paid a fee Will Smith drove an Audi in *I, Robot*.

5. Many people ignore commercials, product placement is hard to miss.

**3. Use a semicolon to connect ideas.** If you want to indicate a close connection—or a strong contrast—between two ideas, use a semicolon.

| | |
|---|---|
| **INCORRECT (FUSED SENTENCE)** | Jhumpa Lahiri is the daughter of immigrants from Calcutta she won the Pulitzer Prize for her first book. |
| **INCORRECT (COMMA SPLICE)** | Jhumpa Lahiri is the daughter of immigrants from Calcutta, she won the Pulitzer Prize for her first book. |
| **CORRECT (IDEAS CONNECTED WITH SEMICOLON)** | Jhumpa Lahiri is the daughter of immigrants from Calcutta; she won the Pulitzer Prize for her first book. |

**PRACTICE**

**19-5**    Correct each of the following run-ons by using a semicolon to connect ideas. Do not use a capital letter after the semicolon unless the word that follows is a proper noun.

**Example:** Energy drinks have become popular among teenagers and young adults; the high levels of caffeine and various additives give them a boost of energy.

1. Caffeine is the primary ingredient in most energy drinks it stimulates the central nervous system and increases alertness.

2. Energy drinks appeal to students and professionals, they need a quick and easy way to fight mental and physical fatigue.

3. Advertisements for energy drinks stress this boost of energy, Red Bull uses the slogan "Red Bull gives you wings."

4. Red Bull owns approximately 40 percent of the energy drink market, large corporations and many smaller companies also sell energy drinks.

5. Some scientists worry about the dangers of consuming energy drinks in one study, drinking Red Bull was shown to raise the risk of heart attack.

**4. Use a semicolon followed by a transitional word or phrase to connect ideas.** To show a specific relationship between two closely related ideas, add a transitional word or phrase after the semicolon.

---

### Some Frequently Used Transitional Words and Phrases

| | | |
|---|---|---|
| as a result | in fact | still |
| finally | moreover | therefore |
| for example | nevertheless | thus |
| however | now | usually |
| in addition | | |

---

**INCORRECT (FUSED SENTENCE)**    The human genome project is very important it may be the most important scientific research of the last hundred years.

**INCORRECT (COMMA SPLICE)**    The human genome project is very important, it may be the most important scientific research of the last hundred years.

**CORRECT (IDEAS CONNECTED WITH SEMICOLON AND *IN FACT*)**    The human genome project is very important; in fact, it may be the most important scientific research of the last hundred years.

WORD POWER

**genome** a complete set of chromosomes and its associated genes

### PRACTICE
### 19-6

Correct each of the following run-ons by using a semicolon, followed by the transitional word or phrase in parentheses, to connect ideas. Be sure to put a comma after the transitional word or phrase.

**Example:**    Theodor Seuss Geisel never received his doctorate<sub>_; however,_</sub> the world knows him by his pen name, "Dr. Seuss." (however)

1. Geisel wrote many of his books as poetry, he illustrated most of his own books. (in addition)

2. He used a small number of words to encourage children to read his publisher made lists of words for Geisel to use. (in fact)

3. *The Cat in the Hat* uses about 220 different words *Green Eggs and Ham* uses only 50 words. (in contrast)

4. Political issues were important to Geisel, *The Lorax* warns readers about the dangers facing the environment. (for example)

5. Geisel died in 1991, Dr. Seuss lives on in books, in movies, in cartoons, and in the musical *Seussical*. (however)

## FYI

### Connecting Ideas with Transitional Words and Phrases

A run-on often occurs when you use a transitional word or phrase to join two sentences but do not include the required punctuation.

| | |
|---|---|
| **INCORRECT (FUSED SENTENCE)** | It is easy to download information from the Internet however it is not always easy to evaluate the information. |
| **INCORRECT (COMMA SPLICE)** | It is easy to download information from the Internet, however it is not always easy to evaluate the information. |

To correct this kind of run-on, put a semicolon before the transitional word or phrase, and put a comma after it.

| | |
|---|---|
| **CORRECT** | It is easy to download information from the Internet; however, it is not always easy to evaluate the information. |

**5. Use a dependent word to connect ideas.** When one idea is dependent on another, you can connect the two ideas by adding a dependent word.

### Some Frequently Used Dependent Words

| | | |
|---|---|---|
| after | eventually | when |
| although | if | which |
| as | then | who |
| because | unless | |
| even though | until | |

| | |
|---|---|
| **INCORRECT (FUSED SENTENCE)** | J. K. Rowling is now the best-selling author of the Harry Potter books not too long ago she was an unemployed single mother. |
| **INCORRECT (COMMA SPLICE)** | J. K. Rowling is now the best-selling author of the Harry Potter books, not too long ago she was an unemployed single mother. |
| **CORRECT (IDEAS CONNECTED WITH *ALTHOUGH*)** | Although J. K. Rowling is now the best-selling author of the Harry Potter books, not too long ago she was an unemployed single mother. |

| INCORRECT (FUSED SENTENCE) | Harry Potter is an orphan he is also a wizard with magical powers. |
|---|---|
| INCORRECT (COMMA SPLICE) | Harry Potter is an orphan, he is also a wizard with magical powers. |
| CORRECT (IDEAS CONNECTED WITH *WHO*) | Harry Potter, who is an orphan, is also a wizard with magical powers. |

## PRACTICE

**19-7** Correct each of the run-ons below in one of the following ways—by creating two separate sentences, by connecting ideas with a comma followed by a coordinating conjunction, by connecting ideas with a semicolon, or by connecting ideas with a semicolon and a transitional word or phrase. Be sure the punctuation is correct. Remember to put a semicolon before, and a comma after, each transitional word or phrase.

**Example:** All over the world, people eat flatbreads, *and* different countries have different kinds.

1. Flatbread is bread that is flat usually it does not contain yeast.

2. One example of a flatbread is the pancake, many Americans eat pancakes with maple syrup.

3. The tortilla is a Mexican flatbread tortillas are made of corn or wheat.

4. A favorite flatbread in the Middle East is the pita, it often has a pocket to be filled with vegetables or meat.

5. Italians eat focaccia, it is similar to pizza crust.

6. Crackers are another kind of flatbread the dough is baked until crisp.

7. Indian cooking has several kinds of flatbreads, all of them are delicious.

8. Matzoh resembles a large, square cracker, it is a traditional food for the Jewish holiday of Passover.

9. Fifty years ago, most people ate only the flatbreads from their native lands, today flatbreads are popular all over the world.

10. Many American grocery stores sell tortillas, pitas, and other flatbreads Americans love flatbread sandwiches.

**PRACTICE**

**19-8** Correct each of the following run-ons (fused sentences and comma splices) by connecting ideas with a dependent word from the list on page 270.

**Examples:** Many call centers are located in Bangalore ~~it~~ $\overset{, which}{}$ is a large city in southern India.

$\overset{Even\ though}{}$ Bangalore call centers have been successful, they have posed some problems for companies, consumers, and workers.

1. Large international companies turned to call centers in Bangalore they wanted to offer their customers less expensive help.

2. U.S. customers have sometimes complained about Indian call center employees they are hard to understand.

3. English is one of the languages of India, Indian English sounds quite different from American English.

4. Many workers in Bangalore call centers go through accent training this aims for a "neutral accent."

5. Of course, accents are not the only obstacle, cultural differences (for example, ideas about what is polite or rude in conversation) may also cause problems.

6. Many call center workers leave, they work for just one or two years.

7. Turnover is high, the work is stressful.

8. The worker finishes a call, he or she gets another call right away.

9. Most shifts are at night, this is daytime in the United States.

10. India is losing some call center jobs these jobs are moving to other countries, such as the Philippines.

**WORD POWER**

**obstacle** something that stands in the way

**PRACTICE**

**19-9** Review the five strategies for correcting run-ons. Then, correct each fused sentence or comma splice below in the way that best indicates the relationship between ideas. Be sure to use appropriate punctuation.

**Example:** Stories about Robin Hood have existed since medieval times$\overset{.\ They}{}$ ~~they~~ tell of a thief living in the king's forest.

1. In modern stories, Robin Hood steals from the rich to give to the poor, in the original stories, Robin Hood keeps what he steals.

2. The original Robin Hood does show kindness to the lower classes, he tells his men not to steal from farmers.

3. The Robin Hood stories refer to specific places, many people think he was a real person.

4. Historians have not yet identified the real Robin Hood, he is lost among hundreds of others with the same name.

5. The name "Robin Hood" was common, it eventually became a nick-name for any outlaw.

## Skills Check

Look back at your response to the Seeing and Writing prompt on page 263. Reread it, and then answer the following questions.

- Have you joined any two sentences without any punctuation?
- Have you joined any two sentences with just a comma?

Correct each run-on you find.

## TEST · Revise · Edit

Starting with TEST, revise your paragraph. Then, edit and proofread your work.

## EDITING PRACTICE

Read the following student paragraph. Then, revise it by carefully correcting each run-on. Be sure to use appropriate punctuation. The first error has been corrected for you.

### Pigeons

To most people, pigeons are an annoyance. Many city parks are full of pigeons; they are also found on building ledges and on monuments. Pigeons soil cars, sidewalks, and buildings, they also have unique abilities. There are several different types of pigeons one of the most interesting, the passenger pigeon, is now extinct. Passenger pigeons were used during wartime they carried messages in capsules attached to their legs. A pigeon named Cher Ami (French for "dear friend") became famous during World War I for saving two hundred American soldiers lost behind enemy lines, he delivered a message identifying their location. A pigeon with similar abilities is the homing pigeon, it will travel hundreds of miles to get back home. No one is sure how these birds find their way perhaps they follow the lines in the earth's magnetic field. Maybe they use the sun and stars maybe they simply use their excellent senses of sight, smell, and hearing. Pigeons have many talents, most people still consider them a nuisance.

## EDITING PRACTICE

Read the following student paragraph. Then, revise it by carefully correcting each run-on. Be sure to use appropriate punctuation. The first error has been corrected for you.

### Stripes

*As old-fashioned*
~~Old-fashioned~~ ideas about prison life are becoming popular again the striped prison uniform is making a comeback. Most American prisons abandoned striped uniforms more than fifty years ago, at the time, wearing stripes was seen as humiliating. However, there is a reason for bringing back striped uniforms. These uniforms can help people identify escaped prisoners. Most people outside of

prisons do not wear jumpsuits with horizontal stripes. Some other popular prison uniforms, however, resemble everyday clothing. Denim is a popular uniform material in prisons, denim blends in too well with clothing worn by people on the street. Orange jumpsuits may be noticeable, they also may look too much like the uniforms worn by some sanitation workers. Escaped prisoners in striped suits are easy to spot, even at night, the stripes are highly visible. Some people still object to striped uniforms they argue that these uniforms are designed to humiliate prisoners. However, in states using striped uniforms, they are popular with voters. Some think prison life is too easy, they want prisoners to be treated more harshly. Only time will tell if striped uniforms will catch on nationwide.

# review checklist

## Run-Ons

- A run-on is an error that occurs when two sentences are incorrectly joined. (See 19a.)

- A fused sentence occurs when two sentences are incorrectly joined without any punctuation. A comma splice occurs when two sentences are incorrectly joined with just a comma. (See 19a.)

- You can correct a run-on in one of five ways.

  - by creating two separate sentences

  - by connecting ideas with a comma followed by a coordinating conjunction

  - by connecting ideas with a semicolon

  - by connecting ideas with a semicolon and a transitional word or phrase

  - by connecting ideas with a dependent word (See 19b.)

# 20 Fragments

© Richard B. Levine / The Image Works

## seeing and writing

The picture above shows people registering to vote. Why do you think many young people don't vote? Look at the picture, and then write a paragraph explaining why you think this situation exists. Try to use the Word Power words in your paragraph.

In this chapter, you will learn

- to recognize fragments (20a)
- to correct missing-subject fragments (20b)
- to correct phrase fragments (20c)
- to correct incomplete-verb fragments (20d)
- to correct infinitive fragments (20e)
- to correct dependent clause fragments (20f)

**PREVIEW**

## 20a  Recognizing Fragments

A **fragment** is an incomplete sentence. Every complete sentence must do the following.

- Every sentence must include at least one subject.
- Every sentence must include at least one verb.
- Every sentence must express a complete thought.

If a group of words does not do *all* these things, it is a fragment and not a sentence—even if it begins with a capital letter and ends with a period.
The following is a complete sentence.

**e macmillanhighered.com
/foundationsfirst**
LearningCurve > Fragments
Additional Grammar
Exercises > Recognizing
Fragments

> SENTENCE  A new U.S. <u>president</u> <u>was elected</u>. (includes both a subject and a verb and expresses a complete thought)

The following groups of words are not sentences.

> FRAGMENT
> (NO VERB)  A new U.S. president. (What point is being made about the president?)
>
> FRAGMENT
> (NO SUBJECT)  Was elected. (Who was elected?)
>
> FRAGMENT
> (INCOMPLETE
> THOUGHT)  When the new U.S. president was elected. (What happened when the new president was elected?)

### PRACTICE

**20-1**  Each of the following items is a fragment because it lacks a subject, a verb, or both. Add any words needed to turn the fragment into a complete sentence.

**Example:**  The sparkling lake.

*The sparkling lake reflected the sunlight.*

_____

1. Eats sunflower seeds for breakfast.

_____

_____

2. A terrible scream.

_____

_____

3. Ate quickly, hoping to win the pie-eating contest.

_____

_____

4. Answered the question.

_____

_____

5. Wore a purple and pink tutu and waved a magic wand.

_____

_____

6. Harold and Sally, the king and queen of the prom.

_____

_____

7. The old house on the hill, dark and empty.

_____

_____

8. The last two pieces of dental floss.

_____

_____

9. Skidded off the road into a ditch.

_____

_____

10. The leaves with their beautiful fall colors.

_____

_____

# FYI

## Identifying Fragments

Fragments almost always appear right next to complete sentences.

┌──── COMPLETE SENTENCE ────┐  ┌──── FRAGMENT ────┐
Okera majored in two subjects. English and philosophy.

You can often correct a fragment by attaching it to an adjacent sentence.

Okera majored in two subjects, English and philosophy.

WORD POWER

**adjacent** next to; adjoining

## PRACTICE

### 20-2

In the paragraph on the following page, some of the numbered groups of words are missing a subject, a verb, or both. First, underline each fragment. Then, decide how each fragment could be attached to an adjacent word group to create a complete new sentence. Finally, rewrite the entire paragraph, using complete sentences, on the lines provided.

**Example:**   John Goodman did the voice of Sully in *Monsters University*. An animated film that also featured the voices of Billy Crystal, Steve Buscemi, and Helen Mirren.

**Rewrite:**   *John Goodman did the voice of Sully in* Monsters University, *an animated film that also featured the voices of Billy Crystal, Steve Buscemi, and Helen Mirren.*

(1) The main characters in most animated movies today. (2) Have the voices of celebrities. (3) Producers cast stars in a film. (4) To bring in a bigger audience. (5) And to increase the movie's chances of financial success. (6) Generally, famous names do not matter to children. (7) But are important to adults. (8) For instance, Johnny Depp fans went to see *Rango* not just to watch a gun-slinging chameleon in action. (9) But also to hear a favorite actor's voice. (10) All in all, celebrity voices help make animated films more popular.

**Rewrite:** _____

_____

_____

_____

_____

## 20b  Missing-Subject Fragments

Every sentence must include a subject and a verb. If the subject is missing, a sentence is incomplete.

In the following example, the first group of words is a sentence. It includes a subject (*I*) and a verb (*had*). However, the second group of words is a fragment. It includes a verb (*worked*) but no subject.

> ┌─── SENTENCE ───┐
> Last summer, I had a job at an amusement park.
> ┌─ FRAGMENT ─┐
> INCORRECT   And also worked at a diner.

The best way to correct this kind of fragment is usually to attach it to the sentence that comes right before it. (This sentence often contains the missing subject.)

> CORRECT   Last summer, I had a job at an amusement park and also worked at a diner.

Another way to correct a missing-subject fragment is to add a new subject.

> CORRECT   Last summer, I had a job at an amusement park. I also worked at a diner.

### PRACTICE
### 20-3

Each of the following items includes a missing-subject fragment. Using one of the two methods explained above, correct each fragment.

**Example:**   Job seekers can expand their opportunities by networking. And also strengthen their résumés by taking classes.

*Job seekers can expand their opportunities by networking. They can also*

*strengthen their résumés by taking classes.*

1. Guide dogs have sweet personalities. And are also true professionals.

   _____

   _____

2. This sports car can accelerate and brake quickly. But can carry only two passengers.

   _____

   _____

3. The concert entertained the audience. And also raised money for charity.

   _____

   _____

4. Honeybees communicate through smell. And also communicate through a special movement called a "waggle dance."

   _____

   _____

5. Walt Disney created the cartoon characters Mickey Mouse and Donald Duck. And also founded Disneyland.

   _____

   _____

6. The blockbuster film attracted huge audiences. But was not praised by critics.

   _____

   _____

7. To meet new friends, some people go to meetups. Or volunteer in their community.

   _____

   _____

8. Tulips grew everywhere. But did not bloom where I had planted them.

_____

_____

9. Social networks are a great place to share good news. But should not be used to complain about friends or coworkers.

_____

_____

10. I bought lunch from a sidewalk vendor. And ate a bowl of cereal for dinner.

_____

_____

## 20c Phrase Fragments

Every sentence must include a subject and a verb. A **phrase** is a group of words that is missing a subject or a verb or both, so it cannot stand alone as a sentence. When you punctuate a phrase as if it is a sentence, you create a fragment.

To correct a phrase fragment, add the words needed to make it a complete sentence. (You will often find these words in an adjacent sentence.)

**INCORRECT**  The horse jumped. ⌐ PHRASE FRAGMENT ¬ Over the fence.

**CORRECT**  The horse jumped over the fence.

**INCORRECT**  We arrived at last. ⌐ PHRASE FRAGMENT ¬ Safe and sound.

**CORRECT**  We arrived at last, safe and sound.

**INCORRECT**  The first *Die Hard* movie had two stars. ⌐ PHRASE FRAGMENT Bruce Willis and Alan Rickman.

**CORRECT**  The first *Die Hard* movie had two stars, Bruce Willis and Alan Rickman.

**INCORRECT**  Sequels have been made for many popular action movies. ⌐ PHRASE FRAGMENT ¬ Such as *Lethal Weapon, Die Hard, Terminator,* and *The Matrix*.

**CORRECT**  Sequels have been made for many popular action movies, such as *Lethal Weapon, Die Hard, Terminator,* and *The Matrix*.

**PRACTICE**

**20-4** Each of the following phrases is a fragment because it lacks a subject, a verb, or both. Correct each fragment by adding any words needed to turn the fragment into a complete sentence.

**Example:** With a loud crash.

*The bookcase fell to the floor with a loud crash.*

_____

1. In a ten-story apartment building.

_____

_____

2. On the ledge outside the window.

_____

_____

3. Happy to be home.

_____

_____

4. At the beginning of football season.

_____

_____

5. Such as a bag of pretzels and a giant bottle of Gatorade.

_____

_____

6. During the announcement.

_____

_____

7. Such as a brand-new washing machine.

_____

_____

8. With a pile of books in her arms.

_____

_____

9. Cold as ice.

_____

_____

10. Along the banks of the river.

_____

_____

## PRACTICE
**20-5** In the following paragraph, some of the numbered groups of words are phrase fragments. First, identify each fragment by labeling it _F_. Then, decide how each fragment could be attached to an adjacent word group to create a complete new sentence. Finally, rewrite the entire paragraph, using complete sentences, on the lines provided.

**Example:** Frida Kahlo was married to fellow artist Diego Rivera.

_____ A mural painter. ___F___

**Rewrite:** _Frida Kahlo was married to fellow artist Diego Rivera, a mural_

_painter._

(1) Mexican artist Frida Kahlo lived and painted. _____ (2) In the first half of the twentieth century. _____ (3) She is famous for her many self-portraits. _____ (4) In these portraits, Kahlo is usually dressed up. _____ (5) In colorful clothes. _____ (6) She is also adorned. _____ (7) With jewelry and flowers. _____ (8) The scenes that surround her are often exotic. _____ (9) With a dreamlike atmosphere. _____ (10) Kahlo's paintings express the reality of her own life. _____ (11) A life of great beauty and great pain. _____

**Rewrite:**

_____

_____

_____

_____

_____

## 20d  Incomplete-Verb Fragments

Every sentence must include a subject and a verb. If the verb is missing or incomplete, a word group is a fragment, not a sentence.

An *-ing* verb, such as *rising*, cannot stand alone in a sentence without a **helping verb** (*is rising*, *was rising*, *were rising*, and so on). When you use an *-ing* verb without a helping verb, you create a fragment.

┌──── FRAGMENT ────┐

**INCORRECT**   The moon was full and round. Rising over the ocean.

The simplest way to correct an *-ing* fragment is usually to attach it to the sentence that comes right before it. (This sentence often includes the missing subject and verb.)

**CORRECT**   The moon was full and round, rising over the ocean.

Another way to correct the fragment is to add a subject and a helping verb.

**CORRECT**   The moon was full and round. It was rising over the ocean.

## FYI

### Incomplete-Verb Fragments with *Being*

The *-ing* verb *being* is often used incorrectly as if it were a complete verb.

**INCORRECT**   I was twenty minutes late for my job interview. The result being that I didn't get the job.

To correct this kind of fragment, substitute a form of the verb *be* that can stand alone in a sentence—for example, *is, was, are,* or *were.*

**CORRECT**   I was twenty minutes late for my job interview. The result was that I didn't get the job.

ⓔ **macmillanhighered.com /foundationsfirst**
Additional Grammar
Exercises > Incomplete
Verb Fragments

### PRACTICE

**20-6**   Each of the following items is an *-ing* fragment. Turn each fragment into a sentence by adding the words needed to complete it. (You can either add a subject and a helping verb or add a new sentence before or after the fragment.)

**Example:**   Driving a new car that runs on hydrogen fuel.

**Revised:**   *My boss is now driving a new car that runs on hydrogen fuel.*

1. Looking for Spanish-language websites. _____

_____

2. Wearing jeans and a T-shirt. _____

_____

3. Living in Phoenix for the summer. _____

_____

4. Telling me not to get a tattoo. _____

_____

5. Always complaining about how much work he has to do. _____

_____

## 20e  Infinitive Fragments

An **infinitive** consists of *to* plus the **base form** of the verb (*to be, to live*). An infinitive is not a complete verb. An infinitive phrase (*to be free, to live happily ever after*) is not a complete sentence because it does not include a subject or a complete verb.

> **INCORRECT**    Sonia decided to leave school. To become a musician.

The simplest way to correct an infinitive fragment is usually to attach it to the sentence that comes right before it. (This sentence often includes the missing subject and verb.)

> **CORRECT**    Sonia decided to leave school to become a musician.

Another way to correct an infinitive fragment is to add a subject and a complete verb.

> **CORRECT**    Sonia decided to leave school. She wanted to become a musician.

### PRACTICE
**20-7**    Each of the following items is an infinitive fragment. Turn each fragment into a complete sentence by adding a subject and a complete verb.

**Example:**   To run the Boston marathon again.

*Bob was determined to run the Boston marathon again.*

1. To enter the karaoke contest.

 

 

2. To become financially independent.

 

 

3. To go where no man has gone before.

 

 

4. To graduate with honors.

 

 

5. To see every movie about zombies.

 

 

## 20f    Dependent Clause Fragments

Every sentence must include a subject and a verb. A sentence must also express a complete thought.

A **dependent clause** is a group of words that is introduced by a dependent word, such as *although, because,* or *after.* A dependent clause includes a subject and a verb, but it does not express a complete thought. Therefore, it cannot stand alone as a sentence.

> FRAGMENT    After Jeanette got a full-time job.

This fragment includes a subject (*Jeanette*) and a complete verb (*got*), but it does not express a complete thought. Readers expect the thought to continue, but it stops short. What happened after Jeanette got a full-time job? Was the result positive or negative? To turn this fragment into a sentence, you need to complete the thought.

> SENTENCE    After Jeanette got a full-time job, she was able to begin paying off her loans.

- Some dependent clauses are introduced by dependent words called **subordinating conjunctions** (*although, because, if,* and so on).

> FRAGMENT    Although many students study French in high school.

This fragment includes a subject (*many students*) and a complete verb (*study*), but it does not express a complete thought.

To correct this kind of fragment, add an **independent clause** (a simple sentence) to complete the thought and finish the sentence.

> SENTENCE    Although many students study French in high school, Spanish is more popular.

■ Other dependent clauses are introduced by dependent words called **relative pronouns** (*who, which, that,* and so on).

FRAGMENT    Marc Anthony, who is Puerto Rican.

FRAGMENT    Zimbabwe, which was called Rhodesia at one time.

FRAGMENT    One habit that has been observed in many overweight children.

Each of the three fragments above includes a subject (*Marc Anthony, Zimbabwe, habit*) and a complete verb (*is, was called, has been observed*). However, they are not sentences because they do not express complete thoughts.

To correct each of these fragments, add the words needed to complete the thought.

SENTENCE    Marc Anthony, who is Puerto Rican, records in both English and Spanish.

SENTENCE    Zimbabwe, which was called Rhodesia at one time, is a country in Africa.

SENTENCE    One habit that has been observed in many overweight children is excessive television viewing.

**PRACTICE**

**20-8**    Correct each of these dependent clause fragments by attaching it to the sentence before or after it. If the dependent clause comes at the beginning of a sentence, place a comma after it.

**Example:**    Although several insects produce silk. Only moth silk is harvested for clothing.

*Although several insects produce silk, only moth silk is harvested for clothing.*

_____

1. Even though a chocolate bar may only have 100 calories. It is not a healthy food.

_____

_____

2. He received a standing ovation. Whenever he performed his comedy routine.

_____

_____

3. Because Adriana's goals were ambitious. She gave herself plenty of time to achieve them.

_____

_____

4. After the scientists analyzed the satellite images. They announced their findings.

_____

_____

5. The college welcomes applications. Until its deadline in December.

_____

_____

**PRACTICE**

**20-9** Turn each of the following dependent clause fragments into a complete sentence by adding a group of words that completes the thought.

**Example:**   Because he wanted to get married.

**Revised:**   _He needed to find a job because he wanted to get married._

_____

1. This young man, who has a very promising future.

Revised: _____

_____

2. After the music had stopped.

Revised: _____

_____

3. A snake that was trying to find water.

Revised: _____

_____

4. Even though hang gliding is a dangerous sport.

Revised: _____

_____

5. Although most people think of themselves as good drivers.

Revised: _____

_____

6. Parents who do not set limits for their children.

Revised: _____

_____

7. Frequent-flier miles, which can sometimes be traded for products as well as for airline tickets.

Revised: _____

_____

8. Whenever Margaret woke up late.

Revised: _____

_____

9. While she searched the crowd frantically.

Revised: _____

_____

10. The mayor, who has raised millions for his campaign.

Revised: _____

_____

**PRACTICE**

**20-10**    All of the following are fragments. Turn each fragment into a complete sentence, and write the revised sentence on the lines below the fragment. Consider different possible revisions for each fragment before you write down your revised sentence.

**Example:**    When a huge bat flew out of the closet.

**Revised:**    *I was just climbing into bed when a huge bat flew out of the closet.*

_____

OR

**Revised:**    *When a huge bat flew out of the closet, I decided to check out of*

*the hotel.*

1. Finding a twenty-dollar bill on the sidewalk.

   Revised: _____

   _____

2. And disappeared without a trace.

   Revised: _____

   _____

3. The tiny plastic ballerina spinning inside the music box.

   Revised: _____

   _____

4. Anyone who has ever worked for tips.

   Revised: _____

   _____

5. The basket, which was filled with exotic tropical fruits.

   Revised: _____

   _____

6. To be banned from the sport for life.

   Revised: _____

   _____

7. But left without his hat or coat.

   Revised: _____

   _____

8. Continuing to play with her toys.

   Revised: _____

   _____

9. Returning to the scene of the crime.

   Revised: _____

   _____

10. Below the surface of the muddy river.

    Revised: _____

potentially major benefits. For the 20 percent of Americans who are disabled and for our society as a whole. What has it accomplished so far? Above all, the ADA has helped change attitudes. Bringing about greater acceptance for people with disabilities. People who otherwise might have been isolated at home. Now graduate from college and work in challenging jobs. The specific effects of the ADA are evident throughout our daily lives. In wheelchair lifts on public buses, curb and building ramps, braille signs, and captioning of TV shows. In addition, colleges may now assign a note taker or allow extra time to complete a test. To give students with disabilities the support they need. However, people with disabilities still face significant barriers. As a result, unemployment rates are still much higher for people with disabilities. Than for other groups. In the future, advances in technology may help. To bring down some of the remaining barriers.

## review checklist

### Fragments

- A fragment is an incomplete sentence. Every sentence must include a subject and a verb and must express a complete thought. (See 20a.)
- Every sentence must include a subject. (See 20b.)
- Phrases cannot stand alone as sentences. (See 20c.)
- Every sentence must include a complete verb. (See 20d and 20e.)
- Dependent clauses cannot stand alone as sentences. (See 20f.)

# 21 Subject-Verb Agreement

© Danita Delimont/Alamy

## seeing and writing

The picture above shows the Mount Rushmore National Memorial in the Black Hills of South Dakota. Look at the picture, and then write a paragraph describing what you see. Use present tense verbs throughout, and try to use the Word Power words in your paragraph.

In this chapter, you will learn
- to understand subject-verb agreement (21a)
- to understand agreement with *be*, *have*, and *do* (21b)
- to understand agreement with compound subjects (21c)
- to understand agreement when words come between the subject and the verb (21d)
- to understand agreement with indefinite pronouns as subjects (21e)
- to understand agreement when the verb comes before the subject (21f)

# 21a Understanding Subject-Verb Agreement

A sentence's subject (a noun or a pronoun) and verb must **agree**: singular subjects take singular verbs, and plural subjects take plural verbs.

Most subject-verb agreement problems occur in the present tense, with third-person singular subjects (*he, she,* and *it*). To form the third-person singular, add *-s* or *-es* to the **base form** of the verb (the present tense form that is used with *I*).

macmillanhighered.com
/foundationsfirst
LearningCurve > Subject-Verb
Agreement; Additional
Grammar Exercises >
Understanding Subject-Verb
Agreement

### Subject-Verb Agreement

|            | SINGULAR        | PLURAL              |
|------------|-----------------|---------------------|
| 1st person | I walk          | Alex and I/we walk  |
| 2nd person | you walk        | you walk            |
| 3rd person | he/she/it walks | they walk           |
|            | the dog walks   | the dogs walk       |
|            | Alex walks      | Alex and Sam walk   |

**PRACTICE**

**21-1** Underline the correct form of the verb in each of the following sentences. Make sure that the verb agrees with the subject.

**Example:** Every Valentine's Day, people (buys/<u>buy</u>) millions of little Conversation Hearts for their sweethearts.

(1) Most people (knows/know) the New England Confectionery Company by the name NECCO. (2) This long-established candy company (makes/make) NECCO Wafers, Sweethearts Conversation Hearts, and Sky Bar Candy Bars, as well as many other sweets. (3) The wafers and hearts (remains/remain) NECCO's best-known products. (4) Year after year, the recipe (stays/stay) the same. (5) As a result, the sugary candies (tastes/taste)

the same as they did 150 years ago. (6) They also (continues/continue) to come in the same colors. (7) Surprisingly, NECCO still (produces/produce) its candy in Massachusetts, where the company was founded in 1847. (8) NECCO regularly develops new products and (updates/update) the sayings on its Conversation Hearts. (9) The playful phrases (continues/continue) to be especially popular on Valentine's Day. (10) As long as Valentine's Day (exists/exist), it seems NECCO will exist as well.

**PRACTICE**

**21-2**   Fill in the blank with the correct present tense form of the verb in parentheses.

**Example:**   Hiroshima's Peace Memorial Park _____*covers*_____ (cover) a large area of city land.

(1) In many ways, present-day Hiroshima, Japan, _____ (seem) like any other busy, modern city. (2) Tall buildings, buses, and crowds _____ (fill) the active downtown. (3) On summer nights, the baseball stadium _____ (roar) with the sounds of excited Hiroshima Carp fans. (4) However, powerful reminders of the past _____ (exist) as well. (5) The Peace Memorial Park and Museum now _____ (stand) where the atomic bomb struck in 1945. (6) The park _____ (contain) dozens of monuments, statues, ponds, and memorials, including the Children's Peace Monument. (7) This monument _____ (honor) Sadako, one of the children who died of leukemia as a result of the bomb's radiation. (8) Every year, schoolchildren _____ (show) their support for world peace by bringing millions of paper cranes to this statue of Sadako. (9) At the other end of the park, the Peace Memorial Museum _____ (provide) information about World War II, the development of the atomic bomb, the bomb's effects, and the peace movement. (10) By maintaining this large memorial park, the people of Hiroshima _____ (hope) to stop a similar event from happening again.

## 21b  *Be*, *Have*, and *Do*

The verbs *be, have,* and *do* form the present tense in special ways. You can avoid problems with these verbs by memorizing their forms.

### Subject-Verb Agreement with *Be*

|  | SINGULAR | PLURAL |
|---|---|---|
| 1st person | I am | we are |
| 2nd person | you are | you are |
| 3rd person | he/she/it is | they are |
|  | Tran is | Tran and Ryan are |
|  | the boy is | the boys are |

### Subject-Verb Agreement with *Have*

|  | SINGULAR | PLURAL |
|---|---|---|
| 1st person | I have | we have |
| 2nd person | you have | you have |
| 3rd person | he/she/it has | they have |
|  | Shana has | Shana and Robert have |
|  | the student has | the students have |

**ie macmillanhighered.com /foundationsfirst**
Additional Grammar
Exercises > Be, Have, and Do

### Subject-Verb Agreement with *Do*

|  | SINGULAR | PLURAL |
|---|---|---|
| 1st person | I do | we do |
| 2nd person | you do | you do |
| 3rd person | he/she/it does | they do |
|  | Ken does | Ken and Mia do |
|  | the book does | the books do |

**PRACTICE**

**21-3**   Fill in the blank with the correct present tense form of the verb *be*.

**Example:**   The Tour de France _____*is*_____ a popular bicycle race.

1. Every July, the Tour de France _____ broadcast all over the world.

2. The Tour de France _____ the world's largest annual sporting event.

3. The winner of the race _____ the person with the shortest overall time.

4. Teams that compete in the race _____ mostly professional.

5. Most cyclists who race in the Tour _____ slim and light, but the Swedish rider Magnus Backstedt, the heaviest cyclist, weighed 208 pounds.

### PRACTICE
**21-4**  Fill in the blank with the correct present tense form of the verb *have*.

**Example:**  You ___*have*___ to be cautious when shopping for a used car.

1. An educated car shopper _____ a better chance of getting a high-quality vehicle.

2. The car salespeople _____ their own interests in mind.

3. For this reason, buyers _____ to look out for themselves.

4. Fortunately, the Internet _____ a lot to offer people who want to buy a used car.

5. Many sites _____ customer reviews of the best used cars.

### PRACTICE
**21-5**  Fill in the blank with the correct present tense form of the verb *do*.

**Example:**  Therapy animals ___*do*___ many different kinds of community-service work.

1. For example, many dogs _____ important work in hospitals.

2. Animals _____ not do their work alone, of course.

3. A person _____ therapy along with the animal.

4. First, you _____ an evaluation to make sure the animal is a good candidate.

5. Other animals besides dogs _____ therapy as well.

**PRACTICE
21-6**    Fill in the blank with the correct present tense form of the verb *be, have,* or *do.*

**Example:**   All over the world, soccer _____*is*_____ (be) a popular sport.

(1) Soccer _____ (do) not have the popularity in the United States that it _____ (have) in most other places, but the World Cup _____ (have) more and more U.S. fans every year. (2) The World Cup _____ (be) the most important international soccer tournament. (3) Like Olympic events, World Cup matches _____ (be) contests between countries, and fans _____ (have) a patriotic loyalty to their teams. (4) To make its country proud, a team _____ (do) its best to win. (5) The United States _____ (have) men's and women's soccer teams that play in the World Cup. (6) When our teams _____ (do) well, we _____ (be) interested in the tournament. (7) Fortunately, our teams _____ (be) internationally competitive. (8) The women _____ (do) particularly well. (9) The U.S. women's team _____ (be) almost always one of the top four teams in the world. (10) They _____ (have) first-place trophies from both the 1991 and 1999 World Cups.

macmillanhighered.com
/foundationsfirst
LearningCurve > Subject-Verb
Agreement; Additional
Grammar Exercises >
Compound Subjects

# 21c  Compound Subjects

The subject of a sentence is not always a single word. It can also be a **compound subject**, which consists of two or more words connected by *and* or *or*. To avoid agreement problems with compound subjects, follow these rules.

■ When the parts of a compound subject are connected by *and*, use a plural verb.

Every day, <u>Sarah and Tom</u> <u>drive</u> to school.

■ When the parts of a compound subject are connected by *or*, the verb agrees with the word that is closer to it. If the word closer to the verb is singular, use a singular verb. If the word closer to the verb is plural, use a plural verb.

Every day, <u>Sarah or her friends</u> <u>drive</u> to school.

Every day, <u>her friends or Sarah</u> <u>drives</u> to school.

**PRACTICE 21-7**  Underline the correct verb in each of the following sentences.

**Example:**  My sisters or my mother (mows/mow) the lawn every weekend.

1. Bag lunches and carpools (is/are) good ways to save money.

2. A Republican or a Democrat always (wins/win) the presidential election.

3. Rosa Parks and Martin Luther King Jr. (continues/continue) to be honored for their roles in the Montgomery bus boycott of 1955–1956.

4. As the experience of Pete Rose illustrates, if a baseball player or coaches (bets/bet) on their own sport, they will be banned from the game.

5. In the documentary *Country Boys*, Appalachian teenagers Chris and Cody (struggles/struggle) to overcome their difficult childhoods.

## 21d  Phrases between Subject and Verb

Do not be confused if a **prepositional phrase** (a phrase that begins with *of, in, between,* and so on) comes between the sentence's subject and verb. These words do not affect subject-verb agreement.

A box of chocolates makes a very good gift.

High levels of radon occur in some houses.

An easy way to identify the subject of a sentence is to cross out the prepositional phrase.

A box of chocolates makes a very good gift.

High levels of radon occur in some houses.

macmillanhighered.com /foundationsfirst
LearningCurve > Subject-Verb Agreement; Additional Grammar Exercises > Phrase between Subject and Verb

## FYI

### Phrases between Subject and Verb

Watch out for phrases that begin with *as well as, in addition to,* or *along with*. A noun or pronoun that is part of such a phrase cannot be the subject of a sentence.

The mayor, as well as members of the city council, supports the pay increase. (*Mayor, not members, is the subject.*)

**PRACTICE**

**21-8**　In each of the following sentences, cross out the prepositional phrase that separates the subject and the verb. Then, underline the simple subject of the sentence once and the verb that agrees with the subject twice.

**Example:**　Some <u>people</u> ~~in China~~ (commutes/<u><u>commute</u></u>) by bicycle.

1. Often, a resident of one of China's cities (travels/travel) a long distance to work.

2. Westerners in China (expects/expect) to see many bicycles.

3. A black bicycle (is/are) no longer a common sight in China.

4. The streets in large cities like Beijing (has/have) bicycle lanes.

5. Today, the economy of China (is/are) booming.

6. Chinese citizens with high-paying jobs (is/are) not likely to commute by bicycle.

7. A worker with a long commute (does/do) not want to spend hours bicycling to work.

8. A bus, as well as private cars, (pollutes/pollute) the air.

9. Many Chinese people under age thirty (does/do) not even know how to ride a bicycle.

10. A Chinese store with a stock of bicycles (rents/rent) the old-fashioned black ones, mainly to tourists.

# 21e　Indefinite Pronoun Subjects

Most **indefinite pronouns**—*anybody, everyone,* and so on—are singular and take singular verbs.

<u>Everyone</u> <u><u>likes</u></u> ice cream.

<u>Each</u> of the boys <u><u>carries</u></u> a beeper.

<u>Neither</u> of the boys <u><u>misses</u></u> class.

<u>Nobody</u> <u><u>wants</u></u> to see the team lose.

> ### Singular Indefinite Pronouns
>
> | | | | |
> |---|---|---|---|
> | anybody | either | neither | one |
> | anyone | everybody | no one | somebody |
> | anything | everyone | nobody | someone |
> | each | everything | nothing | something |

However, some indefinite pronouns—*many, several, few, both, others*—are plural and take plural verbs.

Few <u><u>watch</u></u> the nightly news on television.

Many <u><u>get</u></u> their news from the Internet.

**PRACTICE
21-9**   Underline the correct verb in each of the following sentences.

**Example:**   After a year in AmeriCorps, everybody (<u>receives</u>/receive) a small grant to help pay for college or graduate school.

(1) To become an AmeriCorps volunteer, one (has/have) to make a pledge to "get things done" for America. (2) Everyone in this service organization (joins/join) because of a desire to help others. (3) Each of the volunteers (makes/make) a commitment to serve for ten to twelve months. (4) Many (spends/spend) their year of service teaching, tutoring, or mentoring. (5) Others (chooses/choose) to work on improving public health or the environment. (6) Everything (is/are) funded by the government's Corporation for National and Community Service. (7) Almost anybody (is/are) eligible to apply to be an AmeriCorps volunteer. (8) To be considered, somebody (needs/need) only to be seventeen or older and a lawful resident of the United States. (9) Something about this organization (inspires/inspire) hope and determination in people. (10) Few (regrets/regret) the decision to become an AmeriCorps volunteer.

## 21f Verbs before Subjects

A verb agrees with its subject even if it comes *before* the subject, as it does in questions.

$$\overset{\text{V}}{\text{Where is}} \text{ the } \overset{\text{S}}{\underline{\text{ATM}}}?$$

$$\overset{\text{V}}{\text{Where are}} \overset{\text{S}}{\underline{\text{Zack and Angela}}}?$$

$$\text{Why } \overset{\text{V}}{\underline{\text{are}}} \overset{\text{S}}{\underline{\text{they}}} \text{ running?}$$

If you have trouble identifying the subject, answer the question with a statement.

$$\overset{\text{V}}{\text{Where is}} \text{ the } \overset{\text{S}}{\underline{\text{ATM}}}? \text{ The } \overset{\text{S}}{\underline{\text{ATM}}} \overset{\text{V}}{\underline{\text{is}}} \text{ inside the bank.}$$

**e** macmillanhighered.com
/foundationsfirst
LearningCurve > Subject-Verb
Agreement; Additional
Grammar Exercises > Verbs
before Subjects

# FYI

### *There is* and *There are*

When a sentence begins with *there is* or *there are*, the word *there* is not the subject of the sentence. The subject comes after the form of the verb *be*.

$$\text{There } \overset{\text{V}}{\underline{\text{is}}} \text{ still one } \overset{\text{S}}{\underline{\text{ticket}}} \text{ available for the playoffs.}$$

$$\text{There } \overset{\text{V}}{\underline{\text{are}}} \text{ still ten } \overset{\text{S}}{\underline{\text{tickets}}} \text{ available for the playoffs.}$$

**PRACTICE**

**21-10** First, underline the simple subject of each sentence. Then, circle the correct form of the verb.

**Example:** What (is/are) your reasons for applying to this college?

1. There (is/are) an excellent nursing program here.

2. What (does/do) the students here usually like best about the school?

3. What (has/have) been the most popular major in the last five years?

4. There (is/are) more people taking business courses today than there were twenty years ago.

5. How many years (does/do) an average student take to graduate?

# Skills Check

Look back at your response to the Seeing and Writing prompt on page 295. Reread it, and complete the following tasks.

- Underline every subject once.
- Underline every verb twice.

If you spot a subject-verb agreement error, cross out the incorrect verb form, and write the correct form above the line.

# TEST · Revise · Edit

Starting with TEST, revise your paragraph. Then, edit and proofread your work.

## EDITING PRACTICE

Read the following student paragraph. If the underlined verb does not agree with its subject, cross out the verb, and write in the correct form. If it does agree, write *C* above the verb. The first sentence has been done for you.

Great Smoky Mountains National Park

            *C*
The United States has fifty-nine national parks. The largest park is Alaska's Wrangell–St. Elias National Park and Preserve, but the most visited park are Great Smoky Mountains National Park, in Tennessee and North Carolina. There is many reasons why this park attract people. It run along the beautiful Great Smoky Mountains, the Appalachian Trail go through it, and it supports thousands of species of wildlife. Because it maintain more than thirty-one species of salamanders, some people call the park "the salamander capital of the world." Visitors to the park enjoys many different activities. Some likes to hike, others enjoy fishing, and many does nothing but relaxes and sightsee. Children have fun visiting the historic buildings that is preserved in the park's most popular attraction, Cades Cove. Unfortunately, like many natural areas, the park have a problem with air pollution. Another environmental issue are the loss of hemlock trees that provides shade over streams. As shade disappear, water temperatures rises, and this endangers the different species that depends on cooler water, such as salamanders.

## EDITING PRACTICE

Read the following student paragraph. If the underlined verb does not agree with its subject, cross out the verb, and write in the correct form. If it does, write *C* above the verb. The first sentence has been done for you.

Credit Card Debt

          *C*
Although it is one of the most expensive ways to be in debt, many people in this country carries a large credit-card balance. The average credit-card interest rate is almost 16 percent. This kind of debt often develops before we

realize it <u>are</u> happening. Despite our best efforts, balances <u>creep</u> upward. The problem <u>is</u> that the companies that <u>issues</u> credit cards <u>make</u> them very easy to get. Once people <u>has</u> credit cards, it <u>is</u> easy for them to spend more than they <u>should</u>. Most companies <u>offers</u> benefits for using their cards. Some companies <u>gives</u> clients free airfare or merchandise when they <u>spend</u> a certain amount. Either points or a small payment <u>get</u> you the benefits. Sometimes we <u>forget</u>, however, that the credit-card companies <u>wants</u> to keep us in debt. Too many people <u>falls</u> into this trap, but there <u>is</u> ways to prevent it from happening. First, everyone <u>need</u> to learn how credit-card companies <u>makes</u> their money. For example, the minimum payment <u>is</u> often not much more than the interest owed on the balance. By paying just the minimum, users never <u>gets</u> out of debt even if they <u>pay</u> their bills. If we <u>want</u> to use credit cards, we <u>needs</u> to take the time to read the rules.

# review checklist

## Subject-Verb Agreement

- Singular subjects (nouns and pronouns) take singular verbs, and plural subjects take plural verbs. (See 21a.)

- The irregular verbs *be*, *have*, and *do* often present problems with subject-verb agreement in the present tense. (See 21b.)

- Compound subjects can cause problems in agreement. (See 21c.)

- Words that come between the subject and the verb do not affect subject-verb agreement. (See 21d.)

- Most indefinite pronouns, such as *no one* and *everyone*, are singular and take a singular verb when they serve as the subject of the sentence. (See 21e.)

- A verb agrees with its subject even if the verb comes before the subject. (See 21f.)

# 22 Illogical Shifts

© Syracuse Newspapers / The Image Works

## seeing and writing

The picture above shows a female soldier. Look at the picture, and then write a paragraph in which you consider whether or not women should serve as front-line combat troops. Consider both sides of the issue before you write your paragraph. Try to use the Word Power words in your paragraph.

**In this chapter, you will learn**
- to avoid illogical shifts in tense (22a)
- to avoid illogical shifts in person (22b)
- to avoid illogical shifts in voice (22c)

A **shift** occurs whenever a writer changes *tense*, *person*, or *voice* in a sentence or a paragraph. As you write and revise, make sure that any shifts you make are **logical**—that is, that they occur for a reason.

**LOGICAL SHIFT IN TENSE**   In high school, I just wanted to have fun, but now I want to become a graphic artist. (shift in tense indicates that the writer's attitude has changed)

# 22a  Shifts in Tense

**Tense** is the form a verb takes to show when an action took place or a situation occurred. The three basic tenses are *past*, *present*, and *future*. An **illogical shift in tense** occurs when a writer shifts from one tense to another for no good reason.

**ILLOGICAL SHIFT**   We sat at the table for more than an hour before a server comes and takes our order. (shift from past tense to present tense)

**REVISED**   We sat at the table for more than an hour before a server came and took our order. (consistent use of past tense)

**e** macmillanhighered.com
/foundationsfirst
LearningCurve > Shifts;
Additional Grammar
Exercises > Shifts in Tense

**PRACTICE**

**22-1**   Underline the verbs in the following sentences. Then, correct any illogical shifts in tense by rewriting the verb in the correct tense above the line. If a sentence is correct, write *C* in the blank after the sentence.

**Examples**

                                                          *was*
Nelson Mandela <u>died</u> in 2013 when he ~~is~~ ninety-five. _____
                                                          ∧

When I <u>started</u> college, I <u>took</u> out several student loans, and now I <u>have</u>

to pay them back. ___*C*___

1. After Eduardo worked on his car, we go on a road trip together. _____

2. People are now able to discuss their hobbies online if they choose.

   _____

3. We told her not to eat the cookies, but she eats them anyway. _____

4. Anthony and Alexis took a vacation before the baby arrives. _____

5. In 1994, hotel manager Paul Rusesabagina saved over a thousand people when he shelters Tutsi refugees at his hotel in Rwanda. _____

6. Your teacher told me that you receive the highest grade in the class last semester. _____

7. Megan wanted to help people, so she became a public defender. _____

8. Before I scheduled the meeting, I review my notes. _____

9. A small road ran through this town before they build the highway.

_____

10. Yesterday, I had biology lab, and today I have play rehearsal. _____

## 22b Shifts in Person

**Person** is the form a pronoun takes to indicate who is speaking, spoken about, or spoken to.

### Person

|  | SINGULAR | PLURAL |
|---|---|---|
| 1st person | I | we |
| 2nd person | you | you |
| 3rd person | he, she, it | they |

An **illogical shift in person** occurs when a writer shifts from one person to another for no clear reason.

ILLOGICAL SHIFT    Before someone gets a job in the computer industry, you have to take a lot of courses. (shift from third person to second person)

REVISED    Before someone gets a job in the computer industry, he or she has to take a lot of courses. (consistent use of third person)

ILLOGICAL SHIFT    The students were told that you had to attend a conference each week. (shift from third person to second person)

REVISED    The students were told that they had to attend a conference each week. (consistent use of third person plural)

macmillanhighered.com
/foundationsfirst
LearningCurve > Shifts;
Additional Grammar
Exercises > Shifts in Person

**PRACTICE**

**22-2**   Correct any illogical shifts in person in the following sentences. If necessary, change any verbs that do not agree with the new subjects. If a sentence is correct, write *C* in the blank.

**Example:**   I stopped at the computer store because ~~you~~ could recycle
                                                        ^I^

empty printer cartridges there. _____

1. Some people may decide not to buy a Toyota because you can buy a similar Hyundai for less money. _____

2. Students can learn Spanish by taking a class, but you can also learn Spanish by listening to CDs. _____

3. Before you buy an airline ticket, you should compare prices by checking several websites. _____

4. Kyra worked on an assembly line where you could not spend more than thirty seconds on each task. _____

5. Brian said that he bought all his furniture on eBay. _____

6. When someone prepares a stir-fry, you have to prepare all the ingredients before starting to cook. _____

7. The instructor informed his students that you should proofread carefully. _____

8. Even though Patrick is careful with his personal information, he is still afraid of identity theft. _____

9. Most people know that they can buy inexpensive furniture at a Salvation Army store. _____

10. Scientists tell us that you can suffer bone loss if I do not have enough calcium in your diet. _____

## 22c   Shifts in Voice

macmillanhighered.com /foundationsfirst
LearningCurve > Shifts; Additional Grammar Exercises > Shifts in Voice

**Voice** is the form a verb takes to indicate whether the subject is acting or is acted upon.

When a sentence is in the **active voice**, the subject *performs* the action. When a sentence is in the **passive voice**, the subject *receives* the action—that is, it is acted upon.

ACTIVE VOICE    Pablo Neruda <u>won</u> the Nobel Prize in literature in 1971.

PASSIVE VOICE   The Nobel Prize in literature <u>was won</u> by Pablo Neruda in 1971.

An **illogical shift in voice** occurs when a writer shifts from active to passive voice or from passive to active voice for no good reason.

ILLOGICAL SHIFT   The jazz musician John Coltrane <u>played</u> the tenor sax, and the soprano sax <u>was</u> also <u>played</u> by him. (active to passive)

REVISED   The jazz musician John Coltrane <u>played</u> the tenor sax, and he also <u>played</u> the soprano sax. (consistent use of active voice)

ILLOGICAL SHIFT   *Fences* <u>was written</u> by August Wilson, and he also <u>wrote</u> *The Piano Lesson*. (passive to active)

REVISED   August Wilson <u>wrote</u> *Fences*, and he also <u>wrote</u> *The Piano Lesson*. (consistent use of active voice)

# FYI

## Changing from Passive to Active Voice

You should use the active voice in most of your college writing because it is stronger and more direct than the passive voice. To change a sentence from passive to active voice, determine who or what performs the action, and make this noun the subject of this new sentence.

PASSIVE VOICE   Three world <u>records</u> in track <u>were set</u> by Jesse Owens in a single day. (Jesse Owens performed the action.)

ACTIVE VOICE   Jesse Owens <u>set</u> three world records in track in a single day.

### PRACTICE
### 22-3

Correct any illogical shifts in voice in the following sentences, using active voice wherever possible. Change any verb that does not agree with its new subject. If a sentence is correct, write *C* in the blank.

**Example:**   Whenever that song comes on the radio, ~~I am made~~ happy. ^it makes me^

~~by it.~~ _____

1. The sandwich special was ordered by Anna, and Dave ordered the chef's salad. _____

2. Although they all know English, Portuguese is spoken by them at home. _____

3. In 1910, Camp Fire Girls was founded by Luther Gulick, and the organization still exists today. _____

4. Because the essay was written by Jeremy, it has few mistakes.
   _____

5. The Kingdom of Lesotho does have a king, but the country is governed
   by the prime minister. _____

6. Whenever we give my dad a present, he always pretends he likes it.
   _____

7. Camouflage is worn by soldiers and hunters so that they blend in with
   their surroundings. _____

8. The judges could not decide, so the prize was given by them to both
   skaters. _____

9. A settlement was discussed by the lawyers, but the defendant refused
   it. _____

10. Many young people do not vote, and most politicians want that to
    change. _____

## Skills Check

Look back at your response to the Seeing and Writing prompt on page
308. Reread it, and underline every verb twice. Then, answer the following questions.

- Can you identify any illogical shifts in tense?
- Can you identify any illogical shifts in person?
- Can you identify any illogical shifts in voice?

Cross out any illogical shifts, and write the correct forms above them.

## TEST · Revise · Edit

Starting with TEST, revise your paragraph. Then, edit and proofread
your work.

## EDITING PRACTICE

Read the following student paragraph, which contains illogical shifts in tense, person, and voice. Then, edit the paragraph to correct the illogical shifts, making sure subjects and verbs agree. The first sentence has been edited for you.

Graphic Novels

    Today, many people are reading graphic novels, and ~~we~~ *they* are taking them more seriously than ever before. Graphic novels are book-length comics, and classic comic techniques are used by graphic novelists. These artists tell all kinds of complex stories through their illustrated panels. For example, in his books *Maus* and *Maus II*, Art Spiegelman writes about the Holocaust and told his father's story of survival. In *Persepolis* and *Persepolis 2*, Marjane Satrapi tells the story of her childhood in Iran in the 1970s and 1980s when the country was gripped by the Islamic Revolution. Although these writers focus on real events, others focused on their own invented worlds. For instance, many people love Frank Miller's *Sin City* series because you feel as if you are in a world of shadowy streets. Another favorite graphic novelist who creates alternate realities is Alan Moore; his books included *Watchmen*, *V for Vendetta*, and the *League of Extraordinary Gentlemen* series. As more and more people read these books and discover that they are not just comics, more attention and respect are gained by graphic novels. And, as readers acknowledge the importance of these books, you are beginning to see graphic novels as required reading.

## EDITING PRACTICE

Read the following student paragraph, which contains illogical shifts in tense, person, and voice. Then, edit the paragraph to correct the illogical shifts, making sure subjects and verbs agree. The first sentence has been edited for you.

Taboo Topics

People meeting for the first time should avoid certain topics, especially

*first impressions make*

because a strong impact ~~is made by first impressions.~~ Taboo topics vary across

cultures, so people who travel need to be particularly aware of what you should

not say. In the United States, experts agree on general topics to avoid, although

some specifics are disagreed on by them. Topics to avoid include money, politics,

religion, sex, death, health issues, and family problems. For example, people can

ask a new acquaintance about work, but you should not ask about salary. Politics

and religion are obvious danger areas. After all, people have definite political

views, and their strong religious beliefs are held by many people. Sex is too

intimate a topic. Many first dates became last dates when one person makes

sexual remarks. Death and health and family matters are also often too intimate.

On making a casual reference to such matters, people might touch a nerve you do

not know about. For example, someone might make a joke about death and then

finds out that a new acquaintance's mother is dying. Fortunately, people who

avoid taboo topics will find that they still have a lot to talk about when meeting

someone for the first time.

## review checklist

### Illogical Shifts

- An illogical shift in tense occurs when a writer shifts from one verb tense to another for no apparent reason. (See 22a.)

- An illogical shift in person occurs when a writer shifts from one person to another for no apparent reason. (See 22b.)

- An illogical shift in voice occurs when a writer shifts from active to passive voice or from passive to active voice for no apparent reason. (See 22c.)

# 23 Dangling and Misplaced Modifiers

**The Bernsteins**

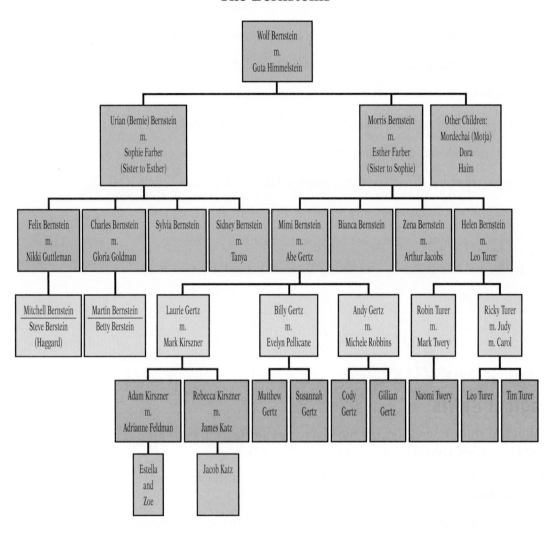

Laurie Kirszner

# seeing and writing

The diagram above shows a family tree. Look at the picture, and then write a paragraph in which you tell a story from your own family's history. If possible, discuss the significance this story has for your family. Try to use the Word Power words in your paragraph.

A **modifier** is a word (or word group) that identifies or describes another word in a sentence. To avoid confusion, a modifier should be placed as close as possible to the noun or pronoun it modifies—ideally, directly before or directly after it.

<u>Holding on tightly</u>, the movers lifted the piano. (The *-ing* modifier describes *the movers.*)

<u>Shocked by the verdict</u>, the lawyer said she would appeal. (The *-ed* modifier describes *the lawyer.*)

WORD POWER

**modify** to describe, limit, or qualify

## 23a Correcting Dangling Modifiers

A **dangling modifier** "dangles" because the word it is supposed to modify does not appear in the sentence. Often, a dangling modifier comes at the beginning of a sentence and seems to modify the word that follows it. Look at the following sentence.

DANGLING MODIFIER    <u>Working overtime</u>, my salary almost doubled.

In the sentence above, the modifier *working overtime* seems to be modifying *salary*. But this makes no sense. How can salary work overtime? Here is a correct sentence.

REVISED    <u>Working overtime</u>, I almost doubled my salary.

As the example above illustrates, the easiest way to correct a dangling modifier is to supply the word (a noun or pronoun) that the dangling modifier should actually modify. Here are some other examples.

macmillanhighered.com
/foundationsfirst
Additional Grammar
Exercises > Identifying
Dangling Modifiers

DANGLING MODIFIER    <u>Living in England</u>, a collection of poems was published. (Did the poetry collection live in England?)

REVISED    <u>Living in England</u>, Robert Frost published a collection of poems.

DANGLING MODIFIER    <u>Distracted by my cell phone</u>, my car almost drove off the road. (Did the phone distract the car?)

REVISED    <u>Distracted by my cell phone</u>, I almost drove my car off the road.

**PRACTICE**

**23-1**   Each of the following sentences contains a dangling modifier. Correct each sentence by adding a noun or pronoun to which the modifier can logically refer.

**Example:**   Watching from the bleachers, my daughter hit a home run.

*Watching from the bleachers, I saw my daughter hit a home run.*

_____

1. Coming home from a long day of mowing lawns, an ice cream cone sounded perfect.

   _____

   _____

2. Following the recipe, the cake was easy to make.

   _____

   _____

3. Convinced by friends to leave her current job, a new job was found in two weeks.

   _____

   _____

4. Wanting to buy a home in 1935, a Sears mail-order house was thought to be the best choice.

   _____

   _____

5. Working full-time at the coffee shop, my homework did not always get finished.

   _____

   _____

6. Talking on his cell phone, the staircase was blocked.

   _____

   _____

7. Honoring the animals that pulled pioneer wagons across the West, the mule was declared Missouri's state animal in 1995.

   _____

   _____

8. Reading the eyewitness accounts, the weaknesses in the prosecutor's argument were obvious.

_____

_____

9. Working for several months as a hotel desk clerk, her ability to deal calmly with unhappy customers had improved greatly.

_____

_____

10. Responding to complaints from students, the rules about cell phones in the classroom were changed.

_____

_____

**PRACTICE**

**23-2**  Complete the following sentences, making sure to include a noun or pronoun to which each modifier can logically refer.

**Example:**  Begging for forgiveness, *Kate's husband swore that he would*

*never again forget their wedding anniversary.*

1. Frightened out of her wits, _____

_____

2. Seeing a strange object fall to earth, _____

_____

3. Thinking that he must be dreaming, _____

_____

4. Jumping into the deep end of the pool, _____

_____

5. Kissing the sleeping princess, _____

_____

6. Alerted by sounds from the next room, _____

_____

7. Slamming down the cover of her laptop, _____

_____

8. Finishing the assignment early, ⎯⎯⎯⎯⎯⎯⎯⎯⎯⎯⎯

⎯⎯⎯⎯⎯⎯⎯⎯⎯⎯⎯⎯⎯⎯⎯⎯⎯⎯⎯⎯⎯⎯⎯⎯⎯⎯

9. Stopped for speeding, ⎯⎯⎯⎯⎯⎯⎯⎯⎯⎯⎯⎯⎯⎯⎯

⎯⎯⎯⎯⎯⎯⎯⎯⎯⎯⎯⎯⎯⎯⎯⎯⎯⎯⎯⎯⎯⎯⎯⎯⎯⎯

10. Changing the oil every six thousand miles, ⎯⎯⎯⎯⎯⎯

⎯⎯⎯⎯⎯⎯⎯⎯⎯⎯⎯⎯⎯⎯⎯⎯⎯⎯⎯⎯⎯⎯⎯⎯⎯⎯

## 23b Correcting Misplaced Modifiers

**macmillanhighered.com
/foundationsfirst**
Additional Grammar
Exercises > Identifying
Misplaced Modifiers

Ideally, a modifier should come right before or right after the word it modifies. A **misplaced modifier** appears to modify the wrong word because it is placed incorrectly in the sentence. To correct this problem, move the modifier so that it is as close as possible to the word it is supposed to modify.

MISPLACED
MODIFIER
I ran to the window wearing my bathrobe. (Was the window wearing the bathrobe?)

REVISED
Wearing my bathrobe, I ran to the window.

MISPLACED
MODIFIER
The dog ran down the street frightened by the noise. (Was the street frightened by the noise?)

REVISED
Frightened by the noise, the dog ran down the street.

### PRACTICE
### 23-3
Rewrite the following sentences, which contain misplaced modifiers, so that each modifier clearly refers to the word it is supposed to modify.

**Example:** Splashing in a cool mud bath, Mr. Phelps scratched the back of the prize pig.

*Mr. Phelps scratched the back of the prize pig splashing in a cool mud bath.*

⎯⎯⎯⎯⎯⎯⎯⎯⎯⎯⎯⎯⎯⎯⎯⎯⎯⎯⎯⎯⎯⎯⎯⎯⎯⎯

1. Bucking wildly, the rodeo rider was thrown by the angry bull.

⎯⎯⎯⎯⎯⎯⎯⎯⎯⎯⎯⎯⎯⎯⎯⎯⎯⎯⎯⎯⎯⎯⎯⎯⎯⎯

⎯⎯⎯⎯⎯⎯⎯⎯⎯⎯⎯⎯⎯⎯⎯⎯⎯⎯⎯⎯⎯⎯⎯⎯⎯⎯

2. The trick-or-treaters rang every doorbell carrying enormous bags of candy.

_____

_____

3. Blushing furiously, the bathroom door was quickly closed by Henry.

_____

_____

4. Attracted to the bright light, the candles were surrounded by moths.

_____

_____

5. A car is not likely to be damaged by rust parked in a garage.

_____

_____

6. Suffering from a headache, the exam was too much for Stacey.

_____

_____

7. Chasing a Frisbee, the football field was quickly crossed by the Labrador retriever.

_____

_____

8. Starved after a climb up the mountain, the food that was meant to last two days was devoured by the hikers.

_____

_____

9. Walking to the park, a rainstorm soaked Max.

_____

_____

10. The horse won the race covered with a blanket of roses.

_____

The History of Popcorn

*Most*

~~Usually eaten in a movie theater, most~~ Americans do not think much about

*, usually eaten in a movie theater.* ^

popcorn/ However, popcorn has a long and interesting history. Popcorn is a truly

American food. Exploring a cave in New Mexico, ears of popping corn more than

five thousand years old were found. Arriving from Europe, native peoples offered

to sell popcorn to Columbus and his crew. In addition, transported by the native

Americans, the Pilgrims ate popcorn at the first Thanksgiving. Liking this local

food, popcorn was eaten as a breakfast food by early English colonists. By the

nineteenth century, street vendors sold popcorn from pushcarts. Sold in movie

theaters, movies were soon associated with popcorn. The popularity of the fluffy

white snack continued through the Great Depression. Arriving in the 1940s, the

movie business was hurt by television, and people ate less popcorn. However,

things soon changed. Preparing their favorite snack at home, popcorn was made

popular again. In the 1950s, people made popcorn in pots on the stove. In the

1960s, popcorn was made in prepackaged foil pans that puffed up as the popcorn

popped. Today, popcorn is made in the microwave. Popped in a microwave, in a

prepackaged container, or in a pot on the stove, Americans today like to eat

popcorn while they watch TV. Wherever they eat it, most Americans are unaware

of the long history of popcorn.

# review checklist

## Dangling and Misplaced Modifiers

Correct a dangling modifier by supplying a word to which the dangling modifier can logically refer. (See 23a.)

Avoid misplaced modifiers by placing modifiers as close as possible to the words they modify. (See 23b.)

Read the following student essay, which includes some common sentence problems. Revise any incorrect sentences to eliminate run-ons, fragments, errors in subject-verb agreement, illogical shifts, and dangling and misplaced modifiers. The first sentence has been edited for you.

### No-Glove Softball

Softball was invented in Chicago in 1887 *when* some football fans got together. To hear the score of a game between their teams. Waiting inside on a cold Thanksgiving Day, the time passed slowly. They decided to entertain themselves by playing baseball. They used a broomstick for a bat, and a tied-up boxing glove was used for a ball. Today, everyone know about softball, and many plays the game at school, in leagues, or at picnics. However, few is aware of how it was originally played.

The first softball was called a "mush ball" or a "cabbage ball." The reason for this name being that it was 16 inches around and soft. Fielders did not need gloves, and catchers do not need special protective equipment. The softness of the balls were one reason for the game's popularity in the 1930s. During the Depression, people wanted to play sports. However, expensive equipment were not an option. People liked no-glove softball because it required just a ball and a bat. Also, surrounded by homes and streets, the game could be played in small parks. A ball was not likely to land in the street or break a window that was so large and soft.

People enjoyed playing the new game, they also enjoyed watching it. The Windy City League was established in Chicago, no-glove softball fans were thrilled. They could now watch the best players compete. The League built stadiums and admission was charged for games. The number of fans at these games were astounding. Sometimes exceeding the number at Cubs or White Sox games.

Over time, softball became more like baseball. The ball shrank. To its current size of 10 or 12 inches around. A smaller ball could go farther, the outfield was expanded. In addition, gloves and catcher's gear was added. However, many people still play no-glove softball who like the simplicity of the old-style game. New Orleans and Chicago has the most players.

In 1995, 16-inch softball became a lettered sport in Chicago high schools. Requiring skill but not size, many students are attracted to the game. A student is too small to make the football or basketball teams, he or she can still excel at 16-inch softball. These varsity players are part of a long history in Chicago. In 2009, several Chicago businesses funded a park. Filled with sculptures and plaques to memorialize the heroes of the game's past.

# 24 Verbs: Past Tense

MAN
ON THE
MOON

NASA

## seeing and writing

The picture above shows astronaut Neil Armstrong planting the American flag on the moon in 1969. Select a newsworthy event that occurred during your lifetime, and write a one-paragraph news story about it. Include a headline, and be sure to use the past tense. Try to use the Word Power words in your paragraph.

**In this chapter, you will learn**

- to understand regular verbs in the past tense (24a)
- to understand irregular verbs in the past tense (24b)
- to deal with problem verbs in the past tense (24c and 24d)

**Tense** is the form a verb takes to show when an action or situation takes place. The **past tense** indicates that an action happened in the past.

## 24a Regular Verbs

**Regular verbs** form the past tense by adding -*d* or -*ed* to the **base form** of the verb (the present tense form of the verb that is used with *I*).

# FYI

### Regular Verbs in the Past Tense

- Most regular verbs form the past tense by adding -*d* or -*ed* to the base form of the verb.

  I <u>edited</u> my paper.

  Last summer they <u>biked</u> through northern California.

- Regular verbs that end in -*y* form the past tense by changing the *y* to *i* and adding -*ed*.

  try        tried

  vary        varied

macmillanhighered.com /foundationsfirst

LearningCurve > Verbs: Past Tense; Additional Grammar Exercises > Regular Verbs

**PRACTICE**

**24-1** Some of the verbs in the following sentences are in the present tense, and some are in the past tense. First, underline the verb in each sentence. Then, on the line after each sentence, write *present* if the verb is present tense and *past* if the verb is past tense.

**Examples**

The design of the French flag <u>influenced</u> the design of the Italian flag.

_____past_____

President Obama <u>owns</u> boxing gloves autographed by Muhammad Ali.

   *present*

1. My grandmother showed us how to sprinkle pepper at the door to prevent ants from entering. _____

2. The Mall of America employs about 12,000 people. _____

3. Unfortunately, late payments on rent and utilities lower your credit score. _____

4. Deaf students at Gallaudet University invented the football huddle.

   _____

5. Many small libraries allow people to order books from a larger regional collection. _____

6. I talked to an adviser about my career plans. _____

7. Dairy cows named Mooley Wooley and Miss Wayne lived at the White House during the Taft administration. _____

8. The real estate agent recommended that we paint our walls white to make the rooms seem larger. _____

9. General Robert E. Lee surrendered to General Ulysses S. Grant on April 9, 1865. _____

10. The last known Tasmanian tiger died in captivity in 1936. _____

**PRACTICE**

**24-2** Change the present tense verbs in the following passage to past tense. Cross out the present tense form of each underlined verb, and write the past tense form above it.

**Example:**  Before the existence of the Food and Drug Administration,

                       *regulated*

        very few laws ~~regulate~~ the sale of medicines.

          ^

(1) The Food and Drug Administration <u>start</u> in an interesting way. (2) In the nineteenth century, Chinese workers <u>help</u> to build the transcontinental railroad across the United States. (3) When they <u>experience</u> joint pain, they <u>rub</u> on snake oil. (4) Salesmen for other pain medications <u>claim</u> that it <u>seems</u> ridiculous to use worthless substances like snake oil. (5) Soon people <u>use</u> the term *snake oil* to mean any medicine with

mysterious ingredients that <u>seem</u> to work miracles. (6) In 1906, after the use of poisonous medicines <u>result</u> in some fatalities, President Theodore Roosevelt <u>signs</u> a law that <u>creates</u> a government bureau with the power to regulate medicines. (7) In 1930, this bureau <u>becomes</u> the Food and Drug Administration (FDA). (8) In the 1930s, more fatalities <u>occur</u>. (9) As a result, the FDA <u>receives</u> more power from President Franklin Delano Roosevelt. (10) The FDA's power <u>increases</u> again in 1962 after pregnant women's use of the drug thalidomide <u>causes</u> serious birth defects in babies.

## 24b Irregular Verbs

Unlike regular verbs, **irregular verbs** do not form the past tense by adding -*d* or -*ed*. Instead, they use special irregular past tense forms that may look very different from their present tense forms.

The chart that follows lists the base forms and the past tense forms of the most common irregular verbs.

**macmillanhighered.com /foundationsfirst**
LearningCurve > Verbs: Past Tense; Additional Grammar Exercises > Irregular Verbs

### Irregular Verbs in the Past Tense

| BASE FORM | PAST TENSE | BASE FORM | PAST TENSE |
|---|---|---|---|
| awake | awoke | fall | fell |
| be | was, were | feed | fed |
| become | became | feel | felt |
| begin | began | fight | fought |
| bet | bet | find | found |
| bite | bit | fly | flew |
| blow | blew | forgive | forgave |
| break | broke | freeze | froze |
| bring | brought | get | got |
| build | built | give | gave |
| buy | bought | go | went |
| catch | caught | grow | grew |
| choose | chose | have | had |
| come | came | hear | heard |
| cost | cost | hide | hid |
| cut | cut | hold | held |
| dive | dove, dived | hurt | hurt |
| do | did | keep | kept |
| draw | drew | know | knew |
| drink | drank | lay (to place) | laid |
| drive | drove | lead | led |
| eat | ate | leave | left |

| BASE FORM | PAST TENSE | BASE FORM | PAST TENSE |
|---|---|---|---|
| let | let | sleep | slept |
| lie (to recline) | lay | speak | spoke |
| light | lit | spend | spent |
| lose | lost | spring | sprang |
| make | made | stand | stood |
| meet | met | steal | stole |
| pay | paid | stick | stuck |
| quit | quit | sting | stung |
| read | read | swear | swore |
| ride | rode | swim | swam |
| ring | rang | take | took |
| rise | rose | teach | taught |
| run | ran | tear | tore |
| say | said | tell | told |
| see | saw | think | thought |
| sell | sold | throw | threw |
| send | sent | understand | understood |
| set | set | wake | woke, waked |
| shake | shook | wear | wore |
| shine | shone, shined | win | won |
| sing | sang | write | wrote |
| sit | sat | | |

**PRACTICE**

**24-3**  Use the list of irregular verbs above to help find the correct past tense forms of the irregular verb in parentheses. Then, write the correct form in the space provided.

**Example:** The defendant _____*swore*_____ (swear) that he had never entered the room.

1. Alan _____ (know) the answer even before the teacher finished asking the question.

2. I accidentally _____ (leave) my cat behind when I moved out of my old apartment.

3. The river _____ (freeze) early last year because it was unusually cold.

4. She _____ (teach) her son to play the piano as soon as he was old enough to sit on the bench and reach the keys.

5. Huyn _____ (find) a silver bracelet under her chair at the restaurant.

**PRACTICE**

**24-4** In the following passage, fill in the correct past tense form of the irregular verb in parentheses. Refer to the list of irregular verbs on pages 332–33.

> **Example:** In 2006, the WNBA ____*chose*____ (choose) its All-Decade Team, a true dream team.

(1) The Women's National Basketball League (WNBA) _____ (begin) in 1997. (2) In its first season, the WNBA _____ (have) eight teams, a number that _____ (rise) and then _____ (fall) over the years; it currently has twelve teams. (3) From the start, as a women's professional sports league, the WNBA _____ (be) more than just another league. (4) It _____ (give) the top women college basketball players a chance to play, and these women _____ (become) role models for young girls interested in sports. (5) The Houston Comets _____ (win) the first WNBA championship. (6) In the years that followed, one team after another rose to dominance and captured the imagination of fans. (7) In 2007, ESPN _____ (make) an agreement with the league to pay the teams for rights to show the games; this agreement has been extended through 2022. (8) Also, a new generation of players, including Candace Parker and Maya Moore, _____ (come) to the game and _____ (bring) their own brand of thrills. (9) These younger players also _____ (set) new records and helped raise the level of WNBA play. (10) Many people _____ (think) the WNBA would never last, and while its future is not guaranteed, the league is almost twenty years old and still going strong.

## 24c Problem Verbs: *Be*

The irregular verb *be* can cause problems for writers because it has two different past tense forms—*was* for singular subjects and *were* for plural subjects. The only way to make certain that you use these forms correctly is to memorize them.

Jackie <u>was</u> interested in becoming a physical therapist. (singular)

The <u>plants</u> <u>were</u> harmless to human beings but poisonous to animals. (plural)

---

### Past Tense Forms of the Verb *Be*

| | SINGULAR | PLURAL |
|---|---|---|
| 1st person | I <u>was</u> tired. | We <u>were</u> tired. |
| 2nd person | You <u>were</u> tired. | You <u>were</u> tired. |
| 3rd person | He <u>was</u> tired. | |
| | She <u>was</u> tired. | They <u>were</u> tired. |
| | It <u>was</u> tired. | |

---

### PRACTICE

**24-5**  In each of the following sentences, circle the correct form of the verb *be*.

macmillanhighered.com /foundationsfirst Additional Grammar Exercises > Problem Verbs: Be

**Example:**  The toy fire engine (was/were) surprisingly loud.

1. Julio (was/were) thrilled to win a freshman honors scholarship.

2. The contestants (was/were) told to eat as many hot dogs as they could in five minutes.

3. I (was/were) determined not to complain during the difficult hike.

4. The Sears Tower (was/were) renamed Willis Tower in 2009.

5. Engineering students across the country (was/were) challenged to design a car that blind people could someday drive.

6. We (was/were) the first on our street to install solar panels.

7. The children (was/were) fascinated by the kites that flew overhead.

8. Roberto (was/were) the best goalkeeper in our league.

9. You (was/were) still carving your pumpkin when the first trick-or-treaters arrived.

10. My watch (was/were) programmed to measure the distance I ran.

### PRACTICE

**24-6**  Edit the following passage for errors in the use of the verb *be*. Cross out any underlined verbs that are incorrect, and write the correct forms above them. If a verb form is correct, label it *C*.

**Example:**   In 1947, the House Un-American Activities Committee (HUAC) began questioning people in the movie industry who ~~was~~ *were* suspected of being Communists.

(1) HUAC's investigation of Hollywood was one result of the fear of Communism that defined the Cold War between the United States and the Soviet Union. (2) HUAC were concerned that Communists were using films to spread their ideas. (3) Many people in the Hollywood community was called to testify in front of HUAC. (4) Several Hollywood stars, including actors Humphrey Bogart and Lauren Bacall, were so angered by this treatment that they flew to Washington to protest the investigation. (5) Despite their objections, the members of HUAC was determined to continue their questioning. (6) Ten of the people questioned refused to say whether they were Communists; instead of answering, they read statements claiming that the investigation was unconstitutional. (7) These people, later named "The Hollywood Ten," was sent to jail for contempt of Congress. (8) Other suspected Communists in the film industry were blacklisted, which meant they was not allowed to work in the industry. (9) Some blacklisted screenwriters used false names and was able to continue making movies. (10) The blacklist was not broken until 1960, when Dalton Trumbo, the blacklisted screenwriter of the movie *Spartacus,* were publicly acknowledged.

## 24d   Problem Verbs: *Can/Could* and *Will/Would*

The helping verbs *can/could* and *will/would* can cause problems for writers because their past tense forms are sometimes confused with their present tense forms.

macmillanhighered.com
/foundationsfirst
Additional Grammar
Exercises > Problem Verbs:
Can/Could and Will/Would

### *Can/Could*

*Can,* a present tense verb, means "is able to" or "are able to." *Could,* the past tense of *can,* means "was able to" or "were able to."

Students can use the copy machines in the library.

Columbus told the queen he could find a short route to India.

*Could* is also used to express a possibility or a wish.

The president wishes he could balance the budget.

## Will/Would

*Will*, a present tense verb, talks about the future from a point in the present. *Would*, the past tense of *will*, talks about the future from a point in the past.

I will finish writing the report tomorrow.

Last week, I told my boss that I would work an extra shift today.

*Would* is also used to express a possibility or a wish.

If we moved to the country, we would be able to have a garden.

Felicia would like to buy a new car.

# FYI

## *Can/Could* and *Will/Would*

*Can/could* and *will/would* never change form, no matter what the subject is.

I can/he can/they can

I could/he could/they could

I will/he will/they will

I would/he would/they would

**PRACTICE**

**24-7**   In each of the following sentences, circle the correct form of the helping verb.

**Example:**   When I was in high school, I (can/could) run a six-minute mile.

1. If you get lost, this map and compass (will/would) help you find your way home.

2. Marisol (can/could) remember the name of every video game she has ever played.

3. When Kim was pregnant, she (can/could) not fit into any of my jeans.

4. I wish my company (will/would) pay for more of my courses.

5. Kevin (can/could) get his degree in May if he completes all his spring classes.

**PRACTICE 24-8**    In the following paragraph, circle the correct form of the helping verb from the choices in parentheses.

**Example:**  In a survey, many Facebook users reported that they (will/(would)) use Facebook if they were bored.

(1) Today, Facebook has over 1 billion users, probably because it (can/could) help people meet two basic needs. (2) First, users (can/could) present themselves the way they want; second, they (can/could) feel a sense of belonging. (3) Of course, if you asked people why they used Facebook, not many (will/would) give these two reasons. (4) Instead, they (will/would) say something like "to let my friends know what I'm doing" or "to see what my friends were up to." (5) Facebook users (will/would) sometimes find that using Facebook (can/could) have negative effects. (6) For example, a user who checked up on friends (can/could) learn that he or she wasn't invited to a party. (7) Psychologists (will/would) like to find out when Facebook use makes people happy or unhappy. (8) Some psychologists wonder if a major factor (can/could) be active use versus passive use of Facebook. (9) If people posted something or "liked" something, they (will/would) be using Facebook actively. (10) However, if people only read other people's Facebook pages without doing anything, they (will/would) be using Facebook passively. (11) According to studies, when people use Facebook actively, they (will/would) probably feel good, but when they use it passively, they (will/would) probably feel lonely.

## Skills Check

Look back at your response to the Seeing and Writing prompt on page 329. Reread it, and complete the following tasks.

- Underline every past tense verb you have used.
- Check to make sure that you have used the correct past tense form in each case.

Cross out any incorrect forms, and write the correct form above the line.

## TEST · Revise · Edit

Starting with TEST, revise your paragraph. Then, edit and proofread your work.

## EDITING PRACTICE

Read the following student paragraph, which contains errors in past tense verb forms, and decide whether each of the underlined past tense verbs is correct. If the verb is correct, write *C* above it. If it is not, cross out the verb, and write the correct past tense form. The first error has been corrected for you. (If necessary, consult the list of irregular verbs on pp. 332–33.)

### Crazy Horse

Crazy Horse <u>was</u> [*C*] the greatest Sioux leader. He <u>was</u> [*C*] someone who ~~want~~ [*wanted*] to preserve Sioux traditions and ways of life. Along with other chiefs, such as Sitting Bull and Red Cloud, Crazy Horse <u>resist</u> the invasion of white settlers. For many years, he successfully <u>defended</u> the Black Hills and <u>keeped</u> them from U.S. military control. The American government <u>want</u> to move the Sioux to a reservation. However, Crazy Horse <u>knew</u> that the government could not be trusted, and he <u>fight</u> hard to keep his people on their land. Crazy Horse <u>won</u> many battles. His most famous victory <u>were</u> over General George Custer. In 1876, Crazy Horse <u>meeted</u> Custer at the Battle of Little Bighorn. Custer <u>plan</u> to surprise Sitting Bull at his camp next to the Little Bighorn River. However, Custer was not <u>prepared</u> for what he <u>encounter</u>, and Crazy Horse and Sitting Bull <u>wipe</u> out his entire unit. After defeating Custer, Crazy Horse <u>continued</u> to fight the U.S. Army, but less than a year after the Battle of Little Bighorn, Crazy Horse <u>surrender</u> to the army. The Sioux finally <u>agree</u> to move to a reservation. Then, shortly after the army <u>moved</u> him and his people to a reservation, Crazy Horse <u>were</u> arrested. The army <u>accuse</u> him of planning a revolt, and once they <u>had</u> him in custody, they <u>kill</u> him. Many people <u>thinked</u> Crazy Horse was a hero because he <u>defended</u> his people and <u>sticked</u> to his beliefs. To honor him, a huge memorial was proposed in 1948. The Native Americans who commissioned the sculpture <u>wanted</u> everyone to know about their hero.

## review checklist

### Verbs: Past Tense

- The past tense of a verb indicates that an action happened in the past. (See 24a.)

- Regular verbs form the past tense by adding either -*d* or -*ed* to the base form of the verb. (See 24a.)

- Irregular verbs have irregular forms in the past tense. (See 24b.)

- *Be* is the only verb in English that has two different forms in the past tense—one for singular and one for plural. (See 24c.)

- *Could* is the past tense of *can*. *Would* is the past tense of *will*. (See 24d.)

# 25 Verbs: Past Participles

AP Photo/John Minchillo

## seeing and writing

The picture above shows a winner at the Nathan's Hot Dog Eating Contest in Coney Island. Look at the picture, and then write a paragraph about something you really wanted to achieve and finally did. Explain whether you now believe the goal you achieved was worth the struggle. Try to use the Word Power words in your paragraph.

In this chapter, you will learn

- to identify regular past participles (25a)
- to identify irregular past participles (25b)
- to use the present perfect tense (25c)
- to use the past perfect tense (25d)
- to use past participles as adjectives (25e)

## 25a Regular Past Participles

Every verb has a **past participle** form. The past participle form of a *regular verb* is the same as the past tense form. Both are formed by adding *-d* or *-ed* to the base form of the verb (the present tense form of the verb used with *I*).

macmillanhighered.com
/foundationsfirst
LearningCurve > Verbs:
The Past and Perfect
Tenses; Additional Grammar
Exercises > Regular Past
Participles

PAST TENSE

He wondered.

PAST PARTICIPLE

He has wondered.

Combined with a helping verb, such as *has* or *had*, past participles form the **present perfect** and **past perfect** tenses.

HELPING VERB    PAST PARTICIPLE

PRESENT PERFECT TENSE    She has repaired her own car for years.

HELPING VERB    PAST PARTICIPLE

PAST PERFECT TENSE    She told him that she had repaired her own car.

In the examples above, note that the past participle always has the same form: *She has repaired*/*She had repaired*; only the helping verb changes form to agree with the subject.

### PRACTICE

**25-1** Below are the base forms of ten regular verbs. In the spaces, write the appropriate present tense form, past tense form, and past participle form.

**Example**
shout

*present:* She ___*shouts*___ every day.

*past:* They ___*shouted*___ yesterday at the game.

*past participle:* I have always ___*shouted*___ too much.

1. agree

   *present:* He always _____ with me.

   *past:* We _____ yesterday.

   *past participle:* They had _____ before the summit meeting.

2. love

   *present:* She _____ her new iPod.

   *past:* You _____ those cupcakes last week.

   *past participle:* He has _____ her for years.

3. drop

   *present:* He always _____ the ball.

   *past:* I _____ that course last semester.

   *past participle:* She has always _____ the children off at day care before work.

4. cry

   *present:* The baby _____ every night.

   *past:* He _____ when she left.

   *past participle:* He had also _____ the night before.

5. work

   *present:* It _____ every time.

   *past:* I _____ the late shift last year.

   *past participle:* You have _____ since you were fourteen years old.

**PRACTICE**

**25-2**   Fill in the correct past participle form of each verb in parentheses.

**Example:**   An energetic and engaging performer, Cuban singer Celia Cruz had ___*gained*___ (gain) the devotion of fans all over the world.

1. By the time she died in 2003, Celia Cruz had _____ (live) in the United States for more than forty years.

2. She had _____ (start) her career in Cuba, where she was one of her country's biggest stars.

3. She had _____ (escape) to the United States in 1959, fleeing the Communist regime in Cuba.

4. Cruz had always _____ (refuse) to return to Cuba as long as Castro was in power.

5. Over the years, her many recordings have _____ (help) to make her music popular in Europe as well as in the United States.

6. Because of her singing, many people around the world have _____ (learn) to love salsa music.

7. Her music has also _____ (inspire) many young Latina singers.

8. By the time of her death at the age of seventy-nine, Celia Cruz had _____ (record) more than seventy albums.

9. She had also _____ (earn) many awards, including five Grammys, two Latin Grammys, three honorary doctorates, and a National Medal of Arts.

10. For her many contributions to Latin music, she had also _____ (acquire) the title "The Queen of Salsa."

## 25b  Irregular Past Participles

*Irregular verbs* do not form the past participle by adding *-d* or *-ed* to the base form of the verb. Verbs that are irregular in the past tense nearly always have irregular past participle forms.

macmillanhighered.com
/foundationsfirst
LearningCurve > Verbs:
The Past and Perfect
Tenses; Additional Grammar
Exercises > Irregular Past
Participles

| BASE FORM | PAST TENSE | PAST PARTICIPLE |
|-----------|-----------|-----------------|
| choose | chose | chosen |
| sing | sang | sung |
| wear | wore | worn |

The following chart lists the base form, the past tense form, and the past participle of the most common irregular verbs.

## Irregular Past Participles

| BASE FORM | PAST TENSE | PAST PARTICIPLE |
| --- | --- | --- |
| awake | awoke | awoken |
| be (am, are) | was, were | been |
| beat | beat | beaten |
| become | became | become |
| begin | began | begun |
| bet | bet | bet |
| bite | bit | bitten |
| blow | blew | blown |
| break | broke | broken |
| bring | brought | brought |
| build | built | built |
| buy | bought | bought |
| catch | caught | caught |
| choose | chose | chosen |
| come | came | come |
| cost | cost | cost |
| cut | cut | cut |
| dive | dove, dived | dived |
| do | did | done |
| draw | drew | drawn |
| drink | drank | drunk |
| drive | drove | driven |
| eat | ate | eaten |
| fall | fell | fallen |
| feed | fed | fed |
| feel | felt | felt |
| fight | fought | fought |
| find | found | found |
| fly | flew | flown |
| forgive | forgave | forgiven |
| freeze | froze | frozen |
| get | got | got, gotten |
| give | gave | given |
| go | went | gone |
| grow | grew | grown |
| have | had | had |
| hear | heard | heard |
| hide | hid | hidden |
| hold | held | held |
| hurt | hurt | hurt |
| keep | kept | kept |
| know | knew | known |
| lay (to place) | laid | laid |
| lead | led | led |
| leave | left | left |

| BASE FORM | PAST TENSE | PAST PARTICIPLE |
|---|---|---|
| let | let | let |
| lie (to recline) | lay | lain |
| light | lit | lit |
| lose | lost | lost |
| make | made | made |
| meet | met | met |
| pay | paid | paid |
| put | put | put |
| quit | quit | quit |
| read | read | read |
| ride | rode | ridden |
| ring | rang | rung |
| rise | rose | risen |
| run | ran | run |
| say | said | said |
| see | saw | seen |
| sell | sold | sold |
| send | sent | sent |
| set | set | set |
| shake | shook | shaken |
| shine | shone, shined | shone, shined |
| sing | sang | sung |
| sit | sat | sat |
| sleep | slept | slept |
| speak | spoke | spoken |
| spend | spent | spent |
| spread | spread | spread |
| spring | sprang | sprung |
| stand | stood | stood |
| steal | stole | stolen |
| stick | stuck | stuck |
| sting | stung | stung |
| swear | swore | sworn |
| swim | swam | swum |
| take | took | taken |
| teach | taught | taught |
| tear | tore | torn |
| tell | told | told |
| think | thought | thought |
| throw | threw | thrown |
| understand | understood | understood |
| wake | woke, waked | woken, waked |
| wear | wore | worn |
| win | won | won |
| write | wrote | written |

**PRACTICE**

**25-3**　Below are the base forms of ten irregular verbs. In the spaces after each verb, write the appropriate present tense form, past tense form, and past participle form. If necessary, refer to the chart on pages 346–47.

**Example**

sleep

*present:* He _____*sleeps*_____ late every Sunday morning.

*past:* Until she was three years old, she _____*slept*_____ in a crib.

*past participle:* The dog has _____*slept*_____ on our bed since he was a small puppy.

1. take

   *present:* She _____ cream in her coffee.

   *past:* The hospital emergency room _____ more patients than it could handle.

   *past participle:* It has _____ three months to straighten out my credit score.

2. say

   *present:* Walter _____ he knows how to ski, but I'm not sure I believe him.

   *past:* The teacher _____ we had to write all our answers in complete sentences.

   *past participle:* Until this year, every graduation speaker had _____ that we graduates were the hope of the future.

3. spend

   *present:* I _____ more and more on gas every week.

   *past:* Last year, the United States _____ hundreds of millions of dollars on AIDS prevention and treatment.

   *past participle:* Because they had _____ more than they earned for several years, they had to declare bankruptcy.

4. read

   *present:* She _____ three newspapers every day.

*past:* She _____ in the paper that state legislators voted themselves a raise.

*past participle:* He has already _____ most of the books for the course.

5. choose

*present:* Every Sunday, the minister _____ a subject for the sermon.

*past:* They _____ the best players for the All-Star team.

*past participle:* He had _____ an engagement ring before he proposed, but his girlfriend didn't like it.

**PRACTICE**

**25-4**   Fill in the correct past participle form of each irregular verb in parentheses below. Refer to the chart on pages 346–47 as needed.

**Example:**   The popularity of karaoke has ___*spread*___ (spread) over the past twenty years.

(1) Karaoke, formerly a primarily Asian pastime, has _____ (become) very popular worldwide. (2) Karaoke, which means "empty orchestra" in Japanese, has _____ (grow) with the many advances in technology since its invention in the 1960s. (3) There has _____ (be) disagreement about who invented the first karaoke machine, but it was most likely Japanese musician Daisuke Inoue in 1971. (4) Although it has been a common pastime in Japan since the 1970s, karaoke has only _____ (become) popular in the United States in the last two decades. (5) As more songs have become available for karaoke systems, the karaoke bar has _____ (catch) on as a fun destination. (6) A game where players choose a song at random and then must sing it has _____ (come) to be known as "Kamikazi Karaoke." (7) Karaoke has _____ (take) various forms in the United States, including live karaoke with a band and private karaoke done in spaces rented by the hour. (8) Portland, Oregon, has _____ (hold) the unofficial title of "karaoke capital of

the U.S." for several years. (9) "Angels," a song by the British pop singer Robbie Williams, has _____ (break) the world record for most people singing karaoke. (10) Despite its popularity, some people think that karaoke has reached its peak and has _____ (begin) to decline.

## 25c The Present Perfect Tense

The **present perfect tense** consists of the present tense of the helping verb *have* plus the past participle.

macmillanhighered.com
/foundationsfirst
LearningCurve > The Past and
Perfect Tenses; Additional
Grammar Exercises > The
Present Perfect Tense

### The Present Perfect Tense (*have* or *has* + past participle)

| SINGULAR | PLURAL |
| --- | --- |
| I have gained. | We have gained. |
| You have gained. | You have gained. |
| He has gained. | They have gained. |
| She has gained. | |
| It has gained. | |

■ Use the present perfect tense to indicate that an action began in the past and continues into the present.

> PRESENT PERFECT TENSE    The Gallup poll has predicted elections since the 1930s. (*The predicting began in the past and continues into the present.*)

■ Use the present perfect tense to indicate that an action has just occurred.

> PRESENT PERFECT TENSE    I have just voted. (*The voting has just now occurred.*)

### PRACTICE
**25-5** In the following paragraph, form the present perfect tense by filling in the correct form of *have* and the correct past participle form of the verb in parentheses.

**Example:** The invention of the cochlear implant ___*has*___ ___*given*___ (give) many deaf people the chance to get back some of their hearing.

(1) The cochlear implant, an electronic device that is surgically implanted in the inner ear, _____ _____ (be) available since the 1980s. (2) Although an implant cannot fully bring back a person's hearing, it _____ _____ (make) it easier for some people to function in the hearing world. (3) People who _____ _____ (choose) to get cochlear implants can usually hear well enough to use a telephone. (4) Children who get the implants early enough _____ _____ (be) able to learn to speak. (5) However, this device _____ _____ (cause) a heated debate within the deaf community. (6) Many deaf people _____ _____ (speak) out against cochlear implants. (7) They are proud of their deafness and feel that they _____ _____ (lead) full and satisfying lives using American Sign Language (ASL) as their main means of communication. (8) They think that cochlear implants _____ _____ (hurt) deaf culture. (9) So, although some people _____ _____ (welcome) cochlear implants, others have not. (10) The invention of this device _____ _____ (cause) more controversy than anyone ever thought possible.

**PRACTICE**

**25-6** Circle the appropriate verb tense (past tense or present perfect) from the choices in parentheses.

**Example:** In 2012, massive open online courses (MOOCs) (received/ have received) wide attention for the first time.

(1) MOOCs (became/have become) a popular trend in education. (2) The earliest forerunners of MOOCs (were/have been) correspondence courses, which (emerged/have emerged) in the nineteenth century. (3) When radio broadcasts (became/have become) popular, colleges (offered/have offered) courses over the radio. (4) Later, people (took/have taken) television courses. (5) In the 1990s, computers and the Internet (gave/have given) distance learning a boost. (6) Since then, many students (earned/ have earned) undergraduate and graduate degrees by taking courses in "distance education" degree programs. (7) Stephen Downes and George

Siemens (taught/have taught) the first MOOC in 2008, and MOOCs (expanded/have expanded) rapidly since then. (8) From their beginning to the present, MOOCs (developed/have developed) characteristics that set them apart from other types of distance learning. (9) Most notably, MOOCs (became/have become) massive, with thousands of students taking courses over the Internet. (10) In 2012, a Stanford University MOOC on artificial intelligence (attracted/has attracted) more then 160,000 students in 190 countries, and a current MOOC on computer programming (had/has had) the largest enrollment to date: more than 300,000 students.

## 25d The Past Perfect Tense

The **past perfect tense** consists of the past tense of the helping verb *have* plus the past participle.

**e** macmillanhighered.com
/foundationsfirst
LearningCurve > Verbs:
The Past and Perfect Tenses;
Additional Grammar
Exercises > The Past
Perfect Tense

### The Past Perfect Tense (*had* + past participle)

| SINGULAR | PLURAL |
|---|---|
| I had returned. | We had returned. |
| You had returned. | You had returned. |
| He had returned. | They had returned. |
| She had returned. | |
| It had returned. | |

Use the past perfect tense to indicate that one past action occurred before another past action.

PAST                 PAST PERFECT

**PAST PERFECT
TENSE**   The job applicant told the receptionist that he had arrived. *(The job applicant arrived at the interview before he talked to the receptionist.)*

**PRACTICE
25-7**   Circle the appropriate verb tense (present perfect or past perfect) from the choices in parentheses.

**Example:** Many states (have established)/had established) restrictions on secretly recording conversations, but they (have passed)/had passed) no laws against hidden cameras.

1. The American Civil Liberties Union (ACLU) (has argued/had argued) that hidden cameras in public places are an invasion of privacy.

2. During the 1990s, surveillance cameras were bulky, and it was obvious where they (has been/had been) installed in stores and on the street.

3. More recently, cameras (have shrunk/had shrunk), making them harder to spot.

4. In the past, images from surveillance cameras (have been/had been) fuzzy; however, newer technology (has increased/had increased) the quality of the image.

5. With better clarity, along with new zoom and tilt features, the number of surveillance cameras (has soared/had soared).

6. By 2010, concerned citizens (have counted/had counted) many thousands of surveillance cameras on Manhattan streets.

7. The ACLU argues that widespread surveillance (has led/had led) to police abuses, such as the creation of video files that track participants in legal street demonstrations.

8. However, legal experts (have noted/had noted) that an individual's right to privacy does not extend to public spaces.

9. Others (have pointed/had pointed) out that surveillance (has had/had had) benefits; for example, it helped the police identify perpetrators in the Oklahoma City and London Underground bombings.

10. Many of those who (have wished/had wished) for privacy in public places now realize that, for better or worse, their public lives are often on view.

### PRACTICE
### 25-8
Fill in the appropriate tense (past tense or past perfect) of the verb in parentheses.

**Example:** No one ___had crossed___ (cross) Antarctica before Sir Ernest

Shackleton ____did____ (do).

(1) In 1914, Shackleton _____ (set) out with twenty-seven men to cross the Antarctic continent. (2) However, he _____

(fail) to reach his goal. (3) Early in the journey, his ship, called the *Endurance*, _____ (run) into ice in the Weddell Sea. (4) The ice _____ (destroy) the ship and _____ (halt) the expedition. (5) Although Shackleton _____ (plan) to end the journey on the other side of Antarctica, the team never even _____ (make) it to the Antarctic continent. (6) After they _____ (lose) the *Endurance*, the crew _____ (have) only three small lifeboats. (7) They _____ (spend) the next year trying to get back to their starting point. (8) Their difficult journey home through the dark, frozen sea _____ (become) one of the greatest survival stories of all time. (9) Miraculously, by 1916, the entire crew _____ (arrive) home safely. (10) None of them _____ (die). (11) On earlier expeditions, Shackleton _____ (show) himself to be an excellent leader; this time, he _____ (prove) that he could lead a group safely through the most hostile territory on earth.

## 25e Past Participles as Adjectives

**e** macmillanhighered.com
/foundationsfirst
Additional Grammar
Exercises > Past Participles
as Adjectives

In addition to functioning as verbs, past participles can function as **adjectives**, modifying nouns that follow them.

My aunt sells painted furniture.

I like fried chicken.

The past participle is also used as an adjective after a **linking verb**—such as *be*, *become*, or *seem*. (A linking verb connects a subject to the word that describes it.)

Mallory was surprised.

My roommate became depressed.

The applicant seemed qualified for the job.

**PRACTICE**

**25-9** The following paragraph contains errors in past participle forms used as adjectives. Cross out any underlined participle that is incorrect, and write the correct form above it. If the participle form is correct, label it *C*.

**Example:** The telegram was <u>invented</u> by Samuel F. B. Morse in 1844.
*(C above invented)*

(1) For more than 150 years, the telegram was <u>use</u> by people who wanted to send messages in the fastest way. (2) Samuel Morse created Morse Code, a system of dots and dashes that were <u>transmit</u> by skilled operators. (3) Before the first transcontinental telegraph line was <u>completed</u>, the fastest way to send a message from New York to California was by Pony Express, which took about ten days. (4) With a telegram, that message could be <u>receive</u> almost immediately. (5) For many years, the Western Union Company, with its teams of 14,000 uniformly <u>dress</u> messenger boys, was the most famous telegraph company. (6) At first, the dots and dashes of the Morse Code messages were <u>wrote</u> out by clerks. (7) In 1914, the teletype was <u>create</u>, allowing Morse Code to be automatically decoded on a strip of ticker tape. (8) For many years, people received <u>unexpected</u> bad news by telegram, so they learned to fear a knock at the door by a Western Union messenger. (9) After World War II, long-distance telephone calls became easier and cheaper to make, and the telegram was <u>need</u> less and less. (10) In 2001, the last telegram was <u>deliver</u>.

# Skills Check

Look back at your response to the Seeing and Writing prompt on page 342. Reread it, and complete the following tasks.

- Underline the helping verbs and past participles.
- Check to make sure that you have used verb tenses correctly.
- Cross out any incorrect verb forms, and write your corrections above the line.

# TEST · Revise · Edit

Starting with **TEST**, revise your paragraph. Then, edit and proofread your work.

## EDITING PRACTICE

Read the following student paragraph, which contains errors in the use of past participles and in the use of the past, present perfect, and past perfect tenses. Decide whether each of the underlined verb forms is correct. If it is correct, write *C* above it. If it is not, cross it out, and write in the correct verb form. The first sentence has been done for you.

*The Boondocks*

When *The Boondocks* started in 1997, Aaron McGruder, its creator, ~~have~~ *had* not yet graduated *(C)* from college. McGruder wants to draw a comic strip that examined serious subjects, especially racial issues. Since *The Boondocks* begun, it had amused many people. It has also maked many people angry. Through the eyes of two African-American brothers who have moved from Chicago to an all-white suburb, *The Boondocks* has comment on many controversial topics. The comic strip had often criticized politicians and pop icons, including black entertainers. For example, one of the brothers, Huey, is name after Huey P. Newton, a black radical of the 1960s. Huey is often anger by people's ignorance of black issues, especially among blacks themselves. He has disapprove of former Secretary of State Condoleezza Rice and actor Cuba Gooding Jr. The other brother, Riley, is fascinated by the "thug life" that some rappers glamorize even though *The Boondocks* has condemn this lifestyle. The comic strip had been very successful. An animated series on the Cartoon Network featuring *The Boondocks* begun in 2005 and ended in 2014. In 2006, the series was nominate by the NAACP Image Awards for the Most Outstanding Comedy Series.

## Verbs: Past Participles

- The past participle form of a regular verb adds -*d* or -*ed* to the base form of the verb. (See 25a.)

- Irregular verbs usually have irregular past participles. (See 25b.)

- The present perfect tense consists of the present tense of *have* plus the past participle. It shows a continuing action, usually one that began in the past and continues into the present. (See 25c.)

- The past perfect tense consists of the past tense of *have* plus the past participle. It describes a past action that occurred before another past action. (See 25d.)

- The past participle can function as an adjective. (See 25e.)

# 26 Nouns

## WORD POWER

**memento** a reminder of the past; a keepsake (the plural form is *mementos*)

**memorabilia** objects valued because of their link to historical events or culture

## seeing and writing

The photo above shows a World War II veteran with his treasured wartime memorabilia. What objects do you treasure? Why? Look at the picture, and then write a paragraph in which you answer these questions. Try to use the Word Power words in your paragraph.

In this chapter, you will learn

• to identify nouns (26a)
• to recognize singular and plural nouns (26b)
• to form plural nouns (26c)

PREVIEW

## 26a Nouns

A **noun** is a word that names a person (*actor, Denzel Washington*), an animal (*elephant, Babar*), a place (*city, Houston*), an object (*game, Monopoly*), or an idea (*theory, Darwinism*).

## FYI

### Common and Proper Nouns

Most nouns, called **common nouns**, name general classes of people, places, or things. Common nouns begin with lowercase (not capital) letters.

    prince        holiday

Some nouns, called **proper nouns**, name particular people, places, or things. A proper noun always begins with a capital letter.

    Prince Charming      Memorial Day

 macmillanhighered.com
/foundationsfirst
LearningCurve > Parts of
Speech: Nouns and Pronouns

**PRACTICE
26-1** In each of the following sentences, underline every noun. Label common nouns *C* and proper nouns *P*.

                      P                 C                 P
**Example:**  Day of the Dead is a holiday celebrated in Mexico and in

                    C             P
        other countries in Latin America.

1. This holiday is celebrated every year to honor the spirits of the dead.

2. The celebration occurs in early November, just after people in the United States celebrate Halloween.

3. This holiday was started by the Aztecs, who had a similar ritual.

4. However, the holiday now includes Christian as well as Indian traditions.

5. Today, people observe the Day of the Dead differently in different regions.

1. The doctor wrote a prescription after <u>she</u> examined the patient.

   _____

2. Skunks are best known for the horrible scent <u>they</u> produce.

   _____

3. The mechanic presented <u>his</u> estimate. _____

4. Mr. and Mrs. Thomas were worried about <u>their</u> retirement fund.

   _____

5. When Tim got a new job, his friends surprised <u>him</u> with a party.

   _____

**PRACTICE**

**27-3**   In the following passage, circle the antecedent of each under-lined pronoun. Then, draw an arrow from the pronoun to its antecedent.

**Example:** In recent decades, some (Americans) have been dissatisfied with the education that <u>their</u> children are getting in public school.

(1) The charter school movement arose as a way to give students an alternative to <u>their</u> neighborhood public schools. (2) Charter schools are financed with tax money, like traditional public schools, but <u>they</u> are privately run. (3) As a result, an administrator of a charter school has more flexibility in designing <u>its</u> curriculum and setting rules. (4) With over two million children now attending more than six thousand charter schools, the movement has had <u>its</u> successes. (5) However, from the beginning, educators have been divided in <u>their</u> views. (6) Although some educators feel that charter schools provide a valuable alternative to traditional public schools, others feel that <u>they</u> deprive <u>them</u> of funds. (7) Recent studies compared test scores of students in charter schools with those of <u>their</u> neighbors in traditional public schools. (8) When the two groups' scores are examined, <u>they</u> are not very different overall. (9) However, poor minority students in charter schools seem to do better than <u>their</u> peers in traditional public schools. (10) These results

suggest that charter schools can be an important part of public education but that we need to learn more about when and how <u>they</u> work best.

## 27b Special Problems with Pronoun-Antecedent Agreement

Three kinds of antecedents can cause problems for writers because they are not easy to identify as singular or plural—*compound antecedents, indefinite pronoun antecedents*, and *collective noun antecedents*.

## Compound Antecedents

A **compound antecedent** consists of two or more words connected by *and* or *or*: *England <u>and</u> the United States; Japan <u>or</u> China*.

macmillanhighered.com
/foundationsfirst
Additional Grammar
Exercises > Pronoun
Antecedent Agreement with
Compound Antecedents

■ Compound antecedents connected by *and* are always plural. They are always used with plural pronouns.

> England and the United States drafted soldiers into <u>their</u> armies.

■ Compound antecedents connected by *or* may take a singular or a plural pronoun. The pronoun always agrees with the word that is closer to it.

> When will European nations or our own country use <u>its</u> [not *their*] resources to fight famine in Africa?

> When will our own country or European nations use <u>their</u> [not *its*] resources to fight famine in Africa?

**PRACTICE
27-4**   In each of the following sentences, underline the compound antecedent, and circle the connecting word (*and* or *or*). Then, circle the appropriate pronoun in parentheses.

**Example:**   Street vendors (and) ballpark concession workers usually

say the hot dog is one of (its/their) top-selling foods.

(1) Both Frankfurt, Germany, and Vienna, Austria, claim that (it/they) invented the frankfurter or wiener—what Americans call a hot dog. (2) Before forks and knives made (its/their) appearance at the dinner table, sausages were eaten as finger foods in these cities. (3) As early as

the 1480s, when men and women gathered at festivals, (he or she/they) were often given small sausages to eat. (4) Even earlier, the Romans used to combine various spices and ground meat and then stuff (it/them) into a pig's intestines, creating an early version of a pork sausage. (5) Frankfurters and wieners finally made (its/their) way to the United States in the 1860s. (6) Soon, outdoor vendors began wrapping the hot wiener or frankfurter in a bun so that (it/they) would not burn the customer's hands. (7) According to legend, either the cartoonist Thomas Dorgan or the vendor Adolf Gehring coined the term "hot dog" while (he/they) was at a baseball game. (8) A sporting event and a busy city street corner are the two most popular places to find a hot dog because (it/they) are always full of hungry people in search of a quick bite to eat. (9) However, some fast-food chains and restaurants also specialize in hot dogs, and (it/they) can be appealing destinations for customers who like unusual toppings. (10) For example, chili and baked beans cannot usually be found in a street corner cart, but (it/they) may be available at a hot dog specialty restaurant.

## Indefinite Pronoun Antecedents

Most pronouns refer to a specific person or thing. **Indefinite pronouns**, however, do not refer to any particular person or thing.

Most indefinite pronouns are singular, but some are plural.

ℹ macmillanhighered.com
/foundationsfirst
Additional Grammar
Exercises > Pronoun-
Antecedent Agreement
with Indefinite Pronouns

### Singular Indefinite Pronouns

| | | | |
|---|---|---|---|
| another | either | neither | somebody |
| anybody | everybody | no one | someone |
| anyone | everyone | nobody | something |
| anything | everything | nothing | |
| each | much | one | |

### Plural Indefinite Pronouns

| | |
|---|---|
| both | others |
| few | several |
| many | some |

7. Others have us

create artificial

8. DNA evidence

someone get (h

9. An organizatio

imprisoned peo

10. Several of the

row at the time

## Collective Noun

**Collective nouns**
a group of people
antecedents are use

The band was

In the sentence ab
vidual musicians, b
it is used with the

**Frequently**

army
association
band
class
club

**PRACTICE**

**27-7** In each
the ante
circle the correct p

**Example:** Th

1. Last night, our

2. Our police offic

3. The class appla

4. The jury gave (

5. Some people m

---

■ When an indefinite pronoun antecedent is singular, use a singular pronoun to refer to it.

Something was out of *its* usual place. (*Something* is singular, so it is used with the singular pronoun *its*.)

■ When an indefinite pronoun antecedent is plural, use a plural pronoun to refer to it.

The whole group wanted to go swimming, but few had brought their bathing suits. (*Few* is plural, so it is used with the plural pronoun *their*.)

Note that indefinite pronouns are sometimes used in phrases with *of*— *each of, either of, neither of, one of, some of, both of, several of*, and so on. Even if an indefinite pronoun is followed by such a phrase, you still need to use a singular pronoun to refer to a singular indefinite pronoun and a plural pronoun to refer to a plural indefinite pronoun.

Each of the games has *its* [not *their*] own rules.

Some of the games have *their* [not *its*] own rules.

## FYI

### Using *His or Her* with Indefinite Pronouns

Singular indefinite pronouns that refer to people—such as *anybody*, *anyone*, *everybody*, *everyone*, *somebody*, and *someone*—require a singular pronoun.

However, using the singular pronoun *his* suggests that the indefinite pronoun refers to a male and using *her* suggests that the indefinite pronoun refers to a female. Using *his or her* is more accurate because the indefinite pronoun may refer to either a male or a female.

Everyone must revise his or her work.

When used over and over again, however, *his or her* can create wordy passages. To avoid this problem, use a plural noun instead of the indefinite pronoun.

All students must revise their work.

**PRACTICE**

**27-5** Edit the following sentences for errors in pronoun-antecedent agreement. In some sentences, substitute *his or her* for *their* when the antecedent is singular and could refer to a person of either gender. In other sentences, replace the antecedent with a plural word or phrase.

## Reflexive Pronouns

**Reflexive pronouns** always end in *-self* (singular) or *-selves* (plural). These pronouns indicate that people or things did something to themselves or for themselves.

Christina bought herself a new watch.

You need to pace yourself when you exercise.

Eliza and Megan made themselves a plate of nachos.

## Intensive Pronouns

**Intensive pronouns** also end in *-self* or *-selves*. Unlike reflexive pronouns, however, they always appear directly after their antecedents. Intensive pronouns are used for emphasis.

I myself have a friend with an eating disorder.

The actor himself did all the dangerous stunts.

They themselves questioned their motives.

### Reflexive and Intensive Pronouns

**Singular Forms**

| ANTECEDENT | REFLEXIVE OR INTENSIVE PRONOUN |
|---|---|
| I | myself |
| you | yourself |
| he | himself |
| she | herself |
| it | itself |

**Plural Forms**

| ANTECEDENT | REFLEXIVE OR INTENSIVE PRONOUN |
|---|---|
| we | ourselves |
| you | yourselves |
| they | themselves |

**PRACTICE**

**27-14**   In each of the following sentences, fill in the correct reflexive or intensive pronoun.

**Example:** You two should take _____*yourselves*_____ out for dinner to celebrate your anniversary.

1. She _____ had always walked to school, so she told her children that they should too.

2. The legislators voted _____ a raise.

3. The cat licked _____ and then dozed off.

4. Einstein _____ could not have solved that problem.

5. After my haircut, I caught a frightening glimpse of _____ in the mirror.

6. My sister weighs _____ every morning.

7. If you fall, pick _____ up and start over again.

8. You _____ told me that this material would not be on the final exam.

9. The toddlers covered _____ with mud before their mother could stop them.

10. They bought the property for thousands of dollars, but they tore down the house _____ almost immediately afterward.

# Skills Check

Look back at your response to the Seeing and Writing prompt on page 367, and underline every pronoun you used. Reread your paragraph, and answer the following questions.

- Do all your pronouns and antecedents agree?
- Are any of your pronouns vague or unneccesary?
- Have you used the correct pronoun case?

Make any necessary corrections.

# TEST · Revise · Edit

Starting with TEST, revise your paragraph. Then, edit and proofread your work.

## EDITING PRACTICE

Read the following student paragraph, which contains pronoun errors. Check for errors in pronoun case and pronoun-antecedent agreement as well as for any vague or unnecessary pronouns. Then, make any editing changes you think are necessary. The first sentence has been corrected for you.

James Cameron: High and Deep

James Cameron, he is the only person *who* ~~whom~~ has climbed to the highest peak of Hollywood success and explored the deepest part of the Pacific Ocean. In 1998, the Academy of Motion Pictures awarded Cameron their Oscar for Best Director for his film *Titanic*, and in 2012 he descended nearly seven miles alone in a small submarine to the bottom of the Mariana Trench. Cameron's adventurous life began in 1954, in Ontario, Canada. The 1968 film *2001: A Space Odyssey*, impressed the young Cameron, whom later said: "As soon as I saw that, I knew I wanted to be a filmmaker." Too often, a young person spends his time just dreaming about success, but Cameron did more. He wrote screenplays and taught himself about special effects. In 1978, after he made a short film, they gave him work on special effects for Hollywood films. Then, one night in 1981, he had a frightening dream about a robot sent from the future to kill him, and this became the plot of his first hit film, *The Terminator* (1984). Since then, Cameron has made successful films such as *Aliens* (1986), *True Lies* (1994), *Titanic* (1997), and *Avatar* (2009). Each of Cameron's films has their fans, and us moviegoers have all probably seen at least one or two of his blockbusters. Him and his films have been awarded more than twenty Oscars, and the Hollywood Foreign Press Association has given him three of their Golden Globe awards.

# review checklist

## Pronouns

☐ A pronoun is a word that refers to and takes the place of a noun or another pronoun. (See 27a.)

☐ The word to which a pronoun refers is called the pronoun's antecedent. (See 27a.)

☐ Compound antecedents connected by *and* are plural and are used with plural pronouns. Compound antecedents connected by *or* may take singular or plural pronouns. (See 27b.)

☐ Most indefinite pronoun antecedents are singular and are used with singular pronouns. A few indefinite pronoun antecedents are plural and are used with plural pronouns. (See 27b.)

☐ Collective noun antecedents are singular and must be used with singular pronouns. (See 27b.)

☐ A pronoun should always refer to a specific antecedent. (See 27c.)

☐ When a pronoun directly follows its antecedent, it is usually unnecessary. (See 27c.)

☐ Personal pronouns can be in the subjective, objective, or possessive case. (See 27d.)

☐ Pronouns present special problems when they are used in compounds and comparisons. The pronouns *who* and *whom* also cause problems. (See 27e.)

☐ Reflexive pronouns and intensive pronouns must agree with their antecedents in person and number. (See 27f.)

# 28 Adjectives and Adverbs

© Ocean/Corbis

## seeing and writing

The picture above shows people at a masquerade party. Look at the picture, and then write a paragraph in which you describe the costume you would wear to this party. Try to use the Word Power word in your paragraph.

In this chapter, you will learn
- to identify adjectives and adverbs (28a)
- to understand comparatives and superlatives (28b)
- to identify demonstrative adjectives (28c)

**PREVIEW**

## 28a  Identifying Adjectives and Adverbs

Adjectives and adverbs are words that **modify** (describe or identify) other words. Adjectives and adverbs make your sentences more specific and more interesting.

e macmillanhighered.com
/foundationsfirst
LearningCurve > Parts of
Speech: Verbs, Adjectives,
and Adverbs; Additional
Grammar Exercises >
Identifying Adjectives and
Adverbs

### Identifying Adjectives

An **adjective** answers the question *What kind? Which one?* or *How many?* Adjectives modify nouns or pronouns.

The Spanish city of Madrid has exciting nightlife. (The adjective *Spanish* modifies the noun *city*; the adjective *exciting* modifies the noun *nightlife*.)

It is lively because of its many clubs and tapas bars. (The adjective *lively* modifies the pronoun *it*.)

**PRACTICE**

**28-1**  In each of the blanks in the following paragraph, copy one adjective from the list below. Cross each adjective off the list as you use it. Be sure to choose an adjective that makes sense in each sentence.

**Example:**  The Florida Highwaymen left a ____*distinctive*____ mark on

the American art world.

| | | | |
|---|---|---|---|
| growing | original | deserted | energetic |
| ~~distinctive~~ | attractive | steamy | serious |
| bold | hardworking | sticky | several |

(1) Led by the young and _____ painter Alfred Hair, a group of twenty-six African-American artists painted Florida's undeveloped landscape in the 1960s. (2) Their images of _____ beaches and _____ swamps have a dreamlike quality. (3) The Florida Highwaymen, as they came to be called, sold these _____ landscape paintings from their cars and door-to-door. (4) Hair and his _____ colleagues could each produce up to twenty paintings a day. (5) The

Highwaymen's works were often sold while the paint was still _____. (6) With their _____ use of color, the Highwaymen developed a unique style. (7) Their vibrant paintings were greatly admired by Florida's tourists and its _____ population. (8) At first, _____ art collectors did not consider the paintings to be remarkable. (9) However, after being forgotten for _____ decades, the paintings have now reemerged as collectibles. (10) Although an _____ Highwaymen painting cost only $25 in the 1960s, today it could be worth as much as $5,000.

## Identifying Adverbs

An **adverb** answers the question *How? Why? When? Where?* or *To what extent?* Adverbs modify verbs, adjectives, or other adverbs.

The huge Doberman barked angrily. (*The adverb* angrily *modifies the verb* barked.)

Still, we felt quite safe. (*The adverb* quite *modifies the adjective* safe.)

Very slowly, we held out a big juicy steak. (*The adverb* very *modifies the adverb* slowly.)

**PRACTICE**
**28-2** In each of the blanks in the following paragraph, copy one adverb from the list below. Cross each adverb off the list as you use it. Be sure to choose an adverb that makes sense in each sentence.

**Example:** I waited _____*wearily*_____ for the train.

| quickly | heavily | easily | unusually | uncomfortably |
| noisily | rudely | bravely | really | ~~wearily~~ |

(1) The subway train screeched _____ into the station. (2) The doors _____ slid open, and departing passengers _____ pushed their way out. (3) Entering passengers struggled _____ to get through the narrow doors. (4) It was _____ hot for April, and people were sweating _____ in the steamy underground tunnel. (5) Jammed _____ in the middle of the car, I hoped I'd

be able to squeeze out _____ when I reached my stop. (6) What a

_____ great way to start the work day!

## Telling Adjectives and Adverbs Apart

Many adverbs are formed by adding the ending -*ly* to an adjective.

| ADJECTIVE | ADVERB |
|-----------|--------|
| bad | badly |
| nice | nicely |
| quick | quickly |
| quiet | quietly |
| real | really |
| slow | slowly |

Because the adjective and adverb forms of the words in the list above are similar, you may sometimes be confused about which form to use in a sentence. Remember, adjectives modify nouns or pronouns; adverbs modify verbs, adjectives, or other adverbs.

ADJECTIVE   Kim likes the slow dances. (*Slow modifies the noun dances.*)

ADVERB   Kim likes to dance slowly. (*Slowly modifies the verb dance.*)

ADJECTIVE   Mark Twain's real name was Samuel L. Clemens. (*Real modifies the noun name.*)

ADVERB   It was really generous of him to donate his time. (*Really modifies the adjective generous.*)

### PRACTICE
**28-3**   In the following paragraph, circle the correct form (adjective or adverb) from the choices in parentheses.

**Example:**   In certain parts of the world, eating insects is a (common)/ commonly) practice.

(1) Some people in Latin America, Asia, and Africa (regular/regularly) eat insects. (2) In Mexico, for example, some (traditional/traditionally) recipes include butterfly larvae, ants, or beetles. (3) Villagers might roast the insects, fry them (light/lightly), and use them as a filling for a taco or an omelet. (4) In China and other parts of Asia, insects such as

crickets and termites are (common/commonly) fried, roasted, and stewed. (5) Some Pacific islanders (happy/happily) dine on dragonflies, while Cambodians eat tarantulas and Indonesians eat grubs. (6) A (popular/ popularly) African dish is made from caterpillar guts, which are boiled in salt water and then dried. (7) Although they may not sound appetizing to us, insects are (actual/actually) an important part of many peoples' diets. (8) They provide protein, vitamins, and minerals to people in places where meat, fish, and poultry are not (wide/widely) available. (9) Because insects are so abundant and reproduce so (quick/ quickly), they are also a much more ecologically responsible food choice than beef and chicken. (10) Who knows? Maybe our next (environmental/ environmentally) friendly trend will be to eat fried grasshoppers for breakfast.

# FYI

## Good and Well

Be careful not to confuse *good* and *well*. Unlike regular adjectives, whose adverb forms add -*ly*, the adjective *good* is irregular. Its adverb form is *well*.

**ADJECTIVE**  John Steinbeck was a good writer. (*Good* modifies the noun *writer*.)

**ADVERB**  He wrote particularly well in the novel *The Grapes of Wrath*. (*Well* modifies the verb *wrote*.)

Always use *well* when you are describing someone's health.

He wasn't at all *well* [not *good*] after his trip.

macmillanhighered.com
/foundationsfirst
Additional Grammar
Exercises > Good and Well

**PRACTICE 28-4**  In the following passage, circle the correct form (*good* or *well*) in parentheses.

**Example:** Have Americans treated U.S. veterans (good/well) enough?

(1) Some U.S. veterans of twentieth-century wars were treated (good/ well); others, unfortunately, were not. (2) In the 1940s, most American

veterans of World War II came home to a (good/well) life. (3) No one doubted that these men and women had done a (good/well) thing by going to war. (4) The G.I. Bill ensured that many of them were able to get a (good/well) education. (5) In the strong postwar economy, (good/well) jobs were not difficult to find. (6) Unfortunately, things did not go as (good/well) for the veterans who returned from the Vietnam War. (7) Many Americans felt that the U.S. involvement in that war was not a (good/well) idea. (8) Some blamed the soldiers even though most of them had done their jobs (good/well). (9) Rather than being (good/well) respected, the returning veterans were sometimes treated badly. (10) In addition, injured soldiers often ended up in veterans' hospitals that were not (good/well) staffed. (11) By comparison, veterans of the wars in Iraq and Afghanistan have been (good/well) received when they returned home. (12) Even people who did not support these wars do not take out their anger on the soldiers who fought so (good/well). (13) Still, veterans of today's wars must continue to deal with underfunded veterans' hospitals, and improvements are much needed and (good/well) deserved. (14) No matter what the public may think of a war, it is important to treat veterans (good/well) when they return home.

## 28b Comparatives and Superlatives

Adjectives and adverbs are sometimes used to compare two or more people or things.

The **comparative form** of an adjective or adverb compares *two* people or things. The **superlative form** of an adjective or adverb compares *more than two* people or things. Special forms of the adjectives and adverbs are used to indicate these comparisons.

macmillanhighered.com
/foundationsfirst
Additional Grammar
Exercises > Comparatives
and Superlatives

ADJECTIVE     These shoes are ugly.

COMPARATIVE   The brown shoes are uglier than the black ones.

SUPERLATIVE   The purple ones are the ugliest of all.

ADVERB Will you be able to get home soon?

COMPARATIVE I may not be home until midnight, but I will try to get there sooner.

SUPERLATIVE Unfortunately, the soonest I can leave work is 7:30.

*Note:* Some adverbs—such as *almost, very, somewhat, quite, extremely, rather,* and *moderately*—do not have comparative or superlative forms.

## Forming Comparatives and Superlatives

Adjectives and adverbs form the comparative with *-er* or *more* and the superlative with *-est* or *most.*

### Adjectives

■ To form the comparative of a one-syllable adjective, add *-er*. To form the superlative of a one-syllable adjective, add *-est*.

young younger youngest

■ To form the comparative of an adjective that has two or more syllables, use *more*. To form the superlative of an adjective that has two or more syllables, use *most*.

beautiful more beautiful most beautiful

### Adverbs

■ To form the comparative of an adverb that ends in *-ly*, use *more*. To form the superlative of an adverb that ends in *-ly*, use *most*.

slowly more slowly most slowly

■ Some other adverbs form the comparative with *-er* and the superlative with *-est*.

soon sooner soonest

## Solving Special Problems with Comparatives and Superlatives

The following four rules will help you avoid errors with comparatives and superlatives.

1. Never use both *-er* and *more* to form the comparative.

   The comic could have been a lot funnier. (*not more funnier*)

2. Never use both *-est* and *most* to form the superlative.

   *Scream* was the scariest [*not most scariest*] movie I ever saw.

3. Never use the superlative when you are comparing only two things.

> Beth is the younger [*not youngest*] of the two sisters.

4. Never use the comparative when you are comparing more than two things.

> This is the worst [*not worse*] part-time job I ever had.

## PRACTICE
### 28-5
In the blank at the right, fill in the comparative form of each adjective or adverb.

**Examples**

rich _____*richer*_____

embarrassed _____*more embarrassed*_____

1. strong _____

2. quickly _____

3. traditional _____

4. neat _____

5. neatly _____

6. gently _____

7. new _____

8. easy _____

9. easily _____

10. useful _____

## PRACTICE
### 28-6
In the blank at the right, fill in the superlative form of each adjective or adverb.

**Examples**

rich _____*richest*_____

embarrassed _____*most embarrassed*_____

1. strong _____

2. quickly _____

3. traditional _____

4. neat _____

5. neatly _____

6. gently _____

7. new _____

8. easy _____

9. easily _____

10. useful _____

## PRACTICE
### 28-7
Fill in the correct comparative form of the word in parentheses.

**Example:**   In the 1960s, the salaries of American athletes were not much _____*greater*_____ (great) than the average salary of other Americans.

1. The salaries of professional athletes have grown far _____ (rapidly) than salaries in other professions.

2. Salaries differ across sports: the average salary in the NBA ($5.2 million) is considerably _____ (high) than the average in the NFL ($1.75 million) or in major league baseball ($2.5 million).

3. Revenue is _____ (great) for the NFL than for the NBA, but football teams are much _____ (large) than basketball teams.

4. Averages are deceptive; top players have generous contracts, but the earnings of many other players are far _____ (low) than average.

5. As athletes' salaries have grown, the debate over salaries has become _____ (heated).

6. Some people argue that something is wrong with a society that pays athletes so much _____ (generously) than it pays its teachers or soldiers.

7. Others reply that if athletes' pay is so much _____ (high) than others, it is because athletes are special.

8. These people also point out that athletic contests are not only _____ (entertaining) than many other activities but also _____ (inspiring).

9. They add that athletes' professional lives are _____ (dangerous) than most peoples' and that their careers are significantly _____ (short), often because of injury.

10. Both sides of the debate make good points; it would be hard to say that one position is _____ (strong) than the other.

**PRACTICE
28-8**    Fill in the correct superlative form of the word in parentheses.

**Example:** Participants in extreme sports are among the _____*most obsessive*_____ (obsessive) people in the world.

(1) Some contests seem to be designed to show which participant is

the _____ (crazy). (2) For example, the world record holder for

the _____ (high) wingsuit jump jumped from a hot-air balloon at

37,000 feet. (3) Motocross riders compete to see who can drive a motorized

bike the _____ (fast) on a dirt track filled with steep jumps. (4) In

kitesurfing, one of the goals is to travel the _____ (far), and the

world record holder crossed over 200 miles of open sea in twelve hours.

(5) The human obsession with extremes is not new, however; records show-

ing who was the _____ (strong) weightlifter or the _____

(quick) sprinter go back more than a century. (6) People who lack skill in

the _____ (familiar) extreme sports can still set a world record

by finding an event in *Guinness World Records* that they can compete in.

(7) One man ironed for the _____ (long) period on record

(55 hours and 5 minutes). (8) The same man also had the _____

(large) number of bridesmaids (79) at his wedding. (9) Standing on one

foot or peeling an apple is not an extreme sport, but people have set some

of the _____ (surprising) records in events like these. (10) After

looking through *Guinness World Records*, many people might conclude

that extreme sports are not the _____ (bizarre) activities in which

people can participate.

# FYI

## *Good/Well* and *Bad/Badly*

The adjectives *good* and *bad*, and their adverb forms *well* and *badly*, are irregular. They do not form the comparative and superlative in the same way that other adjectives and adverbs do. Because their forms are so irregular, you must memorize them.

| ADJECTIVE | COMPARATIVE FORM | SUPERLATIVE FORM |
| --- | --- | --- |
| good | better | best |
| bad | worse | worst |

| ADVERB | COMPARATIVE FORM | SUPERLATIVE FORM |
| --- | --- | --- |
| well | better | best |
| badly | worse | worst |

**macmillanhighered.com /foundationsfirst**
Additional Grammar Exercises > The Comparative and Superlative of Good/Well and Bad/Badly

**PRACTICE
28-9**    Fill in the correct comparative or superlative form of *good*, *well*, *bad*, or *badly*.

**Example:**    Historians' _____*best*_____ (good) guess is that poker originated in Persia, France, or Great Britain.

1. Poker may be one of the _____ (good) card games ever invented.

2. The game was carried all over the world by American soldiers, who often competed to see who were the _____ (good) poker players.

3. After the World Series of Poker started in 1970, poker fans saw that if they were _____ (good) players than their opponents, they could win a lot of money.

4. During the 1970s, new books on poker strategy helped fans play _____ (well) than ever.

5. It seemed that even the _____ (good) players could learn a lot from the experts.

6. With online poker, those who played _____ (badly) than their friends could play at home without embarrassing themselves.

7. With cameras that showed players' cards to the audience, TV poker shows became a _____ (good) experience for viewers.

8. Winning at poker requires skill, but even the _____ (good) players need luck to win.

9. To a poker player, there is nothing _____ (bad) than having good cards and still losing.

10. Some people fear that the increased popularity of poker is making gambling addictions _____ (bad).

## 28c  Demonstrative Adjectives

**Demonstrative adjectives** do not describe other words. These adjectives—*this*, *that*, *these*, and *those*—simply identify particular nouns.

*This* and *that* identify singular nouns.

This book is much more interesting than that one.

*These* and *those* identify plural nouns.

These books are novels, but those books are biographies.

macmillanhighered.com /foundationsfirst
Additional Grammar Exercises > Demonstrative Adjectives

**PRACTICE 28-10**

In the following paragraph, circle the correct form of the demonstrative adjective in parentheses.

**Example:**   The names of (this/these) Motown groups often had two parts—the lead singer and the backup group.

(1) (That/Those) African-American musicians who came out of Detroit in the 1960s had a unique sound. (2) (That/Those) special sound came to be known as Motown, after Motown Records, which in turn was named for Detroit, the "Motor City." (3) The sound was created when powerful lead vocals were combined with a strong rhythm section and (that/those) well-known gospel-style backup singing. (4) Some of the artists who recorded in (this/these) style are Diana Ross and the Supremes, Gladys Knight and the Pips, and Smokey Robinson and the Miracles. (5) (This/These) kind of group became famous under the direction of Motown Records owner Berry Gordy. (6) Recently, the record company's in-house band, the Funk Brothers, was finally recognized for helping to create (that/those) recognizable Motown sound. (7) The movie *Standing in the Shadows of Motown* highlights the work of (this/these) band. (8) The plot of *Dreamgirls*, another recent film loosely based on Motown Records, suggests that bribery

was what enabled (that/those) record label to succeed. (9) In (that/those) award-winning movie, a fictional Detroit record-label owner is portrayed as an unethical thug. (10) After Berry Gordy and some Motown artists complained, saying (that/those) kind of portrayal was harmful and untruthful, the film's producers issued a public apology.

## Skills Check

Look back at your response to the Seeing and Writing prompt on page 388. Reread it, and underline every adjective and adverb you used. Then, answer the following questions.

- Have you used the correct comparative and superlative forms?
- Have you used demonstrative adjectives correctly?

Correct any errors you find. Then, add or substitute descriptive words if necessary to make your writing more specific and more interesting.

## TEST · Revise · Edit

Starting with TEST, revise your paragraph. Then, edit and proofread your work.

## EDITING PRACTICE

Read the following student paragraph, which contains errors in the use of adjectives and adverbs. Make any changes necessary to correct adjectives that are incorrectly used instead of adverbs, adverbs that are incorrectly used instead of adjectives, errors in the use of comparatives and superlatives, and errors in the use of demonstrative adjectives. You may also add adjectives or adverbs that you feel would make the writer's ideas clearer or more specific. The first sentence has been edited for you.

### Craigslist: A Website for the People

In the online world, where changes happen at ~~more and more~~ *faster and* faster speeds, Craigslist has had amazing success while hardly changing its way of doing business or the look of its website. The main reason Craigslist has done so good is that it is a site for the people. Also, sometimes more simpler is better than more complicated. Craigslist was started informally in 1995 by Craig Newmark, who had recent moved to San Francisco, as a way for people to let others know about local events. By 1999, Craigslist was a company, and the people of San Francisco could post free classified ads in many different categories. Over the next few years, the company grew quick, developing other local sites. Today, there are more than seven hundred local sites in seventy countries. Unfortunately, over the years Craigslist ads have been associated with serious problems. Critics have charged that Craigslist does not do a well enough job of protecting its users from scams and serious crimes. This may be inevitable because Craigslist has over eighty million new classified ads each month—the most greatest number of classified ads anywhere. Of websites in the United States, Craigslist ranks eighth in traffic, ahead of sites like ESPN, whose staffs are far more big. Furthermore, Craigslist looks differently from many other sites, not just because of its simple design but also because it does not have banner advertisements. In addition to going without these revenue from outside advertisers, Craigslist still does not charge for most of the ads people post. Between making a profit and helping users, its CEO says, helping users is by far the most important of the two goals.

## Adjectives and Adverbs

☐ Adjectives modify nouns or pronouns. (See 28a.)

☐ Adverbs modify verbs, adjectives, or other adverbs. (See 28a.)

☐ To compare two people or things, use the comparative form of an adjective or adverb. To compare more than two people or things, use the superlative form of an adjective or adverb. (See 28b.)

☐ Adjectives and adverbs form the comparative with -er or *more* and the superlative with -est or *most*. (See 28b.)

☐ The adjectives *good* and *bad* and their adverb forms, *well* and *badly*, have irregular comparative and superlative forms. (See 28b.)

☐ Demonstrative adjectives—*this, that, these,* and *those*—identify particular nouns. (See 28c.)

# 29 Grammar and Usage Issues for ESL Writers

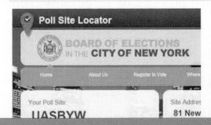

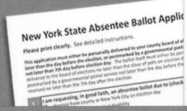

Courtesy of the Board of Elections in the City of New York.

## seeing and writing

The picture above shows the home page of the Board of Elections in the City of New York website, with some information in English, Spanish, Chinese, and other languages. Do you think U.S. election information should be available in languages other than English? If not, why not? If so, what languages should be represented? Why? Look at the picture, and then write a paragraph that answers these questions. Try to use the Word Power words in your paragraph.

**In this chapter, you will learn**

- how subjects are used in sentences (29a)
- to understand count and noncount nouns (29b)
- to use determiners with count and noncount nouns (29c)
- to understand articles (29d)
- to form negative statements and questions (29e)
- to indicate verb tense (29f)
- to recognize stative verbs (29g)
- to use gerunds (29h)
- to choose prepositions (29i)
- to use prepositions in phrasal verbs (29j)

Learning English as a second language involves more than just learning grammar. In fact, if you have been studying English as a second language, you may know more English grammar than many native speakers do. Still, you will need to learn conventions and rules that many native speakers already know. This chapter covers the grammar and usage issues that give nonnative speakers the most trouble.

# 29a  Subjects in Sentences

e macmillanhighered.com
/foundationsfirst
Additional Grammar
Exercises > Special Problems
with Subjects

English requires that every sentence state its subject. In fact, every dependent clause must also have a subject.

**INCORRECT**  My parents do not make much money although work hard. (Who works hard?)

**CORRECT**  My parents do not make much money although they work hard.

When the real subject follows the verb and the normal subject position before the verb is empty, it must be filled by a "dummy" subject, such as *it* or *there*.

**INCORRECT**  Is very hot today.

**CORRECT**  It is very hot today.

**INCORRECT**  Are tall mountains in my country.

**CORRECT**  There are tall mountains in my country.

Standard English also does not permit a two-part subject in which the second part of the subject is a pronoun referring to the same person or thing as the first part.

**INCORRECT**  My sister she is a cardiologist.

**CORRECT**  My sister is a cardiologist.

**PRACTICE**

**29-1**   The following sentences contain problems with subjects. Rewrite each sentence correctly on the lines provided. (Some of the sentences can be corrected in more than one way.)

**Example:**   Are no roads in the middle of the jungle.

*There are no roads in the middle of the jungle.*

1. The old woman she sells candles in the shop downstairs.

2. Are six kinds of rice in the cupboard.

3. Dmitri he rides his bicycle ten miles every day.

4. The doctor says is hope for my father.

5. My neighbor she watches my daughter in the evenings.

## 29b   Count and Noncount Nouns

macmillanhighered.com/foundationsfirst
LearningCurve > Multilingual Articles and Types of Nouns; Additional Grammar Exercises > Count and Noncount Nouns

A **count noun** names one particular thing or a group of particular things: *a teacher, a panther, a bed, an ocean, a cloud; two teachers, five panthers, three beds, two oceans, fifteen clouds*. A **noncount noun**, however, names things that cannot be counted: *gold, cream, sand, blood, smoke*.

Count nouns usually have a singular form and a plural form: *cloud, clouds*. Noncount nouns usually have only a singular form: *smoke*. Note how the nouns *cloud* and *smoke* differ in terms of how they are used in sentences.

CORRECT     The sky is full of clouds.

CORRECT     The sky is full of smoke.

INCORRECT   The sky is full of smokes.

**CORRECT** I see ten clouds in the distance.

**CORRECT** I see some smoke in the distance.

**INCORRECT** I see ten smokes in the distance.

In many cases, you can use either a count noun or a noncount noun to communicate the same idea.

| COUNT | NONCOUNT |
|---|---|
| people (plural of *person*) | humanity (not *humanities*) |
| tables, chairs, beds | furniture (not *furnitures*) |
| letters | mail (not *mails*) |
| supplies | equipment (not *equipments*) |
| facts | information (not *informations*) |

Some nouns can be either count or noncount, depending on the meaning intended.

**COUNT** Students in this course are expected to submit two papers.

**NONCOUNT** These artificial flowers are made of paper.

## FYI

### Count and Noncount Nouns

Here are some general guidelines for using count and noncount nouns.

- Use a count noun to refer to a living animal, but use a noncount noun to refer to the food that comes from that animal.

  **COUNT** There are several live lobsters in the tank.

  **NONCOUNT** This restaurant specializes in lobster.

- If you use a noncount noun for a substance or class of things that can come in different varieties, you can often make that noun plural if you want to talk about those varieties.

  **NONCOUNT** Cheese is a rich source of calcium.

  **COUNT** Many different cheeses come from Italy.

- If you want to shift from a general concept to specific examples of it, you can often use a noncount noun as a count noun.

  **NONCOUNT** You have a great deal of talent.

  **COUNT** My talents do not include singing.

**PRACTICE**

**29-2**   In each of the following sentences, identify the underlined word as a count or noncount noun. If it is a noncount noun, circle the *N* following the sentence, but do not write in the blank. If it is a count noun, circle the *C*, and then write the plural form of the noun in the blank.

**Examples**

She was filled with admiration for the turtle.  Ⓝ C _____

A seagull watched from a safe distance.  N Ⓒ ____ *seagulls* ____

1. Rosa walked across the sand.  N C _____

2. The moon shone brightly.  N C _____

3. The moon was reflected in the water.  N C _____

4. A sea turtle came out of the waves.  N C _____

5. The turtle crawled slowly up the beach and dug a hole for her eggs.

   N C _____

6. Rosa had heard that a turtle egg feels like leather.  N C _____

7. Rosa felt sympathy for the turtle.  N C _____

8. An enemy could be nearby, waiting to attack the turtle or eat her eggs.

   N C _____

9. The enemy could even be a human being who likes to eat turtle.

   N C _____

10. Rosa sighed with relief when the turtle finished laying her eggs and

    swam away.  N C _____

## 29c  Determiners with Count and Noncount Nouns

ⓔ macmillanhighered.com /foundationsfirst
Additional Grammar Exercises > Determiners with Count and Noncount Nouns

**Determiners** are adjectives that *identify* rather than describe the nouns they modify. Determiners may also *quantify* nouns (that is, indicate an amount or a number).

Determiners include the following groups of words.

- Articles: *a, an, the*
- Demonstrative adjectives: *this, these, that, those*
- Possessive adjectives: *my, our, your, his, her, its, their*

**Example:**   Moths are living in my closet.

*Question:*   _Are moths living in my closet?_

*Negative statement:*   _Moths are not living in my closet._

1. I answered her email immediately.

   *Question:* _____

   *Negative statement:* _____

2. The porcupine attacked my dog.

   *Question:* _____

   *Negative statement:* _____

3. Final exams will be given during the last week of school.

   *Question:* _____

   *Negative statement:* _____

4. Gunnar saw the robbery at the convenience store.

   *Question:* _____

   *Negative statement:* _____

5. He is working on the problem right now.

   *Question:* _____

   *Negative statement:* _____

## 29f Verb Tense

macmillanhighered.com
/foundationsfirst
LearningCurve > Multilingual
Verbs

In English, a verb's form indicates its **tense**—when the action referred to by the verb took place (for instance, in the past or in the present). Be sure to use the appropriate tense of the verb even if the time is obvious or if the sentence includes other indications of time (such as *two years ago* or *yesterday*).

INCORRECT   Yesterday, I get a letter from my sister Yunpi.

CORRECT   Yesterday, I got a letter from my sister Yunpi.

## FYI

See Chapter 24 for information on the past tense and Chapter 25 for information on past participles.

## 29g  Stative Verbs

**Stative verbs** usually tell us that someone or something is in a state that will not change, at least for a while.

macmillanhighered.com /foundationsfirst
Additional Grammar Exercises > Stative Verbs

Hiro knows American history very well.

Most English verbs show action, and these action verbs can be used in the progressive tenses. The **present progressive** tense consists of the present tense of *be* plus the present participle (*I am going*). The **past progressive** tense consists of the past tense of *be* plus the present participle (*I was going*). Stative verbs, however, are rarely used in the progressive tenses.

INCORRECT   Hiro is knowing American history very well.

CORRECT   Hiro knows American history very well.

# FYI

## Stative Verbs

Stative verbs—for example, *know, understand, think, believe, want, like, love,* and *hate*—often refer to mental states. Other stative verbs include *be, have, need, own, belong, weigh, cost,* and *mean*. Certain verbs of sense perception, like *see* and *hear*, are also stative even though they can refer to momentary events rather than to unchanging states.

Many verbs have more than one meaning, and some of these verbs are active with one meaning but stative with another. An example is the verb *weigh*.

ACTIVE   The butcher weighs the meat.

STATIVE   The meat weighs three pounds.

In the first sentence above, the verb *weigh* means "to put on a scale"; it is active, not stative, as the use of the present progressive tense shows. In the second sentence, however, the same verb means "to have weight," so it is stative, not active. It would be incorrect to say, "The meat is weighing three pounds."

### PRACTICE
### 29-6
In each of the following sentences, circle the verb. Then, correct any problems with stative verbs by crossing out the incorrect verb tense and writing the correct verb tense above the line. If a sentence is correct, write *C* in the blank after the sentence.

**Example:** Ahmed ~~is wanting~~ *wants* to take advanced calculus next semester. ____

1. Ahmed is studying mathematics in college. ____

2. He is also knowing a lot about astronomy. ____

3. He is understanding the movements of planets and stars. ____

4. He was being president of the Astronomy Club last year. ____

5. Ahmed is working his way through school. ____

6. He is having a job at a gas station. ____

7. He is hating the long hours that he works there. ____

8. Ahmed is needing the money for his tuition. ____

9. Little by little, he is earning enough to help his family. ____

10. Ahmed is knowing he has to keep his job for now. ____

## 29h  Gerunds

**ⓔ macmillanhighered.com
/foundationsfirst**
Additional Grammar
Exercises > Gerunds

A **gerund** is a verb form ending in *-ing* that always acts as a noun.

Reading the newspaper is one of my favorite things to do on Sundays.

Just like a noun, a gerund can be used as a subject, a direct object, a subject complement, or the object of a preposition.

## FYI

### Gerunds

- A gerund can be a subject.

    Playing soccer is one of my hobbies.

- A gerund can be a direct object.

    My brother influenced my playing.

- A gerund can be a subject complement.

    The most important thing is winning.

- A gerund can be the object of a preposition.

    The crowd cheered him for trying.

**PRACTICE**
**29-7**   To complete the sentences below, fill in the blanks with the gerund form of the verb provided in parentheses.

**Example:** _____*Wearing*_____ (wear) a thick leather glove helps bull

riders prevent rope burn.

1. _____ (walk) through the garden, I admired the azaleas.

2. On my way to school, I enjoy _____ (listen) to music.

3. The dentist warned me against _____ (drink) too much soda.

4. _____ (bring) your dog to a bar is legal in Portland, Oregon.

5. For Ben, _____ (pass) chemistry was the hardest thing he

had ever done.

## 29i  Choosing Prepositions

A **preposition** is a word that introduces a noun or pronoun and links it to other words in the sentence. The word the preposition introduces is called the **object of the preposition**.

A preposition and its object combine to form a **prepositional phrase**: *on the table, near the table, under the table*. Thus, prepositions show the precise relationships between words—for example, whether a book is *on*, *near*, or *under* a table.

> I thought I left the book on the table or somewhere near the table, but I found it under the table.

The prepositions *at*, *in*, and *on*, which identify the location of a place or an event, sometimes cause problems for nonnative speakers of English.

- The preposition *at* specifies an exact point in space or time.

  > Please leave the package with the janitor at 150 South Street. I will pick it up at 7:30 tonight.

- Expanses of space or time are treated as containers and therefore require *in*.

  > Jean-Pierre went to school in the 1970s.

- *On* must be used in two cases: with names of streets (but not with exact addresses) and with days of the week or month.

  > We will move into our new office on 18th Street either on Monday or on March 12.

## FYI

### Using Prepositions in Familiar Expressions

Below is a list of familiar expressions that have similar meanings. They are often used in the same contexts.

acquainted with/familiar
  with
addicted to/hooked on
angry with (a person),
  upset with
bored with/tired of
capable of/able to
consist of/have, contain,
  include
deal with/address (a problem)
depend on/rely on
differ from (something else),
  be different from
differ with (someone else)/
  disagree
emigrate from/move from
  (another country)
grateful for (a favor)/
  thankful for

immigrate to/move to
  (another country)
interested in/fascinated by
interfere with/disrupt
meet with/get together with
object to/oppose
pleased with/happy with
protect against/guard
  against
reply to/answer
responsible for/accountable for
similar to/almost the
  same as
succeed in/attain success in
take advantage of/use an
  opportunity to
wait for (something to
  happen)/expect
wait on (in a restaurant)/serve

**PRACTICE**

**29-8**    In the following paragraph, fill in each blank with the correct preposition.

**Example:**    Naomi's family lives _____*in*_____ a small house _____*on*_____

Parsons Street.

(1) Naomi emigrated _____ Ghana when she was a teenager.

(2) Her family settled _____ New Jersey, _____ the East Coast

of the United States. (3) Naomi had studied English _____ Ghana,

but she was not prepared for the kind of English spoken _____ the

United States. (4) The other students _____ her class sometimes

laughed _____ her pronunciation. (5) Still, she studied hard, and her high school teachers were pleased _____ her progress. (6) Naomi was interested _____ attending college and getting a nursing degree. (7) She knew that she was capable _____ doing well _____ college classes if she could continue to improve her English. (8) Before sending an application _____ a local college, Naomi met _____ an admissions officer to discuss her application. (9) Everyone _____ the admissions office was encouraging, and Naomi decided to take advantage _____ their offers to help her. (10) _____ April 12, Naomi's mother called her _____ her after-school job to tell her that the college had accepted her.

## 29j  Prepositions in Phrasal Verbs

A **phrasal verb** consists of two words, a verb and a preposition, that are joined to form an idiomatic expression. Many phrasal verbs are **separable**. This means that a direct object can come between the verb and the preposition. However, some phrasal verbs are **inseparable**; that is, the preposition must always come immediately after the verb.

**macmillanhighered.com /foundationsfirst**
Additional Grammar Exercises > Prepositions in Phrasal Verbs

### Separable Phrasal Verbs

In many cases, phrasal verbs may be split, with the direct object coming between the two parts of the verb. When the direct object is a noun, the second word of the phrasal verb can come either before or after the object. In the sentences below, *turn off* is a phrasal verb. Because the object of the verb *turn off* is a noun (*printer*), the second word of the verb can come either before or after the verb's object.

**CORRECT**   Please turn off the printer.

**CORRECT**   Please turn the printer off.

When the object of a transitive verb is a pronoun, however, these two-word verbs must be split, and the pronoun must come between the two parts.

**CORRECT**   Please turn it off.

**INCORRECT**   Please turn off it.

### Some Common Separable Phrasal Verbs

| | | | |
|---|---|---|---|
| ask out | hang up | put back | think over |
| bring up | leave out | put off | throw away |
| call up | let in | put on | try out |
| carry out | let out | set aside | turn down |
| drop off | look over | shut off | turn off |
| fill out | make up | take down | wake up |
| give away | put away | take off | |

Remember, when the object of the verb is a pronoun, these two-word verbs must be split, and the pronoun must come between the two parts: *take it down, put it on, let it out, make it up,* and so on.

## Inseparable Phrasal Verbs

Some phrasal verbs cannot be separated; that is, the preposition cannot be separated from the verb. This means that a direct object cannot come between the verb and the preposition.

CORRECT    Please go over the manual carefully.

INCORRECT    Please go the manual over carefully.

Notice that in the correct sentence above, the direct object (*manual*) comes right after the preposition (*over*).

### Some Common Inseparable Phrasal Verbs

| | | |
|---|---|---|
| come across | go over | see to |
| get along | run across | show up |
| give in | run into | stand by |

### PRACTICE
### 29-9

Consulting the lists of inseparable and separable phrasal verbs above, decide whether the preposition is placed correctly in each of the following sentences. If a sentence is correct, write *C* in the blank after the sentence. If it is not correct, edit the sentence.

**Example:**   Before she called the taxi, Chong looked up the phone

number in the phone book. ___*C*___

1. Chong had never traveled alone, and she wanted to try out it. _____

2. She planned to stay away for at least a week. _____

3. Chong went over her instructions for her family before she left on her

trip. _____

4. On the kitchen counter, she left out a list of chores for her family to do while she was away. _____

5. She told her husband that the children had to get to school early on Friday and that he should wake up them at 6:30 a.m. _____

6. She warned him not to give to them in if they wanted to watch cartoons on Saturday morning. _____

7. When her husband and children asked how long she would be gone, Chong put off them. _____

8. Before she left, she collected some of her old clothes and gave away them. _____

9. She also dropped off her husband's shirts at the cleaners. _____

10. After three days, Chong missed her family so much that she called up them and said that she was coming home right away. _____

## Skills Check

Look back at your response to the Seeing and Writing prompt on page 403. Reread it, and complete the following tasks.

- Review the grammatical issues covered in this chapter.
- Make any necessary grammar and usage corrections to your writing.

## TEST · Revise · Edit

Starting with **TEST**, revise your paragraph. Then, edit and proofread your work.

## EDITING PRACTICE

Read the following student paragraph, which contains errors in the use of subjects, articles and determiners, stative verbs, and idiomatic expressions containing prepositions. Look carefully at each underlined word or phrase. If it is not used correctly, cross it out and write the correct word or phrase above the line. If the underlined word or phrase is correct, write *C* above it. The first sentence has been edited for you.

### The Electoral College

Many Americans ~~are believing~~ *believe* that the winning candidate is the person who has gotten the most votes, but when an election is ~~being~~ very close, the candidate who gets the greatest number of votes may not win the presidency. The president is actually selected by the Electoral College, a group consisting with "electors" from every state. The Electoral College was created by the Continental Congress on 1787, before George Washington was elected president. Since those time, United States has depended for the Electoral College to select the president. If the no candidate wins a majority of Electoral College votes, the House of Representatives decides the election. In 1824, John Quincy Adams was elected by the House of Representatives even though he had received only the third of the popular vote. Were two more elections in the nineteenth century in which the apparent winner lost in the Electoral College. At 1876, Electoral College chose Rutherford B. Hayes, who had lost for Samuel Tilden in the popular vote. In 1888, Benjamin Harrison got fewer votes than Grover Cleveland, but Harrison got more electoral votes and became president. Americans are becoming very interested with the Electoral College when an election is close. For example, in 2000 George W. Bush got more electoral votes and defeated Al Gore even though Gore won the popular vote. Most Americans think that every vote should be equally important in the democracy. Some people feel that the Electoral College system is not fair. Perhaps some twenty-first-century Congress will finally object on the system enough to try out a new one.

# review checklist

## Grammar and Usage Issues for ESL Writers

☐ In almost all cases, English sentences must state their subjects. (See 29a.)

☐ English nouns may be count nouns or noncount nouns. A count noun names one particular thing or a group of particular things (*a teacher, oceans*). A noncount noun names something that cannot be counted (*gold, sand*). (See 29b.)

☐ Determiners are adjectives that identify rather than describe the nouns they modify. Determiners may also indicate amount or number. (See 29c.)

☐ The definite article *the* and the indefinite articles *a* and *an* are determiners that indicate whether the noun that follows is one readers can identify (*the book*) or one they cannot yet identify (*a book*). (See 29d.)

☐ To form a negative statement, add the word *not* directly after the first helping verb of the complete verb. To form a question, move the helping verb that follows the subject to the position directly before the subject. (See 29e.)

☐ A verb's form must indicate when the action referred to by the verb took place. (See 29f.)

☐ Stative verbs indicate that someone or something is in a state that will not change, at least for a while. Stative verbs are rarely used in the progressive tenses. (See 29g.)

☐ A gerund is a verb form ending in *-ing* that is always used as a noun. (See 29h.)

☐ Many familiar expressions end with prepositions. The prepositions *at, in*, and *on* sometimes cause problems for nonnative speakers of English. (See 29i.)

☐ A phrasal verb consists of two words, a verb and a preposition, that are joined to form an idiomatic expression. (See 29j.)

Read the following student essay, which includes some basic grammatical errors. Correct any errors you find in the use of the past tense, past participles, nouns, pronouns, adjectives, and adverbs. The first error has been corrected for you.

## The Peace Corps: A Way to Give Back

Americans often say that they are interested in promoting world peace. In 1960, John F. Kennedy ~~has~~ had the idea that the U.S. government could give ordinary citizens a way to do just that. Beginning in 1961, Americans have had a chance to become Peace Corps volunteers. Today, people continue to volunteer for the Peace Corps for these reasons. First, they could travel. Second, they got valuable experience. Most important, they have the chance to help others.

One reason to join the Peace Corps is to travel. Members of the Peace Corps have been send all over the world by the U.S. government, which pays their costs. For example, the Peace Corps had had volunteers in the nation of Kazakhstan since 1993. Kazakhstan used to be a Communist country, but the Peace Corps has helped the people of Kazakhstan to move to a free-market system and to practice democracy. Peace Corps volunteers always work close with ordinary people. Before they are sent to Kazakhstan or any other country, every volunteer studies the local language. During their stay, he or she eats the local food and participates in local activitys, such as village meetings and weddings. In some countries, members of the Peace Corps live with host families; in others, he or she lives alone in small huts. Running water and electricity may be available, or conditions may be more difficult. These are not typical tourist experiences; they are priceless opportunitys to learn about people in another part of the world.

Another reason to join the Peace Corps is to learn skills for future. Living in another country is a life-changing experience for Peace Corps volunteers. This volunteers have to become more self-reliant and self-confident. Far from home, they learn to get along with many different kinds of people. The volunteers they learn how to deal with frustration and how to survive and thrive in a new environment. Most Peace Corps volunteers had became fluent in another language and familiar with another culture—skills that corporations and government value. If former Peace Corps members want to go to graduate school, he or she can sometimes get financial aid. Therefore, someone whom is thinking about the future may find that their Peace Corps experience will be very valuable.

The most important reason to join the Peace Corps is to help others. Peace Corps volunteers can make especially important contributions in education and agriculture. In the developing world, many people have little education, yet they need to be well educate. Peace Corps volunteers not only teach academic subjects like English and math but also provide vital health information. Volunteers can even teach a local resident to be teachers themselves. In this way, the volunteers' contributions can continue after they have return to the United States. Agriculture is another area where Peace Corps volunteers can make a real significant difference; after all, increasing the food supply is essential for most developing countries. Peace Corps volunteers they also help with business skills, community development, and information technology. The Peace Corps makes it possible for its volunteers to work on projects that contribute to positive change.

Joining the Peace Corps offers several benefits. First, volunteers get to travel and live in a foreign country. Second, Peace Corps experience gives volunteers skills that can help them find rewarding employment. Third, and more important, the Peace Corps gives volunteers the opportunity to do well. Often, Americans want to "give something back" and share some of their advantages with others. They can do this by becoming Peace Corps volunteers.

unit

**6**

# Understanding Punctuation, Mechanics, and Spelling

# 30 Using Commas

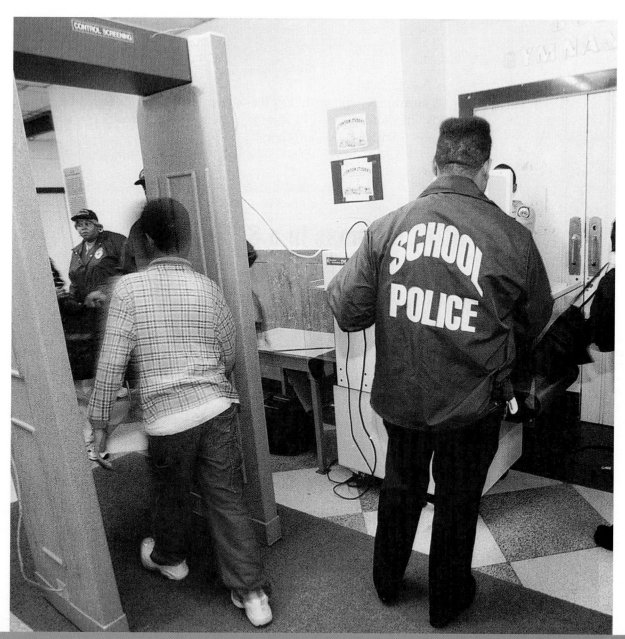

Dan Loh/AP Images

## seeing and writing

The picture above shows a security checkpoint in a public high school. What kind of security do you think is needed in U.S. high schools? Why? Look at the picture, and then write a paragraph in which you answer these questions. Try to use the Word Power words in your paragraph.

WORD POWER

**altercation** angry quarrel
**surveillance** the close observation of a person or a group of people, especially a person or group under suspicion

In this chapter, you will learn
- to use commas in a series (30a)
- to use commas with introductory and transitional elements (30b)
- to use commas with appositives (30c)
- to use commas with nonrestrictive clauses (30d)
- to use commas in compound and complex sentences (30e)
- to use commas in dates and addresses (30f)

A **comma** is a punctuation mark that separates words or groups of words within sentences. In this way, commas help readers by keeping ideas distinct from one another.

# 30a Commas in a Series

Use commas to separate items in a **series** of three or more words, phrases, or clauses.

macmillanhighered.com
/foundationsfirst
LearningCurve > Commas;
Additional Grammar
Exercises > Commas
in a Series

*Hamlet*, *Macbeth*, and *Othello* are tragedies by William Shakespeare.

Brian read *Hamlet*, started *Macbeth*, and skimmed *Othello*.

*Hamlet* is a tragedy, *Much Ado about Nothing* is a comedy, and *Richard III* is a history play.

## FYI

### Using Commas in a Series

Newspapers and magazines usually leave out the comma before the coordinating conjunction in a series of three or more items. However, your writing is clearer when you use a comma before the coordinating conjunction (*and*, *or*, *but*, and so on) in this situation.

UNCLEAR  The party had two hundred guests, great food and rock music blaring from giant speakers. (*Did food as well as music come from the speakers?*)

CLEAR  The party had two hundred guests, great food, and rock music blaring from giant speakers.

**PRACTICE**

**30-1**   Edit the following sentences for the correct use of commas in a series. If the sentence is correct, write *C* in the blank.

**Example:**   We stowed our luggage, took our seats‸and fastened our

seat belts. _____

1. The street was crowded with buses cars and trucks. _____

2. The boys are either in the house, in the yard or at the park. _____

3. Jo Ellen took a walk Roger cleaned the house and Phil went to the

movies. _____

4. Volunteers collected signatures accepted donations and answered

phones. _____

5. We did not know whether to laugh, cry, or cheer. _____

## 30b  Commas with Introductory and Transitional Elements

## Introductory Words and Phrases

Use a comma to set off an **introductory phrase** from the rest of the sentence.

For best results, take this medicine with a full glass of water.

In case of fire, keep calm.

After the concert, we walked home through the park.

Hot and tired, we stopped for a cold drink.

Clearly, she is the most talented contestant.

Whistling a tune, he thought about the concert.

To get good grades, you need to work hard.

macmillanhighered.com
/foundationsfirst
Additional Grammar
Exercises > Commas
with Introductory and
Transitional Elements

**PRACTICE**

**30-2**   Edit the following sentences for the correct use of commas with introductory phrases. If the sentence is correct, write *C* in the blank.

**Example:**   After school‸Thieu went to soccer practice. _____

The artist who was formerly known as Prince is now known as Prince again.

In the sentence above, the highlighted words provide essential information: they tell readers which particular artist is now known as Prince again. Without the clause *who was formerly known as Prince*, the sentence does not communicate the same idea.

The artist is now known as Prince again. (Which artist is known as Prince?)

## FYI

### *Which*, *That*, and *Who*

- *Which* always introduces a nonrestrictive clause.

  NONRESTRICTIVE   Natural disasters, which can be terrifying, really appeal to movie audiences. (clause set off by commas)

- *That* always introduces a restrictive clause.

  RESTRICTIVE   They wanted to see the movie that had the best special effects. (no commas)

- *Who* can introduce either a nonrestrictive or a restrictive clause.

  NONRESTRICTIVE   Wally Lamb, who wrote a novel recommended by Oprah's Book Club, saw his book become a best-seller. (clause set off by commas)

  RESTRICTIVE   Many people who watched *Oprah* have bought the books her book club recommended. (no commas)

## PRACTICE

**30-6**   In each of the following sentences, decide whether the underlined words are essential to the sentence's meaning. Then, add commas to set off nonrestrictive clauses. If the sentence is correct, write *C* in the blank.

### Examples

My boss who loves fishing has a picture of his boat in his office. _____

The train that derailed yesterday was empty. ___*C*___

1. A clock that ticks loudly can be irritating. _____

2. The reader who graded my essay gave me an A. _____

3. My new tablet which was a birthday present is easy to use. _____

4. Fish that live in polluted water are unsafe to eat. _____

5. The artist who painted this picture is famous for her landscapes. _____

6. Boxing which requires quick reflexes can be exciting to watch. _____

7. Rafael who finishes work at 5:30 met Carla for dinner at 7:00. _____

8. The Thai restaurant that opened last month is supposed to be excellent.

    _____

9. Gray wolves which many ranchers dislike are making a comeback in

    the West. _____

10. The Broadway star who has also appeared in films has many devoted

    fans. _____

**PRACTICE**

**30-7**  Edit the sentences in the following paragraph so that commas set off all nonrestrictive clauses. (Remember, commas are *not* used to set off restrictive clauses.) If the sentence is correct, write *C* in the blank.

**Example:**  The Rupununi Weavers Society‸which is based in Guyana‸

runs an Internet business. _____

(1) Many people who live in developing countries have difficulty making a living. _____ (2) Modern technology which of course includes the Internet is changing that. _____ (3) In fact, businesses that use the Internet can reach customers around the world. _____ (4) For example, a group of women who live in Guyana started an Internet business. _____ (5) The women who call themselves the Rupununi Weavers Society needed buyers for their products. _____ (6) These products which they make themselves are handwoven hammocks. _____ (7) A company, that sells satellite telephones, donated some phone lines to the weavers. _____ (8) The same company which also sells computers helped the women

connect to the World Wide Web. _____ (9) The weavers who could find no customers in their own village soon sold many of their hammocks to customers in other regions. _____ (10) These women changed the economy of a village that had long been in poverty. _____

**PRACTICE**

**30-8**    Edit the sentences in the following paragraph so that commas set off all nonrestrictive clauses. If the sentence is correct, write *C* in the blank.

> **Example:** Before 1965, discriminatory laws, which were called Jim Crow laws, existed in many states. _____

(1) The March on Washington for Jobs and Freedom which took place on August 28, 1963 was an important event in the U.S. civil rights movement. _____ (2) Between 200,000 and 300,000 marchers participated which made it one of the largest demonstrations for human rights in U.S. history. _____ (3) Many people predicted violence and disorder, but the march was peaceful and well organized. _____ (4) Marchers gathered on the National Mall which has the Washington Monument at one end and the Lincoln Memorial at the other. _____ (5) After speeches by fifteen other civil rights leaders, Martin Luther King Jr. who was president of the Southern Christian Leadership Conference delivered his "I Have a Dream" speech. _____ (6) The speech which lasted about seventeen minutes was widely considered the high point of the occasion. _____ (7) In a 1999 poll, scholars who study public speeches ranked it first among twentieth-century American speeches. _____ (8) It is most famous for the repetition of "I have a dream" which occurs eight times in the second half of the speech. _____ (9) The "dream" is about an America that will keep its promise of equality and freedom for all. _____ (10) This country which elected an African-American president in 2008 and 2012 has made great progress toward fulfilling King's dream, but more work remains to be done. _____

**ℯ macmillanhighered.com /foundationsfirst**
Additional Grammar Exercises > Commas in Compound and Complex Sentences

# 30e   Commas in Compound and Complex Sentences

In Chapters 15 and 16, you learned how to use commas in compound and complex sentences. Here is a brief review.

## Compound Sentences

A **compound sentence** is made up of two or more independent clauses (simple sentences) joined by a coordinating conjunction (*and, or, nor, but, for, so, yet*), by a semicolon, or by a transitional word or phrase. When a coordinating conjunction joins two independent clauses, always use a comma before the coordinating conjunction.

> Morocco is in North Africa, <u>but</u> Senegal is in West Africa.

## Complex Sentences

A **complex sentence** is made up of an independent clause and one or more dependent clauses. The clauses are joined by a subordinating conjunction or a relative pronoun. Use a comma after the dependent clause when it comes *before* the independent clause.

> <u>Although</u> the African-American men called the Buffalo Soldiers fought bravely in World War II, most were never honored for their heroism.

**PRACTICE**

**30-9**   Edit the sentences in the following paragraph for the correct use of commas in compound and complex sentences. If the sentence is correct, write *C* in the blank.

**Example:**   The Alaska Statehood Act was signed by President Eisenhower in 1958, and Alaska became a state the following year. ___*C*___

(1) Travel in Alaska is difficult so people often rely on airplanes for transportation. _____ (2) Alaska's population is small but it is a very large state. _____ (3) Although many people live in Alaska's cities many others live in small villages. _____ (4) Such villages are scattered across the state and roads do not always reach them. _____ (5) Moreover, travel by road is not always possible because the state's Arctic weather can be severe. _____ (6) Even though air travel is expensive it is often the best

option available. _____ (7) Alaska's bush pilots use small planes because these planes can take off and land in tight spots. _____ (8) When a landing strip is not available a pilot may land on snow or even on open water. _____ (9) Most of Alaska's air passengers are locals, but visiting hunters and sightseers also fly with bush pilots. _____ (10) Until residents find a better means of transportation bush pilots will enjoy a brisk business in Alaska. _____

**macmillanhighered.com /foundationsfirst** Additional Grammar Exercises > Commas in Dates and Addresses

# 30f Commas in Dates and Addresses

## Dates

Use commas in dates to separate the day of the week from the month and to separate the day of the month from the year.

> The first Christmas that Elena's son celebrated was Saturday, December 25, 1999.

When a date that includes commas falls in the middle of a sentence, place a comma after the date.

> Saturday, December 25, 1999, was the first Christmas that Elena's son celebrated.

## Addresses

Use commas in addresses to separate the street address from the city and to separate the city from the state or country.

> The British prime minister lives at 10 Downing Street, London, England.

When an address that includes commas falls in the middle of a sentence, place a comma after the address.

> The residence at 10 Downing Street, London, England, has been home for Winston Churchill and for Margaret Thatcher.

**PRACTICE 30-10** Edit the following sentences for the correct use of commas in dates and addresses. Add any missing commas, and cross out any unnecessary commas. If the sentence is correct, write *C* in the blank.

**Examples**

Atif was born on August 15 1965. _____

Islamabad Pakistan is near his hometown. _____

1. Atif is from Lahore Pakistan. _____

2. On March 12, 1995 his family arrived in the United States. _____

3. Their first home was at 2122 Kent Avenue Brooklyn New York. _____

4. Atif and his wife became citizens of the United States in December, 1999. _____

5. They wanted to move to Boston Massachusetts where Atif's cousins lived. _____

6. On Tuesday June 6 2000 the family moved to the Boston area. _____

7. Their new address was 14 Arden Street Allston Massachusetts. _____

8. Atif's daughters started school there on September 5. _____

9. The school is located at 212 Hope Street, Allston. _____

10. Atif's older daughter graduated from the sixth grade on Friday June 28 2002. _____

# Skills Check

Look back at your response to the Seeing and Writing prompt on page 429. Reread it, and complete the following tasks.

- Circle every comma in your writing.
- Then, review this chapter, and decide whether each comma is necessary.
- If you decide any commas are unnecessary, cross them out.
- Reread your work again to make sure you have not left out any necessary commas.

# TEST · Revise · Edit

Starting with **TEST**, revise your paragraph. Then, edit and proofread your work.

## EDITING PRACTICE

Read the following student paragraph, which contains some errors in the use of commas. Add commas where necessary between items in a series and with introductory phrases, transitional words or phrases, appositives, and nonrestrictive clauses. Cross out any unnecessary commas. The first sentence has been edited for you.

### The Battles of Elizabeth Cady Stanton

In the 1860s, two human rights campaigns divided public opinion. One was abolition the movement to end slavery. The other was women's suffrage the movement to allow women to vote. Elizabeth Cady Stanton was an important figure in both struggles and she helped to bring about their success. Her work toward abolition which included lobbying Congress went on for more than twenty years. At the same time she wanted to improve the lives of women. Women, who had almost no legal rights were treated as the property of men. Cady Stanton believed women would never be equal to men, until they had the right to vote. Although the suffrage movement was an uphill fight she devoted herself to it for more than fifty years. She wrote to Congress spoke about women's rights, and published a newspaper called *The Revolution*. Elizabeth Cady Stanton's work which she did while raising seven children changed women's lives. Obviously her important place in history is well deserved.

## review checklist

### Using Commas

☐ Use commas to separate elements in a series of three or more words, phrases, or clauses. (See 30a.)

☐ Use commas to set off introductory and transitional elements. (See 30b.)

☐ Use commas to set off an appositive from the rest of the sentence. (See 30c.)

☐ Use commas to set off nonrestrictive clauses. (See 30d.)

☐ Use commas in compound and complex sentences. (See 30e.)

☐ Use commas to separate parts of dates and addresses. (See 30f.)

# 31 Using Apostrophes

© Spencer Grant/Photo Researchers, Inc.

## seeing and writing

The picture above shows a female firefighter. Do you believe that men and women are equally qualified for all jobs, or do you think that some jobs should be "men's jobs" or "women's jobs"? Look at the picture, and then write a paragraph in which you explain your position. Try to use the Word Power words in your paragraph.

**In this chapter, you will learn**

- to use apostrophes to form contractions (31a)
- to use apostrophes to form possessives (31b)
- to revise incorrect use of apostrophes (31c)

An **apostrophe** is a punctuation mark that is used in two situations: to form a contraction and to form the possessive of a noun or an indefinite pronoun.

macmillanhighered.com
/foundationsfirst
LearningCurve > Apostrophes;
Additional Grammar
Exercises > Apostrophes
in Contractions

# 31a Apostrophes in Contractions

A **contraction** is a word that uses an apostrophe to combine two words. The apostrophe takes the place of the letters that are left out.

I didn't [*did not*] understand the question.

It's [*it is*] sometimes hard to see the difference between right and wrong.

### Frequently Used Contractions

| | | | | | | | |
|---|---|---|---|---|---|---|---|
| I | + | am | = I'm | could | + | not | = couldn't |
| we | + | are | = we're | do | + | not | = don't |
| you | + | are | = you're | does | + | not | = doesn't |
| it | + | is | = it's | will | + | not | = won't |
| I | + | have | = I've | should | + | not | = shouldn't |
| I | + | will | = I'll | would | + | not | = wouldn't |
| there | + | is | = there's | let | + | us | = let's |
| is | + | not | = isn't | that | + | is | = that's |
| are | + | not | = aren't | who | + | is | = who's |
| can | + | not | = can't | | | | |

### PRACTICE
### 31-1

Edit the following paragraph so that apostrophes are used correctly in contractions.

**Example:** Kentucky's Berea College ~~doesnt~~ *doesn't* require its students to pay tuition.

(1) Berea College students from low-income families who cant pay for school can still get a college education. (2) In fact, Berea wont accept anyone who has the ability to pay. (3) The college wants only students who

wouldnt otherwise be able to afford to attend a four-year college. (4) There arent many other colleges or universities that offer this kind of support. (5) Berea has made itself unusual in other ways as well, in ways that other schools arent. (6) For example, the college has a community-service program thats very well respected. (7) Its not unusual for Berea students to spend many hours every week volunteering in their Appalachian community. (8) Theyre also all required to have on-campus jobs. (9) This school offers students a rare opportunity in an age where income tends to determine whos able to attend college and who isnt. (10) Its unfortunate that more schools havent decided to follow Berea's lead.

**PRACTICE**

**31-2** In each of the following sentences, add apostrophes to contractions, if needed, and edit to make sure all apostrophes are placed correctly. If a sentence is correct, write *C* in the blank.

> **Example:** Thousands of people die in car accidents each year be-
> cause of drivers who ~~arent~~ *aren't* paying attention. _____

1. Were all guilty of distracted driving at one time or another. _____

2. For example, changing the radio station doesnt require much concentration, but it can still take our attention off the road. _____

3. One distraction that's especially hazardous is texting. _____

4. Anyone who has tried to send a text while driving knows it is'nt easy.

   _____

5. Texting while driving has increased in recent years, primarily among teenagers who do'nt have much driving experience. _____

6. Some groups have told lawmakers that it's not safe to mix texting and driving. _____

7. As a result, many states dont allow drivers to text while driving. _____

8. In a few states, only new drivers are prohibited from texting while driving, and its legal for experienced drivers to text. _____

9. Some members of Congress feel that texting while driving should'nt be legal for anyone in any state. _____

10. Most Americans agree theres no reason to text and drive, and they believe its' a good idea to pass a federal law banning texting while driving. _____

## 31b Apostrophes in Possessives

**Possessive** forms show ownership. **Nouns** (names of people, animals, places, objects, or ideas) and **indefinite pronouns** (words like *everyone* and *anything*) use apostrophes to show ownership.

## Singular Nouns and Indefinite Pronouns

To form the possessive of singular nouns (including names), add an apostrophe plus an *s*.

The game's score [the score of the game] was very close.

Coach Nelson's goal [the goal of Coach Nelson] was to win.

Some singular nouns end in *-s*. Even if a singular noun already ends in *-s*, add an apostrophe plus an *s* to form the possessive.

The class's new computers were unpacked on Tuesday.

Carlos's computer crashed on Wednesday.

## FYI

### Indefinite Pronouns

Indefinite pronouns—words like *everyone* and *anything*—form possessives in the same way singular nouns do: they add an apostrophe and an *s*.

Rodney was everyone's choice [the choice of everyone] for quarterback.

## Plural Nouns

Most nouns form the plural by adding *-s*. To form the possessive of plural nouns (including names) that end in *-s*, add just an apostrophe. Do *not* add an apostrophe plus an *s*.

The two televisions' features [the features of the two televisions] were very different.

The Thompsons' house [the house of the Thompsons] is on the corner.

Some irregular plural nouns do not end in -*s*. If a plural noun does not end in -*s*, add an apostrophe plus an *s* to form the possessive.

The children's room is upstairs.

**PRACTICE**

**31-3**   Rewrite the following groups of words, changing the singular noun or indefinite pronoun that follows *of* to the possessive form.

**Example:**   the plot of the book _____*the book's plot*_____

1. the owner of the shop _____

2. the pilot of the plane _____

3. the cat of my neighbor _____

4. the surface of the desk _____

5. the cell phone of Indira _____

6. the engine of the truck _____

7. the sister of Chris _____

8. the guess of anyone _____

9. the opinion of our class _____

10. the waiting room of the doctor _____

**PRACTICE**

**31-4**   Rewrite the following groups of words, changing the plural noun that follows *of* to the possessive form.

**Example:**   the rhythm of the dancers _____*the dancers' rhythm*_____

1. the bags of the travelers _____

2. the quills of the porcupines _____

3. the faces of the women _____

4. the room of the men _____

5. the car of the ministers _____

6. the bills of the customers _____

7. the apartment of the Huangs _____

## EDITING PRACTICE

The following student paragraph includes errors in the use of semicolons, colons, dashes, and parentheses. (Some are used incorrectly; others have been omitted where they are needed.) Correct any errors you find. The first sentence has been corrected for you.

### An Alligator for a Neighbor

The alligator is a popular symbol in Florida the University of Florida even uses one as its mascot. However, alligators are: wild animals that can sometimes hurt humans. As we build our homes closer to animal habitats; we may find we have an alligator for a neighbor. Human construction often forces alligators out of their natural habitat swamps and other wetlands. The destruction of their homes and hunting grounds means alligators must find shelter close to human habitats in parks, in golf ponds, or even in swimming pools. This means the animals come much closer to humans than they should. An alligator can seriously harm or even kill a human, but following a few rules should keep you safe if you encounter an alligator. The first rule is the most important leave the alligator alone. Most attacks occur after people have tried to feed or touch the alligator. Second, stay away from alligator nests a mother will always fight to defend her young. If an alligator does attack you; try to strike it in its most vulnerable areas the eyes or nose. Hit the alligator on the nose to make it let go often, alligators open their jaws when hit on the snout. Any scrapes or bites from an alligator no matter how small should be immediately treated by a doctor. As we build closer to the alligator's natural habitat; we may have more encounters with these animals. For this reason: it is important to understand the challenges of having an alligator for a neighbor.

☐ Use semicolons to separate two simple sentences (independent clauses). (See 32a.)

☐ Use colons to introduce quotations, explanations, clarifications, examples, and lists. (See 32b.)

☐ Use dashes and parentheses to set off material from the rest of the sentence. (See 32c.)

# 33 Understanding Mechanics

© Warner Bros/Photofest

## seeing and writing

The picture above shows Bugs Bunny facing his longtime enemy, Elmer Fudd. Look at the picture. Then, write a paragraph in which you describe your favorite cartoon or comic strip. Be sure to name the most important characters, and try to quote some dialogue that you remember. Try to use the Word Power words in your paragraph.

In this chapter, you will learn

- to capitalize proper nouns (33a)
- to punctuate direct quotations (33b)
- to set off titles (33c)

**PREVIEW**

## 33a Capitalizing Proper Nouns

A **proper noun** names a particular person, animal, place, object, or idea. Proper nouns are always capitalized. The list that follows explains and illustrates the rules for capitalizing proper nouns.

**macmillanhighered.com /foundationsfirst**
LearningCurve > Capitalization; Additional Grammar Exercises > Capitalizing Proper Nouns

- Always capitalize **names of races**, **ethnic groups**, **tribes**, **nationalities**, **languages**, and **religions**.

   The census data revealed a diverse community of Caucasians, African Americans, and Asian Americans, with a few Latino and Navajo residents. Native languages include English, Korean, and Spanish. Most people identified themselves as Catholic, Protestant, or Muslim.

- Capitalize **names of specific people** and **any titles that go along with those names**.

   From 2000 until 2006, President Vicente Fox led Mexico.

In general, do not capitalize titles that are used without a name.

   The student body president met with the dean.

- Capitalize **names of specific family members** and **their titles**.

   Cousin Matt and Cousin Susie are the children of Mom's brother, Uncle Bill.

Do not capitalize words that identify family relationships, including those introduced by possessive pronouns.

   My cousins Matt and Susie are the children of my mother's brother Bill, who is my uncle.

- Capitalize **names of specific countries**, **cities**, **towns**, **bodies of water** (**lakes**, **rivers**, **oceans**), **streets**, and so on.

   The Liffey runs through Dublin.

Do not capitalize words that identify unnamed places.

   The river runs through the city.

- Capitalize **names of specific geographical regions**.

   Louis L'Amour's novels are set in the American West.

Do not capitalize such words when they refer to a direction.

> We got lost after we turned west off the freeway.

■ Capitalize **names of specific groups, clubs, teams,** and **associations.**

> Members of the Teamsters' Union worked at the Democratic Party convention, the Backstreet Boys concert, and the Sixers-Pacers game.

Do not capitalize general references to groups of individuals.

> Members of the union worked at the party's convention, the rock group's concert, and the basketball teams' game.

■ Capitalize **brand names.**

> Jan put on her Rollerblades and skated off to Xerox her paper.

Do not capitalize general references to kinds of products.

> Jan put on her in-line skates and skated off to photocopy her paper.

■ Capitalize **titles of specific academic courses.**

> Calvin registered for English 101 and Psychology 302.

Do not capitalize names of general academic subject areas, except for proper nouns—for example, the name of a language or a country.

> Calvin registered for English and psychology.

■ Capitalize **days of the week, months of the year,** and **holidays.**

> Christmas, Chanukah, and Kwanzaa all fall in December.

Do not capitalize the names of the seasons (*summer, fall, winter, spring*).

> Christmas, Chanukah, and Kwanzaa all fall in the winter.

***Note:*** Also capitalize the names of specific buildings and monuments; specific historical periods, events, and documents; and names of businesses, government agencies, schools, and other institutions.

**PRACTICE**

**33-1**    Edit the following sentences, capitalizing letters and changing capitals to lowercase letters where necessary.

**Example:**    Archaeologists study the Ojibwa at ᴹmackinac State Historic

Park in ᴹmichigan, a ˢ$tate where many of the Ojibwa live.

1. The Ojibwa are the largest native american group in north america.

2. Today, they live near the Great lakes in the united states and canada.

3. The Ojibwa migrated to the midwest from their original homes near the atlantic ocean.

4. Many modern Ojibwa live in the cities of Detroit and duluth and on rural Reservations.

5. Activist Winona LaDuke, who served as the Principal of an Ojibwa school, ran for Vice President on the green party ticket in 2000.

**PRACTICE**

**33-2**  Write a sentence that includes each of the following pairs of words. Capitalize where necessary. Each sentence should be at least six or seven words long.

**Example:**  valentine's day/holiday

*Graham's least favorite holiday is Valentine's Day.*

1. aunt mary/aunt

_____

2. johnson's department store/store

_____

3. reverend jackson/minister

_____

## 33b  Punctuating Quotations

A **direct quotation** reproduces the *exact* words of a speaker or writer. Direct quotations are always placed in quotation marks. A direct quotation is usually accompanied by an **identifying tag** (sometimes called a signal phrase), a phrase that tells who is being quoted. In the following sentences, the identifying tag is underlined.

macmillanhighered.com /foundationsfirst
Additional Grammar Exercises > Punctuating Quotations

Brian said, "I've decided to go to business school."

Tolstoy wrote, "Happy families are all alike; every unhappy family is unhappy in its own way."

When a quotation is a complete sentence, it begins with a capital letter and ends with a period, a question mark, or an exclamation point. When a quotation falls at the end of a sentence (as it does in the previous examples), the period is placed *inside* the quotation marks.

If the quotation is a question or an exclamation, the question mark or exclamation point is also placed *inside* the quotation marks.

Howie asked, "Is that your final answer?"

When the vampire attacked, Ted cried, "Help me!"

---

### Punctuating Direct Quotations with Identifying Tags

- Identifying tag at the beginning

  Jamie announced, "I really need to cut up all my credit cards."

- Identifying tag at the end

  "I really need to cut up all my credit cards," Jamie announced.

  "Do I really need to cut up all my credit cards?" asked Jamie.

- Identifying tag in the middle

  "I'll cut up all my credit cards," Jamie promised, "and then I'll start over."

  Note that because the part of the quotation that follows the identifying tag is not a new sentence, it does not begin with a capital letter.

- Identifying tag between two sentences

  "Doing without credit cards will be good for me," Jamie decided. "Paying cash for everything will help me stick to my budget."

  Note that because the part of the quotation that follows the identifying tag is a complete sentence, it begins with a capital letter.

---

## FYI

### Indirect Quotations

A direct quotation reproduces someone's *exact* words, but an **indirect quotation** simply summarizes what was said or written. Do not use quotation marks with indirect quotations.

| | |
|---|---|
| **DIRECT QUOTATION** | Martin Luther King Jr. said, "I have a dream." |
| **INDIRECT QUOTATION** | Martin Luther King Jr. said that he had a dream. |

**PRACTICE**

**33-3**  Rewrite each of the following sentences twice. In the first version, place the identifying tag at the end of the sentence. In the second version, place the identifying tag in the middle of the sentence. Be sure to check punctuation and capitalization carefully.

**Example:**  Joe said, "The grapes don't taste as good as they look."

*"The grapes don't taste as good as they look," Joe said.*

*"The grapes," Joe said, "don't taste as good as they look."*

1. The senator promised, "I will do my best to defeat the new immigration bill."

    _____

    _____

2. The mayor announced, "Everyone should evacuate before the hurricane strikes."

    _____

    _____

3. Sunita said, "I wonder if we will ever have a woman president of the United States."

    _____

    _____

**PRACTICE**

**33-4**  In the following sentences containing direct quotations, first underline the identifying tag. Then, punctuate the quotation correctly, adding capital letters where necessary.

**Example:**  Injustice anywhere, said Dr. Martin Luther King Jr., is a threat to justice everywhere.

1. The guide announced whatever you do, don't leave the group.

2. Why does it always rain on my birthday Patrice asked.

3. Move along, everyone the officer shouted.

4. The game isn't over till it's over said baseball legend Yogi Berra.

5. If we get separated Paul asked where should I meet you?

macmillanhighered.com
/foundationsfirst
Additional Grammar
Exercises > Setting
Off Titles

# 33c    Setting Off Titles

Some titles are enclosed in quotation marks; others are *italicized*. (When you write by hand, underline to indicate italics.)

The following box indicates which titles should be italicized and which should be enclosed in quotation marks.

---

### Italics or Quotation Marks?

| ITALICIZED TITLES | TITLES IN QUOTATION MARKS |
|---|---|
| Books: *The Joy Luck Club* | Book chapters: "Writing a Paragraph" |
| Newspapers: *Los Angeles Times* | Short stories: "The Lottery" |
| Magazines: *People, Latina* | Essays and newspaper and magazine articles: "Shooting an Elephant" |
| Record albums: *Motown Legends* | Short poems: "The Road Not Taken" |
| Long poems: *Paradise Lost* | Songs and speeches: "The Star-Spangled Banner"; "I Have a Dream" |
| Plays: *Our Town, Death of a Salesman* | Individual episodes of television or radio series: "The Montgomery Bus Boycott" (episode of *Eyes on the Prize*) |
| Films: *Lord of the Rings* | |
| Television and radio series: *Eyes on the Prize* | |
| Paintings and sculpture: *American Gothic*; *Pietà* | |
| Video games: *Halo 4*; *Call of Duty: Black Ops* | |

---

**PRACTICE**

**33-5**    In each of the following sentences, underline titles to indicate italics or insert quotation marks around titles. (Remember that titles of books and other long works are underlined and that titles of stories, essays, and other shorter works are enclosed in quotation marks.)

**Example:**    Stephen King's book <u>Just after Sunset</u> includes the short stories "Rest Stop" and "Harvey's Dream."

1. For an audience in New York, Jay-Z and Alicia Keys performed their song Empire State of Mind from the album Blueprint 3.

2. The movie Slumdog Millionaire is based on the novel Q & A by Vikas Swarup.

3. The first chapter of Max Brooks's book The Zombie Survival Guide is called The Undead: Myths and Realities.

4. The book Guinness World Records 2010 has a section called Planet Earth and another called Human Achievements.

5. The author of the vampire novels Twilight, New Moon, Eclipse, and Breaking Dawn was interviewed for the newspaper USA Today.

# FYI

## Capitalizing Words in Titles

Capitalize the first letters of all important words in titles. Do not capitalize an **article** (*a*, *an*, or *the*), a **preposition** (*to*, *of*, *around*, and so on), or a **coordinating conjunction**—unless it is the first or last word of the title (*On the Road*; *No Way Out*).

**PRACTICE 33-6** Edit the following sentences, capitalizing letters where necessary in titles.

**Example:** The hit song "my heart will go on" by Celine Dion was featured in the soundtrack for the film *titanic*.

1. Some of Disney's most successful animated films include *finding nemo*, *the lion king*, and *snow white and the seven dwarfs*.

2. Reality shows like *dancing with the stars* and *america's next top model* are popular among all age groups.

3. The documentary film *this is it* includes footage from Michael Jackson's last concert.

4. The American literature class discussed stories such as Kate Chopin's "the story of an hour" and Flannery O'Connor's "a good man is hard to find."

5. The magazine *rolling stone* provides in-depth coverage of musicians with articles like "lenny kravitz: just like starting over" and "rivers cuomo grows up."

## Skills Check

Look back at your response to the Seeing and Writing prompt on page 460. Reread it, and answer the following questions.

- Have you capitalized all proper nouns?
- Have you used quotation marks correctly to set off direct quotations?
- Have you punctuated direct quotations correctly?
- Have you italicized the title of the cartoon you chose to write about and used capital letters in the title where necessary?

Correct any errors in mechanics.

## TEST · Revise · Edit

Starting with TEST, revise your paragraph. Then, edit and proofread your work.

## EDITING PRACTICE

Read the following student paragraph, which contains errors in mechanics. Then, edit the passage to correct the errors. The first sentence has been edited for you.

### The Nobel Peace Prize

The Nobel Peace Prize is one of the best known Awards in the world. It was first awarded in 1901 and has been presented in all but nineteen years since then. The prize was awarded just once during world war I and just once during world war II, and both times the winner was the International Committee Of The Red Cross. Sometimes, the Award has been controversial, as it was when former vice President Al Gore shared the Prize with the intergovernmental panel on climate change. Gore's book, "Earth In The Balance," and his Movie, "an Inconvenient Truth," advocated action to combat the effects of Climate Change, but some people disagreed with his claim that climate change was a serious danger to humanity. Perhaps the greatest controversy associated with the nobel peace prize involved mahatma Gandhi, not because he received the Award but because he did not, despite being nominated for it five times. On october 9, 2009, many were surprised when president Barack Obama won the Nobel peace prize after less than a year in office. Obama said, I will accept this award as a call to action." Like the red cross, other organizations have also won the award. For example, the 2013 award went to the Organization for the Prohibition of Chemical Weapons.

## review checklist

### Understanding Mechanics

☐ Capitalize proper nouns. (See 33a.)

☐ Always place direct quotations within quotation marks. (See 33b.)

☐ In titles, capitalize all important words, as well as the first and the last words. Use quotation marks or italics to set off titles. (See 33c.)

# 34 Understanding Spelling

AP Images

## seeing and writing

The picture above shows a man smoking outside his place of work. Look at the picture, and then write a paragraph in which you discuss whether you think laws that prohibit smoking in public places are fair. Try to use the Word Power words in your paragraph.

In this chapter, you will learn

- to become a better speller (34a)
- to know when to use *ie* and *ei* (34b)
- to understand prefixes (34c)
- to understand suffixes (34d)

PREVIEW

## 34a Becoming a Better Speller

Teachers and employers will expect you to be able to recognize and correct misspelled words. The following suggestions can help you become a better speller.

- *Use a spell checker.* Always use a spell checker. It will identify and correct many typos and misspelled words. However, keep in mind that spell checkers will not identify typos that create words (*form* instead of *from*) or words that you have used incorrectly (*there* for *their*).

- *Look up unfamiliar words.* As you proofread, circle words whose spellings you are not sure of. Look up these words to make sure they are spelled correctly.

- *Proofread carefully.* Proofread first for misspellings. Then, go back and check for other errors. (Try starting with the last sentence of your paper and reading backward to the beginning. This strategy enables you to concentrate on one word at a time without being distracted by your paper's content.)

- *Keep a personal spelling list.* Write down all the words you misspell. Also, keep a record of the words your spell checker highlights, and write down any misspelled words that your instructor identifies. (These will usually be circled or marked *sp.*)

- *Learn the basic spelling rules.* Memorize the spelling rules outlined in this chapter. Each rule you learn can help you spell many words correctly.

- *Review commonly confused words.* Study the commonly confused words in Chapter 35. If any of these words give you trouble, add them to your personal spelling list.

- *Use memory cues.* Think of a memory cue that will help you remember how to spell each particularly troublesome word. For example, remembering that *definite* contains the word *finite* will help you remember that *definite* is spelled with an *i*, not an *a*.

- *Learn how to spell the most frequently misspelled words.* Study the words on the following list. If a word gives you trouble, add it to your personal spelling list.

## Some Frequently Misspelled Words

| | | | |
|---|---|---|---|
| across | disappoint | loneliness | reference |
| address | early | medicine | restaurant |
| a lot | embarrass | minute | roommate |
| all right | entrance | necessary | secretary |
| argument | environment | noticeable | sentence |
| beautiful | everything | occasion | separate |
| becoming | exercise | occur | speech |
| beginning | experience | occurred | studying |
| believe | finally | occurrences | surprise |
| benefit | forty | occurring | tomato |
| calendar | fulfill | occurs | tomatoes |
| cannot | generally | personnel | truly |
| careful | government | possible | until |
| careless | grammar | potato | usually |
| cemetery | harass | potatoes | Wednesday |
| certain | height | prejudice | weird |
| crowded | holiday | prescription | window |
| definite | integration | privilege | withhold |
| definitely | intelligence | probably | woman |
| dependent | interest | professor | women |
| describe | interfere | receive | writing |
| develop | judgment | recognize | written |

## FYI

### Vowels and Consonants

Knowing which letters are vowels and which are consonants will help you understand the spelling rules presented in this chapter.

| | |
|---|---|
| **VOWELS** | *a, e, i, o, u* |
| **CONSONANTS** | *b, c, d, f, g, h, j, k, l, m, n, p, q, r, s, t, v, w, x, z* |

The letter *y* may be considered either a vowel or a consonant, depending on how it is pronounced. In *young, y* acts as a consonant because it has the sound of *y;* in *truly,* it acts as a vowel because it has the sound of *ee.*

macmillanhighered.com
/foundationsfirst
Additional Grammar
Exercises > *ie* and *ei*

## 34b *ie* and *ei*

Memorize this rule: *i* before *e,* except after *c,* or when *ei* sounds like *ay* (as it does in *neighbor* and *weigh*).

| I BEFORE E | EXCEPT AFTER C | OR WHEN *EI* IS PRONOUNCED *AY* |
|---|---|---|
| achieve | ceiling | eight |
| believe | conceive | freight |
| friend | deceive | neighbor |
| | | weigh |

# FYI

## Exceptions to the "*i* before *e*" Rule

The following exceptions to the "*i* before *e*" rule follow no pattern, so you must memorize them.

| | | | |
|---|---|---|---|
| ancient | foreign | neither | society |
| caffeine | height | science | species |
| conscience | leisure | seize | weird |
| either | | | |

**PRACTICE**

**34-1**  In each of the following sentences, proofread the underlined words for correct spelling. If a correction needs to be made, cross out the incorrect word, and write the correct spelling above it. If the word is spelled correctly, write *C* above it.

**Example:**   The winner of the college <u>science</u> competition will ~~recieve~~ *receive*
          a full scholarship.

1. If you <u>believe</u> in yourself, you will find it easier to <u>acheive</u> your goals.

2. Sometimes, an emergency can turn <u>nieghbors</u> into <u>friends</u>.

3. <u>Niether</u> one of these dresses fits, and the colors aren't flattering <u>either</u>.

4. The <u>frieght</u> charge depends on the <u>wieght</u> of the package.

5. In the future, people will have more <u>leisure</u> than we can <u>conceive</u> of.

6. The children could not control <u>thier</u> <u>grief</u> over the death of the dog.

7. The wealthy <u>soceity</u> of <u>ancient</u> Rome depended on slave labor.

8. The <u>hieght</u> of the <u>cieling</u> was striking.

9. A criminal may confess to <u>releive</u> a guilty <u>conscience</u>.

10. That unusual <u>species</u> of butterfly must have come here from a <u>foriegn</u>
    country.

## 34c   Prefixes

A **prefix** is a group of letters added to the beginning of a word that changes the word's meaning. Adding a prefix to a word does not change the spelling of the original word.

| | |
|---|---|
| dis + service = disservice | pre + heat = preheat |
| un + able = unable | un + natural = unnatural |
| co + operate = cooperate | over + rate = overrate |

**PRACTICE**

**34-2**   Write in the blank the new word that results when the given prefix is added to each of the following words.

**Example:**   pre + view = _____*preview*_____

1. un + easy = _____

2. dis + satisfied = _____

3. co + exist = _____

4. pre + war = _____

5. tele + communications = _____

## 34d   Suffixes

A **suffix** is a group of letters added to the end of a word that changes the word's meaning or its part of speech. Adding a suffix to a word can change the spelling of the original word.

### Words Ending in Silent *e*

A **silent *e*** is an *e* that is not pronounced. If a word ends with a silent *e*, drop the *e* if the suffix you are adding begins with a vowel.

**DROP THE *E***

| | |
|---|---|
| hope + ing = hoping | dance + er = dancer |
| continue + ous = continuous | insure + able = insurable |

**EXCEPTIONS**

| | |
|---|---|
| change + able = changeable | courage + ous = courageous |
| notice + able = noticeable | replace + able = replaceable |

Keep the *e* if the suffix begins with a consonant.

**KEEP THE *E***

hope + ful = hopeful          bore + dom = boredom

excite + ment = excitement          same + ness = sameness

**EXCEPTIONS**

argue + ment = argument          true + ly = truly

judge + ment = judgment          nine + th = ninth

**PRACTICE**

**34-3** Write in the blank the new word that results when the given suffix is added to each of the following words.

**Examples**

decide + ing = _____*deciding*_____

lone + ly = _____*lonely*_____

1. adore + able = _____          6. invite + ation = _____

2. definite + ly = _____          7. true + ly = _____

3. judge + ment = _____          8. dine + ing = _____

4. care + ful = _____          9. insure + ance = _____

5. whistle + ed = _____          10. dedicate + ion = _____

# Words Ending in *y*

When you add a suffix to a word that ends in -*y*, change the *y* to an *i* if the letter before the *y* is a consonant.

**CHANGE *Y* TO *I***

beauty + ful = beautiful          busy + ly = busily

try + ed = tried          friendly + er = friendlier

**EXCEPTIONS**

■ Keep the *y* if the suffix starts with an *i*.

cry + ing = crying          baby + ish = babyish

■ Keep the *y* when you add a suffix to some one-syllable words.

shy + er = shyer          dry + ness = dryness

■ Keep the *y* if the letter before the *y* is a vowel.

**KEEP THE *Y***

annoy + ance = annoyance          enjoy + ment = enjoyment

play + ful = playful          display + ed = displayed

**EXCEPTIONS**

day + ly = daily                   say + ed = said

gay + ly = gaily                   pay + ed = paid

**PRACTICE**

**34-4** Write in the blank the new word that results when the given suffix is added to each of the following words.

**Examples**

cry + ed = _____cried_____

fry + ing = _____frying_____

employ + ment = _____employment_____

1. try + ing = _____        6. annoy + ance = _____

2. pay + ed = _____         7. dry + ness = _____

3. noisy + ly = _____       8. play + ful = _____

4. buy + er = _____         9. tiny + er = _____

5. destroy + ed = _____     10. happy + ness = _____

# Doubling the Final Consonant

When you add a suffix that begins with a vowel—for example, *-ed*, *-er*, or *-ing*—double the final consonant in the original word if you can answer "yes" to *both* these questions.

1. Do the last three letters of the word have a consonant-vowel-consonant pattern (cvc)?
2. Does the word have only one syllable (or place the stress on the last syllable)?

**FINAL CONSONANT DOUBLED**

cut        +   ing   =   cutting (*cvc — one syllable*)

bat        +   er    =   batter (*cvc — one syllable*)

pet        +   ed    =   petted (*cvc — one syllable*)

commit     +   ed    =   committed (*cvc — stress is on last syllable*)

occur      +   ing   =   occurring (*cvc — stress is on last syllable*)

**FINAL CONSONANT NOT DOUBLED**

answer     +   ed    =   answered (*cvc — but stress is not on last syllable*)

happen     +   ing   =   happening (*cvc — but stress is not on last syllable*)

act        +   ing   =   acting (*one syllable — but no cvc*)

**PRACTICE**

**34-5**  Write in the blank the new word that results when the given suffix is added to each of the following words.

**Examples**

hit + ing = _____hitting_____

slow + er = _____slower_____

1. shop + er = _____

2. squeak + ing = _____

3. prefer + ed = _____

4. thin + est = _____

5. climb + ed = _____

6. wrap + ing = _____

7. fair + est = _____

8. regret + ed = _____

9. begin + ing = _____

10. star + ed = _____

# Skills Check

Look back at your response to the Seeing and Writing prompt on page 470. Type the paragraph you wrote, and run a spell check. Then, answer the following questions.

- Which errors did the spell check identify?
- Which errors did the spell check miss?

Correct any errors you find.

# TEST · Revise · Edit

Starting with TEST, revise your paragraph. Then, edit and proofread your work.

## EDITING PRACTICE

Read the following student paragraph, which contains spelling errors. As you read, identify the words you think are misspelled. Then, check the list on page 472. If you do not find them there, check a dictionary. Finally, cross out each incorrectly spelled word, and write the correct spelling above the line. The first error has been corrected for you.

Body Language

Body language is the gestures and facial expressions by which a person

communicates with others. Body and facial ~~movments~~ *movements* can certanly tell alot about

a person. In fact, some sceintists claim that body language comunicates more

than speach does. Gestures, smiles, posture, eye contact, and even the position

of a person's head, arms, and legs can all revele whether the person is honest

or lying, interested or bored, defensive or coperative. Body language can be

especialy important in a job interview. The first thing to remember is to keep

eye contact with the interviewer but not to stare. The point is to look intrested

without harrassing the interviewer. Experts also say that it is alright to use your

hands to show enthusiasm. Again, the trick is not to overdo it because this can

make you seem agressive or just plain wierd. One suprising recommendation is

not to cross your arms. This can make you look stuborn. Finaly, at the end of

the interview, give the interviewer a firm handshake. This gesture shows that

you are honest and trustworthy. These tips about body language can come in

handy at a job interveiw. They can also help you acheive sucess in other

situations as well.

# review checklist

## Understanding Spelling

☐ Follow the steps to becoming a better speller. (See 34a.)

☐ *I* comes before *e*, except after *c* or in any *ay* sound, as in *neighbor* and *weigh*. (See 34b.)

☐ Adding a prefix to a word does not affect the word's spelling. (See 34c.)

☐ Adding a suffix to a word can change the word's spelling. (See 34d.)

☐ When a word ends with a silent *e*, drop the *e* if the suffix begins with a vowel. Keep the *e* if the suffix begins with a consonant. (See 34d.)

☐ When you add a suffix to a word that ends with a -*y*, change the *y* to an *i* if the letter before the *y* is a consonant. Keep the *y* if the letter before the *y* is a vowel. (See 34d.)

☐ When you add a suffix that begins with a vowel, double the final consonant in the original word if (1) the last three letters of the word have a consonant-vowel-consonant pattern (cvc), and (2) the word has one syllable, or the last syllable is stressed. (See 34d.)

# 35 Learning Commonly Confused Words

© Jeff Greenberg/The Image Works

## seeing and writing

The picture above shows a group of people taking the oath of allegiance at a naturalization ceremony for new U.S. citizens. Look at the picture, and then write a paragraph in which you discuss what the United States of America means to you. Try to use the Word Power words in your paragraph.

Some English words cause spelling problems because they look or sound like other words. The following word pairs are often confused. Learning to distinguish them can help you become a better speller.

**Accept/Except**   *Accept* means "to receive something." *Except* means "with the exception of."

> "I accept your challenge," said Alexander Hamilton to Aaron Burr.

> Everyone except Darryl visited the museum.

**Affect/Effect**   *Affect* is a verb meaning "to influence." *Effect* is a noun meaning "result" and sometimes a verb meaning "to bring about."

> Jodi's job could affect her grades.

> Overexposure to sun can have a long-term effect on skin.

> Commissioner Williams tried to effect changes in police procedure.

macmillanhighered.com /foundationsfirst
Additional Grammar Exercises > Learning Commonly Confused Words

**All ready/Already**   *All ready* means "completely prepared." *Already* means "previously, before."

> Serge was all ready to take the history test.

> Gina had already been to Italy.

**Brake/Break**   *Brake* means "a device to slow or stop a vehicle." *Break* means "to smash" or "to detach."

> Peter got into an accident because his foot slipped off the brake.

> Babe Ruth bragged that no one would ever break his home-run record.

**Buy/By**   *Buy* means "to purchase." *By* is a preposition meaning "close to" or "next to" or "by means of."

> Tina wanted to buy an iPad.

> He drove by but didn't stop.

> He stayed by her side all the way to the hospital.

> Malcolm X wanted "freedom by any means necessary."

**PRACTICE**

**35-1**   Proofread the underlined words in the following sentences for correct spelling. If a correction needs to be made, cross out the incorrect word, and write the correct spelling above it. If the word is spelled correctly, write *C* above it.

**Example:**   The ~~breaks~~ *brakes* on this car work well, <u>except</u> *C* on icy roads.

1. The sign in the shop read, "If you <u>break</u> anything, you have to <u>buy</u> it."

2. Brad was <u>already</u> for the beach <u>except</u> that he forgot his sunglasses.

3. Some medications <u>effect</u> concentration <u>by</u> causing drowsiness.

4. If we hope to <u>affect</u> change in our government, we have to <u>except</u> our responsibility to vote.

5. The college basketball player had <u>already</u> <u>accepted</u> an offer from a professional team <u>by</u> the end of his junior year.

6. Gervase plans to <u>buy</u> a used car with antilock <u>breaks</u>.

7. <u>Buy</u> the way, I've <u>all ready</u> taken that course.

8. Mild stress can <u>effect</u> a person in a positive way, whereas long-term stress can have a negative <u>affect</u>.

9. The excited contestant was <u>all ready</u> to <u>accept</u> the prize money she had won.

10. Participating in sports can <u>affect</u> young people strongly and <u>affect</u> a change for the better in their ability to get along with others.

**Conscience/Conscious**   *Conscience* refers to the part of the mind that urges a person to choose right over wrong. *Conscious* means "aware" or "deliberate."

> After he cheated at cards, his conscience started to bother him.
>
> As she walked through the woods, she became conscious of the hum of insects.
>
> Elliott made a conscious decision to stop smoking.

**Everyday/Every day**   *Everyday* is a single word that means "ordinary" or "common." *Every day* is two words that mean "occurring daily."

> *I Love Lucy* was a successful comedy show because it appealed to everyday people.
>
> Every day, Lucy and Ethel would find a new way to get into trouble.

**Fine/Find**   *Fine* means "superior quality" or "a sum of money paid as a penalty." *Find* means "to locate."

> He sang a fine solo at church last Sunday.
>
> Demi had to pay a fine for speeding.
>
> Some people still use a willow rod to find water.

**Hear/Here**   *Hear* means "to perceive sound by ear." *Here* means "at or in this place."

> I moved to the front so I could hear the speaker.
>
> My great-grandfather came here in 1883.

**Its/It's**    *Its* is the possessive form of *it*. *It's* is the contraction of *it is* or *it has*.

The airline canceled its flights because of the snow.

It's twelve o'clock, and we're late.

Ever since it's been in the accident, the car has rattled.

### PRACTICE

**35-2**    Proofread the underlined words in the following sentences for correct spelling. If a correction needs to be made, cross out the incorrect word, and write the correct spelling above it. If the word is spelled correctly, write *C* above it.

       *C*    *find*

**Example:** Every day, we fine new challenges to face.

1. Sarita became <u>conscience</u> of someone staring at her.

2. "<u>Its</u> been a long time since I've seen you <u>here</u>," Tony said.

3. Sarita smiled as she said, "<u>Its</u> a great place to <u>here</u> jazz."

4. Paul hated paying the <u>fine</u> for parking in a disabled spot, but his <u>conscious</u> bothered him more than losing the money.

5. <u>Everyday</u>, the dog eats <u>it's</u> dinner at precisely 12:00 noon.

6. As soon as a child becomes <u>conscious</u> of right and wrong, his or her <u>conscience</u> begins to develop.

7. This week, <u>everyday</u> has been <u>fine</u> weather.

8. You will <u>fine</u> an outstanding collection of American art right <u>hear</u> in the college museum.

9. The restaurant made a <u>conscience</u> effort to enforce <u>it's</u> "no smoking" policy.

10. The wind had stopped <u>its</u> roaring, but in my mind, I could still <u>hear</u> it.

**Know/Knew/New/No**    *Know* means "to have an understanding of" or "to have fixed in the mind." *Knew* is the past tense form of the verb *know*. *New* means "recent or never used." *No* expresses a negative response.

I know there will be a lunar eclipse tonight.

He knew how to install a new light switch.

Is anything wrong? No.

**Lie/Lay**  *Lie* means "to rest or recline." The past tense of *lie* is *lay*. *Lay* means "to put or place something down." The past tense of *lay* is *laid*.

> Every Sunday, I lie in bed until noon.
>
> They lay on the grass until it began to rain, and then they went home.
>
> Tammy told Carl to lay his cards on the table.
>
> Brooke and Cassia finally laid down their hockey sticks.

**Loose/Lose**  *Loose* means "not fastened" or "not attached securely." *Lose* means "to misplace."

> In the 1940s, many women wore loose-fitting pants.
>
> Sometimes, I lose my keys.

**Mine/Mind**  *Mine* is a possessive pronoun that indicates ownership. *Mind* can be a noun meaning "human consciousness" or "intelligence" or a verb meaning "to obey" or "to attend to."

> That red mountain bike is mine.
>
> A mind is a terrible thing to waste.
>
> "Mind your manners when you visit your grandmother," Dad said.

**Passed/Past**  *Passed* is the past tense of the verb *pass*. It means "moved by" or "succeeded in." *Past* is a noun meaning "earlier than the present time."

> The car that passed me must have been doing more than eighty miles an hour.
>
> David finally passed his driving test.
>
> The novel was set in the past.

**Peace/Piece**  *Peace* means "the absence of war" or "calm." *Piece* means "a part of something."

> The prime minister thought he had achieved peace with honor.
>
> My peace of mind was destroyed when the flying saucer landed.
>
> "Have a piece of cake," said Marie.

**PRACTICE**

**35-3**  Proofread the underlined words in the following sentences for correct spelling. If a correction needs to be made, cross out the incorrect word, and write the correct spelling above it. If the word is spelled correctly, write *C* above it.

> *know*        *C*
> **Example:**  Heads of state ~~no~~ that peace is hard to achieve.

1. Everyone was amazed when the troops lay down their weapons and

   went home in peace.

2. He <u>new</u> he should not eat another <u>peace</u> of candy, but he ate it anyway.

3. In the <u>passed</u>, it was more important to <u>mine</u> one's manners than it is today.

4. Jamal <u>past</u> his chemistry final with a high grade, as we <u>knew</u> he would.

5. I <u>loose</u> my way every time I drive to the mall.

6. The car <u>passed</u> us so quickly it was clear that the driver did not <u>no</u> the speed limit.

7. Janet decided to <u>lay</u> on a lounge chair and enjoy the <u>peace</u> of the garden.

8. The violinist was able to finish playing the <u>piece</u> even though one string had come <u>loose</u>.

9. The <u>new</u> dog had to be trained not to <u>lay</u> on the couch.

10. The children were warned to <u>mine</u> the babysitter.

**Plain/Plane**   *Plain* means "simple, not elaborate." *Plane* is the shortened form of *airplane*.

Sometimes, the Amish are called the plain people.
Chuck Yeager was the first person to fly a plane faster than the speed of sound.

**Principal/Principle**   *Principal* means "first" or "highest" or "the head of a school." *Principle* means "a law or basic assumption."

She had the principal role in the movie.
I'll never forget the day the principal called me into his office.
It was against his principles to tell a lie.

**Quiet/Quit/Quite**   *Quiet* means "free of noise" or "still." *Quit* means "to leave a job" or "to give up." *Quite* means "actually" or "very."

Jane looked forward to the quiet evenings at the lake.
Sammy quit his job and followed the girls into the parking lot.
"You haven't quite got the hang of it yet," she said.
After practicing all summer, Tamika got quite good at softball.

**Raise/Rise**   As a verb, *raise* means "to elevate" or "to increase in size, quantity, or worth." The past tense of *raise* is *raised*. *Rise* means "to stand up" or "to move from a lower position to a higher position." The past tense of *rise* is *rose*. As a noun, *raise* means "an increase in salary."

Carlos raises his hand whenever the teacher asks for volunteers.
They raised the money for the down payment.

The fans rise every time their team scores a touchdown.

Erin rose before dawn so she could see the sunrise.

Her boss gave her a raise.

**Right/Write**    *Right* means "correct" or "the opposite of left." *Write* means "to form letters with a writing instrument."

If you turn right at the corner, you will be going in the right direction.

All students are required to write three short papers.

**Sit/Set**    *Sit* means "to assume a sitting position." The past tense of *sit* is *sat*. *Set* means "to put down or place" or "to adjust something to a desired position." The past tense of *set* is *set*.

I usually sit in the front row at the movies.

They sat at the clinic waiting for their names to be called.

Every semester I set goals for myself.

Elizabeth set the mail down on the kitchen table and left for work.

**Suppose/Supposed**    *Suppose* means "to consider" or "to assume." *Supposed* is both the past tense and the past participle of *suppose*. *Supposed* also means "expected" or "required." (Note that when *supposed* has this meaning, it is followed by *to*.)

Suppose researchers found a cure for AIDS tomorrow.

We supposed the movie would be over by ten o'clock.

You were supposed to finish a draft of the report by today.

**PRACTICE**

**35-4**    Proofread the underlined words in the following sentences for correct spelling. If a correction needs to be made, cross out the incorrect word, and write the correct spelling above it. If the word is spelled correctly, write *C* above it.

**Example:**    Everyone in the creative writing class was ~~suppose~~ *supposed* to

~~write~~ *C* a short story.

1. You are <u>supposed</u> to <u>raise</u> from your seat when an older person enters

   the room.

2. The school board hasn't <u>quite</u> selected a new <u>principle</u> for the high

   school yet.

3. The dress Lindsay is making started out <u>plane</u> but is now <u>quite</u> fancy.

4. We watched as the <u>plane</u> <u>raised</u> slowly and disappeared in the clouds.

5. All she wanted was a <u>quite</u> place to <u>set</u> and think for a while.

6. I <u>suppose</u> I should <u>sit</u> this glass on a coaster so as not to damage the wood table.

7. <u>Set</u> the dial to the <u>right</u> level for the kind of fabric you are ironing.

8. Although Yuki was usually <u>quiet</u>, she spoke up to defend her <u>principals</u>.

9. Do you <u>suppose</u> Raoul will be chosen for the <u>principle</u> role in the play?

10. If the candidate cannot <u>rise</u> enough money, she will have to <u>quite</u> the race for mayor.

**Their/There/They're**   *Their* is the possessive form of *they*. *There* means "at or in that place." *There* is also used in the phrases *there is* and *there are*. *They're* is a contraction meaning "they are."

Jane Addams helped poor people improve their living conditions.

I put the book over there.

There are three reasons why I will not eat meat.

They're the best volunteer firefighters I've ever seen.

**Then/Than**   *Then* means "at that time" or "next in time." *Than* is used to introduce the second element in a comparison.

He was young and naive then, but now he knows better.

I went to the job interview and then stopped off for a burger.

My dog is smarter than your dog.

**Threw/Through**   *Threw* is the past tense of *throw*. *Through* means "in one side and out the opposite side" or "finished."

Satchel Paige threw a baseball faster than ninety-five miles an hour.

It takes almost thirty minutes to go through the tunnel.

"I'm through," he said, storming out of the office.

**To/Too/Two**   *To* means "in the direction of." *Too* means "also" or "more than enough." *Two* denotes the numeral 2.

During spring break, I am going to Disney World.

My roommates are coming too.

The microwave popcorn is too hot to eat.

"If we get rid of the tin man and the lion, the two of us can go to Oz," said the scarecrow to Dorothy.

**Use/Used**   *Use* means "to put into service" or "to consume." *Used* is both the past tense and the past participle of *use*. *Used* also means "accustomed." (Note that when *used* has this meaning, it is followed by *to*.)

I use a soft cloth to clean my glasses.

"Hey! Who used all the hot water?" he yelled from the shower.

Mary had used all the firewood during the storm.

After living in Alaska for a year, they got used to the short winter days.

**PRACTICE**

**35-5** Proofread the underlined words in the following sentences for correct spelling. If a correction needs to be made, cross out the incorrect word, and write the correct spelling above it. If the word is spelled correctly, write *C* above it.

> *There*           *C*
> **Example:** ~~Their~~ are at least two good reasons not to rent that apart-
> ^
> ment.

1. It was hard to get use to the cold when they first came to New York from there home in Puerto Rico.

2. The shortstop threw the ball to second base, but it flew on through the air and landed in the stands.

3. I'm threw with the two of them and all they're nonsense!

4. Her blind date was more fun then she expected although it was too early to tell if she really liked him.

5. "They're used to staying up until nine," Mrs. Tsang told the babysitter.

6. Four-year-old Zachary got spaghetti sauce all over his face and than use his T-shirt to wipe it off.

7. If they had known then what problems there car would have, they never would have bought it.

8. As a new teacher, Spencer use to feel tired at the end of the day.

9. Is there any reason to risk driving after drinking to much at a party?

10. I don't like the food at that restaurant, and it's two expensive too.

**Weather/Whether**   *Weather* refers to the state of the atmosphere with respect to temperature, humidity, precipitation, and so on. *Whether* means "if it is so that; if the cause is that."

> The *Farmer's Almanac* says that the weather this winter will be severe. Whether this prediction will be correct is anyone's guess.

**Where/Were/We're**   *Where* means "at or in what place." *Were* is the past tense of *are*. *We're* is a contraction meaning "we are."

> Where are you going, and where have you been?

Charlie Chaplin and Mary Pickford were popular stars of silent movies.

We're doing our back-to-school shopping early this year.

**Whose/Who's**   *Whose* is the possessive form of *who*. *Who's* is a contraction meaning "who is" or "who has."

My roommate asked, "Whose book is this?"

"Who's there?" squealed the second little pig.

"Who's been sleeping in my bed?" asked Goldilocks.

**Your/You're**   *Your* is the possessive form of *you*. *You're* is a contraction meaning "you are."

"You should have worn your running shoes," said the hare as he passed the tortoise.

"You're too kind," replied the tortoise sarcastically.

**PRACTICE**

**35-6**   Proofread the underlined words in the following sentences for correct spelling. If a correction needs to be made, cross out the incorrect word, and write the correct spelling above it. If the word is spelled correctly, write *C* above it.

> *C*          *whether*
> **Example:**   We're not sure ~~weather~~ this is the right road to take.

1. "Whose going to the party," Tracey asked, "and whose car are we taking?"

2. Orlando, were we went on vacation, has good weather and great beaches.

3. "Your late for you're appointment," the receptionist said.

4. Someone who's had experience buying cameras can tell you whether to buy that one.

5. Where you surprised at the sudden change in the weather?

6. Do you know whose left this laptop were anyone might take it?

7. By the time your finished with school and work, your energy is all gone.

8. Whether you like it or not, no one is going to make you're decisions for you.

9. Who's car is parked in the spot were my car usually is?

10. Were you excited when you're letter to the editor was printed?

# Skills Check

Look back at your response to the Seeing and Writing prompt on page 480. Reread it, and complete the following tasks.

- Use the Search or Find function on your computer to locate any words in this chapter that you think you might have misspelled or used incorrectly.
- Check the spelling and usage of each of those words. Cross out any misspelled or misused words, and write the correct words above the line.

# TEST · Revise · Edit

Starting with **TEST**, revise your paragraph. Then, edit and proofread your work.

## EDITING PRACTICE

Read the following student paragraph, which contains errors in word usage. Identify the words you think are used incorrectly, and then find them in this chapter or look them up. Finally, cross out each word that is used incorrectly, and write the correct word above the line. The first sentence has been done for you.

### The Minimum Wage

As someone who has had minimum-wage jobs, I strongly believe in the *principle* ~~principal~~ of a living wage. How in good conscious can employers not pay workers enough to support themselves? Many employers say that rising the minimum wage would have a negative affect on there companies. In addition, some business owners think that the minimum wage is all ready to high. I do not agree with these arguments. A minimum wage is suppose too be enough to supply a person's basic needs. Its also true that higher wages can increase a worker's morale. I realize that the definition of a fair minimum wage depends on the person your talking to. They're is also the question of weather the minimum hourly wage should be enough to support one person or an entire family. In the United States, forty-five states have minimum-wage laws. The federal government first past a minimum-wage law in 1938. About 80 percent of all private industries are all ready covered by federal law. To often, however, self-employed workers and employees of small businesses are not effected by this law. This is a complex problem that will not be easily layed to rest. As lawmakers try to fine a solution, they must except the fact that everyone needs a living wage.

## review checklist

### Learning Commonly Confused Words

Memorize the differences between the most commonly confused words.

Read the following student essay, which includes errors in the use of punctuation, mechanics, and spelling. Correct any errors you find. The first sentence has been edited for you.

Helicopter Parents

Are your parents obsessed with ~~you're~~ *your* every ~~acheivement?~~ *achievement?* Do they dispare whenever you fail a test? Do you ever feel as if your never allowed to make an independent decision? If this sounds familiar you may be the child of helicopter parents. When we think of a helicopter, we imagine a loud aircraft hovering overhead. Helicopter parents are parents, who hover over their children watching every move protecting them from failure and pressuring them to succeed. Helicopter parents can have a disturbing affect on children of any age babies and toddlers, school-age children, and even college students.

Pediatricians can sometimes identify helicopter parents' even before the children are born. These parents are very commited to having read everthing they can about how to create the best child posible. Hoping to improve the babys inteligence, they play classical music while the baby is still in the womb. Once the child is born, these parents read books about child development, and frantically call the pediatrician, whenever they think that their child isnt reaching developmental milestones. In fact they expect their child to be much better than average. They drive their children to carefully chosen play dates; and by only educational toys.

When their children go to school; helicopter parents interfear even more. They harrass alot of the teachers, questioning there judgements about testing and placment, and they are not shy about demanding, that there children be given a different teacher or be placed in a more advanced class. Although all parents are encouraged to supervize their childrens' homework some helicopter parents actually sieze the homework and do it for them. The days when children could dissappear for long hours — playing or daydreaming — are long gone. Instead, children of helicopter parents are ferryed from school to piano lessons to soccer practice to gymnastics. If their on a team that looses, they get a trophy anyway.

Once there children go to college, helicopter parents can be nightmares for administrator's. They accompany their children through registration and complain when a certian class is closed. When a child has an arguement with a roomate, helicopter parents demand a new roommate and they call the proffessor when they're child gets a low grade. Because these children have never used an alarm clock (their parents used to get them up every morning), the parents call everyday to make sure that their getting ready for class. These students have little chance to learn the coping skills they need. As Sue shellenbarger says in the july 29 2005 Wall street journal Online, Some of these hovering parents, whose numbers have been rising for several years, are unwittingly undermining their children's chances of success.

Its clear that good parenting involves a careful balance between concern for the childs' well being, and the need to let go. Every child needs the freedom to make mistakes — or even fail. Helicopter parents do not allow there children too have this important freedom. The dangers are that the children will never learn how to make their own decitions and that they will feel to much pressure to meet their parents expectations. Good parents need to care deeply about their children but they also need to know when its' time to let go.

# 36 Readings for Writers

The following sixteen essays by student and professional writers are designed to give you interesting material to read, react to, think critically about, discuss, and write about.

Each essay is accompanied by a short introduction that tells you something about the reading and its author. Definitions of some of the words used in the essay appear in **Word Power** boxes in the margins. Following each essay are four **Thinking about the Reading** discussion questions and two or three **Writing Practice** prompts.

**Preview** these essays, and then **highlight** and **annotate** them to better understand what you are reading. (Previewing, highlighting, and annotating are discussed in Chapter 1.) Then, reread the essays more carefully in preparation for class discussion and writing.

## Readings

# It's Possible to Graduate Debt-Free. Here's How
## Rebekah Bell

Student loan debt is one of the most common types of debt in the United States. Rebekah Bell, a freelance writer, addresses this problem in her article "It's Possible to Graduate Debt-Free. Here's How." Published in the *Wall Street Journal* in July 2013, the article highlights Bell's strategies for avoiding student loan debt. Bell graduated from Biola University in La Mirada, California.

1    In 2009, when I was applying to my dream college, my parents had one stipulation: graduate without debt. I burst out laughing.

**WORD POWER**

**stipulation** requirement
**feasible** possible

2    There was no feasible way that a middle-class 19-year-old with average grades could attend a college with a price tag of nearly $40,000 a year without taking out loans. But now that I've graduated loan-free, I realize how lucky I am that my parents made this seemingly ridiculous demand.

3    Figures from the Federal Reserve Bank of New York reveal that 37 million Americans have student loan debt. About two-thirds of students receiving bachelor's degrees borrow to fund their education, with the average student debt at an all-time high of $26,000. Total student-loan debt is estimated to be $1 trillion.

4    Only 38% of borrowers are making payments on their loans. The rest are either still in school, postponing payments or not paying them back. Almost one in 10 students who started repayment in 2009 defaulted within two years. At least 40% of student borrowers put off a major purchase such as a car or home because they couldn't afford it, and many are delaying marriage and families.

5    The lesson here is that students should do everything within their power to avoid this kind of debt. Although attending school without loans is difficult, it is not impossible. Here's what I learned about avoiding the debt trap:

- Think creatively. I attended a college close to home during my freshman year because it offered a scholarship. I also took classes online to save money. Some of my friends completed dual-enrollment classes during high school, got college credits from the College-Level Examination Program in subjects where they were already proficient, or attended a less expensive community college before moving to a four-year school. Others attended trade or vocational schools instead of college. The aim should always be: Reduce the number of credits you're paying for at the premium rate.

- Look hard for scholarships. I received an academic scholarship and need-based aid through my university. I also received several community and church scholarships and a matching grant through my father's workplace. Searching for scholarships and aid is tiring but can definitely pay off.

- Use your skills. Figure out a way to use your college interests to earn extra money—and to beef up your résumé and gain real-world experience. I competed on my university's speech team and worked as a videographer for the college newspaper in exchange for several thousand dollars' worth of scholarship money. Some of my friends received athletic or theater scholarships. A friend who was an English major worked in the on-campus tutoring center.

- Generate income. There are creative ways to make money. For me, it meant raising and selling cattle (one of the perks of being raised as a 4-H kid on a farm). One friend became a wedding photographer, earning cash and working only on weekends. My older sister taught piano lessons. A tech-savvy friend did Web design. These were all jobs that brought in money without interfering with classes.

- Make the most of summers. I worked full-time but also spent time interning for film companies. Some of my friends found paid internships during the summer, worked at camps, or took classes at community college for a fraction of the cost. One friend who did this was able to graduate a semester early, thereby saving several thousand dollars on tuition.

- Live frugally. I had a 10-meal per week plan and bought groceries for the rest of my meals. I also lived in a less expensive dorm and had two roommates instead of one, which saved money on room and board. Figure out simple ways to save money. Even if it's only $20 or $30 a month, it adds up over a year.

> **WORD POWER**
>
> **frugally** not extravagantly
> **naysayers** those who take a negative view

More than one financial-aid counselor told me it would be impossible to graduate debt-free. It often seemed like the naysayers were right. But persistence helped me pull it off. And even if I had fallen short, I still would have had to borrow much less than the average student. I may not have had as much free time as some classmates, but I enjoyed a rich and fulfilling college experience while also graduating debt-free. Graduating without debt means that now I can apply for jobs that I really want—instead of feeling like I have to grab the first one that will help me start paying off a student loan. Today, I'm indebted only to my parents for being so unreasonable.   6

## Thinking about the Reading

1. In paragraph 5, referring to student loans, Bell says, "The lesson here is that students should do everything within their power to avoid this kind of debt." Do you agree with her? Why, or why not? What argument could you make against this position?
2. Which of the suggestions Bell lists in paragraph 5 make the most sense to you? Which, if any, seem unrealistic?
3. What did Bell gain by graduating debt-free? What, if anything, do you think she might have lost?
4. Why is Bell grateful to her parents?

## Writing Practice

1. Interview a few classmates to learn how they are financing their education. Then, write an article for your school newspaper that gives an overview of the different ways college students can pay for college.
2. What strategies have you used to keep your educational debt under control? How successful have those strategies been? Write a letter to a younger sibling or some other relative giving him or her advice about how to keep from accumulating too much debt.

# Don't Hang Up, That's My Mom Calling

## Bobbi Buchanan

*Telemarketers' sales calls often interrupt our already hectic lives. Bobbi Buchanan's article reminds us that there is a real, and sometimes familiar, person on the other end of every telemarketing call. Buchanan, whose writing has appeared in the* New York Times *and the* Louisville Review, *is the editor of the online journal* New Southerner. *This article was first published in the* New York Times *in 2003.*

1    The next time an annoying sales call interrupts your dinner, think of my 71-year-old mother, LaVerne, who works as a part-time telemarketer to supplement her Social Security income. To those Americans who have signed up for the new national do-not-call list, my mother is a pest, a nuisance, an invader of privacy. To others, she's just another anonymous voice on the other end of the line. But to those who know her, she's someone struggling to make a buck, to feed herself and pay her utilities—someone who personifies the great American way.

2    In our family, we think of my mother as a pillar of strength. She's survived two heart surgeries and lung cancer. She stayed at home her whole life to raise the seven of us kids. She entered the job market unskilled and physically limited after my father's death in 1998, which ended his pension benefits.

3    Telemarketing is a viable option for my mother and the more than six million other Americans who work in the industry. According to the American Teleservices Association, the telemarketing work force is mostly women; 26 percent are single mothers. More than 60 percent are minorities; about 5 percent are disabled; 95 percent are not college graduates; more than 30 percent have been on welfare or public assistance. This is clearly a job for those used to hardship.

4    Interestingly enough, the federal list exempts calls from politicians, pollsters, and charities, and companies that have existing business relationships with customers can keep calling. Put this in perspective. Are they not the bulk of your annoying calls? Telemarketing giants won't be as affected by the list but smaller businesses that rely on this less costly means of sales will. The giants will resort to other, more expensive forms of advertisement and pass those costs along to you, the consumer.

5    My mother doesn't blame people for wanting to be placed on the do-not-call list. She doesn't argue the fairness of its existence or take offense when potential clients cut her off in mid-sentence. All her parenting experience has made her impervious to rude behavior and snide remarks, and she is not discouraged by hang-ups or busy signals. What worries my mother is that she doesn't know whether she can do anything else at her age. As it is, sales are down and her paycheck is shrinking.

6    So when the phone rings at your house during dinnertime and you can't resist picking it up, relax, breathe deeply and take a silent oath to be polite. Try these three painless words: "No, thank you."

7    Think of the caller this way: a hard-working, first-generation American; the daughter of a Pittsburgh steelworker; a survivor of the Great Depression; the widow of a World War II veteran; a mother of seven, grandmother of eight, great-grandmother of three. It's my mother calling.

**WORD POWER**

**viable** able to survive; capable of success

**WORD POWER**

**exempts** frees from an obligation that others are subject to

**WORD POWER**

**impervious** impossible to affect

## Thinking about the Reading

1. What specific things does Buchanan want readers to know about her mother? Why are these things important?

2. In paragraph 3, Buchanan says that telemarketing is "clearly a job for those used to hardship." What does she mean?

3. What is Buchanan's objection to the national do-not-call list? Do you agree with her? Why or why not?

4. What was your opinion of telemarketers before you read this essay? Has the essay changed your mind in any way? If so, how?

## Writing Practice

1. Write an email to Buchanan arguing that although telemarketers may be nice people who need the income, they are still annoying invaders of our privacy.

2. What do you think can be done to achieve a compromise between telemarketers' need for employment and our desire not to be bothered by their calls? Suggest some ways to make such calls less annoying.

3. Imagine you have just accepted a job as a telemarketer, and your friends are critical of your decision. Respond to their criticisms, explaining why you took the job and what you hope to get out of it.

# Tortillas

## José Antonio Burciaga

José Antonio Burciaga was born in El Paso, Texas, in 1940, and his Chicano identity is the main subject of his poems, stories, and essays. In this essay, he explores his childhood memories — as well as the cultural significance — of tortillas. Tortillas, thin, round, griddle cakes made of cornmeal, are a staple of Mexican cooking.

My earliest memory of *tortillas* is my *Mamá* telling me not to play with them. I had bitten eyeholes in one and was wearing it as a mask at the dinner table.

As a child, I also used *tortillas* as hand warmers on cold days, and my family claims that I owe my career as an artist to my early experiments with *tortillas*. According to them, my clowning around helped me develop a strong artistic foundation. I'm not so sure, though. Sometimes I wore a *tortilla* on my head, like a *yarmulke*, and yet I never had any great urge to convert from Catholicism to Judaism. But who knows? They may be right.

For Mexicans over the centuries, the *tortilla* has served as the spoon and the fork, the plate and the napkin. *Tortillas* originated before the Mayan civilizations, perhaps predating Europe's wheat bread. According to Mayan mythology, the great god Quetzalcoatl, realizing that the red ants knew the secret of using maize as food, transformed himself into a black ant, infiltrated the colony of red ants, and absconded with a grain of corn. (Is it any wonder that to this day, black ants and red ants do not get along?) Quetzalcoatl then put maize on the lips of the first man and woman, Oxomoco and

> **WORD POWER**
>
> **maize** corn
> **absconded** left quickly and secretly to avoid punishment

Cipactonal, so that they would become strong. Maize festivals are still celebrated by many Indian cultures of the Americas.

4    When I was growing up in El Paso, *tortillas* were part of my daily life. I used to visit a *tortilla* factory in an ancient adobe building near the open *mercado* in Ciudad Juárez. As I approached, I could hear the rhythmic slapping of the *masa* as the skilled vendors outside the factory formed it into balls and patted them into perfectly round corn cakes between the palms of their hands. The wonderful aroma and the speed with which the women counted so many dozens of *tortillas* out of warm wicker baskets still linger in my mind. Watching them at work convinced me that the most handsome and *deliciosas tortillas* are handmade. Although machines are faster, they can never adequately replace generation-to-generation experience. There's no place in the factory assembly line for the tender slaps that give each *tortilla* character. The best thing that can be said about mass-producing *tortillas* is that it makes it possible for many people to enjoy them.

5    In the *mercado* where my mother shopped, we frequently bought *taquitos de nopalitos*, small tacos filled with diced cactus, onions, tomatoes, and *jalapeños*. Our friend Don Toribio showed us how to make delicious, crunchy *taquitos* with dried, salted pumpkin seeds. When you had no money for the filling, a poor man's *taco* could be made by placing a warm *tortilla* on the left palm, applying a sprinkle of salt, then rolling the *tortilla* up quickly with the fingertips of the right hand. My own kids put peanut butter and jelly on *tortillas*, which I think is truly bicultural. And speaking of fast foods for kids, nothing beats a *quesadilla*, a *tortilla* grilled-cheese sandwich.

6    Depending on what you intend to use them for, *tortillas* may be made in various ways. Even a run-of-the-mill *tortilla* is more than a flat corn cake. A skillfully cooked homemade *tortilla* has a bottom and a top; the top skin forms a pocket in which you put the filling that folds your *tortilla* into a taco. Paper-thin *tortillas* are used specifically for *flautas*, a type of taco that is filled, rolled, and then fried until crisp. The name *flauta* means *flute*, which probably refers to the Mayan bamboo flute; however, the only sound that comes from an edible *flauta* is a delicious crunch that is music to the palate. In México *flautas* are sometimes made as long as two feet and then cut into manageable segments. The opposite of *flautas* is *gorditas*, meaning *little fat ones*. These are very thick small *tortillas*.

7    The versatility of *tortillas* and corn does not end here. Besides being tasty and nourishing, they have spiritual and artistic qualities as well. The Tarahumara Indians of Chihuahua, for example, concocted a corn-based beer called *tesgüino*, which their descendants still make today. And everyone has read about the woman in New Mexico who was cooking her husband a *tortilla* one morning when the image of Jesus Christ miraculously appeared on it. Before they knew what was happening, the man's breakfast had become a local shrine.

8    Then there is *tortilla* art. Various Chicano artists throughout the Southwest have, when short of materials or just in a whimsical mood, used a dry *tortilla* as a small, round canvas. And a few years back, at the height of the Chicano movement, a priest in Arizona got into trouble with the Church after he was discovered celebrating mass using a *tortilla* as the host. All of which only goes to show that while the *tortilla* may be a lowly corn cake, when the necessity arises, it can reach unexpected distinction.

## WORD POWER

**versatility** the ability to do many things well

**concocted** mixed various ingredients together

## Thinking about the Reading

1. In one sentence, define *tortilla*.
2. List some of the uses for tortillas that Burciaga identifies.
3. What exactly does the tortilla mean to Burciaga? Why are tortillas important to him?
4. What food in your culture represents for you what the tortilla represents for Burciaga?

## Writing Practice

1. Write about another food that you think is as versatile as tortillas are. Use your imagination to identify as many unusual uses for this food as you can.
2. What foods do you consider to be typically American? Define some of these foods, and explain what makes them "American."
3. Imagine you have met someone who knows nothing about your family's culture. Explain the different ethnic foods eaten by your family. Include information about when and where your family eats these foods and why they are important to your family.

# Learning Tagalog

## Ruel Espejo

Speaking English is one way for first-generation Americans to feel a sense of belonging in the United States. However, as student writer Ruel Espejo discovered, it can also distance people from their heritage and family. In this essay, Espejo explores how language affects both communication and identity.

Like many young adults my age, I have spent nearly eighteen years trying to be like everyone else. For me, a first-generation American, this has meant becoming less Filipino and more American. At the same time, though, the particular circumstances of my life have tugged at me, making me want to hold on to my heritage. Little by little, my parents have helped me to realize that I do not want to leave my culture behind. Because I want to hold on to that culture, I have decided to learn Tagalog, my parents' native language.

Sometimes, late at night, my mother would tell me about her childhood back in the Philippines. I loved listening to her accent become thicker and thicker as she went on about her experiences and the beautiful island she called home. It was through her old stories that I grew to know my grandfather. I could see that he was her hero and that she wished I could see him. I also learned about all the traditional roles that my mother reacted against—she was the first feminist I ever met. Once in a while, though, she would try to describe something—the landscape or a native fruit—in the hybrid language we call "Taglish" (half Tagalog, half English), only to give up, saying, "Well, someday I'll take you home. . . ." After these stories, I

**WORD POWER**

**hybrid** a mix of different things

went to sleep disappointed. I knew that even if I went to the Philippines with her, I would never truly understand what she was talking about.

3    My father would go through the same routine with me almost every day. He would struggle to tell me something, only to be frustrated by his mixed-up words. His inability to express himself embarrassed him, but we'd laugh it off. Gradually, though, as a result of these conversations, I began to see how lacking my relationships with him and with my mother were because of our communication gap. I know that first-generation Americans often reject their parents' culture and embrace American culture, and I know how easy it has been for me to lose touch with my background because I have always been surrounded by all things American. I also know that this rejection results in more than just your ordinary generation gap—it results in a cultural gap, too. But only now do I realize how unfair and wrong this situation is.

**WORD POWER**

**assimilation** blending into the dominant culture

4    I had often read about assimilation, about cultural groups giving up what makes them unique in order to be accepted. But until I really thought about my parents and our communication barrier, it never occurred to me that I was living it. I always thought that I knew a lot about the Filipino culture; my parents exposed me to it early, and they even taught me some of the traditional dances. But lately I have begun to feel it slipping away. I don't want to lose it forever, and so I have decided to learn Tagalog.

5    My favorite English teacher has a method of learning new words she calls "Eighty Flashes." She says that the more you expose yourself to a word, either by sight or by usage, the better you'll learn it. In other words, if you use something every day, it will become the norm. Through this technique, I can learn to communicate more fully with my parents and stay in touch with my background. The easiest way to prevent assimilation is to make Filipino culture the norm—and to do that, I will have to use something from it every day. By learning and speaking Tagalog, I can keep my culture alive. I am proud of being a Filipino American, and I want to celebrate it every day. I don't want to end up being one of those completely assimilated "first generationers" I've read about so often.

**WORD POWER**

**alienation** the state of being alone or separate

6    Without ever telling me what to do, my parents opened up my eyes to my ignorance. Because of them, I have come to realize that I need to keep on being Filipino as well as American, and because of them I have discovered exactly how to do so. When I can speak Tagalog, I will no longer have to watch my father or mother struggle to explain something to me. I will be able to meet them halfway, on a sort of language bridge. The feeling of alienation between us will disappear, and in its place will be a mutual understanding.

7    I know that it will take years to learn Tagalog, and I know that it won't be easy. But because my desire to be close to my parents is stronger than my need to "fit in," and because being close to my parents means being close to my culture, I will take the time and effort to learn our native language. My goal is like any other young person's: to realize my whole self. And by learning and speaking my language, I will be doing just that.

**Thinking about the Reading**

1. Why did Ruel Espejo decide to learn Tagalog? List as many of her reasons as you can.

2. Why did Ruel at first resist learning more about her family's Filipino culture?

3. Explain the "Eighty Flashes" technique (paragraph 5). How did it help Ruel to learn more about the Filipino language and culture?

4. Do you think it is important to keep your ethnic, religious, or cultural heritage—even if it prevents you from being fully assimilated into the larger American culture? Explain your views.

**Writing Practice**

1. List all the things that identify you as a member of a particular ethnic or cultural group—for example, celebrations, language, and religious observances. Then, explain why these things are important to you.

2. Interview an older family member about your family's cultural heritage. Write about the elements of this culture that remain in your own life, and then discuss the elements that have been lost to you.

# A Giant Step

## Henry Louis Gates Jr.

An award-winning writer and critic, Henry Louis Gates Jr. is currently the director of the W. E. B. Du Bois Institute for African and African-American Research at Harvard. In the following essay, which appeared in the *New York Times* in 1990, Gates recalls the ordeals he experienced after a childhood touch football injury.

"What's this?" the hospital janitor said to me as he stumbled over my right shoe. 1

"My shoes," I said. 2

"That's not a shoe, brother," he replied, holding it to the light. "That's a brick." 3

It *did* look like a brick, sort of. 4

"Well, we can throw these in the trash now," he said. 5

"I guess so." 6

We had been together since 1975, those shoes and I. They were orthopedic shoes built around molds of my feet, and they had a 2¼-inch lift. I had mixed feelings about them. On the one hand, they had given me a more or less even gait for the first time in 10 years. On the other hand, they had marked me as a "handicapped person," complete with cane and special license plates. I went through a pair a year, but it was always the same shoe, black, wide, weighing about four pounds. 7

It all started 26 years ago in Piedmont, W.Va., a backwoods town of 2,000 people. While playing a game of touch football at a Methodist summer camp, I incurred a hairline fracture. Thing is, I didn't know it yet. I was 14 and had finally lost the chubbiness of my youth. I was just learning tennis and beginning to date, and who knew where that might lead? 8

Not too far. A few weeks later, I was returning to school from lunch when, out of the blue, the ball-and-socket joint of my hip sheared apart. 9

**WORD POWER**

**orthopedic shoes** shoes made to correct abnormal bone structure

**gait** a way of walking

It was instant agony, and from that time on nothing in my life would be quite the same.

10    I propped myself against the brick wall of the schoolhouse, where the school delinquent found me. He was black as slate, twice my size, mean as the day was long and beat up kids just because he could. But the look on my face told him something was seriously wrong, and—bless him—he stayed by my side for the two hours it took to get me into a taxi.

11    "It's a torn ligament in your knee," the surgeon said. (One of the signs of what I had—a "slipped epithysis"—is intense knee pain, I later learned.) So he scheduled for me a walking cast.

12    I was wheeled into surgery and placed on the operating table. As the doctor wrapped my leg with wet plaster strips, he asked about my school-work.

13    "Boy," he said, "I understand you want to be a doctor."

14    I said, "Yessir." Where I came from, you always said "sir" to white people, unless you were trying to make a statement.

15    Had I taken a lot of science courses?

16    "Yessir. I enjoy science."

17    "Are you good at it?"

18    "Yessir, I believe so."

19    "Tell me, who was the father of sterilization?"

20    "Oh, that's easy, Joseph Lister."

21    Then he asked who discovered penicillin.

22    Alexander Fleming.

23    And what about DNA?

24    Watson and Crick.

25    The interview went on like this, and I thought my answers might get me a pat on the head. Actually, they just confirmed the diagnosis he'd come to.

26    He stood me on my feet and insisted that I walk. When I tried, the joint ripped apart and I fell on the floor. It hurt like nothing I'd ever known.

27    The doctor shook his head. "Pauline," he said to my mother, his voice kindly but amused, "there's not a thing wrong with that child. The problem's psychosomatic. Your son's an overachiever."

28    Back then, the term didn't mean what it usually means today. In Appalachia, in 1964, "overachiever" designated a sort of pathology: the overstraining of your natural capacity. A colored kid who thought he could be a doctor—just for instance—was headed for a breakdown.

29    What made the pain abate was my mother's reaction. I'd never, ever heard her talk back to a white person before. And doctors, well, their words were scripture.

30    Not this time. Pauline Gates stared at him for a moment. "Get his clothes, pack his bags—we're going to the University Medical Center," which was 60 miles away.

31    Not great news: the one thing I knew was that they only moved you to the University Medical Center when you were going to die. I had three operations that year. I gave my tennis racket to the delinquent, which he probably used to club little kids with. So I wasn't going to make it to Wimbledon. But at least I wasn't going to die, though sometimes I wanted to. Following the last operation, which fitted me for a metal ball, I was confined to bed, flat on my back, immobilized by a complex system of weights and pulleys. It was six weeks of bondage—and bedpans. I spent

## WORD POWER

**psychosomatic** relating to a physical illness with a mental cause

**pathology** a deviation from the norm

my time reading James Baldwin, learning to play chess and quarreling daily with my mother, who had rented a small room—which we could ill afford—in a motel just down the hill from the hospital.

I think we both came to realize that our quarreling was a sort of ritual. 32 We'd argue about everything—what time of day it was—but the arguments kept me from thinking about that traction system.

I limped through the next decade—through Yale and Cambridge . . . as 33 far away from Piedmont as I could get. But I couldn't escape the pain, which increased as the joint calcified and began to fuse over the next 15 years. My leg grew shorter, as the muscles atrophied and the ball of the ball-and-socket joint migrated into my pelvis. Aspirin, then Motrin, heating pads and massages, became my traveling companions.

Most frustrating was passing store windows full of fine shoes. I used 34 to dream about walking into one of those stores and buying a pair of shoes. "Give me two pairs, one black, one cordovan," I'd say. "Wrap 'em up." No six-week wait as with the orthotics in which I was confined. These would be real shoes. Not bricks.

In the meantime, hip-joint technology progressed dramatically. But no 35 surgeon wanted to operate on me until I was significantly older, or until the pain was so great that surgery was unavoidable. After all, a new hip would last only for 15 years, and I'd already lost too much bone. It wasn't a procedure they were sure they'd be able to repeat.

This year, my 40th, the doctors decided the time had come.            36

I increased my life insurance and made the plunge.                    37

The nights before my operations are the longest nights of my life—but 38 never long enough. Jerking awake, grabbing for my watch, I experience a delicious sense of relief as I discover that only a minute or two have passed. You never want 6 a.m. to come.

And then the door swings open. "Good morning, Mr. Gates," the nurse 39 says. "It's time."

The last thing I remember, just vaguely, was wondering where amne- 40 siac minutes go in one's consciousness, wondering if I experienced the pain and sounds, then forgot them, or if these were somehow blocked out, dividing the self on the operating table from the conscious self in the recovery room. I didn't like that idea very much. I was about to protest when I blinked.

"It's over, Mr. Gates," says a voice. But how could it be over? I had 41 merely blinked. "You talked to us several times," the surgeon had told me, and that was the scariest part of all.

Twenty-four hours later, they get me out of bed and help me into a 42 "walker." As they stand me on my feet, my wife bursts into tears. "Your foot is touching the ground!" I am afraid to look but it is true: the surgeon has lengthened my leg with that gleaming titanium and chrome-cobalt alloy ball-and-socket-joint.

"You'll need new shoes," the surgeon says. "Get a pair of Dock-Sides; 43 they have a secure grip. You'll need a 3/4-inch lift in the heel, which can be as discreet as you want."

I can't help thinking about those window displays of shoes, those ele- 44 gant shoes that, suddenly, I will be able to wear. Dock-Sides and sneakers, boots and loafers, sandals and brogues. I feel, at last, a furtive sympathy for Imelda Marcos, the queen of soles.

**WORD POWER**

**calcified** hardened with excess calcium
**atrophied** decreased in size, often through disuse
**cordovan** a shade of brown

**WORD POWER**

**furtive** secret

45    The next day, I walk over to the trash can, and take a long look at the brick. I don't want to seem ungracious or unappreciative. We have walked long miles together. I feel disloyal, as if I am abandoning an old friend. I take a second look.

46    Maybe I'll have them bronzed.

### Thinking about the Reading

1. What "mixed feelings" (paragraph 7) does Gates have about his shoes? Do you think he also has mixed feelings about his surgery? Why or why not?

2. "A Giant Step" focuses on Gates's progress toward overcoming a physical disability, but it also traces another kind of change. What do you think is the actual "giant step" Gates refers to in this essay's title?

3. List the personal details that Gates supplies about himself. Given the nature of these details and the fact that Gates today is a respected scholar and university professor, do you think the doctor was justified in calling him "an overachiever" (paragraph 27)? Do you think he would have considered Gates an overachiever if he had been white?

4. At the end of his essay, when Gates looks at his shoes in the trash can, what do you think he sees?

### Writing Practice

1. Identify a situation, characteristic, or physical condition that you believe has handicapped you. Then, write about this disability, focusing either on an incident that made you aware of it or on a time when you were able to overcome it.

2. Write a letter from Gates to his doctor explaining Gates's thoughts about the events recounted in paragraphs 12–30. Imagine the letter is being written just after his successful surgery at the age of forty.

## The Importance of Feeling Seen:
## Why Interracial Families on Commercials Matter

### Roxane Gay

Roxane Gay is a prolific writer of both fiction and nonfiction. Her work has appeared in the *Wall Street Journal* and the *Los Angeles Times*, among many other publications. Her novel *An Untamed State* was published in 2014, as was her essay collection *Bad Feminist*. In this 2013 essay published in *Salon*, Gay examines reactions to a Cheerio's commercial featuring an interracial family and considers what those reactions say about our society as a whole.

1    A boyfriend and I are in Montreal. We are holding hands and walking along Rue Sainte Catherine, mostly window-shopping. The relationship is still relatively new so we are still very fond of each other, affectionate even. Suddenly, an angry man crosses our path, spits and hisses something we don't quite catch. Whatever he has said, we know it isn't nice. We know

why we've angered him. He isn't the first stranger to have some kind of objection to our relationship and he won't be the last, because I am black and my boyfriend is white.

That boyfriend and I have long since broken up but I've never forgotten that moment, the unexpected flash of anger a bigoted stranger brought into the private circle of our happiness. It's strange to think that, even in this day and age, interracial relationships beget commentary and, sometimes, controversy.

In 2013, Cheerios debuted a charming commercial, "Just Checking," where a young girl douses her napping father in Cheerios to keep his heart healthy. This commercial was, somehow, both groundbreaking and controversial. Some people took issue with the commercial because the little girl's parents had the nerve to marry even though they had different racial backgrounds. The YouTube comments were so vitriolic the video's comment section was closed. When I first saw the commercial, it didn't even register that the family was in any way remarkable beyond their wholesome good looks and the adorable premise.

It was only in 1967 that the Supreme Court ruled, in *Loving vs. Virginia*, that the state's anti-miscegenation laws were racist—not nearly so long ago as we might assume. Though interracial marriage has risen steadily over the past three and a half decades, society's attitudes, at least as conveyed by popular culture, have been much slower to change.

Interracial relationships on television were something of a taboo for many years. The American public simply wasn't ready to see two people from different races loving each other and maybe having sex. Certainly, there were Lucille Ball and Desi Arnaz in "I Love Lucy" in the 1950s. "The Jeffersons" was innovative not only for depicting an upper-middle-class black family, but also a couple in an interracial relationship—Tom and Helen Willis. The Willis's marriage was routinely the butt of the joke as George Jefferson ridiculed them, but the couple was there; they were seen.

Today, interracial relationships on television are somewhat more common. Shonda Rhimes, in particular, never misses an opportunity to include interracial relationships on her shows, "Private Practice," "Grey's Anatomy" and "Scandal." She recognizes that not all interracial relationships occur between black and white people, a rarity. Most refreshing is that racial difference is not used as a narrative device. The characters simply are who they are and love whom they love. Even a sitting Republican president is getting in on the act, on "Scandal," where Fitz and the impeccably dressed Olivia Pope are passionately in love and kept apart by forces greater than themselves. They face so many obstacles as a couple that, frankly, race is the least of their worries.

Since seeing "Just Checking" and noting the response, both negative and positive, I've started paying more attention to commercials and the kinds of families who are represented in those commercials. It has been really comforting to see so many interracial families and families of color being represented, being seen. That comfort rises out of seeing more evidence, on television, of the world as it really is, not hopelessly trapped in how it once was.

Clearly, a commercial is just a commercial, but we shouldn't dismiss the importance of inclusion in advertising. When advertisers ignore diversity, it is because they don't think the lives of others matter. There is not

**WORD POWER**

**beget** to cause to exist or occur

**WORD POWER**

**vitriolic** bitterly scathing; caustic

**WORD POWER**

**miscegenation** cohabitation or marriage between people of different races

WORD POWER

**imperative** obligation; duty

enough of a financial imperative for those lives to matter. Though the past few years have brought progress, there is still work to be done. There are all kinds of people who continue to be largely ignored by advertisers, whose lives largely go unseen. They deserve their moment.

9    We continue to have these imperfect but necessary conversations about diverse representation in spheres both great (e.g., our elected leadership) and small (e.g., the entertainment we consume), because it means so much to be seen, to feel seen, to feel acknowledged as a part of this great big world.

### Thinking about the Reading

1. According to Gay, why do "interracial families on commercials matter"? Do you agree that seeing these families in commercials (and on TV) makes a difference to mixed-race families? To others?

2. Gay opens her essay with an anecdote. What is the connection between this story and the point she makes in her essay?

3. In paragraph 8, Gay says, "When advertisers ignore diversity, it is because they don't think the lives of others matter." How else might you explain why advertisers might "ignore diversity"?

4. What purpose does paragraph 4 serve? Is it necessary? Should it be developed further? Explain.

### Writing Practice

1. Find the "Just Checking" commercial on YouTube. Do you agree with Gay that it is "charming" (3), or do you have a different reaction? Do you think it is an effective commercial for Cheerios? Write an analysis of the commercial, evaluating how it conveys its message to its audience.

2. In paragraph 2, Gay says, "It's strange to think that, even in this day and age, interracial relationships beget commentary and, sometimes, controversy." Do you find the reactions Gay describes surprising—that is, "strange . . . in this day and age"? What reactions to such relationships do you observe among your friends? Do you think your parents, or your teachers, might react differently? Write a blog post that conveys your observations and conclusions.

## At the Heart of a Historic Movement

### John Hartmire

As executive director of the National Farmworker Ministry, John Hartmire's father worked closely with Cesar Chavez to fight for social justice for farmworkers. However, his father's dedication to the cause meant that he was absent for most of Hartmire's childhood. In this essay, Hartmire discusses what it is like to make a personal sacrifice for a social cause.

1    When my friend's daughter asked me if I knew anything about the man her school was named after, I had to admit that I did. I told her that in California there are at least twenty-six other schools, seventeen streets, seven

parks, and ten scholarships named after Cesar Chavez. Not only that, I said, I once hit a ground ball through his legs during a softball game, and I watched his two dogs corner my sister's rabbit and, quite literally, scare it to death. I used to curse his name to the sun gods while I marched through one sweltering valley or another knowing my friends were at the beach staring at Carrie Carbajal and her newest bikini.

During those years I wasn't always sure of how I felt about the man, but I did believe Cesar Chavez was larger than life. The impact he had on my family was at once enriching and debilitating. He was everywhere. Like smoke and cobwebs, he filled the corners of my family's life. We moved to California from New York in 1961 when my father was named executive director of the National Farmworker Ministry, and for the next thirty-plus years our lives were defined by Cesar and the United Farm Workers.

During those years my father was gone a lot, traveling with, or for, Cesar. I "understood" because the struggle to organize farmworkers into a viable union was the work of a lifetime, and people would constantly tell me how much they admired what Dad was doing. Hearing it made me proud. It also made me lonely. He organized the clergy to stand up for the union, went to jail defying court injunctions, and was gone from our house for days on end, coming home, my mother likes to say, only for clean underwear. It was my father who fed the small piece of bread to Cesar ending his historic twenty-five-day fast in 1968. It's no wonder Dad missed my first Little League home run.

The experience of growing up in the heart of a historic movement has long been the stuff of great discussions around our dinner table. The memories are both vibrant and difficult. There were times when Cesar and the union seemed to be more important to my father than I was, or my mother was, or my brothers and sister were. It is not an easy suspicion to grow up with, or to reconcile as an adult.

While my friends surfed, I was dragged to marches in the Coachella and San Joaquin valleys. I was taken out of school to attend union meetings and rallies that interested me even less than geometry class. I spent time in supermarket parking lots reluctantly passing out leaflets and urging shoppers not to buy nonunion grapes and lettuce. I used to miss Sunday-afternoon NFL telecasts to canvass neighborhoods with my father. Since my dad wanted his family to be a part of his life, I marched and slept and ate and played with Cesar Chavez's kids. When we grew older his son, Paul, and I would drink beer together and wonder out loud how our lives would have been different had our fathers been plumbers or bus drivers.

But our fathers were fighting to do something that had never been done before. Their battle to secure basic rights for migrant workers evolved into a moral struggle that captured the nation's attention. I saw it all, from the union's grape strike in 1965, to the signing of the first contracts five years later, to the political power gained then lost because, for Cesar, running a union was never as natural as orchestrating a social movement.

My father and Cesar parted company four years before Chavez died in 1993. Chavez, sixty-six at the time of his death, father of eight, grandfather of twenty-seven, leader of thousands, a Hispanic icon who transcended race, left the world a better place than he found it. He did it with the help of a great many good people, and the sacrifice of their families, many of whom believed in his cause but didn't always understand what he was asking of, or taking from, them.

**WORD POWER**

**debilitate** to take away the strength of something or someone

**viable** able to survive; capable of success

**WORD POWER**

**orchestrate** to arrange

**transcend** to be greater than; to go beyond

8     So as students here attend Cesar Chavez Elementary School, as families picnic in a Sacramento park named after him and public employees opt to take off March 31 in honor of his birthday, I try to remember Cesar Chavez for what he was—a quiet man, the father of friends, a man intricately bound with my family—and not what he took from my childhood. Namely, my father. I still wrestle with the cost of my father's commitment, understanding that social change does not come without sacrifice. I just wonder if the price has to be so damn high.

9     Do I truly know Cesar Chavez? I suppose not. He was like a boat being driven by some internal squall, a disturbance he himself didn't always understand, and that carried millions right along with him, some of us kicking and screaming.

### Thinking about the Reading

1. When he was a child, why did Hartmire "curse [Cesar Chavez's] name to the sun gods" (paragraph 1)? Do you think he still feels bitterness about his childhood? If so, at whom is this bitterness directed?

2. In paragraph 2, Hartmire says that Chavez was "larger than life. The impact he had on my family was at once enriching and debilitating. He was everywhere." What does he mean?

3. How has Hartmire's opinion of Chavez changed over the years? Has his opinion of his father also changed?

4. In paragraph 5, Hartmire says that he and Paul Chavez used to try to imagine how their lives might have been different if their fathers had been "plumbers or bus drivers." How do you think their lives would have been different?

### Writing Practice

1. What historical or political figure was "larger than life" for your family? Explain the impact that this person had on you.

2. Who is your greatest living hero? Write a short newspaper profile explaining this person's contributions to society. (If you like, you may write your profile as a recommendation for an award, addressing your remarks to the awards committee.)

3. If your middle school or high school was named after a person, write an article for the school newspaper in which you explain why this individual deserves (or does not deserve) this honor.

# Do What You Love

## Tony Hawk

Tony Hawk, a professional skateboarder since age fourteen, has also developed his own children's clothing line, cocreated a video game, and started the Tony Hawk Foundation — a charitable organization that provides money to build skate parks in low-income neighborhoods. In this essay, he explains why caring about what you do is more important than money or power.

I believe that people should take pride in what they do, even if it is scorned 1
or misunderstood by the public at large.

I have been a professional skateboarder for twenty-four years. For 2
much of that time, the activity that paid my rent and gave me my greatest
joy was tagged with many labels, most of which were ugly. It was a kids'
fad, a waste of time, a dangerous pursuit, a crime.

When I was about seventeen, three years after I turned pro, my high 3
school "careers" teacher scolded me in front of the entire class about
jumping ahead in my workbook. He told me that I would never make it
in the workplace if I didn't follow directions explicitly. He said I'd never
make a living as a skateboarder, so it seemed to *him* that my future was
bleak.

> **WORD POWER**
>
> **explicitly** exactly

Even during those dark years, I never stopped riding my skateboard 4
and never stopped progressing as a skater. There have been many, many
times when I've been frustrated because I can't land a maneuver. I've come
to realize that the only way to master something is to keep at it—despite
the bloody knees, despite the twisted ankles, despite the mocking crowds.

> **WORD POWER**
>
> **maneuver** in
> skateboarding, a trick

Skateboarding has gained mainstream recognition in recent years, but 5
it still has negative stereotypes. The pro skaters I know are responsible
members of society. Many of them are fathers, homeowners, world travelers, and successful entrepreneurs. Their hairdos and tattoos are simply
part of our culture, even when they raise eyebrows during PTA meetings.

> **WORD POWER**
>
> **entrepreneurs** business
> owners
> **obligations** actions owed
> to another

So here I am, thirty-eight years old, a husband and father of three, with 6
a lengthy list of responsibilities and obligations. And although I have many
job titles—CEO, Executive Producer, Senior Consultant, Foundation
Chairman, Bad Actor—the one I am most proud of is Professional Skateboarder. It's the one I write on surveys and customs forms, even though I
often end up in secondary security checkpoint.

My youngest son's preschool class was recently asked what their dads 7
do for work. The responses were things like, "My dad sells money" and
"My dad figures stuff out." My son said, "I've never seen my dad do work."

It's true. Skateboarding doesn't seem like real work, but I'm proud of 8
what I do. My parents never once questioned the practicality behind my
passion, even when I had to scrape together gas money and regarded dinner at Taco Bell as a big night out.

I hope to pass on the same lesson to my children someday. Find the 9
thing you love. My oldest son is an avid skater and he's really gifted for a
thirteen-year-old, but there's a lot of pressure on him. He used to skate for
endorsements, but now he brushes all that stuff aside. He just skates for
fun and that's good enough for me.

> **WORD POWER**
>
> **endorsements** support
> for a product or an action

You might not make it to the top, but if you are doing what you love, 10
there is much more happiness there than being rich or famous.

## Thinking about the Reading

1. Hawk states his thesis in the first sentence of this essay. Restate this
   thesis in your own words. Where in the essay does he repeat this main
   idea?
2. In paragraph 2, Hawk says, "I have been a professional skateboarder
   for twenty-four years." Why do you think he makes this statement
   early in his essay? How do you react to it?

3. What negative stereotypes do you think most people associate with skateboarders? Do you think these stereotypes are accurate? Why, or why not? How is Hawk different from the typical skateboarder?

4. Do you agree with Hawk's thesis? What information can you think of that challenges his position?

### Writing Practice

1. Using Hawk's main idea, write a defense of your own choice of hobby or future profession, something you "take pride in" (paragraph 1).

2. Write about a time when you made an unpopular choice against the advice of friends or family. Would you still make the same choice today? Why, or why not?

3. Do you see skateboarding as a "profession," as "a kids' fad, a waste of time, a dangerous pursuit, a crime" (paragraph 2), or as something else entirely? Explain your views.

# Getting a Tattoo: The Process Step by Step

## Karen L. Hudson

Tattoos have become far more common than ever before. In this About.com article, Karen L. Hudson outlines the process of getting a tattoo, presenting each step along the way. Hudson is the author of *Living Canvas: Your Complete Guide to Tattoos, Piercings, and Body Modification* (2009) and the editor and coauthor of *Chick Ink: 40 Stories of Tattoos — And the Women Who Wear Them* (2007).

1   If you are thinking about getting your first tattoo, but are unfamiliar with the process, the thought might meet you with anticipation. Fear of the unknown can sometimes hold us back from doing things we really want to do. You might be concerned that it will hurt too much. You might be worried that you wouldn't know if the artist was doing something wrong.

2   The best thing you can do is educate yourself on the process of the tattoo application, and that way you will be prepared and know what to expect when you sit in the artist's chair. So, how is a tattoo applied to the skin? From start to finish, this article will tell you exactly how the human skin is transformed into a beautiful work of art.

3   Please keep in mind that the following outline describes the most favorable situation for getting a tattoo. There will always be differences between one artist and the next, but any major deviance from these guidelines could indicate a problem.

### Paperwork and Payment

4   Once you have decided on your tattoo design and your artist, you will be required to show valid identification for proof of age. You may also be asked for your address and phone number, so your artist can contact you

in the future if need be. In most studios, payment must be made before services are rendered. It is up to each studio to decide which methods of payment they accept. Whatever method you pay with, make sure they give you a receipt.

### Sitting in the Chair of Honor

After your paperwork is filled out, you will be seated in the tattoo chair. 5 Sometimes this is in an open work area, and sometimes a private room depending on the location of your tattoo. If you are shy and don't want others to watch, you can request a private room, but be sure you have done this in advance. A lot of studios use dentist-style chairs, some use regular table chairs, and some use benches. Your artist will do his or her best to make you comfortable for the tattoo you have chosen.

### A Clean Shave

Now it is time for the preparation. The area of your body you have chosen 6 for your tattoo will be cleaned, usually with rubbing alcohol. Then, any hair will be removed from the area by shaving it with a new disposable razor which will be discarded after being used. Even the finest of hairs can get in the way and cause problems, so this is a crucial step, even if you can't see any hairs. Then, the area will be cleaned again to make sure it is smooth and ready for the transfer.

### Making and Applying the Stencil Transfer

Most studios today use a wonderful machine called a thermal-fax to make 7 their stencils. This saves on literally hours of tracing time by simply inserting your tattoo design into the machine, and it transfers it onto a special thermal paper in seconds. Once your stencil is ready, it's time to create the transfer onto your skin. Some artists will use soap or water to moisten the skin, and some will use stick deodorant. These aid in making the design transfer better and darker onto your skin. When the paper is pulled away from your skin, it will leave you with a purple-ish blue likeness of your future tattoo!

### Preparing the Tattoo Machine and Other Equipment

It is at this time that your artist will start preparing their tattoo machine. 8 The inks will be placed in little tiny cups called "ink caps," and the needles and tubes will be removed from their sterile pouches and placed in the machine. Clean distilled water will be poured into a cup for cleaning the needles during the tattoo process and to change from one color to the next. Some A&D ointment or Vaseline will be placed on a clean surface for your use only.

### Starting the Linework

Now it is time to get down to serious business. A little ointment will be 9 placed over your transfer design for a few reasons. One is that it helps keep the transfer on longer without accidentally rubbing it off, and it also helps the needle to slide along the skin more smoothly, which is certainly going to be more comfortable to you. After the ointment is applied, it is time for the first line. If you're nervous, don't hold your breath. Some people have passed out during a tattoo, and trust me—it wasn't the pain, it was the panic! Take a nice, slow, deep breath and try to relax. The first minute or so will the be roughest. After that, your skin will kind of get used to it and the pain will begin to subside.

### Shading and Coloring

10   Once all the linework is done, your artist can breathe a little bit easier knowing that they won't have to worry about the transfer anymore. Now it's time to get creative with a little shading and possibly color. Depending on the size of your tattoo, your artist may switch to a different set of needles called "magnums" (or mags) which are designed for coloring and shading. They may even switch tattoo machines altogether. The shading and coloring can go along quite quickly, and before you know it . . . you've got a complete tattoo.

### The Finished Tattoo

11   Your artist may like a picture of your tattoo for their portfolio. They'll clean it up and sometimes even apply a hot towel to it first. Then they'll take a picture, and this is a good time for you to get a shot, too, if you brought a camera along. Taking a photo after the protective ointment is applied causes a glare, so it is best to do it now. If for any reason you do not want the artist to take a photo, just say so. You are not under obligation to let them.

### Dressing and Bandaging

12   Now that your tattoo is finished and clean, it needs to be treated just like a wound. A protective layer of ointment will be applied to the tattoo to prevent invasion of airborne bacteria that can cause infection. Then a bandage will be applied, and it will be taped up to make sure it is secure. It is important that you keep this bandage on for the amount of time your artist instructs, which brings us to our last step: aftercare.

### Receiving Aftercare Instructions

13   Your artist will now give you aftercare instructions. These should be given both verbally and on a piece of paper for you to take home with you. It is important that you listen and follow the instructions you are given. From this point on, it is your responsibility to make sure your tattoo is well taken care of. The artist cannot be blamed if you get an infection because you didn't follow directions.

### A Happy Customer = A Happy Artist

14   You are now the proud owner of a beautiful tattoo. Before you walk out the door, thank your artist, and please don't forget to tip them. Show how much you appreciate their work and dedication. Refer your friends to them. When you go back for your next tattoo, you will have established a good relationship with your artist, and you can be assured they will be there to help you if you ever have any problems or questions in the future.

## Thinking about the Reading

1. What purpose do the boldfaced headings serve in this essay? Are they really necessary? Why or why not?

2. In your own words, list the steps in the process Hudson explains.

3. Do you agree with Hudson that a tattoo can be (or usually is) a "beautiful work of art" (paragraph 2)? Why or why not? Study some of your friends' (or your own) tattoos before you answer.

4. What transitional words and phrases does Hudson use to move readers from one step of the process to the next? Do you think she needs more transitions? If so, where?

## Writing Practice

1. In paragraph 1, Hudson says, "Fear of the unknown can sometimes hold us back from doing things we really want to do." Write about how you carried out a process you feared trying at first but really wanted to do.

2. Rewrite Hudson's process essay to emphasize only the positive (or only the negative) aspects of getting a tattoo. If you want to stress the positive side, omit the cautions and the medical aspects of the procedure. If you want to emphasize the negative side, omit the references to beauty and artistry.

# Forced from Home Yet Never Free of It

## Suki Kim

Suki Kim explores the complicated threads of living far from home in this personal essay, published in 2010 in the *New York Times*. In the essay, Kim remembers her childhood in South Korea, from which she fled with her family when she was twelve years old. Kim is the author of *The Interpreter* (2003), a crime novel set in New York City.

With each year, my childhood house grows bigger in my mind, each nook and corridor casting a longer shadow. The stone steps, about a hundred in total, appear elongated, as if they might reach the sky rather than the front gate. The pomegranate trees and forsythia that had once filled the garden have overgrown into a tropic wilderness, a meteorological miracle for South Korea. The pond, where I looked for the koi with their multiple colors, has turned into a reservoir as deep as the one in Central Park. Rising beyond it all are the peacocks from my father's menagerie, and I wait, as I have always, for the magical fanning of their tails.

I was 12 years old when we fled our home in the dead of night. The moments when my past comes rushing at me and converges with my immediate surroundings should grow fewer as I get older. But even now, decades later, standing in my kitchen on the Upper West Side, I inevitably pause before throwing out leftover salad and think, "Oh, but I must save it for the peacocks."

**WORD POWER**

**elongated** stretched out
**koi** ornamental fish
**menagerie** collection of animals

**WORD POWER**

**converges** comes together from different directions

3    Over the years, I never considered any apartment more than temporary. Each one remained spare, with bare walls and no personal touches—as though I might need to grab everything in a few seconds and run. When I moved into my boyfriend's apartment a few years ago, I came with one small box and some bags of clothes. He asked where the rest of my stuff was. People often ask me where my things are. The question always brings me back there, to South Korea; in my mind I deposit my suitcase at the bottom of those implausibly long steps and look up at the house, towering above.

**WORD POWER**

**imminent** about to occur

4    I believe I had missed my home even when I was living there—the way one might prematurely mourn one's beloved in anticipation of his imminent departure. I recall crying every summer when, as a child, I was sent away to my grandparents' house. My young mother, who had once modeled for a Japanese photographer, always dressed up for the occasion. I remember her standing by the columns at the front door in a tweed dress with matching knee-high boots in dove gray leather. With her long brown hair in a loose bun and a pair of oversize sunglasses, she looked like a movie star as she kissed me once before waving me off into a chauffeured car. But it was the beginning of summer, and her outfit suggested cooler weather, which makes me wonder if I am mixing up moments.

5    I have easily forgotten the summers at my grandparents' house because they preferred my sister, for reasons never explained, and my brother, the son and an heir to our clan of Kim. But I recall with great clarity the flutter in my heart when, at summer's end, the car finally pulled back up to our gate.

**WORD POWER**

**perennial** occurring again and again

6    The house was my father's obsession and was undergoing perennial renovation. Upon returning from our grandparents', we would find the gate positioned at a completely different angle, or the garden lit up like Christmas, with brilliant lanterns hanging from the trees. The orchard appeared as if by magic, with shiny apples that were not there at the start of summer. One year a well was dug, and my father declared, in his usual romantic way, that from now on his children would drink only fresh spring water. Years later, I believe I fell in love with my boyfriend when he bought me a bottle of Evian on our first date.

7    Then there were the animals, which thrilled me. (This surprises me now, since I have grown into an adult with no hankering for pets. For a long time, I was one of the few single women I knew in New York without a cat.) Our house and grounds were filled with pheasants and rock pigeons, turkeys and deer, and, of course, the peacocks. Once, I returned from school to find a spiky ball in the foyer. I had seen porcupines only in mangas and was eager to examine it closely, but my mother was not so amused by this new addition. This was South Korea in the 1970s, and we were not country folks. Soon, my classmates visited the house on school trips, which made me feel special and yet oddly uneasy.

8    On Sundays, the governess would wake us at dawn for the "Tiger Hunt," my father's name for our weekly expedition. The maid would dress us in our "hunting outfits"—corduroy pants and flowery hats much like the ones that Melissa Gilbert wore in "Little House on the Prairie." We would form a line and circle the small hill behind our house as my father made a big show of a shotgun and a fishing rod. If we had no luck with a

tiger sighting, he told us grimly, he might stick some bubble gum on the end of the fishing rod and fling it at the trees to see what else might be up there. My sister and I found this funny and played along, but my little brother was always on the lookout for tigers and was crushed when we inevitably returned home with only cicadas in our bags.

Soon my father had no time for such Sundays. The early '80s in South Korea was a time of political unrest and economic upheaval, and his businesses—from the shipping company and mining ventures to the hotels—collapsed rapidly. The end happened without warning. In the middle of the night, my sister and I were awakened with hushed whispers. I had just started junior high school, and the building was on the same block as the house of a boy I had long harbored a crush on. I always looked for him while waiting for the chauffeur to pick me up after school. On that final night, as I rushed to gather my things before being whisked into a car, it dawned on me that I would never see him again.    9

I may have hesitated before my extensive doll collection, unable to decide which one to bring along, but I am uncertain if that really happened or if such a concrete memory was contrived and imposed later. What I am certain of, however, is that from an end so abrupt and unrequited is born the mantra of what-ifs, which carried me through the darkly vague years that followed.    10

My sister and I were left with my grandparents, while my parents took my brother because he was too young to be separated from them and went into hiding; bankruptcy in South Korea was punishable by a hefty jail term, and the police were after them. When we were finally reunited with our parents at Kennedy Airport a few months after I turned 13, everything had changed.    11

They had borrowed money to find their way to America and were working around the clock to pay it back. My mother looked thinner and noticeably aged from a series of manual jobs, and my father was no longer wearing a suit. My brother seemed not so little anymore. The first house my parents rented was a shabby one-bedroom apartment in Queens that, no matter how I try, I cannot recall clearly. Those years are also marked by silence. My mother tongue was gone suddenly and replaced by an unfamiliar sound called the English language, with which, despite my relentless struggle, I have never felt quite at home.    12

> **WORD POWER**
>
> **relentless** steady and persistent

Years later, during a visit to South Korea, I did attempt to return to my home. I had reached the age my mother must have been when she stood at that front door looking picture perfect, as though she belonged there and nowhere else. The bus and taxi rides felt interminable. When the car finally pulled onto a narrow street between concrete apartment blocks, I paused in my seat, unable to move. A couple of old women peered in to ask if I was lost. When I rolled down the window a little and told them my old address, they said I was parked right near it.    13

> **WORD POWER**
>
> **interminable** unending

Through the window, I glanced toward the empty space at which they were pointing. There might have been a house, or the remnants of a house perhaps. A temple in ruins, one of the women might have said, although I cannot be sure because I never did get out of the car. I sat in that strange corner of the world, which held no glimmer of recognition, before finally telling the driver to take me back to where I came from.    14

> **WORD POWER**
>
> **remnants** things left over

**Thinking about the Reading**

1. Why do you think Kim "never considered any apartment more than temporary" (paragraph 3)?
2. What are some of Kim's most pleasant childhood memories? What does she miss most?
3. What events ended Kim's idyllic childhood? What changed for her and for her family? Why?
4. When Kim returned to South Korea as an adult, why didn't she revisit her childhood home?

**Writing Practice**

1. In your own words, using third person (*she* instead of *I*), retell the story that Kim tells in paragraphs 8 through 11.
2. Find photographs of some of the places (neighborhoods, streets, houses, or rooms) you have lived in since you were a child, and write the story of your family's movement from place to place.

# Eating Chilli Peppers

## Jeremy MacClancy

Jeremy MacClancy is a professor in social anthropology at Oxford Brookes University. He is the author or editor of a number of books, including *Consuming Culture* (1993), *Exotic No More* (2002), and *Anthropology in the Public Arena* (2013). In addition to analyzing the experience of eating chilli peppers, "Eating Chilli Peppers" also explains why people enjoy them so much.

1 How come over half of the world's population have made a powerful chemical irritant the center of their gastronomic lives? How can so many millions stomach chillies?

2 Biting into a tabasco pepper is like aiming a flame-thrower at your parted lips. There might be little reaction at first, but then the burn starts to grow. A few seconds later the chilli mush in your mouth reaches critical mass and your palate prepares for liftoff. The message spreads. The sweat glands open, your eyes stream, your nose runs, your stomach warms up, your heart accelerates, and your lungs breathe faster. All this is normal. But bite off more than your body can take, and you will be left coughing, sneezing, and spitting. Tears stripe your cheeks, and your mouth belches fire like a dragon celebrating its return to life. Eater beware!

3 As a general stimulant, chilli is similar to amphetamines—only quicker, cheaper, non-addictive, and beneficial to boot. Employees at the tabasco plant in Louisiana rarely complain of coughs, hay fever, or sinusitis. (Recent evidence, however, suggests that too many chillies can bring on stomach cancer.) Over the centuries, people have used hot peppers as a folk medicine to treat sore throats or inflamed gums, to relieve respiratory distress, and to ease gastritis induced by alcoholism. For aching muscles and tendons, a chilli plaster is more effective than one of mustard, with the added advantage that it does not blister the skin. But people do not eat tabasco, jalapeno,

**WORD POWER**

**gastronomic** relating to food and drink

**WORD POWER**

**palate** roof of the mouth

or cayenne peppers because of their pharmacological side-effects. They eat them for the taste—different varieties have different flavors—and for the fire they give off. In other words, they go for the burn.

Eating chillies makes for exciting times: the thrill of anticipation, the extremity of the flames, and then the slow descent back to normality. This is a benign form of masochism, like going to a horror movie, riding a roller coaster, or stepping into a cold bath after a sauna. The body flashes danger signals, but the brain knows the threat is not too great. Aficionados, self-absorbed in their burning passion, know exactly how to pace their whole chilli eating so that the flames are maintained at a steady maximum. Wrenched out of normal routines by the continuing assault on their mouths, they concentrate on the sensation and ignore almost everything else. They play with fire and just ride the burn, like experienced surfers cresting along a wave. For them, without hot peppers, food would lose its zest and their days would seem too dull. A cheap, legal thrill, chilli is the spice of their life.

4

**WORD POWER**

**masochism** the deriving of pleasure from pain
**aficionados** enthusiastic followers; fans

In the rural areas of Mexico, men can turn their chilli habit into a contest of strength by seeing who can stomach the most hot peppers in a set time. This gastronomic test, however, is not used as a way to prove one's machismo, for women can play the game as well. In this context, chillies are a non-sexist form of acquired love for those with strong hearts and fiery passions—a steady source of hot sauce for their lives.

5

The enjoyable sensations of a running nose, crying eyes, and dragon-like mouth belching flames are clearly not for the timorous.

6

More tabasco, anyone?

7

**WORD POWER**

**timorous** timid; apprehensive

## Thinking about the Reading

1. MacClancy opens his essay with two questions. Does he answer these questions? If so, where? If not, how would you answer them?

2. Over the years, what health benefits have been associated with eating chilli peppers?

3. Why, according to MacClancy, do people eat chilli peppers?

4. In this essay, MacClancy uses a number of vivid **similes**—comparisons that use the word *like*. For example, in paragraph 2, he says eating chilli peppers is "like aiming a flame-thrower at your parted lips." Identify several other similes in this essay. Can you identify any **metaphors**—comparisons that do not use *like* or *as*? How do these figures of speech get across the impression of chilli peppers that MacClancy is trying to convey here?

## Writing Practice

1. Although this essay describes the experience of eating chilli peppers, it does not actually explain what they look like. Find a few photos on Google Images, and write a physical description of a chilli pepper.

2. In paragraph 2, MacClancy describes what it is like to eat chilli peppers. Choose another very flavorful food that could be described in a similarly dramatic way (for example, a food that is intensely sweet, sour, salty, or spicy), and describe what eating it is like.

# The Little Pretzel Lady

## Sara Price

For some children, adult responsibility comes early in life. Student writer Sara Price recounts her experience as a ten-year-old working a Saturday job with her brother. For three years, to help their financially strapped family, Sara and her brother sold pretzels in a local shopping center.

1   When I was ten years old, selling pretzels at the corner of a shopping center was not my favorite weekend activity. Unfortunately, however, I had no alternative. My father had recently been injured on the job, and we had been experiencing severe financial difficulties. His disability payments and my mother's salary were not enough to support four children and my grandparents. When my parents could not pay our monthly mortgage, the bank threatened to take our house.

2   Knowing we had to find jobs to help, my older brother and I asked the local soft pretzel dealer to give us work on Saturdays. At first he refused, saying we were too young. But we simply would not take no for an answer because our parents desperately needed financial help. When we persisted, the pretzel dealer agreed to let us start the next week. In return for his kindness, my brother and I agreed to work faithfully for the next three years.

3   On the first Saturday morning, my brother and I reported promptly to our positions in front of the Cool-Rite appliance shop at the Academy Plaza shopping center. When Tom, our dealer, arrived with three hundred pretzels, he set up the stand and gave us instructions to sell each pretzel for a quarter, and five for a dollar. Then, Tom wished us luck and said he would be back later to pick up the table and the money. The arrangement with him was that we would get one-third of the total sales.

4   On that first Saturday, after selling our three hundred pretzels, my brother and I earned ten dollars each. (We also received a two-dollar tip from a friendly man who bought fifteen pretzels.) Our first day was considered a good one because we sold out by 4 p.m. However, the days that followed were not always as smooth as the first. When the weather was bad, meaning rain or snow, sales decreased; there were times when we had to stay as late as 7 p.m. until the last pretzel was sold.

5   To my regular customers, I was the little pretzel lady. But to my classmates, I was the target of humiliation. My worst nightmare came true when they found out that I ran a pretzel stand. Many of the boys made fun of me by calling out nasty names and harassing me for free pretzels. It was extremely embarrassing to see them walk by and stare while I stood like a helpless beggar on the street. I came to dread weekends and hate the sight of pretzels. But I was determined not to give up because I had a family that needed support and a three-year promise to fulfill. With that in mind, I continued to work.

6   Although winter was the best season for sales, I especially disliked standing in the teeth-chattering cold. I still remember that stinging feeling when the harsh wind blew against my cheeks. In order to survive the hours of shivering, I usually wore two or three pairs of socks and extra-thick clothing. Many times, I felt like a lonesome, leafless tree rooted to one spot and unable to escape from the bitter cold of winter.

## WORD POWER

**persist** to continue to do something despite setbacks

The worst incident of my pretzel career occurred when I was selling alone because my brother was sick. A pair of teenage boys came up to the stand, called me offensive names, and squirted mustard all over the pretzels. My instant reaction was total shock, and before I could do anything else, they quickly ran away. A few minutes later, I discarded the pretzels, desperately fighting back the tears. I felt helpless and angry because I could not understand their actions.

7

> **WORD POWER**
>
> **offensive** hurtful; disagreeable; unpleasant

The three years seemed like forever, but finally they were over. Even though selling pretzels on the street was the worst job I ever had, I was grateful for it. The money I earned each Saturday accumulated over the three years and helped my family. Selling pretzels also taught me many important values, such as responsibility, teamwork, independence, and appreciation for hard-earned money. Today, as I pass the pretzel vendors on my way to school, I think of a time not too long ago when I was the little pretzel lady.

8

> **WORD POWER**
>
> **accumulate** to gather or pile up little by little

## Thinking about the Reading

1. What emotions did you experience as you read "The Little Pretzel Lady"? Which parts of the essay caused the strongest reactions? Why?

2. Children are often cruel to one another. What do you think caused the cruelty that Sara Price experienced?

3. Sara says that she sometimes felt like "a lonesome, leafless tree rooted to one spot and unable to escape from the bitter cold of winter" (paragraph 6). Explain how this image suits Sara's situation.

4. Do you think that Sara's experience as a "pretzel lady" was more hurtful than beneficial to her? Give reasons to support your answer.

## Writing Practice

1. Write about a time in your childhood when you were teased or bullied by other children.

2. Write about the "little pretzel lady" and her experiences from the point of view of a clerk in the Cool-Rite appliance shop who watches the two children sell pretzels every Saturday.

3. Write about an experience you had at work that made you like or dislike your job. Be sure to include details about the workplace, your job responsibilities, the other people involved, and any conversations you remember.

# El Hoyo

## Mario Suárez

Mario Suárez was born and raised by Mexican immigrants in Arizona, where he became familiar with "El Hoyo," the name for the Mexican-American barrio in Tucson. Meaning "the hole" in English, it is the setting for most of Suárez's writing, much of which appeared in *Arizona Quarterly* in the 1950s. A collection of his work, called *Chicano Sketches*, was published in 2004.

1    From the center of downtown Tucson the ground slopes gently away to Main Street, drops a few feet, and then rolls to the banks of the Santa Cruz River. Here lies the section of the city known as El Hoyo. Why it is called El Hoyo is not very clear. In no sense is it a hole as its name would imply; it is simply the river's immediate valley. Its inhabitants are chicanos who raise hell on Saturday night and listen to Padre Estanislao on Sunday morning. While the term *chicano* is the short way of saying Mexicano, it is not restricted to the paisanos who came from old Mexico with the territory or the last famine to work for the railroad, labor, sing, and go on relief. Chicano is the easy way of referring to everybody. Pablo Gutierrez married the Chinese grocer's daughter and now runs a meat department; his sons are chicanos. So are the sons of Killer Jones who threw a fight in Harlem and fled to El Hoyo to marry Cristina Mendez. And so are all of them. However, it is doubtful that all these spiritual sons of Mexico live in El Hoyo because they love each other—many fight and bicker constantly. It is doubtful they live in El Hoyo because of its scenic beauty—it is everything but beautiful. Its houses are simple affairs of unplastered adobe, wood, and abandoned car parts. Its narrow streets are mostly clearings which have, in time, acquired names. Except for some tall trees which nobody has ever cared to identify, nurse, or destroy, the main things known to grow in the general area are weeds, garbage piles, dark-eyed chavalos, and dogs. And it is doubtful that the chicanos live in El Hoyo because it is safe—many times the Santa Cruz has risen and inundated the area.

2    In other respects living in El Hoyo has its advantages. If one is born with weakness for acquiring bills, El Hoyo is where the collectors are less likely to find you. If one has acquired the habit of listening to Octavio Perea's Mexican Hour in the wee hours of the morning with the radio on at full blast, El Hoyo is where you are less likely to be reported to the authorities. Besides, Perea is very popular and sooner or later to everyone "Smoke In The Eyes" is dedicated between the pinto beans and white flour commercials. If one, for any reason whatever, comes on an extended period of hard times, where, if not in El Hoyo, are the neighbors more willing to offer solace? When Teofila Malacara's house burned to the ground with all her belongings and two children, a benevolent gentleman carried through the gesture that made tolerable her burden. He made a list of five hundred names and solicited from each a dollar. At the end of a month he turned over to the tearful but grateful señora one hundred dollars in cold cash and then accompanied her on a short vacation. When the new manager of a local store decided that no more chicanas were to work behind the counters, it was the chicanos of El Hoyo who, on taking their individually small but collectively great buying power elsewhere, drove the manager out and the girls returned to their jobs. When the Mexican Army was en route to Baja California and the chicanos found out that the enlisted men ate only at infrequent intervals, it was El Hoyo's chicanos who crusaded across town with pots of beans and trays of tortillas to meet the train. When someone gets married, celebrating is not restricted to the immediate friends of the couple. Everybody is invited. Anything calls for a celebration and a celebration calls for anything. On Memorial Day there are no less than half a dozen good fights at the Riverside Dance Hall. On Mexican Independence Day more than one flag is sworn allegiance to amid cheers for the queen.

**WORD POWER**

**adobe** sun-dried brick made of clay or straw

**chavalos** young men

**WORD POWER**

**solace** comfort in sorrow or distress

And El Hoyo is something more. It is this something more which brought Felipe Sanchez back from the wars after having killed a score of Vietnamese with his body resembling a patchwork quilt to marry Julia Armijo. It brought Joe Zepeda, a gunner, . . . back to compose boleros. He has a metal plate for a skull. Perhaps El Hoyo is proof that those people exist, and perhaps exist best, who have as yet failed to observe the more popular modes of human conduct. Perhaps the humble appearance of El Hoyo justifies the indifferent shrug of those made aware of its existence. Perhaps El Hoyo's simplicity motivates an occasional chicano to move away from its narrow streets, babbling comadres, and shrieking children to deny the bloodwell from which he springs and to claim the blood of a conquistador while his hair is straight and his face beardless. Yet El Hoyo is not an outpost of a few families against the world. It fights for no causes except those which soothe its immediate angers. It laughs and cries with the same amount of passion in times of plenty and of want.

Perhaps El Hoyo, its inhabitants, and its essence can best be explained by telling a bit about a dish called capirotada. Its origin is uncertain. But, according to the time and the circumstance, it is made of old, new, or hard bread. It is softened with water and then cooked with peanuts, raisins, onions, cheese, and panocha. It is fired with sherry wine. Then it is served hot, cold, or just "on the weather" as they say in El Hoyo. The Sermeños like it one way, the Garcias another, and the Ortegas still another. While it might differ greatly from one home to another, nevertheless it is still capirotada. And so it is with El Hoyo's chicanos. While being divided from within and from without, like the capirotada, they remain chicanos.

**WORD POWER**

**bolero** a kind of slow-tempo Latin music

## Thinking about the Reading

1. What does the word *chicano* mean? How is it used in "El Hoyo"?
2. In paragraph 1, Suárez enumerates the reasons that, he says, do *not* explain why people live in El Hoyo. What are some of these reasons? Despite these reasons, why do people live in El Hoyo—and why do they keep coming back?
3. List the key physical features of El Hoyo. Are these features largely positive or negative?
4. What is the significance of the last paragraph's description of *capirotada*? How does the description of this dish explain the point Suárez is making about the people of El Hoyo?

## Writing Practice

1. Write about the advantages or the disadvantages of living in your own neighborhood, community, or hometown. Be sure to describe specific physical characteristics as well as people and events.
2. Write a description of a spot on your campus—a room, a building, or an outdoor area—that makes you feel happy, confident, and secure—or anxious, uncomfortable, and uneasy.

# The Online Alternative

## Marc Williams

As more and more schools offer online courses, students must think carefully about the costs and benefits of enrolling in them. In the following essay, student writer Marc Williams compares and contrasts an online class and a traditional class.

1    Last semester, my friend Jason and I decided to sign up for a course called Twentieth-Century African-American Literature. We were both interested in the course's subject, and we thought we could study for exams together, share our notes, and maybe even buy just one set of books. When the course schedule came out, I realized I had a problem. The course was scheduled for Monday, Wednesday, and Friday at noon—a convenient time for Jason but impossible for me because I was working the lunch shift in the cafeteria. When I told my advisor my problem, she had an idea: she suggested that I take the course online. This seemed like a good idea, so I signed up. However, when Jason and I compared notes at the end of the semester, I realized that online learning was not for me.

2    In some ways, the two courses were a lot alike. For example, Jason and I had the same teacher and the same writing assignments. We had to read the same short stories, plays, poems, and articles, as well as *Invisible Man*, a novel by Ralph Ellison. The course materials were posted on the course's website for both traditional and online students. And, of course, we would both take exams (although mine would be given in the campus testing center, not given in class). According to the course syllabus (also the same), our final grades would depend on the same thing: papers, exams, and class participation. Also, we both got three credits for the course. Despite these similarities, the two courses were very different from day one.

3    On the first day of his class, Jason met the instructor and the other students taking the course. The students talked about other literature classes they had taken, works by African-American writers they had read, and their experiences with writing papers about literature. They also asked questions about the syllabus and the course materials. My introduction to the course was different. The instructor emailed me information about how the online course would work. She set up a bulletin board on Blackboard, and students in the class could introduce themselves there and tell why they were taking the course. (This bulletin board would stay up all term so we could talk informally about the class if we wanted to.) So, the first thing I did was log on and write a little bit about myself. Then, I read what other students had written. Although it was possible to chat with other students, I didn't want to take the time.

4    As the semester continued, I realized that the two courses were run very differently. In Jason's class, the instructor gave short lectures about various writers and works and provided historical background when necessary. She also answered questions as they came up and helped move the class discussion along. In my course, the instructor posted a lecture every week, along with a set of questions. Our assignment was to read the lecture material and email her our answers to the questions. Class "dis-

cussion" was also different. In Jason's class, students exchanged ideas in person. In my class, everything happened online. The teacher posted questions for online discussion, and then the students in the class would all log on at a prearranged time and have a discussion about the posted questions. We could also ask questions about the assigned readings during this time.

Contact with the instructor was also different. For Jason, contact was 5 whatever he wanted it to be. He could email the instructor, drop in or call during her office hours, or schedule an appointment. For online students, contact was more limited. Although we could set up face-to-face conferences, this wasn't encouraged. So, I was limited to emailing and to phone calls during the two hours a week that were set aside for online students. When I needed face-to-face help with my papers, I went to the Writing Center.

The hardest thing for me to get used to was the lack of real interaction 6 with other students. Jason set up study groups with other students. In class, they watched and discussed a DVD of Alice Walker's short story "Everyday Use," acted out scenes from *A Raisin in the Sun*, read Yusef Komunyakaa's poetry out loud, and critiqued drafts of other students' papers. Although some of these things were also possible in my online class, it just wasn't the same. Arranging an online discussion with other students in real time was hard because of our different school and work schedules. We could watch films on our own, but we couldn't all discuss the film together right after we saw it. And I missed the chance to see other students' physical reactions and expressions and hear their voices.

At the end of the semester, when Jason and I talked about our classes, 7 it was easy for me to see the positive side of my online course. The most important advantage was convenience. Instead of having to attend classes during specific hours each week, I could log on whenever I had time. Still, I didn't feel I got as much out of my course as Jason got out of his. In regular classes, when I have something to say, I raise my hand and say it, and I get instant feedback from other students and from the instructor. In the online class, I usually had to wait to get an email reply to a posting. I also missed being able to drop by the instructor's office to talk about a problem. Most of all, I missed the chance to get to know other students in the class by working with them in study groups, collaborating with them on projects, or talking to them informally outside of class. For me, taking the online class was definitely worth it because this was the only way I could take the class at all. But I don't think I'll do it again.

## Thinking about the Reading

1. Where does Marc Williams discuss the *similarities* between online and traditional courses?

2. List the *differences* Marc identifies between online and traditional courses.

3. What advantages does Marc's course have over Jason's more traditional course? What disadvantages does Marc identify?

4. What advantages of online courses can you think of that Marc doesn't mention? What additional disadvantages can you think of?

**Writing Practice**

1. Write an email to Marc's instructor suggesting ways to improve her online course.
2. Imagine that the writing course you are now taking was conducted online. How would it be different? (If you are now taking an online writing course, compare it to a traditional writing class.)
3. Interview a few students who have taken online courses, and write a summary of their views on the advantages and disadvantages this kind of learning has over traditional classes.

# What Are Friends For?

## Marion Winik

Marion Winik, who has published eight books, teaches creative writing at the University of Baltimore and has served as a commentator for the National Public Radio show *All Things Considered*. In this excerpt from her essay collection *Telling: Confessions, Concessions, and Other Flashes of Light* (1995), Winik describes different levels of friendship and explains how each type of friend affects our lives.

1   I was thinking about how everybody can't be everything to each other, but some people can be something to each other, thank God, from the ones whose shoulder you cry on to the ones whose half-slips you borrow to the nameless one you chat with in the grocery line.

2   Buddies, for example, are the workhorses of the friendship world, the people out there on the front lines, defending you from loneliness and boredom. They call you up, they listen to your complaints, they celebrate your successes and curse your misfortunes, and you do the same for them in return. They hold out through innumerable crises before concluding that the person you're dating is no good, and even then understand if you ignore their good counsel. They accompany you to a movie with subtitles or to see the diving pig at Aquarena Springs. They feed your cat when you are out of town and pick you up from the airport when you get back. They come over to help you decide what to wear on a date. Even if it is with that creep.

3   What about family members? Most of them are people you just got stuck with, and though you love them, you may not have very much in common. But there is that rare exception, the Relative Friend. It is your cousin, your brother, maybe even your aunt. The two of you share the same views of the other family members. Meg never should have divorced Martin. He was the best thing that ever happened to her. You can confirm each other's memories of things that happened a long time ago. Don't you remember when Uncle Hank and Daddy had that awful fight in the middle of Thanksgiving dinner? Grandma always hated Grandpa's stamp collection; she probably left the windows open during the hurricane on purpose.

4   While so many family relationships are tinged with guilt and obligation, a relationship with a Relative Friend is relatively worry-free. You don't even have to hide your vices from this delightful person. When you slip out Aunt Joan's back door for a cigarette, she is already there.

> **WORD POWER**
>
> **workhorses** horses bred and used for labor
> **innumerable** too many to be counted

> **WORD POWER**
>
> **tinged** slightly colored or tinted

Then there is that special guy at work. Like all the other people at the    5
job site, at first he's just part of the scenery. But gradually he starts to
stand out from the crowd. Your friendship is cemented by jokes about
coworkers and thoughtful favors around the office. Did you see Ryan's
hair? Want half my bagel? Soon you know the names of his turtles, what
he did last Friday night, exactly which model CD player he wants for his
birthday. His handwriting is as familiar to you as your own.

Though you invite each other to parties, you somehow don't quite fit    6
into each other's outside lives. For this reason, the friendship may not
survive a job change. Company gossip, once an infallible source of entertainment, soon awkwardly accentuates the distance between you. But
wait. Like School Friends, Work Friends share certain memories which
acquire a nostalgic glow after about a decade.

A Faraway Friend is someone you grew up with or went to school with    7
or lived in the same town as until one of you moved away. Without a Faraway Friend, you would never get any mail addressed in handwriting. A
Faraway Friend calls late at night, invites you to her wedding, always says
she is coming to visit but rarely shows up. An actual visit from a Faraway
Friend is a cause for celebration and binges of all kinds. Cigarettes, Chips
Ahoy, bottles of tequila.

Faraway Friends go through phases of intense communication, then may    8
be out of touch for many months. Either way, the connection is always there.
A conversation with your Faraway Friend always helps to put your life in
perspective: When you feel you've hit a dead end, come to a confusing fork
in the road, or gotten lost in some crackerbox subdivision of your life, the
advice of the Faraway Friend—who has the big picture, who is so well acquainted with the route that brought you to this place—is indispensable.

Another useful function of the Faraway Friend is to help you remem-    9
ber the things from a long time ago, like the name of your seventh-grade
history teacher, what was in that really good stir-fry, or exactly what happened that night on the boat with the guys from Florida.

Ah, the Former Friend. A sad thing. At best a wistful memory, at worst    10
a dangerous enemy who is in possession of many of your deepest secrets.
But what was it that drove you apart? A misunderstanding, a betrayed
confidence, an unrepaid loan, an ill-conceived flirtation. A poor choice of
spouse can do in a friendship just like that. Going into business together
can be a serious mistake. Time, money, distance, cult religions: all noted
friendship killers. You quit doing drugs, you're not such good friends with
your dealer anymore.

And lest we forget, there are the Friends You Love to Hate. They call    11
at inopportune times. They say stupid things. They butt in, they boss you
around, they embarrass you in public. They invite themselves over. They
take advantage. You've done the best you can, but they need professional
help. On top of all of this, they love you to death and are convinced they're
your best friend on the planet.

So why do you continue to be involved with these people? Why do you    12
tolerate them? On the contrary, the real question is, What would you do
without them? Without Friends You Love to Hate, there would be nothing
to talk about with your other friends. Their problems and their irritating
stunts provide a reliable source of conversation for everyone they know.
What's more, Friends You Love to Hate make you feel good about yourself,

**WORD POWER**

**infallible** unable to fail
**accentuates** makes
something more noticeable
**nostalgic** yearning for
happiness in a former time
or place

**WORD POWER**

**wistful** wished for, dreamy

**WORD POWER**

**inopportune** poorly timed

since you are obviously in so much better shape than they are. No matter what these people do, you will never get rid of them. As much as they need you, you need them too.

<sup>13</sup>   At the other end of the spectrum are Hero Friends. These people are better than the rest of us, that's all there is to it. Their career is something you wanted to be when you grew up—painter, forest ranger, tireless doer of good. They have beautiful homes filled with special handmade things presented to them by villagers in the remote areas they have visited in their extensive travels. Yet they are modest. They never gossip. They are always helping others, especially those who have suffered a death in the family or an illness. You would think people like this would just make you sick, but somehow they don't.

<sup>14</sup>   A New Friend is a tonic unlike any other. Say you meet her at a party. In your bowling league. At a Japanese conversation class, perhaps. Wherever, whenever, there's that spark of recognition. The first time you talk, you can't believe how much you have in common. Suddenly, your life story is interesting again, your insights fresh, your opinions valued. Your various shortcomings are as yet completely invisible.

<sup>15</sup>   It's almost like falling in love.

> **WORD POWER**
>
> **spectrum** the range that falls between one point and another point

> **WORD POWER**
>
> **tonic** a healing element

### Thinking about the Reading

1. List the categories of friends that Winik identifies. What other categories can you think of that she does not mention?

2. Which kind of friend does Winik think is most important? Which category of friend do *you* consider most important?

3. In paragraph 7, Winik says, "An actual visit from a Faraway Friend is a cause for celebration and binges of all kinds. Cigarettes, Chips Ahoy, bottles of tequila." Is she seriously recommending binges of smoking, drinking, and overeating, or is she exaggerating for effect? How can you tell?

4. Create four or five categories of friends you had when you were in middle school and the kinds of friends you have now. How are your categories different? What do these differences reveal about how you have changed?

### Writing Practice

1. Because her essay was written in the 1990s, Winik does not discuss Facebook friends. Write about the different categories of Facebook friends you have, giving each category a name and considering how the categories are different.

2. Write about the different kinds of Relative Friends you have. Create categories based on age, gender, geographical proximity, or some other criterion.

3. Write a letter to a Faraway Friend or a Former Friend (someone you have lost touch with). In your letter, explain why other categories of friends have become more important to you over the years.

# The Transaction

## William Zinsser

William Zinsser has written many articles and books on improving writing and study skills. He has also had a long career as a professional newspaper and magazine writer, drama and film critic, and author of nonfiction books on subjects ranging from jazz to baseball. This excerpt is from his classic book *On Writing Well: An Informal Guide to Writing Nonfiction*, first published in 1976.

1   A school in Connecticut once held "a day devoted to the arts," and I was asked if I would come and talk about writing as a vocation. When I arrived, I found that a second speaker had been invited—Dr. Brock (as I'll call him), a surgeon who had recently begun to write and had sold some stories to magazines. He was going to talk about writing as an avocation. That made us a panel, and we sat down to face a crowd of students, teachers, and parents, all eager to learn the secrets of our glamorous work.

2   Dr. Brock was dressed in a bright red jacket, looking vaguely bohemian, as authors are supposed to look, and the first question went to him. What was it like to be a writer?

3   He said it was tremendous fun. Coming home from an arduous day at the hospital, he would go straight to his yellow pad and write his tensions away. The words just flowed. It was easy. I then said that writing wasn't easy and it wasn't fun. It was hard and lonely, and the words seldom just flowed.

4   Next, Dr. Brock was asked if it was important to rewrite. Absolutely not, he said. "Let it all hang out," he told us, and whatever form the sentences take will reflect the writer at his most natural. I then said that rewriting is the essence of writing. I pointed out that professional writers rewrite their sentences over and over and then rewrite what they have rewritten.

5   "What do you do on days when it isn't going well?" Dr. Brock was asked. He said he just stopped writing and put the work aside for a day when it would go better. I then said that the professional writer must establish a daily schedule and stick to it. I said that writing is a craft, not an art, and that the man who runs away from his craft because he lacks inspiration is fooling himself. He is also going broke.

6   "What if you're feeling depressed or unhappy?" a student asked. "Won't that affect your writing?"

7   Probably it will, Dr. Brock replied. Go fishing. Take a walk. Probably it won't, I said. If your job is to write every day, you learn to do it like any other job.

8   A student asked if we found it useful to circulate in the literary world. Dr. Brock said he was greatly enjoying his new life as a man of letters, and he told several stories of being taken to lunch by his publisher and his agent at Manhattan restaurants where writers and editors gather. I said that professional writers are solitary drudges who seldom see other writers.

9   "Do you put symbolism in your writing?" a student asked me.

**WORD POWER**

**gusto** enthusiasm; lively enjoyment

10    "Not if I can help it," I replied. I have an unbroken record of missing the deeper meaning in any story, play, or movie, and as for dance and mime, I have never had any idea of what is being conveyed.

11    "I *love* symbols!" Dr. Brock exclaimed, and he described with gusto the joys of weaving them through his work.

12    So the morning went, and it was a revelation to all of us. At the end, Dr. Brock told me he was enormously interested in my answers—it had never occurred to him that writing could be hard. I told him I was just as interested in *his* answers—it had never occurred to me that writing could be easy. Maybe I should take up surgery on the side.

13    As for the students, anyone might think we left them bewildered. But in fact, we probably gave them a broader glimpse of the writing process than if only one of us had talked. For there isn't any "right" way to do such personal work. There are all kinds of writers and all kinds of methods, and any method that helps you to say what you want to say is the right method for you. Some people write by day, others by night. Some people need silence, others turn on the radio. Some write by hand, some by word processor, some by talking into a tape recorder. Some people write their first draft in one long burst and then revise; others can't write the second paragraph until they have fiddled endlessly with the first.

14    But all of them are vulnerable and all of them are tense. They are driven by a compulsion to put some part of themselves on paper, and yet they don't just write what comes naturally. They sit down to commit an act of literature, and the self who emerges on paper is far stiffer than the person who sat down to write. The problem is to find the real man or woman behind all the tension.

15    Ultimately, the product that any writer has to sell is not the subject being written about, but who he or she is. I often find myself reading with interest about a topic I never thought would interest me—some scientific quest, perhaps. What holds me is the enthusiasm of the writer for his field. How was he drawn into it? What emotional baggage did he bring along? How did it change his life? It's not necessary to want to spend a year alone at Walden Pond[1] to become deeply involved with a writer who did.

16    This is the personal transaction that's at the heart of good nonfiction writing. Out of it come two of the most important qualities that this book will go in search of: humanity and warmth. Good writing has an aliveness that keeps the reader reading from one paragraph to the next, and it's not a question of gimmicks to "personalize" the author. It's a question of using the English language in a way that will achieve the greatest strength and the least clutter.

17    Can such principles be taught? Maybe not. But most of them can be learned.

1. The place where Henry David Thoreau (1817–1862), an American writer, naturalist, and political activist, lived for two years in a cabin he built himself. He wrote about the experience in his most famous book, *Walden.*

## Thinking about the Reading

1. Why do you think Zinsser chose to use an interview format to compare and contrast his own writing methods and experiences with those of Dr. Brock? Was this a good decision? Why, or why not?

2. What is Zinsser's purpose in comparing his views on the writing process with those of Dr. Brock? Where does he suggest that his work and methods are superior to those of the doctor?

3. Zinsser claims that "rewriting is the essence of writing" (paragraph 4). Use your own experience to support or challenge this statement.

4. Zinsser says that the writer's ability to draw the reader into his subject is the "personal transaction" (paragraph 16)—the exchange between two people that makes writing come alive. Consider the essays in this chapter that you have read. Which ones did not really interest you until you were drawn in by the writer's personal view of the topic?

## Writing Practice

1. Imagine that you have been asked some of the same questions as Zinsser and Dr. Brock—but about your own experience as a college student. How would you respond? Be sure to include answers to the following questions: What is it like to be a student? What do you do when schoolwork or classes are not going well? Does being depressed or unhappy affect your performance in the classroom? How?

2. In paragraph 13, Zinsser writes, "There are all kinds of writers and all kinds of methods." What kind of writer are you? Are you more like Dr. Brock, who finds writing easy, or more like Zinsser, who finds writing hard? What methods do you use to come up with ideas or to get through a particularly difficult assignment? Do you use any of the methods that Zinsser describes in paragraph 13?

3. Zinsser claims that the most successful pieces of writing are produced when the writer really cares about his or her subject. Compare two essays in this chapter in which the writers really seem to care about their subjects. What do the essays have in common that makes them successful?

# Appendix: Building Word Power

Building a vocabulary is an important part of your education. Knowing what words mean and how to use them can help you become a better reader and a better writer. As you have worked your way through *Foundations First*, you have encountered Word Power boxes in each chapter. At this point, you may know the meanings of many of these words, and you have probably used some of them in the Seeing and Writing activities. By continuing to use these and other new words, you can further expand your vocabulary.

## FYI

### Using Context to Build Word Power

You can often figure out what a word means by studying its **context**, the words that surround it. For example, consider the following paragraph.

> Do I truly know Cesar Chavez? I suppose not. He was like a boat being driven by some internal squall, a disturbance he himself didn't always understand, and that carried millions right along with him, some of us kicking and screaming. (John Hartmire, "At the Heart of a Historic Movement")

If you did not know the meaning of the word *squall* (a short, sudden windstorm), you might be able to figure it out by its context. The paragraph above compares United Farmworkers' Union president César Chavez to a boat, and the word *driven* suggests a force that blows the boat around. The phrase "some internal squall, a disturbance . . . " makes it clear that a squall *is* a disturbance, and the rest of the paragraph indicates that this disturbance was powerful enough to affect millions of people. So, even though the paragraph does not explicitly define a squall as a windstorm, the word's context suggests that a squall is a powerful disturbance.

## 1 Using a Dictionary

One of the best ways to improve your vocabulary is to use a dictionary to help understand what new words mean and how to use them in your writing. A **dictionary** (electronic or print) is an alphabetical list of the words in a language. However, a good dictionary is more than just a collection of words. In addition to showing how to spell and pronounce a word and what its most common meanings are, a dictionary can give you a great deal of other information.

An entry from an online dictionary appears below.

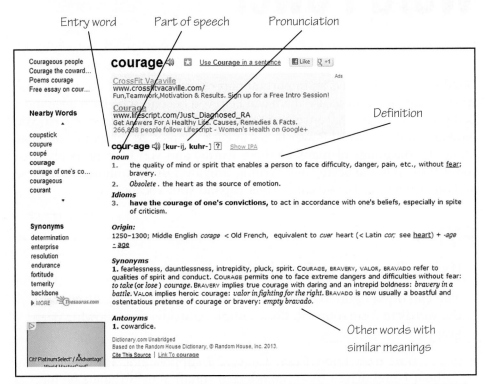

By permission. From Merriam-Webster's Collegiate® Dictionary, 11th Edition © 2014 by Merriam-Webster, Inc. (www.Merriam-Webster.com).

The pages that follow list (in alphabetical order) and define all the words that appear in the Word Power boxes in *Foundations First*. You can use this list as a minidictionary to incorporate these words into your written and spoken vocabulary.

Following the list is a section where you can create a personal vocabulary list, your own list of new words (and their definitions) that you encounter in your reading. Space has been provided for you to write an original sentence for each word so you can remember how it is used.

# 2  Word Power List

This alphabetical list includes all the words, along with their definitions, that appear in the Word Power boxes throughout *Foundations First*.

**absconded** left quickly and secretly to avoid punishment

**accentuates** makes something more noticeable

**accomplishment** things that have been done successfully

**accumulate** to gather or pile up little by little

**achievement** something accomplished successfully

**adjacent** next to; adjoining

**adobe** sun-dried brick made from clay or straw

**advances** actions intended to be sexually inviting

**adversity** difficulty

**aerobic** involving exercise that strengthens the heart and lungs

**affectionate** loving

**aficionados** enthusiastic followers; fans

**alienated** emotionally withdrawn or unresponsive

**alienation** the state of being alone or separate

**altercation** an angry quarrel

**amnesty** a pardon

**annotate** to make explanatory notes on a page

**anticipate** to look forward to

**apathetic** feeling or showing a lack of interest

**apathy** a lack of interest

**arbitrary** based on random choice or personal whim

**arduous** difficult and tiring

**assimilation** blending into the dominant culture

**assistance** money or resources that help someone

**atrophied** decreased in size, often through disuse

**attractions** things that evoke interest

**authoritarian** enforcing strict obedience

**avocation** a hobby or interest pursued for enjoyment rather than for money

**ballot** a written or printed paper on which voters indicate their choices in an election

**ban** to forbid somebody from doing something

**banished** sent away from a place as punishment

**beget** to cause to exist or occur

**bodega** a small grocery store specializing in Hispanic groceries

**bolero** a kind of slow-tempo Latin music

**calcified** hardened with excess calcium

**challenge** something that requires special effort

**characteristics** basic features

**chavalos** young men

**clarify** to make less confusing

**classic** something typical or traditional; an outstanding example of its kind

**cluttered** crowded, disordered

**commemorate** to serve as a memorial to something or someone

**commemoration** a celebration in which a person or an event is remembered

**commend** to express approval of

**commission** to place an order for something

**commitment** devotion or dedication

**competition** a contest

**conceited** self-important

**concocted** mixed various ingredients together

**conflict** a serious disagreement

**conform** to behave as others do

**conscientious** guided by one's conscience; principled

**conscientious objector** someone who refuses to serve in the military for moral reasons

**consolidate** to combine into one thing

**contemporary** current; modern

**context** the words that come before or after another word and clarify its meaning

**convenient** easy, accessible

**converges** comes together from different directions

**coordinating** equal in importance, rank, or degree

**cope** to deal with something difficult

**cordovan** a shade of brown

**courageous** brave

**crave** to have a strong desire for something

**culture** ideas, customs of a group

**curriculum** courses offered in a school or in a field of study

**daring** bold

**debilitate** to take away the strength of something or someone

**destination** the place to which someone is going

**determined** firm; strong-minded

**diction** choice of words; style of expression

**die-casting** a process of forcing very hot metal into a mold

**diehard** determined, loyal

**discipline** to train oneself to do something

**discount** to sell below the usual price

**disenfranchised** denied the right to vote

**disposable** designed to be thrown away

**diverge** to separate and go in different directions

**divulge** to disclose or reveal

**economical** giving good value

**efficient** operating with little waste

**elaborate** rich in detail

**elongated** stretched out

**empower** to give power or confidence

**encouraging** giving support

**endorsements** support for a product or an action

**entrepreneurs** business owners

**environment** surroundings

**envision** to imagine

**equitable** fair, just

**esteem** to have great regard for

**estranged** separated from someone else by feelings of hostility or indifference

**euthanasia** mercy killing

**exaggerate** to overstate

**excessive** extreme

**exempts** frees from an obligation that others are subject to

**exotic** foreign, unusual

**explicitly** exactly

**fatigue** extreme tiredness

**feasible** possible

**feline** relating to cats

**ferocious** fierce

**festive** joyous, merry

**flexible** easy to modify or adapt

**forensics** the study of formal debate

**frugally** not extravagantly

**fulfillment** satisfaction, happiness

**furtive** secret

**fused** melded together

**gait** a way of walking

**gastronomic** relating to food and drink

**gender** sex (male or female)

**generation** a group of individuals born and living at about the same time

**genome** a complete set of chromosomes and its associated genes

**gratification** a source of pleasure

**gusto** enthusiasm; lively enjoyment

**heritage** something passed down from previous generations

**highlight** to mark a page to emphasize important details

**humble** marked by modesty

**hybrid** a mix of different things

**immigrant** a person who comes to a country to permanently settle there

**imminent** about to occur

**imperative** obligation; duty

**impervious** impossible to affect

**improvise** to make do, to manage

**indefensible** hard to defend

**infallible** unable to fail

**ingredients** foods combined to make a particular dish

**innumerable** too many to be counted

**inopportune** poorly timed

**inspire** to make someone want to do something

**institution** a well-known person, place, or thing

**interact** to act together

**interminable** unending

**intimidate** to fill with fear

**invincible** unbeatable

**jargon** words used by a particular group or profession

**koi** ornamental fish

**maize** corn

**maneuver** in skateboarding, a trick

**marooned** stranded

**masochism** the deriving of pleasure from pain

**masquerade** to wear a mask or disguise

**material** having to do with physical objects or money

**mature** full-grown

**mellow** to gain wisdom and tolerance with age

**memento** a reminder of the past; a keepsake (the plural form is mementos)

**memorabilia** objects valued because of their link to historical events or culture

**memorable** worth remembering

**menagerie** collection of animals

**merchandise** goods to be bought and sold

**migrate** to move from one region to another

**miscegenation** cohabitation or marriage between people of different races

**mobility** the ability to move from one social group, class, or level to another

**modify** to describe, limit, or qualify

**monument** a structure built as a memorial

**multicultural** of or relating to many cultures

**naturalization** the process of becoming a citizen

**navigate** to get around a website

**naysayers** those who take a negative view

**network** to cultivate people who can be helpful

**newsworthy** worth reporting in the news

**nostalgic** yearning for happiness in a former time or place

**nurture** to encourage the development of

**nutrition** the process by which a body uses food for growth

**obligations** actions owed to another

**observer** someone who watches attentively

**obsolete** no longer in use

**obstacle** something that stands in the way

**offensive** hurtful; disagreeable; unpleasant

**opportunity** an occasion that makes it possible to do something

**option** the opportunity to choose something

**orchestrate** to arrange

**ornate** excessively ornamented; flowery

**orthopedic shoes** shoes made to correct abnormal bone structure

**ostracize** to exclude from a group

**outlay** an expense

**overwhelm** to overpower

**palate** roof of the mouth

**pandemic** an epidemic that affects many people over a wide area

**parity** equality in power or value

**passive** not actively participating

**pastime** a pleasant activity that fills spare time

**pathology** a deviation from the norm

**peer** someone with equal standing; an equal

**peer pressure** pressure from friends to behave in a way they see as acceptable

**perennial** occurring again and again

**permissive** allowing great freedom

**persist** to continue to do something despite setbacks

**perspective** a view or outlook; the ability to see things as they are

**plight** a difficult situation

**prepare** to put together

**priority** an important or urgent goal

**produce** fruits and vegetables

**prohibit** to forbid

**prudent** acting with care or thought

**psychosomatic** relating to a physical illness with a mental cause

**quota** a number of people or percentage of people set as an upper limit

**reasonable** acting with sound judgment

**recreation** activity done for enjoyment when one is not working; play

**recurring** occurring again and again

**regulate** to control

**relentless** steady and persistent

**remarkable** worthy of notice

**remnants** things left over

**renaissance** a rebirth or revival

**rendered** presented; submitted

**replacement** something that takes the place of another thing

**reputation** the opinion that people have about someone or something

**restrict** to keep within limits

**restrictive** limiting

**reusable** capable of being used again

**rigor** a hardship or difficulty

**role model** a person who serves as a model of behavior

**satisfaction** gratification, fulfillment

**self-esteem** pride in oneself; self-respect

**sentimental** overly romantic

**serendipity** good fortune or luck

**socialize** to mix with others

**solace** comfort in sorrow or distress

**spectacle** a public performance or show; an unusual sight

**spectrum** the range that falls between one point and another point

**splice** a connection made by joining two ends

**stipulation** requirement

**strategy** a plan to achieve a specific goal

**strenuous** requiring great effort or strength

**subordinate** lower in rank or position; secondary in importance

**subsidize** to give financial support to a project

**surveillance** the close observation of a person or a group of people, especially a person or group under suspicion

**symbolism** the use of a symbol (something that stands for something else) in a work of art or literature

**timid** shy, nervous

**timorous** timid; apprehensive

**tinged** slightly colored or tinted

**tonic** a healing element

**tradition** a behavior or custom handed down from generation to generation

**traditional** relating to tradition

**transaction** an exchange or transfer of goods, services, or money; an exchange of thoughts and feelings

**transcend** to be greater than; to go beyond

**transportation** a means of conveyance

**unanticipated** not expected

**unforeseen** not felt or realized before

**unique** the only one; one of a kind

**unwarranted** unnecessary

**vanity** excessive pride in one's appearance or achievements

**vanity plate** a license plate that can be customized for an extra charge

**variety** an assortment of many different things

**versatility** the ability to do many things well

**viable** able to survive; capable of success

**vitriolic** bitterly scathing; caustic

**vocation** an occupation; regular employment

**wistful** wished for, dreamy

**workhorses** horses bred and used for labor

# 3 Your Personal Vocabulary List

To start your personal vocabulary list, write down a brief definition of each word on the lines below, and then use it in a sentence. Continue this list in your journal with words you come across in your reading.

**Example**

Word: _____*memento*_____ Definition: _____*a reminder of the past*_____

_____

Sentence: _*I kept a seashell as a memento of our vacation at the beach.*_

_____

Word: _____ Definition: _____

_____

Sentence: _____

_____

Word: _____ Definition: _____

_____

Sentence: _____

_____

Word: _____ Definition: _____

_____

Sentence: _____

_____

# Acknowledgments

Rebekah Bell. "It's Possible to Graduate Debt-Free." From the *Wall Street Journal*, July 24, 2013. Used by permission.

Bobbi Buchanan. "Don't Hang Up, That's My Mom Calling." Originally published in the *New York Times*, December 8, 2003. Copyright © 2003 Bobbie Buchanan. Reprinted by permission of the author.

José Antonio Burciaga. "Tortillas." Reprinted with permission of Cecilia P. Burciaga.

Henry Louis Gates Jr. "A Giant Step." Copyright © 1990 by Henry Louis Gates Jr. Originally published in the *New York Times Magazine*, December 9, 1990, pp. 34–36. Reprinted by permission of the author.

Roxane Gay. "The Importance of Feeling Seen." From Salon.com, October 25, 2013. Copyright © 2013. Used by permission of Salon.com.

John Hartmire. "At the Heart of a Historic Movement." From *Newsweek*, July 24, 2000. IBT Media. All rights reserved. Used by permission and protected by the copyright laws of the United States. The printing, copying, redistribution, or retransmission of the material without express written permission is prohibited.

Tony Hawk. "Do What You Love." Copyright © 2006 by Tony Hawk. From *This I Believe II: The Personal Philosophies of Remarkable Men and Women*, pp. 103–105. Edited by Jay Allison and Dan Gediman. Copyright © 2008 by This I Believe, Inc. Reprinted by arrangement with Henry Holt and Company, LLC.

Don H. Hockenbury and Sandra Hockenbury. Excerpt from *Psychology*, 6th Ed., pp. 490–491. Copyright © 2012. Used by permission of Worth Publishers, Inc., a division of Macmillan Education.

Karen L. Hudson, "Getting a Tattoo." From About.com. Used by permission.

Suki Kim. "Forced from Home but Never Free of It." From the *New York Times*, December 8, 2010. Copyright © The New York Times, Inc. Used by permission and protected by the copyright laws of the United States. The printing, copying, redistribution, or retransmission of the material without express written permission is prohibited.

Jeremy MacClancy. "Eating Chili Peppers." From *Consuming Culture: Why You Eat What You Eat*. Copyright © 1993 by Henry Holt, Inc. Used by permission of Henry Holt, Inc., a division of Macmillan.

James A. Roark et al. Excerpt from *The American Promise*, 5th Ed., pp. 879–880. Copyright © 2012 by Bedford/St. Martin's. Used by permission of Bedford/St. Martin's, a division of Macmillan Education.

Christine Rosen. "Are Smartphones Turning Us into Bad Samaritans?" From the *Wall Street Journal*, October 25, 2013. Used by permission.

Mario Suarez. "El Hoyo." From *Chicano Sketches: Short Stories by Mario Suarez*. Edited by Francisco A. Lomeli, Cecilia Cota-Robles Suarez, and Juan Jose Casillas-Nunez. Copyright © 2004, The University of Arizona Press. Used by permission.

Marion Winik. "What Are Friends For?" From *Telling: Confessions, Concessions and Other Flashes of Light* by Marion Winik. Copyright © 1994 by Marion Winik. Used by permission of Villard Books, a division of Random House, Inc., and the author.

William Zinsser. "The Transaction." From *On Writing Well*, 7th (30th Anniversary) Ed., by William Zinsser. Copyright © 1976, 1980, 1985, 1988, 1990, 1944, 1998, 2001, 2006 by William K. Zinsser. Reprinted by permission of the author.

# Index

Note: Page numbers in **bold** type indicate pages where terms are defined.

# Index of Rhetorical Patterns

# Preparing a Formal Outline

An informal outline is usually all you need to help you plan a short essay. However, some writers—especially when they are planning a longer, more detailed essay—prefer to use formal outlines.

**Formal outlines** use a combination of numbered and lettered headings to show the relationships among ideas. For example, the most important (and most general) ideas are assigned a Roman numeral; the next most important ideas are assigned capital letters. Each level develops the idea above it, and each new level is indented.

Here is a formal outline for an essay about starting college as a nontraditional student.

---

*Thesis statement:* Although I realized it would be difficult in some ways, I decided that if I really wanted to attend college full-time, I could.

I. Difficulty: Money
  A. Needed to work to live
  B. Didn't have much money saved
  C. Found out about community college (low tuition)
  D. Found out about grants/loans
II. Difficulty: Academic record
  A. Got bad grades in high school
    1. Didn't care
    2. Didn't work
  B. Found out about reasonable admissions requirements at community college
  C. Committed to improving study habits
III. Difficulty: Imagining myself as a student
  A. Had no college graduates in family
  B. Had no friends in school
  C. Felt anxious
    1. Too old
    2. Out of practice at school
  D. Found other students like me
  E. Discovered I like studying

---

# Parts of Speech

The English language has eight basic parts of speech: nouns, pronouns, verbs, adjectives, adverbs, prepositions, conjunctions, and interjections.

Bailey (1993–2010)

**Nouns**  A noun names a person, an animal, a place, an object, or an idea.

Christine brought her dog Bailey to obedience school in Lawndale.
*noun*          *noun  noun*              *noun*        *noun*

**Pronouns**  A pronoun refers to and takes the place of a noun or another pronoun.

Bailey did very well in her lessons and seemed to enjoy them.
*noun*                *pronoun  noun*                        *pronoun*

**Verbs**  A verb tells what someone or something does, did, or will do.

Sometimes Bailey rolls over, but earlier today she refused.
*verb*                                *verb*

Maybe she will change someday.
*verb*

**Adjectives**  An adjective identifies or describes a noun or a pronoun.

This dog is a small beagle with a brown and white coat and long ears.
*adj noun     adj    noun          adj        adj   noun      adj noun*

**Adverbs**  An adverb identifies or describes a verb, an adjective, or another adverb.

Bailey is old now, so she moves very slowly and seldom barks.
*verb  adverb adverb        adverb   verb*

**Prepositions**  A preposition is a word—such as *to*, *on*, or *with*—that introduces a noun or pronoun and connects it to other words in a sentence.

Bailey likes sitting quietly in her box at the foot of the stairs.

**Conjunctions**  A conjunction is a word that connects parts of a sentence.

People say you can't teach an old dog new tricks, but Bailey might be an exception.

**Interjections**  An interjection is a word—such as *Oh!* or *Hey!*—that is used to express emotion.

Wow! Bailey finally rolled over!

The eight basic parts of speech can be combined to form sentences, which always include at least one subject and one verb. The subject tells who or what is being talked about, and the verb tells what the subject does, did, or will do.

Bailey graduated from obedience school at the head of her class.
*s        v*

# Revision Symbols

This chart lists symbols that many instructors use to point out writing problems in student papers. Next to each problem is the chapter or section of *Foundations First* where you can find help with that problem. If your instructor uses different symbols from those shown here, write them in the space provided.

| YOUR INSTRUCTOR'S SYMBOL | STANDARD SYMBOL | PROBLEM |
|---|---|---|
| | *adj* | problem with use of adjective 28 |
| | *adv* | problem with use of adverb 28 |
| | *agr* | agreement problem (subject-verb) 21<br>agreement problem (pronoun-antecedent) 27a, 27b |
| | *apos* | apostrophe missing or used incorrectly 31 |
| | *awk* | awkward sentence structure 22, 23 |
| | *cap or triple underline [example]* | capital letter needed 33a |
| | *case* | problem with pronoun case 27d, 27e |
| | *cliché* | cliché 17d |
| | *coh* | lack of paragraph coherence 3d |
| | *combine* | combine sentences 17b |
| | *cs* | comma splice 30 |
| | *d or wc* | diction (poor word choice) 17c, 35 |
| | *dev* | lack of paragraph development 3b |
| | *frag* | fragment 20 |
| | *fs* | fused sentence 19 |
| | *ital* | italics or underlining needed 33c |
| | *lc or diagonal slash [Example]* | lowercase; capital letter not needed 33a |
| | *para or ¶* | indent new paragraph 2a |
| | *pass* | overuse of passive voice 22c |
| | *prep* | nonstandard use of preposition 29i, 29j |
| | *ref* | pronoun reference not specific 27b |
| | *ro* | run-on sentence 19 |
| | *shift* | illogical shift 22 |
| | *sp* | incorrect spelling 34 |
| | *tense* | problem with verb tense 29f |
| | *trans* | transition needed 3d |
| | *unity* | paragraph not unified 3a |
| | *w* | wordy, not concise 17d |
| | *//* | problem with parallelism 18 |
| | ⊙ | problem with comma use 30 |
| | ⊙ | problem with semicolon use 15b, 32a |
| | " " | problem with quotation marks 33b, 33c |
| | ⊃ *[ex ample]* | close up space |
| | ^ | insert |
| | *[exaample]* | delete |
| | ∽ *[words example]* | reversed letters or words |
| | X | obvious error |
| | ✓ | good point, well put |
| | # *[example words]* | add a space |

# Inside the LaunchPad Solo for *Foundations First*

## LearningCurve

Active and Passive Voice
Apostrophes
Coordination and Subordination
Capitalization
Commas
Fragments
Multilingual—Articles and Types
  of Nouns
Multilingual—Prepositions
Multilingual—Sentence Structure
Multilingual—Verbs
Parallelism
Parts of Speech—Nouns and
  Pronouns
Parts of Speech—Verbs,
  Adjectives, and Adverbs

Parts of Speech—Prepositions
  and Conjunctions
Run-Ons
Shifts
Subject-Verb Agreement
Topic Sentences and Supporting
  Details
Topics and Main Ideas
Patterns of Organization
Verb Tenses
Vocabulary
Word Choice and Appropriate
  Language

## Additional Grammar Exercises

**Chapter 14** Writing Simple Sentences
**Chapter 15** Writing Compound Sentences
**Chapter 16** Writing Complex Sentences
**Chapter 17** Fine-Tuning Your Sentences
**Chapter 18** Using Parallelism
**Chapter 19** Run-Ons
**Chapter 20** Fragments
**Chapter 21** Subject-Verb Agreement
**Chapter 22** Illogical Shifts
**Chapter 23** Dangling and Misplaced Modifiers
**Chapter 24** Verbs: Past Tense
**Chapter 25** Verbs: Past Participles
**Chapter 26** Nouns
**Chapter 27** Pronouns
**Chapter 28** Adjectives and Adverbs
**Chapter 29** Grammar and Usage Issues for ESL Students
**Chapter 30** Using Commas
**Chapter 31** Using Apostrophes
**Chapter 32** Using Other Punctuation Marks
**Chapter 33** Understanding Mechanics
**Chapter 34** Understanding Spelling
**Chapter 35** Learning Commonly Confused Words